D1166832

THE
LEWIS
AND
CLARK
COMPANION

THE

LEWIS

AND

CLARK

COMPANION

*An Encyclopedic Guide to the
Voyage of Discovery*

Stephenie Ambrose Tubbs
WITH CLAY STRAUS JENKINSON

AN OWL BOOK
HENRY HOLT AND COMPANY | NEW YORK

Henry Holt and Company, LLC
Publishers since 1866
115 West 18th Street
New York, New York 10011

Henry Holt® is a registered trademark of
Henry Holt and Company, LLC.

Library of Congress Cataloging-in-Publication Data

Tubbs, Stephenie Ambrose.
    The Lewis and Clark companion : an encyclopedic guide to the voyage of discovery /
Stephenie Ambrose Tubbs, with Clay Straus Jenkinson.— 1st Owl Books ed.
        p.   cm.
    "An Owl book."
    Includes bibliographical references.
    ISBN 0-8050-6725-6 (hc.)—ISBN 0-8050-6726-4 (pbk.)
    1. Lewis and Clark Expedition (1804–1806)—Encyclopedias.   2. West (U.S.)—
Discovery and exploration—Encyclopedias.   3. West (U.S.)—Description and travel—
Encyclopedias.   I. Jenkinson, Clay.   II. Title.

F592.7 .T83 2003
917.804'2'03—dc21   2002037992

Henry Holt books are available for special
promotions and premiums.
For details contact:
Director, Special Markets.

First Owl Books Edition 2003

Designed by Paula Russell Szafransk

Map art © David Cain 2003

Printed in the United States of America

1   3   5   7   9   10   8   6   4   2

To our honored parents,

Stephen and Moira Ambrose

and

Chuck and Mil Jenkinson

Contents

Foreword

Many years ago when Moira and I began taking our children on annual grand adventures camping out west, we kept one purpose primarily in our minds: to learn about the history of a place you have to go there. You have to hike the trails, canoe the rivers, and climb the mountains. It would be hard work, for us and for them, but it would also be incredibly rewarding. We let this purpose guide us as we followed in the footsteps of George Armstrong Custer, Crazy Horse, Little Big Man, Chief Joseph, and of course on the trail of Lewis and Clark. Now, as our country approaches the bicentennial of the Corps of Discovery, there is more interest than ever in seeing the trail as the captains and their party did. People want to know more about their story; they delight in the details of the journals and seek out the scholars who can tell them all about who, what, where, when, and how. This excellently conceived and beautifully achieved companion to the Lewis and Clark Expedition answers the call. Its scope is comprehensive. Its accuracy is complete. It includes the most recent scholarship, from what we think happened to Seaman to York's later years; it includes an examination of Sacagawea, factually tells the story of her husband, Charbonneau, their son, and much more. It is a joy to read, both because one is always encountering something not previously known and because it is delightfully written. I should know. One of the authors, Stephenie Ambrose Tubbs, is our daughter; the other, Clay Jenkinson, is our friend.

Stephenie knows how to write; at the University of Montana she studied under two great western historians, K. Ross Toole and Harry Fritz. Along with our adventures on the Lewis and Clark trail in 1976, during which we all kept journals much as they did on the expedition, she lived in Missoula on a site Meriwether Lewis rode across on his return trip. She now lives in Helena on a site William Clark walked near if not over, and from her home she can see the Gates of the Mountains, named by Meriwether Lewis. She has published several articles on local history and remains deeply involved with the Lewis and Clark world.

North Dakotan Clay Jenkinson also grew up steeped in Lewis and Clark. After attending Oxford University on a Rhodes scholarship and studying at the University of Minnesota, he currently travels the country giving historical interpretations of Meriwether Lewis and Thomas Jefferson, among others. He reads, writes, lectures about, indeed seems to breathe, the Lewis and Clark Expedition. His work *The Character of Meriwether Lewis* is one of the most insightful studies to be written on Lewis. Along with his recent publication on growing up in North Dakota, he has received presidential recognition for his work and has appeared on the Ken Burns PBS series on Thomas Jefferson. He does more than charm his audience; he captures them, entertains them, and educates them.

This companion to the Lewis and Clark Expedition gives descriptions covering a bit of everything in the journals. At one point I could even taste the *boudin blanc* and smell the beaver castor thanks to the thorough text. But for me the greatest delight is the people. Nothing is more fascinating to people than learning about other people. In reading the stories of the major and minor characters encountered in this fascinating journey, we gain a much more complete understanding of the Voyage of Discovery and its motivating force. This companion accomplishes what all such works strive to do—be a complete account of the people, places, and things associated with the Corps of Discovery. In my opinion, from now on it will be the basic reference source in every Lewis and Clark scholar's library.

Stephen E. Ambrose
August 2002

Introduction

The Lewis and Clark Expedition (1803–1806) was the brainchild of Thomas Jefferson. The third president of the United States had a life-long interest in American Indians, the flora and fauna of the New World, and the geography of the American West. Even before he purchased the Louisiana territory from Napoleon Bonaparte in 1803, Jefferson had launched what we call the Lewis and Clark Expedition. Jefferson wanted Captain Meriwether Lewis and his colleagues to map the West, chart its river courses, determine latitude and longitude of significant geographic features of the landscape, study the native peoples who lived in the region, inventory plants, animals, soils, minerals, and climate conditions, persuade the peoples of Louisiana to live in peace with one another under the security umbrella of the United States government, and make preliminary arrangements for trade between Indians and merchants based in St. Louis. President Jefferson's instructions were daunting. He essentially sought to project the Enlightenment onto the American West, and he conceived of Meriwether Lewis and William Clark primarily as data collectors in the wilderness.

Jefferson, like the American Philosophical Society of which he was the president for many years, gave his life to the collection and dissemination of useful knowledge. It is no coincidence that his one published book was not a work of the imagination, but a nonfiction almanac, *Notes on the State of Virginia*.

The Lewis and Clark Expedition was a scientific enterprise, funded by the Congress of the United States, but it was also a military mission into a contested and uncertain country. It was an adventure story, America's first great epic, but it was also a series of carefully planned encounters with the aboriginal peoples of the Missouri and Columbia River valleys. It was the story of friendship between two remarkable young army officers, but it was also an exercise in continental (even global) geopolitics by a nation that believed it had a special destiny in the history of civilization.

Lewis and Clark left St. Louis (actually St. Charles) at the mouth of the Missouri River on May 14, 1804, and returned on September 23, 1806. Their journey has been called the most remarkable exploration mission in American history, and they (and five other known journal keepers) have been called "the writingest explorers of all time."

The Lewis and Clark Companion now takes its place in the extensive and growing literature of the Lewis and Clark Expedition. A book of this sort is inevitably derivative. Our challenge was to synthesize the mass of the existing knowledge about the Lewis and Clark Expedition into a single unified volume. We have, accordingly, read the journals with great care, but we have concentrated our energies on compiling and evaluating the immense secondary literature on Lewis and Clark.

We have attempted to produce an accurate, thoughtful, and reasonably complete companion volume to the journals of Lewis and Clark, a single volume to which any reader can turn for reliable preliminary information about aspects of Lewis and Clark. Some subjects we have omitted to keep this book from swelling out of control. Some subjects we have merely overlooked—we trust our readers will point these out.

We have written this book with the idea that students of Lewis and Clark will have it open before them as they read the journals for themselves. We have sought to provide useful, though not exhaustive, information on subjects that come up in any reading of the Lewis and Clark literature, from the espontoon to the grizzly bear, from Pierre Chouteau to John Colter. We have assumed that general readers would find our entries sufficient to satisfy their curiosity on most or all subjects related to Lewis and Clark, and that serious readers and scholars would find this a satisfactory source of ready reference on subjects they may already know a great deal about. "Mankind," wrote the English lexicographer Samuel Johnson, "requires more often to be reminded than informed."

Every Lewis and Clark scholar is dependent on two essential sources. The University of Nebraska's new edition of the *Journals of the Lewis and Clark Expedition*, edited by Gary E. Moulton, is the indispensable foundation for any serious inquiry into the expedition. Not only has Professor Moulton brought under one compass all the extant journals, including those of John Ordway and Joseph Whitehouse and Lewis's *Fort Mandan Miscellany*, with a uniform standard editorial philosophy, but his introductions and superb annotations have already become the filter through which all subsequent Lewis and Clark scholarship must pass. Our *Lewis and Clark Companion* is inevitably indebted to Professor Moulton's labors on virtually every page.

The second foundation text is Donald Jackson's *Letters of the Lewis and Clark Expedition, with Related Documents* (2 vols.), published in 1962. Jackson's gathering and interpretation of documents related to the expedition provide the contextual matrix in which the Lewis and Clark story must be understood, and it places Thomas Jefferson at the center of the story, where he belongs.

We also freely acknowledge our intellectual debt to a number of seminal secondary studies of Lewis and Clark: narrative treatments such as Stephen Ambrose's *Undaunted Courage: Meriwether Lewis, Thomas Jefferson, and the Opening of the American West*, David Lavender's *The Way to the Western Sea: Lewis & Clark across the Continent*, and David Freeman Hawke's *Those Tremendous Mountains: The Story of the Lewis and Clark Expedition*; and specialist studies such as Paul Russell Cutright's *Lewis and Clark: Pioneering Naturalists*, Donald Jackson's *Thomas Jefferson and the Stony Mountains: Exploring the West from Monticello*, James Ronda's *Lewis and Clark among the Indians*, Roy Appleman's *Lewis and Clark: Historic Places Associated with Their Transcontinental Exploration (1804–06)*, and John Logan Allen's *Passage through the Garden: Lewis and Clark and the Image of the American Northwest*.

Meanwhile, under the able direction of James Merritt, the always informative *We Proceeded On* (*WPO*) has emerged as a serious journal of ideas. We are grateful for the level of scholarship that *WPO* has recently achieved, at the same time that we have depended heavily on the hundreds of useful, particular articles that have been published since its inception in 1975.

This book is in many respects a recasting of the information and insights of other Lewis and Clark scholars in an alphabetical form. We have done very little original research in compiling this book. We see our purpose as expository rather than investigative.

The Lewis and Clark Companion appears as the bicentennial observance of the Lewis and Clark Expedition begins. We wanted it to be available in time to be useful to both scholars and general readers during this period of heightened national interest in the expedition. We are aware, however, that the coming of the Lewis and Clark bicentennial has inspired a wide range of scholars to study aspects of the expedition, and that very little of that new flurry of scholarship was available to us as we compiled this book. It is conceivable that this book would have been fuller had it been published at the end rather than the beginning of the bicentennial period, had it been able to take advantage of the best new scholarship on Lewis and Clark. It is our intention to produce a second edition of *The Lewis and Clark Companion* in a few years and we will, of course, read everything that is published in the interim.

A work of this scope will inevitably contain errors. Some of these will be misinterpretations of the historical material and some will be simple errors of fact. We trust that readers of this book will point out any errors and omissions we have made, and help us to make future editions both more complete and more accurate.

Our hope is that we have made a useful contribution to Lewis and Clark studies, and that our labors will inspire others to investigate this extraordinary story of encounters with landscapes, peoples, the assumptions of the American Enlightenment, and the limits of the English language.

One note: the words in guillemets in some of the entries indicate that those words had been deleted by the authors.

Stephenie Ambrose Tubbs
Clay S. Jenkinson

A

Air gun: A weapon resembling a flintlock rifle that used compressed air to fire its .31-caliber bullet, therefore not issuing smoke or a loud repercussion when discharged. Lewis purchased an air gun in Pennsylvania in 1803, probably from the Philadelphia gunsmith and horologist Isaiah Lukens. Although not reliable as a hunting weapon, the air gun served as an impressive tool in what historian James Ronda called "the Lewis and Clark traveling medicine show," which included items demonstrating the power of magnetism and a spyglass, compass, watch, and burning glass. On one of its first public displays near Pittsburgh, it was inadvertently discharged by Mr. Blaze Cenas, slightly wounding a bystander nearby. Throughout the journals when Lewis mentions the air gun it is usually "astonishing" or "very much surprising the Indians." After meeting up with the Shoshone and putting on the usual display of his authority and power, Lewis writes, "I also shot my air-gun which was so perfectly incomprehensible that they immediately denominated it the great medicine . . . or that in which the power of god is manifest by it's incomprehensible power of action." Several repairs were needed to keep the air gun in working order. John Shields fixed it on June 9, 1805, and Lewis repaired the sights on August 7, 1805. The weapon was used in April 1806 to intimidate the Clackamahas, who were "orderly and kept at a proper distance" after witnessing the gun discharge. Lewis had the gun at the ready after he was wounded by Cruzatte on the return journey and imagined Indians to be his pursuers, "being determined as a retreat was impracticable to sell my life as deerly as possible." The air gun was returned to Lukens after Lewis's death in 1809. Upon the death, in 1846, of the gunsmith, the air gun was sold at auction the following year.

References: Moulton, vols. 5, 7, 8; Russell; Chatters; Beeman

Allen, Paul (1775–1826): Philadelphia journalist. Employed by publishers Bradford and Inskeep at the suggestion of his fellow *Port Folio* writer Nicholas Biddle to finish editing duties on his two-volume *History of the Expedition under the Command of Captains Lewis and Clark.* According to Biddle's instructions Allen was to "take the rude outline as I had left it, add from the original journals whatever had been omitted in the first rapid sketch—mould the whole as he thought best and superintend the publication." Allen received payment of $500 and his name, not Biddle's, appeared on the title page when it was published in 1814. Biddle likely insisted on remaining anonymous because he considered himself too much of a gentleman to garner wages and publicity. Although the true scope of Allen's contribution to the journals remains undetermined, he is credited with extracting a memoir of Lewis from Thomas Jefferson because he wished to "enliven the dulness of the Narrative by something more popular splendid & attractive." Historian Donald Jackson theorized Biddle left much work to be done while another editor of the journals, Rueben Thwaites, considered the Allen effort "typographical and clerical."

    References: Large, "History's Two Nicholas Biddles"; Jackson, Letters; Thwaites, Original Journals, vol. 1; Cutright, History of the Lewis and Clark Journals; Johnson and Malone

American Philosophical Society: Founded in Philadelphia in 1743—the same year that Jefferson was born—by Benjamin Franklin, who based his idea on the model of the Royal Society of London. Members came from Europe as well as from the American colonies and included the most prominent minds in the practical sciences. Thomas Jefferson was a member for forty-seven years and president of the society from 1797 to 1815. He responded to his election calling it "the most flattering incident of my life, and that to which I am most sensible. [I have] no qualification for this distinguished Post, but an ardent desire to see knowledge so disseminated through the mass of mankind, that it may at length reach the extremes of Society, beggars and kings. . . ." In 1793 the society established a fund to send botanist André Michaux in search of the Northwest Passage, but that plan fell through. It was postponed for ten years, until Jefferson approached his personal secretary, Meriwether Lewis, to head the expedition. In preparation for the trip, Jefferson sent Lewis to Philadelphia to receive instruction from several of the society's outstanding members. These included physician and botanist Benjamin Barton, naturalist and professor of anatomy Caspar Wistar, mathematician Andrew Ellicott, and physician Benjamin Rush. When Jefferson gave Lewis his list of instructions, he was reflecting, according to historian Carol Lynn MacGregor, "his desire to accumulate as much knowledge as possible for the practical purposes of commerce, science, and national interests. His methodology mirrors that of the American Philosophical Society, and, in fact, they are one in this endeavor. Jefferson deposited all of the Lewis and Clark journals at his disposal in the archives of the American Philosophical Society where they remain."

Reference: MacGregor, "American Philosophical Society"

Arrowsmith, Aaron (1750–1823): British cartographer who produced a map of North America in 1795 based on the accounts of North West Company explorers Peter Fidler, Samuel Hearne, Alexander Mackenzie, and George Vancouver. The map shows the Missouri unconnected to the "Stony Mountains" or the Mississippi and includes a note indicating the elevation of the mountains, which according to Fidler's Indian informant, The Feathers, was "five ridges in some parts." In 1802 Arrowsmith revised the map showing the mountains near the southern source of the Missouri with another note explaining they divided into "several low ridges." The Arrowsmith map implied an easy crossing of the Rocky Mountains and the close proximity of the Pacific Ocean. Cartographer Nicholas King used both Arrowsmith maps for his chart of the country to be explored by Lewis and Clark. The captains also carried a copy of the 1802 Arrowsmith map with them on their journey and it was the most influential one used in directing the Corps of Discovery to the Pacific Ocean.

Reference: Benson

Au-ho-ne-ga (Au-ho-ning-ga): One of the chiefs and principal men of the Otos and Missouris "made" by Meriwether Lewis and William Clark on August 3, 1804, at Council Bluff.

B

Ba Za conja: One of the chiefs and principal men of the Otos and Missouris designated by Meriwether Lewis and William Clark on August 3, 1804, at Council Bluffs.

Baillet, François: The Philadelphia cook who supplied Meriwether Lewis with 193 pounds of portable soup at a cost of $289.50.
  Reference: Moulton, vol. 5

Barton, Benjamin Smith (1766–1815): Philadelphia physician, naturalist, botany professor, and author of the first American textbook on botany, *Elements of Botany* (1803), which Meriwether Lewis purchased in preparation for his trip west. Thomas Jefferson requested that, while Lewis was in Philadelphia, Professor Barton advise him on the subjects of botany, zoology, and Indian history. Barton complied and also loaned Lewis his copy of DuPratz's *History of Louisiana*. When he returned the book to Barton in May of 1807, Lewis inscribed the book with the following notation: "Dr. Benjamin Smith Barton was so obliging as to lend me this copy of Mons. Du Pratz's history of Louisiana in June 1803. it has been since conveyed by me to the Pacific Ocean through the interior of the Continent of North America on my late tour thither and is now returned to its proprietor by his Friend and Obt. Servt. Meriwether Lewis Philadelphia, May 9th, 1807." The book is owned by the Library Company of Philadelphia and is considered, as Cutright states, "a unique and priceless volume deeply imbued with the colors of American history." Barton was to write the natural history section for the Biddle edition of the journals but poor health forced him to abandon his plans. In a letter to Jefferson in October 1810, Barton wrote, "In regard to Mr. Lewis's papers, I assure you, and I beg you, Sir, to assure his friends, that they will be taken good care of; that it is my sincere wish to turn them as much as I can, to his honour & reputation; and that they shall ultimately be deposited, in good order, in the hands of General Clark, or those of Mr. Conrad, the publisher." He finished the letter with the promise, "I cherish with respect, the memory of your friend; and believe me, Sir, the manner in which you speak of him, in your letter, will act not feebly in making me careful of his fame. His fate was, indeed, melancholy and unhappy: but similar has sometimes been the fate of the best and wisest of men."

References: Cutright, *"Lewis and Clark and Du Pratz"*; Jackson, Letters

Beacon Rock: Landmark and geological feature on the Washington side of the Columbia River measuring 900 feet, the "lava monolith" was sighted and mentioned in the journals on November 2, 1805. The Wahclellah Indians inhabited a village below the rock on the starboard side.

Reference: Moulton, vol. 7

Beaver (*Castor canadensis*): Most valuable trade good on the nineteenth-century frontier, used for hats, coats, muffs, robes, collars, and linings; sold in Europe and the eastern United States. First trapped by the expedition at the mouth of the Kansas River, the size and number of beaver increased as they proceeded to the Rockies. Even before they returned, Lewis and Clark's reports of large populations of beaver in the newly acquired lands of the Louisiana Purchase spurred western exploration and settlement and continued to do so for the next forty years. Indians traditionally used beaver for food and fur, but their harvest methods did not deplete the population until whites came and the value of beaver pelts increased dramatically. Beaver populations declined after 1840. According to Lamar's *New Encyclopedia of the American West*, between 1800 and 1850, one hundred thousand to five hundred thousand beaver pelts were taken per year. The average weight of a mature beaver is thirty-five to fifty pounds. When the fur trade started, trappers could count on four dollars per pound. Fur trade historian Hiram Chittenden wrote that the tributaries of the Missouri were "as rich as if sands of gold covered the bottoms." Natural enemies to the beaver include otter, wolves, coyotes, foxes, and bobcats. Beaver require large bodies of water to thrive. They build large dams and dig canals fortified by the many trees they bring down with their sharp

teeth. Beaver dams and canals can vary from a few yards to a hundred yards long, although *The New Encyclopedia of the American West* states a beaver dam in Montana once measured two thousand feet long. In addition to using trees for building material, beaver also eat willow, aspen, cottonwood, and white birch. The beaver's scientific name, *Castor canadensis*, refers to a yellow waxy material produced by its perineal gland (also known as bark stones, according to Clark), which the beaver uses to keep its fur waterproof and most likely to mark its territory. The animal is a herbivore and does not hibernate. They are mainly nocturnal and usually live fifteen to sixteen years. To signal an alarm, the beaver strikes its tail on the water, which produces a loud slapping sound. Beaver can stay submerged up to fifteen minutes before resurfacing. Young beaver stay with their parents for two years and serve as assistants in building and repairing the dams. A beaver once interfered with communication between the captains at Three Forks by taking a bush or branch that held a note from Lewis to Clark. In another incident Lewis's dog was almost killed when a beaver bit him on the leg and nearly severed an artery. Lewis particularly liked the "tale and liver" and found the beaver "a delacacy . . . I think the tale a most delicious morsal, when boiled it resembles in flavor the fresh tongues and sounds of the codfish and is usually sufficiently large enough to afford a plentifull meal for two men." See Castorium.
References: Chittenden, vol. 2; Lamar; Moulton, vol. 4

Beaver's Head Rock (Beaverhead Rock): Located in Madison County, near present-day Twin Bridges and Dillon, Montana. On August 8, 1805, Lewis recorded, "the Indian woman recognized the point of a high plain to our right which she informed us was not very distant from the summer retreat of her nation on a river beyond the river which runs to the west. this hill she says her nation calls the beaver's head from a conceived remblance of its figure to the head of that animal." The captain described it as a "steep rocky clift of 150 feet high near the Stard. side of the river." The reddish brown rock resembles a beaver's head when viewed from the north; it faces west. According to Alt and Hyndman in *Roadside Geology of Montana*, it is "andesite (a common rock of large volcanos), of unknown age."
References: Moulton, vol. 5; Alt and Hyndman

Beeswax: Used in combination with buffalo tallow and charcoal to seal the stitches of the hides used to cover the iron boat. But "the stitches begin to gape very much since she has began to dry; I am now convinced this would not have been the case had the skins been sewed with a sharp point only." Beeswax was used as part of a poultice given by Captain Clark to treat an abscess on Jean Baptiste's neck in June 1805. On March 9, 1806, Ordway mentions Clatsop Indians bringing "bears wax" to trade. Whitehouse mentions it correctly spelling it "bees wax" in his entry for the same day. While exploring the Columbia River in 1813, Alexander Henry noted, "Great quantities of beeswax continue to be dug out of the sand near this spot and the Indians bring it to trade with us." The Spanish galleon *San Francisco Xavier*, lost at sea near Nehalem Spit in 1705, is the likely source of the beeswax, which can still be found today and has been, according to Ruth and Emory Strong, radiocarbon dated to between 1485 and 1655.

References: Moulton, vols. 4, 11; Strong and Strong; Wood and Thiessen

Benoit, Francis Marie (1768–1819): Fur trader with the Osage, Oto, and Pawnee Indians before the Louisiana Purchase and partner of Manuel Lisa. Benoit, or "Mr. B," incurred the wrath of Meriwether Lewis in the winter of 1803 and the following spring. As he wrote Clark, "Damn Manuel and triply Damn Mr. B. They give me more vexation and trouble than their lives are worth. I have dealt very plainly with these gentlemen, in short have come to an open rupture with them; I think them both great scoundrels, and they have given me abundant proofs of their unfriendly dispositions towards our government and it's measures. These <gentlemen> (no I will scratch it out) these puppies, are not unacquainted with my opinions; and I am well informed that they have engaged some hireling writer to draught a petition and remonstrance to Govr. Claibourne against me; strange indeed that men to appearance in their senses, will <show> manifest such strong sumptoms of insanity, as to be wheting knives to cut their own throats." Lewis's perceived insult did not warrant complete disassociation from the pair as he later became a partner in Lisa's Missouri Fur Company, as did William Clark, in the years following the expedition.

Reference: Jackson, Letters

Bezoar (hair ball): One of the items sent back to Jefferson with Pierre Chouteau and the Osage Indians. Included in the list of articles fowarded to Jefferson along with a rock crystal, a horned lizard from the Osage plains, and a map of the Mississippi from the mouth of the Missouri to New Orleans. It was described as a "specimen of salt formed by concretion, procured at the great Saline of the Osage nation." Cutright defines it as a concretion of hair, often entangling undigested food particles, in stomachs of mammals prone to swallowing hair. Some tribes used it as an antidote to poisons.

References: Thwaites, Original Journals, *vol. 1; Cutright,* Pioneering Naturalists

Biddle, Nicholas (1786–1844): Philadelphia litterateur, scholar, statesman, financier, and editor of the two-volume edition of the *History of the Expedition under the Command of Captains Lewis and Clark* (1814). Biddle entered the University of Pennsylvania at age ten, finished his studies at thirteen, but did not formally graduate until age fifteen. During his graduate studies at Princeton he excelled in the study of the classics, French literature, and writing but chose to pursue the study of law. In 1804, at eighteen years old, Biddle traveled to France to serve as secretary under General John Armstrong, minister to France. He witnessed the coronation of Napoleon and remained in Europe until 1807 as a temporary secretary under the employment of minister James Monroe. Upon his return to Philadelphia, Biddle continued to study law and resumed writing articles (sometimes under the pseudonym Oliver Oldschool) for the first periodical aimed at creating an American literature, *Port Folio.* He entered politics for a short time, serving in the House of Representatives of Pennsylvania, and married an heiress, Jane Craig, of Andalusia. Three months following the death of Meriwether Lewis, and after his (or Jefferson's) first choice in editors fell through, General William Clark approached Biddle to edit the original journals for publication by Philadelphia publisher John Conrad. Biddle worked on the project for a year, despite initial misgivings about his lack of enthusiasm or what he termed his "usual indolence" for the task. Ultimately he latched on to his subject, spending seven or eight hours each day working vigorously. At Clark's invitation Biddle interviewed the general and George Shannon over a period of three weeks, covering some three hundred questions, and combined the various journalists' (Lewis, Clark, Ordway) accounts to weave an accurate and highly readable narrative. Readers of the journals are indebted to Biddle for revealing details unavailable in the originals but by no means insignificant, such as Sacagawea's reunion with Cameahwait, Clark's feelings about his rank, and York's rubdown by Hidatsa chief Le Borgne. When his election to the legislature prevented him from finishing the history, he passed the manuscript to colleague Paul Allen, whom he paid $500 to complete the work. Biddle likely insisted he remain uncredited on the title page. On March 23, 1814, he wrote Clark, "I am content my trouble in the business should be recompensed only by the pleasure which attended it, and by the satisfaction of making your acquaintance, which I shall always value." Although the book did not make a profit for the publishers, or William Clark, it was a critical success, despite Biddle's occasional intrusions, which included references to classical literature and virtually censoring the description of the Buffalo Calling Dance by translating it into Latin. Curiously, Biddle misspelled Clark with an "e" throughout his history. Somehow Biddle managed to misplace Ordway's journal along with Lewis's journal from the Ohio River; a mistake that was not corrected for nearly a century. As president of the Bank of the United States, Biddle maintained a staunch advocacy of reissuing its charter and, along with Albert Gallatin, wrote editorials and articles in support of such legislation. Their effort to secure a new charter failed, but from his home in Andalusia, county seat on the Delaware, Biddle lived the rest of his life at the center of a circle of intellectual friends and visitors. He continued to argue in support of economic practices he felt would be beneficial for all Americans, including shorter hours and higher wages. Biddle's papers are housed in the American Philosophical Society.

References: Jackson, Letters; *Large, "History's Two Nicholas Biddles"; Cutright,* History of the Lewis and Clark Journals; *Johnson and Malone*

Bier (mosquito curtains): *Baire,* a French term for a gauze or net covering used to protect against the swarms of mosquitoes, which the captains and the men frequently found "very troublesome." Each member of the expedition was issued a bier, and Lewis observed on July 21, 1805, "the men are all fortunately supplyed with musquetoe biers otherwise it would be impossible for them to exist under the fatiegues which they daily encounter without their natural rest which they could not obtain for those tormenting insects if divested of their biers." Near Tower Rock, a week before, Lewis wrote, "the Musquetoes are extreemly troublesome this evening and I (have) had left my bier, of course suffered considerably, and promised in my wrath that I will never be guily of a similar peice of negligence while on this voyage."

References: Thwaites, Original Journals, *vol. 2; Moulton, vol. 4*

Big Blue Eyes (Star-gea-hun Ja): Oto chief. At the council on August 19, 1804, Big Blue Eyes chose to return the certificate given to him by the captains as a show of his disapproval at not being included in the distribution of greater presents like tobacco, beads, and medals. He had a change of heart and requested his certificate be presented again; however, Clark wrote, "we would not give the Certft. but rebuked them verry roughly for haveing in object goods and not peace with their neighbours." In the end the certificate was given to Little Thief to "bestow it to the most Worthey, they gave it to him, we then gave them a Dram & broke up the Council." Lewis and Clark learned that the Oto and Missouri nations would not be easily swayed by the white man's promises of peace and pieces of paper; they wanted the valuable trade items and the "milk," or whiskey, the corps had on board. Historian James Ronda writes, "What happened in the Oto-Missouri talks should have been a warning of difficulties ahead."

References: Moulton, vol. 2; Ronda, Lewis and Clark among the Indians

Big Horse: Missouri chief who met with the captains at Council Bluff, or "Handsome Prairie," on August 3, 1804. Big Horse did not appear to care what nationality the whites were; only the quality of their trade goods mattered. He asked for a spoonful of milk (whiskey) from the captains. This council was somewhat disappointing for the captains; they had hoped to impress the natives with their promises and presents.

Reference: Ronda, Lewis and Clark among the Indians

Bighorn (*Argalia*, ibex, mountain sheep, Rocky Mountain bighorn sheep): Recorded by Lewis on April 26, 1805, as having been spotted by Joseph Field on his exploration of the mouth of the Yellowstone River: "he saw several of the bighorned anamals in the couse of his walk but they were so shy he could not get a shot at them; he found a large horn of one of these anamals which he brought with him." Four days later Clark saw "a female and her faun of the Bighorn animal on the top of a Bluff lying, the noise we made allarmed them and they had come down on the Side of the bluff which had but little Slope being nearly purpindicular, I directed two men to kill those anamals, one went on the top and the other man near the water they had two Shots at the doe while in motion without effect, Those animals run & Skiped about with great ease on this declivity & appeared to prefur it to the leavel bottom or plain." Drouillard was the first hunter of the party to bag a skittish bighorn; Clark and Bratton each also shot one. Lewis described the species in characteristically anatomic detail on May 25, 1805, noting, "the whole form is much more delicate than that of the common goat, and there is a great disparity in the size of the male and female than between those of either the deer or the goat." He further commented on the use by natives of the bighorn sheep's horn in constructing their bows. "I have no doubt but it would be eligant and ucefull hair combs, and might probably answer as many valuable purposes to civilized man, as it dose to the savages, who form their watercups spoons and platters of it." Wondering at the bighorn's surefootedness, Whitehouse observed, "They are very Subtle, nimble & Run very fast . . . and their flesh <eat like> had the taste of Mutton." On May 29, 1805, Lewis noted a "great abundance of the Argalia [or, added by Biddle] the Bighorned animals in the high country through which this river passes Cap. C who assended this R. much higher than I did has <thought it proper to> call it Judeith's River." Lewis originally called the river "Big Horn" in his journal entry. After exploring the territory in the Missouri River Breaks, on May 31, Lewis recognized a familiar odor, "the sides of the Clifts where these anamals resort much to lodg have the peculiar smell of sheepfolds." One of the three caches located near the Marias River contained several bighorn sheep horns. On his exploration of the Yellowstone, Clark was able to obtain several specimens of bighorn sheep heads, skins, and bones, which Peale later displayed in the Quadruped Room of his museum in Philadelphia. A bighorn sheep horn was given by Clark to his sister Fanny and her husband and now resides at the Filson Historical Society. In addition two sets of horns purchased from the Mandan Indians were among the items shipped back to Jefferson in the spring of 1805. (Noted in Clark's entry for December 22, 1804.) Lewis observed the Shoshone method of making bows from bighorns in his entry for August 23, 1805: "the bows of the bighorn are formed of small peices laid flat and cemented with gleue, rolled with sinews and glew, and highly ornamented as they are much prized." The bighorn's life span runs to fifteen years and they range from parts of southern British Columbia to southwest Alberta, Idaho, and Montana south to southeast California, Arizona, and New Mexico. Although they are highly adept at avoiding predators, the lambs sometimes fall prey to golden eagles. Lewis and Clark named several creeks and rivers in honor of the bighorn.

References: Burroughs; Cutright, Pioneering Naturalists; Moulton, vols. 4, 5, 11

Bison (*Bison bison*, buffalo): An ungulate that once covered the continent of North America from Alaska to northern Mexico and from the Continental Divide to the forests of Kentucky in numbers estimated at between sixty and seventy-five million. They particularly thrived on the Great Plains where their hooves helped produce an ideal environment for native grasses such as little bluestem, buffalo grass, and sage. Buffalo wandered in large herds, usually moving south before winter and north in the summer. As they traveled, the buffalo were pursued by nomadic Indian tribes who relied on them for food, clothing, and shelter, and included them at the top of their mythology and religion, which held that the earth and the buffalo were one and the same. The trails made by the buffalo were the first roads in America; many of our highways still follow routes laid out by buffalo herds. Private Joseph Field killed the corps's first buffalo on August 23, 1804, in what is now South Dakota; the men knew that as long as they were near buffalo they would never be hungry. Buffalo provided the ingredients for one of Meriwether Lewis's favorite dishes, *boudin blanc*; the captain also appreciated the taste of the buffalo

The number and size of the bison herds encountered by the expedition were a continuous source of amazement; when they traveled through buffalo country the party ate as much as they liked. Engraving by Karl Bodmer, courtesy of the Joslyn Art Museum, Omaha, Nebraska. Gift of Enron Art Foundation.

hump. In addition to consuming its meat, the Plains Indians used almost every part of the buffalo to provide materials; the muscles supplied sinew for sewing, the rawhide supplied moccasins, bull boats, and shields along with rope, containers, and drums. From the hair they made pillow stuffing, saddle pads, and ceremonial objects. Tanned buffalo hide was used for clothes, tipis, robes, blankets, bags, and dolls. The horns provided cups, ladles, and powder horns. The bones made excellent paintbrushes, sleds, tools, hoes, and awls. The paunch could be made into water flasks, and skulls were used for ceremonies. During the course of their journey, Lewis and Clark comment repeatedly on the "immence herds" and "great quantities" of buffalo they observed. One large "gangue" was estimated by Lewis to number twenty thousand. On April 29, 1805, near present-day eastern Montana, Lewis wrote, "we can scarcely cast our eyes in any direction without percieving deer Elk Buffaloe or Antelopes." Buffalo in such numbers apparently took little notice of the men in their midst: "we saw a great quantity of game today particularly of Elk and Buffalo the latter are now so gentle the men frequently throw sticks and stones at them in order to drive them out of the way." Near the Great Falls Clark commented, "Great numbers of Buffalow in every direction, I think 10,000 may be seen in a view." Among the many strange sights associated with the buffalo, and witnessed by the expedition (the journals refer to buffalo some nine hundred times), was the incident the night one almost killed several men by rampaging through the camp. Lewis was once followed a considerable distance by a buffalo calf who was alarmed by Seaman; another time he was nearly killed by three charging buffalo bulls. At the Great Falls the party saw and smelled numerous buffalo carcasses washed over the falls when the animals were getting water. Near the Judith River on May 29, 1805, large numbers of winter-killed bison were observed. Once, the party was forced to wait several hours for a herd of buffalo to get across the river and allow them to pass. Today buffalo are recovering from the near extinction they faced in the late 1800s when their numbers dwindled to only 350 head. As Richard Manning writes in *Grassland: The History, Biology, Politics, and Promise of the American Prairie*, "Bison are a manifestation of a healthy native grassland the way a flower is the healthy manifestation of a healthy plant." According to the Sierra Club there are now two hundred thousand bison in the United States. See Buffalo Calling Dance; Bull boat.

References: Moulton, vol. 4; Hasselstrom; Schneider; Manning

Bissell, Russell (d. 1807): First infantry captain in charge of the men stationed at Kaskaskia, Illinois, on the Mississippi. Bissell served with his brother Daniel who was also a captain stationed at Fort Massac, Illinois, on the lower Ohio River. In letters dated July 2, 1803, they were instructed by Secretary of War Henry Dearborn to "furnish one Sergeant & Eight good men who understand rowing a boat to go with Capt. Lewis as far up the River as they can go & return with certainty before the Ice will obstruct the passage of the river. They should be furnished with the best boat at the Post & take provisions for Capt. Lewis's party and themselves." Historian Ernest Osgood notes this order was not carried out because of the late start on the Missouri.

Lewis wrote to Clark that he would "select by voluntary engagement any men from the Company of Capts. Rl and Dl Bissell and Stoddart's now occupying the posts of Massac & Kaskaskias; from these I think we shall be enabled to form our party without much difficulty." Among those chosen from Captain Russell Bissell's company were Peter Weiser, Richard Windsor, Patrick Gass, John Ordway, and possibly John Collins, although no muster roll exists as to the exact composition of his company. Among Captain Daniel Bissell's men were Joseph Whitehouse and John Newman, who was eventually expelled from the party in October of 1804 for "having uttered repeated expressions of a highly criminal and mutionous nature." The interpreter, George Drouillard, who worked as a civilian employee for Daniel Bissell, was also hired on at Fort Massac. The carpentry skills of Private Patrick Gass made Captain Russell Bissell reluctant to release him, but Gass asked Lewis to intercede on his behalf; he was allowed to sign up with the Corps of Discovery at Camp Dubois in 1803. Patrick Gass later served under Brigadier General Bissell in the War of 1812 and lost an eye, which ended his military career. See Gass, Patrick.

References: Jackson, Letters; Moulton, vol. 2; MacGregor, Journals of Patrick Gass

Bitterroot (*Lewisia rediviva*): A flowering plant of the Portulacaceae family. Discovered by Meriwether Lewis in 1806 and named in his honor by botanist Frederick Pursh. Author and naturalist Jerry DeSanto counts the bitterroot as a food plant of great significance to the native peoples in Montana, Washington, Idaho, and Oregon, equivalent in value to, but not to be confused with, the camas and cous. Called *spitlem* by the Salish, *konah* by the Snake (Shoshone), and *mepemcu* by the Kutenai, the bitterroot grows mainly on the west side of the Continental Divide. The Bitterroot River and Valley represent a traditional gathering spot for tribes to collect the plant, usually during the month of May and only by women. Old women would perform "First Roots Ceremonies" to guarantee a successful harvest of the cherished plant. Most tribes practiced a way of harvesting that encouraged the plant's regenerative properties. Although many negative reviews on its taste exist, various means of cooking and drying, as well as the time of harvest, may affect the flavor and degree of bitterness.

The taste may also be affected by the recipe, as it is said to be very good in certain soups. Lewis discovered the plant at or near the mouth of Lolo Creek in July 1806, having previously tasted it on August 22, 1805, writing "another speceis was much mutilated but appeared to be fibrous; the parts were brittle, hard of the size of small quill, cilindric and white as snow throughout, except some small parts of the hard black rind which they had not seperated in the preperation this the Indians with me informed were always boiled for use. I made the exprement, found that they had become perfectly soft by boiling but had a very bitter taste, which was naucious to my pallate, and I trans-fered them to the Indians (Shoshone) who ate them heartily." Lewis was able to sample and collect the bitterroot in 1806 only because of an unusually late growing season. Upon return to St. Louis, Lewis gave some dried plants to horticulturalist Bernard McMahon and botanist Frederick Pursh in April 1807, including the bitterroot speci-mens he collected at Lolo Creek. Later the collection was stored at McMahon's home in Philadelphia; Pursh took a portion of it to Lon-don. McMahon achieved temporary success in bringing the dried bit-terroot back to life through cultivation, which prompted the second part of the plant's Latin name. Pursh died soon after the 1814 publica-tion of his *Flora*, but he is responsible for crediting Lewis and Clark with the "discovery" of the bitterroot. The specimens disappeared for many years because botanist Benjamin Smith Barton misplaced some of them and gave the rest to Thomas Jefferson. Jefferson transferred them to the American Philosophical Society. There they lay unac-counted for until 1896, when botanist Thomas Meehan located them in poor condition and authenticated them with the help of a Harvard botanist, Dr. Benjamin Robinson. The plants were deposited to their present location, the Academy of Natural Sciences in Philadelphia, in 1898. The Lewis bitterroot specimens returned to Montana briefly in 1929 when a college student, Genevieve Murray, obtained permission from the academy to borrow them for her master's thesis at the Uni-versity of Montana. Her adviser helped her secure permission for the loan as he had been a guide for Elliott Coues in 1893. By statewide vote (including women) the bitterroot has been Montana's state flower since 1895. The low-set blossoms flower in late spring and early summer; leaves go from rose pink to white within a few days.

The present Bitterroot River was called Clark's Fork by the captains. The name Clark's Fork River now refers to the river at Missoula.

References: Moulton, vol. 5; DeSanto, Bitterroot *and* Montana Almanac

Black Buffalo (Black Buffalo Bull, Un-tongar-Sarbar [d. 1813]): Chief of the Teton Sioux. He was given a medal by the captains on September 25, 1804, and invited on board ship along with another, more troublesome Teton chief, the Partisan. In an attempt at social interaction the chiefs were given whiskey, which caused them to feign drunkenness and instigate a squabble aimed at detaining the expedition. Black Buffalo later used his influence to keep his warriors out of trouble and, according to Clark, "doe as we have advised them." On the return trip, after hearing reports from the Mandan of trouble with the same group of Teton Sioux, Clark refused to allow them near the boats.

Reference: Moulton, vol. 3

Black Cat (Posecopsahe): Mandan chief of the Rooptahee village. Encountered the expedition in late October 1804. He was designated or "made" a chief by the captains, who found him friendly and cooperative; they presented him with an American flag, which he later, in 1806, proudly displayed to North West Company traders. On October 31, 1804, Clark recorded, "I walked down and with great cermoney was Seeted on a roab by the Side of the Chief, he threw a handsom Roabe over me and after smoking the pipe with several old men arround the Chief Spoke Said he believed what we had told them and that peace would be general, which not only gave him Satisfaction but all his people they now Could hunt without fear, and ther womin Could work in the fields without looking everry moment for the Enemey and put off their mockersons at night." Black Cat frequently visited Fort Mandan over the winter of 1804–05, sometimes even spending the night. On February 8, 1805, Lewis commented on his character, "this man possesses more integrety, firmness, inteligence and perspicuety of mind than any indian I have met with in this quarter, and I think with a little management he may be made a usefull agent in furthering the views of our government. The black Cat presented me with a bow and apologized for not having completed the shield he had promised alledging that the weather had been too could to permit his making it, I gave him som small shot 6 fishing-hooks and 2 yards of ribbon his squaw also presented me with 2 pair of mockersons for which in return I gave a small lookingglass and a couples of nedles. the chief dined with me and left me in the evening."

Reference: Moulton, vol. 3

Black Moccasin (Omp-se-ha-ra): Awatixa Hidatsa (Minitari) chief of the Metaharta village. Encountered by the expedition in October 1804. On February 25, 1805, Clark observed, "we were Visited by the Black mockerson Chief of the little Village Big Bellies, the Chief of the Shoe Inds and a number of others   those Chiefs gave us Some meat which they packed on their wives." Many years later, in 1833, George Catlin painted Black Moccasin smoking a peace pipe and appearing very regal. He asked Catlin to pass on his best wishes to the Red Hair, otherwise known as William Clark.

References: Moulton, vol. 3; Burns and Duncan

Blue beads: Chief's beads (*tiacomoshack*). Used as ornamentation and highly prized, blue beads were considered the most desirable of the types of beads used for trade among Native American Indian tribes. In Philadelphia Lewis purchased twenty-five pounds of assorted beads thinking that amount would be more than sufficient to see the expedition to the Pacific and back. This was a serious miscalculation on Lewis's part and one to which he referred in his journal, particularly because the beads were inexpensive in Philadelphia and he was aware of the higher value of blue beads before he embarked on his tour, writing in June of 1803, "It is far more valued than the white beads of the same manufacture and answers all the purposes of money." Sergeant Gass described an incident at Fort Clatsop when Lewis and Clark appropriated Sacagawea's blue-beaded belt in exchange for a sea otter robe. "One of the natives here had a robe of sea otter skins, of the finest fur I ever saw; which the Commanding Officers wanted very much, and offered two blankets for it, which the owner refused, and said he would not take five. He wanted beads of the blue colour, of which we had none, but some that were on a belt belonging to our interpreter's squaw; so they gave him the belt for the skins." Although

Clark writes she was reimbursed with a "coate of Blue Cloth," Saca-gawea probably regretted the loss of her belt; oral tradition indicates she was given the belt by the Hidatsa women because she was a hard worker.

References: Jackson, Letters; *Hunsaker; Moulton, vols. 6, 10*

Blunderbuss: Blunderbutts or blunderbushes, according to Clark. The party had two of these swivel guns; they were cached at the Great Falls. One was damaged when a buffalo charged through camp on the night of May 28,1805. Russell describes these weapons as scatterguns with a barrel of approximately twenty-four inches and a flared muzzle two inches in diameter. It is likely they would have been carried on the pirogues, but when the encounter with the Sioux occurred on September 24, 1804, they were mounted on the keelboat. Russell fur-ther theorizes that the blunderbusses would have been mounted on the sentinel's catwalk at Fort Mandan, for maximum effectiveness. The blunderbusses survived their internment in the cache and were likely used as part of the party's defensive armaments on the return journey as well. On September 21, 1806, Clark described the arrival at St. Charles: "the party rejoiced at the Sight of this hospital village plyed thear ores with great dexterity and we Soon arrived opposit the Town, this day being Sunday we observed a number of Gentlemen and ladies walking on the bank, we Saluted the Village by three rounds from our blunderbuts and the Small arms of the party, and landed near the lower part of the town. we were met by great numbers of the inhabi-tants, we found them excessively polite." The blunderbusses were returned to St. Louis two days later.

References: Russell; Moulton, vols. 8, 9

Bodmer, Karl (1809–1893): Swiss painter. Bodmer received art instruction at an early age from his uncle the painter Johann Jakob Meier. He worked as an illustrator for travel albums sold to people touring the Rhine River and became acquainted with Prince Maxim-ilian of Weid, a natural history enthusiast and a seeker of adventure in foreign lands who needed an artist to document his upcoming expedition to the Missouri River. In addition to illustrating, Bodmer assisted the prince in collecting, hunting, and preparing botanical and

Bodmer's view of the Bear Paw Mountains from Fort McKenzie. As they advanced toward the Rocky Mountains the party acquired some sense of the size and scope of the mountain chain they had assumed would be easy to portage. Engraving by Karl Bodmer, courtesy of the Joslyn Art Museum, Omaha, Nebraska. Gift of Enron Art Foundation.

zoological specimens. Despite an early disagreement over salary and copyright of the paintings produced on the voyage, the prince and Bodmer came to terms and set off in May of 1833. An outbreak of cholera changed their original plans to visit New York and Louisiana. On a side trip Bodmer traveled alone to New Orleans and captured on canvas the first of his Native American Indian subjects. When they left St. Louis with the American Fur Company on the steamboat *Yellowstone* (1832), they hoped to meet friendly natives who traded at the posts. Bodmer painted watercolors of the Omahas, Poncas, and Sioux and of Nebraska, along with illustrations of the stark Dakota landscape. While the prince kept a journal, Bodmer rendered the same scenes Lewis and Clark witnessed twenty-eight years before. They steamed up the Missouri to Fort Pierre and boarded the *Yellowstone*'s sister steamboat, the *Assiniboine*, and finally arrived at Fort McKenzie on August 9 via the keelboat *Flora*. While at Fort McKenzie, Bodmer painted some of his finest ethnographic portraits, with his artistic talent and attention to detail producing impressive results. His subjects were enticed to sit for hours through gifts of trinkets and the belief that if Bodmer painted an individual that person received protection or "medicine" in battle. Conditions at the fort proved distressing: the prince suffered from scurvy and nearly died. By May the travelers arrived back in St. Louis and by August 8 they had returned to Europe. The prince wanted to publish a multivolume narrative account of the trip including an atlas of aquatints while Bodmer favored a more popular and timely version. Weid insisted on the expensive edition, and Bodmer went to work in Paris trying to secure and promote sales. The artist was not suited to the role of administrator or to the task of meeting deadlines. This, compounded with family tragedies, produced more missed deadlines and a period of depression in Bodmer's life. He remained friendly with his patron, the prince, although he refused an offer to travel to Russia with him. Their book proved to be a financial loss but the prince and Bodmer did not give up on promoting it, even taking advantage of fellow artist George Catlin's popularity in order to sell it. In the end public interest in the prince's edition could not sustain Bodmer; he left Paris to pursue different styles of artistic expression featuring animals and forest scenery. In Barbizon, an artist's community in France, Bodmer successfully produced his art, if less inspired or original than that of his earlier years. He won prizes for his canvases and exhibited in the nearby salons. When the prince died in 1867, Bodmer had contributed seven engravings to his latest book, *North America in Pictures* (1846). Though Bodmer liked to reminisce about his days in America and his native friends, Indians were not a lifelong obsession for him as for Catlin. In his last years Bodmer contributed illustrations to magazines and journals, but if it were not for a collection of funds obtained for him by the son of a friend, Bodmer would have been insolvent. He had a sad family life and spent his last fifteen years in extreme hardship, eventually going blind and dying in 1893. The winter he spent at Fort Clark would not be equaled creatively. Bodmer's emphasis on detail led later ethnographers to refer to his work as priceless. His paintings are frequently associated with accounts of the expedition.

References: Orr; *"Joslyn Art Museum Is Given Maximilian / Bodmer Collection"*; Freedman

Boley, John: Private from Kaskaskia, Illinois. He transferred from Russell Bissell's company to serve in the expedition and was one of the men who abused the privilege of leaving camp by going to the "whiskey shop" during the period at Camp Dubois. In his detachment orders for March 3, 1804, Lewis writes, ". . . and dose therefore most positively direct, that Colter, Bolye, Wiser, and Robinson do not recieve permission to leave camp for any pretext whatever for ten days, after this order is read on parade, unless otherwise directed here-after by Capt. Clark or himself." He was not a member of the permanent party and returned to St. Louis in 1805. Later that year he joined Zebulon Pike's expedition to find the sources of the Mississippi and in 1806 accompanied Pike to the Rocky Mountains. He avoided capture by the Spanish when he traveled with a party down the Arkansas River, reaching New Orleans in 1807. He may also have served under one of the Bissell brothers.

    Reference: Thwaites, Original Journals, *vol. 1*

Boudin blanc: White sausage pudding. Lewis describes the recipe on May 9, 1805: "from the cow I killed we saved the necessary materials for making what our wrighthand cook Charbono calls the boudin blanc and immediately set him about preparing them for supper; this white pudding we all esteem one of the greatest delacies of the forrest, it may not be amiss therefore to give it a place. About 6 feet of the lower extremity of the large gut is the first mosel that the cook makes love to, this he holds fast at one end with the right hand while with the forefinger and thumb of the left he gently compresses it, and dis-charges what he says is not good to eat, but of which in the squel we get a moderate portion; the mustle lying underneath the shoulder blade next to the back, and fillets are next saught, these are needed up very fine with a good portion of kidney suit; to this composition is then added a just proportion of pepper and salt and a small quantity of flour; thus far advanced, our skillful opporater C——o seizes his recepticle, which has never touched the water, for that would intirely distroy the regular order of the whole procedure; you will not forget that the side you now see is that covered with a good coat of fat pro-vided the anamal be in good order; the operator sceizes the receptacle

I say, and tying it fast at one end turns it inward and begins now with repeated evolutions of the hand and arm and a brisk motion of the finger and thumb to put in what he says is bon pour manger; thus by stuffing and compressing he soon distends the recepticle to the utmost limmits of it's power of expansion, and in the course of the opperation it's longtudinal progress it drives from the other end of the recepticle of a much larger portion of the than was previously discharged by the finger and thumb of the left hand in a former part of the operation; thus when the sides of the recepticle are skilfully exchanged the outer for the iner, and all is compleatly filled with something good to eat, it is tyed at the other end, but not any cut off, for that would make the pattern too scant; it is then baptised in the missouri with two dips and a flirt, and bobbed into the kettle; from whence after it be well boiled it is taken and fryed with bears oil untill it becomes brown, when it is ready to esswage the pangs of a keen appetite or such as travelers in the wilderness are seldom at a loss for." According to Lewis and Clark food expert Leandra Holland, the recipe Charbonneau used would have been common in French-speaking areas of the New World, including St. Louis and New Orleans. Usually pork would be the main ingredient; Charbonneau simply utilized what he had on hand, bison, for his version. Holland feels the variety of organ meats, including the heart, incorporated into the dish gave it the unique flavor Lewis so obviously enjoyed.

Reference: Moulton, vol. 4

Branding iron: Inscribed with the words "U.S. Capt. M. Lewis" and according to historian Roy Appleman probably made by the blacksmith of the party, John Shields. It was found sometime between 1892 and 1894, "on an island in the Columbia River 3½ miles above the Dalles, Oregon." Lewis used it for branding trees, not horses, which were likely branded with stirrups, instead of with the branding iron of his name. On November 22, 1805, Clark states, "Capt Lewis Branded a tree with his name Date &c. I marked my name the Day & year on an Alder tree, the party all Cut the first letters of their names on different trees in the bottom." As the party prepared to leave their horses with the Nez Percé in October of 1805, Ordway recorded, "we branded them on the near fore Shoulder with a Stirrup Iron, and cropped their fore mane So as we may know them at our return." Joseph Whitehouse also noted the branding iron's use on trees: "branded Several trees with the U.S. mark & Capt. M. Lewis & Latd. &c." and he notes the use of the "Stirrup Iron" for branding horses. The Lewis branding iron is owned by the Oregon Historical Society.

References: Appleman; Carrick, "Lewis and Clark Question and Answer"; Moulton, vols. 6, 9, 11

Bratton, William E. (1778–1841): Private. Born in Augusta County, Virginia, of Scottish-Irish descent. The Bratton family migrated to Kentucky in 1790, counting Bratton, or "Bratten" as he was often referred to (also sometimes called "Bret"), as one of the "nine young men from Kentucky." In his youth Bratton apprenticed as a blacksmith. According to historian Olin Wheeler, "It is not improbable that Bratton was one of the blacksmiths that was so successful at Fort Mandan, his trade being that of a gunsmith." He also contributed his skill as a hunter, scout, plant forager, and messenger. When Sergeant Floyd died, Bratton stood out as one of three men with the highest number of votes picked to replace him. When Moses Reed deserted, Bratton accompanied the party sent to bring him back dead or alive. The only man on the voyage who suffered a serious illness for an extended period of time, Bratton's miraculous recovery remains a subject of debate. He joined the Corps of Discovery on October 20, 1803, at the Falls of the Ohio and was one of the enlisted men assigned to court-martial duty in the trial of John Newman. Near present-day Valley County, Montana, Bratton was walking on the shore when chased by a grizzly bear he managed to wound but not kill, prompting Lewis to write, "he arrived so much out of breath that it was several minutes before he could tell what had happened . . . Bratton had shot him through the center of lungs, notwithstanding which he had pursued him near half a mile." By far the most repeated reference to Bratton concerned his health. His stint of prolonged duty in charge of the Salt Camp on the Pacific Ocean took its toll. Under Bratton's command four men, over a period of seven weeks, extracted twenty gallons of salt from the seawater. Bratton discovered the beached whale and brought some of the blubber back to Fort Clatsop. By early February both Gibson and Bratton retreated to the relative comfort of the fort following debilitating illnesses; Gibson had to be carried back on a litter. On February 16, 1806, Lewis noted, "Bratton is still very weak and complains of a pain in the lower part of the back when he moves which I suppose procedes from dability. I gave him barks [cinchona or Peruvian bark]." Clark added saltpeter to the list of remedies. The following day more barks were applied. On March 7, 1806, Lewis observed, "Bratton is much wose today, he complains of a violent pain in the small of his back and is unable in consequence to set up. We gave him one of our flannel shirts, applied a bandage of flannel to the part and bathed and rubbed it well with some vollatile linniment which I prepared with sperits of wine, camphor, castile soap, and a little laudanum. He felt himself better in the evening." Next day Lewis recorded Bratton much better: "his back gives him but little pain." But the relief proved temporary. On March 20, 1806, as the party prepared to leave Fort Clatsop, Lewis mentions Willard and Bratton as still weak, caused, he believed, by lack of proper food. "I expect when we get under way we shall be much more healthy. It has always had that effect on us heretofore." The following day Lewis expressed his doubts: "Bratten is now so much reduced that I am somewhat uneasy with respect to his recovery; the pain of which he complains most seems to be seated in the small of his back and remains obstinate. I believe that it is the rheumatism." On April 20, 1806, Lewis wrote, "Bratton was compelled to ride as he was yet unable to walk." Finally on May 24, 1806, at Camp Chopunnish the men decided to try something different for their stricken comrade. "William Bratton still continues very unwell: he eats heartily and digests his food well, and his recovered flesh almost perfectly yet is so weak in the loins that he is scarcely able to walk four or five steps, nor can he set upright without the greatest pain. We have tried every remedy which our engenuity could devise, or with which our stock of medicines furnished us, without effect. John Shields observed that he had seen men in similar situation restored by violent sweats. Bratton requested that he might be sweated in the manner proposed by Sheilds to which we consented. Sheilds sunk a circular hole of 3 feet diamiter and four feet deep in the earth. he kindled a large fire in the hole and heated well, after which the fire was taken out a seat placed in the center of the hole for the patient with a board at bottom for his feet to rest on; some hoops of willow poles were bent in an arch crossing each other over the hole, on these several blankets were thrown forming a secure and thick orning of about 3 feet high. the patient being striped naked was seated under this orning in the hole and the blankets well secured on every side. the patient was furnished with a vessell of water which he sprinkles on the bottom and sides of the hole and by that means creates as much steam or vapor as he could possibly bear in this situation he was kept about 20 minutes after which he was taken out and suddonly plunged in cold water twise and was then immediately returned to the sweat hole where he was continued three quarters of an hour longer then taken out covered up in several blankets and suffered to cool gradually. during the time of his being in the sweat hole he drank copious draughts of a strong tea of horse mint. . . . Bratton feels himself much better and is walking about today and says he is nearly free from pain." The cure worked so well the captains applied it to a chief of considerable note who lost power of his limbs. The sweat-lodge worked wonders for him as well although Dr. E. G. Chuinard discounts the sweat bath as the deciding factor in either man's recovery. Chuinard suspected Bratton's affliction was not intra-abdominal as some have suggested but more likely a case of intervertebral disc infection, which would be consistent with the course of Bratton's illness including his "spontaneous recovery" with or without the sweat-lodge. Historian Paul Cutright mentions "medical men have suggested sciatica, infectious arthritis, and inflamed sacro-illiac joint . . . undoubtedly aggravated by the months of penetrating damp and cold that characterized the long winter months at Fort Clatsop." On June 8, 1806, Bratton was reported by Lewis as "so far recovered that we cannot well consider him an invalid any longer, he has had a tedious illness which he boar with much fortitude and firmness." As proof of his permanent recovery, upon his return to the United States Bratton settled in Kentucky and Missouri, served in the War of 1812 under General William Henry Harrison, and fought at the Battle of Tippecanoe. He became a farmer and in 1819 at the age of forty-one married Mary H. "Polly" Maxwell. He fathered eight sons and two daughters and established residences in Ohio and Indiana where he served as justice of the peace in Wayne Township. He continued to be active in religious and educational community affairs. William Bratton died in 1841 and is buried in Waynetown, Indiana. When he discharged Private Bratton on October 10, 1806, Lewis wrote, ". . . as a tribute justly due the merits of said William Bratton, I wish with cheerfulness to declare that the ample support which he gave me under every difficulty, the manly firmness which he evinced on every necessary occation, and the fortitude with which he boar the fatigues and painfull sufferings incident to that long Voyage, entitled him to my highest confidence and sincere thanks; while it eminently recommends him to the consideration and rispect of his fellow Citizens." He received, along with his pay of $178.33, a land warrant for 320 acres from the U.S. government, eventually selling it to Samuel Barclay in 1816. His middle initial E. stood for his mother's maiden name of Elliot, which he added later in life to distinguish himself from a relative also named William Bratton. In later years, Bratton related frequently to his children that instead of switches the men used their ramrods on a culprit sentenced to lashes well laid on.

References: Biddle; Moulton, vols. 4, 6, 7; Cutright, Pioneering Naturalists; Jackson, Letters; Clarke; Wheeler

Breadroot (*Pisoralea esculenta*, white apple or pomme de prairie, pomme blanc): Turniplike plant scientifically described by Lewis on May 5, 1805; "The white apple is found in great abundance in this neighbourhood; it is confined to the highlands principally. The whiteapple, so called by the French Engages, is a plant which rises to the hight of 6 or 9 Inchs. rarely exceeding a foot; it puts forth one to four and sometimes more stalks from the same root, but is generally found with one only. . . . This root forms a considerable article of food with the Indians of the Missouri, who for this purpose prepare them in several ways. they are esteemed good at all seasons of the year, but are best from the middle of July to the latter end of Autumn when they are sought and gathered by the provident part of the natives for their winter store. . . . thus prepared they thicken their soope with it; sometimes they also boil these dryed roots with their meat without breaking them; when green they are generally boiled with their meat, sometimes mashing them or otherwise as they think proper. . . . they also eat this root roasted and frequently make hearty meals of it raw without sustaining any inconvenience or injury therefrom. The White or brown bear feed very much on this root, which their tallons assist them to procure very readily. the white apple appears to me to be a tasteless insipid food of itself tho' I have no doubt but our epicures would admire this root very much, it would serve in their ragouts and gravies in stead of the truffles morella." While under Lewis's care for high fever and abdominal pain, Sacagawea felt well enough to gather "a considerable quantity of the white apples of which she eat so heartily in their raw state, together with a considerable quantity of dryed fish without my knowledge that she complained very much and her fever again returned. I rebuked Sharbono severely for suffering her to indulge herself with such food he being privy to it and having been previously told what she must only eat."

Reference: Moulton, vol. 4

Broken Arm (Tunnachemootoolt): Nez Percé war chief engaged in a war party against the Shoshone on the south branch of Lewis's River. When Lewis and Clark first arrived in his country, the Clearwater area, he was given a flag by Lewis and Clark, which he proudly displayed outside his tipi. Broken Arm made a treaty of friendship with the Americans but refused to send a delegation with the expedition. He did give Clark his shirt and two pipes, the fancier one as a present for the Shoshone, as a sign of good intentions. Broken Arm was one of the three chiefs (the others were Cut Nose and Twisted Hair) involved in a dispute over the care of the corps's horses while they had possession of them. Among other articles the captains gave him was a vial of eyewash, and "he was much pleased with this present." According to historian Gary Moulton, little is known of Broken Arm beyond what is written in the journals. Lewis ranked the four chiefs in this order: Tunnachemootoolt (Broken Arm), Neeshneparkeeook, Yoomparkkartim, and Hohots Ilppip.

Reference: Moulton, vol. 7

Buffalo Calling Dance (Red Stick Ceremony): Sacred Mandan ceremony believed to entice the buffalo to come closer to the hunters' villages on the Missouri River. Historian James Ronda explains it was an example of the Native American belief that sexual relations could be a "pipeline to power" and that, by offering their young wives to the elder men of the village, young men received some of the wisdom and strength of these men. Whites usually viewed such ceremonies as superstition, but for the Mandan and Hidatsa nations the dance represented a critical part of their religion and survival. Artist George Catlin, who spent a winter with the Mandan in the 1830s, witnessed that "the dance always has the desired effect. It never fails. Nor can it, for it cannot be stopped, going incessantly day and night until 'buffalo come.' Drums beat and rattles shake, songs and yells are shouted, and lookers-on stand ready with masks on their heads and weapons in hand to take the place of each dancer as he becomes fatigued, and jumps out of the ring. . . . These dances sometimes continue two or three more weeks without stopping an instant, until the joyful moment when buffaloes made their appearance. So they never fail and they believe the dance has been the means of bringing the buffalo." Clark matter-of-factly recorded his observations of the ceremony: "a Buffalow Dance (or Meidson) for 3 nights passed in the 1st village, a curious custom the old men arrange themselves in a circle & after Smoke a pipe, which is handed them by a young man, Dress up for the purpose, the young men who have their wives in a circle to one of the old men with a whining tone and the old man to take his wife (who presents necked except a robe) and—(or Sleep with him) the Girl then takes the old man (who very often can scarcely walk) and leades him to a Convenient place for the business, after which they return to the lodge, if the Old man (or a white man) returns to the lodge without gratifying the man & his wife, he offers her again and again; it is often the case that after the 2d time (he) without kissing the husband throws a nice robe over the old man & begs him not to dispise him, & his wife." Biddle later changed the passage to imperfect Latin. The enlisted men of the expedition were enthusiastic if unbelieving participants in the ritual. One lucky participant was given four young women. Later, trapper Pierre Antoine Tabeau would write the men were "untiringly zealous in attracting the cow" and the Mandan credited their zealousness with a successful hunting season the following spring.

References: Abel, Tabeau's Narrative; *Catlin,* Letters and Notes; *Moulton, vol. 3*

A bull boat, constructed by the Mandan Indians from buffalo skins and willow branches. In August 1806 Sergeant Pryor and three men used bull boats to catch up to the main party after their horses were stolen by the Crow. Montana Historical Society, Helena.

Bull boat: Watercraft made of buffalo skin and used by the Mandan and Hidatsa people for transportation on the Missouri River and as ventilation covers for their earth lodge chimneys. The captains were amazed at the stability of the bull boats, which they called "canoes made of a Single buffalow Skin with 2 and 3 Squars Cross the river to day in waves as high as ever I saw them on this river, quite uncomposed. . . ." On July 24, 1806, Clark sent Sergeant Pryor and Privates Shannon, Hall, and Windsor to take horses to the Mandans. On the way they encountered some Crow Indians who managed to steal the horses. Under the instruction of Sergeant Pryor, they constructed two bull boats to float down the Yellowstone and onto the Missouri River, one for the four men and one in reserve: "2 sticks of 1¼ inches diameter is tied together So as to form around hoop of the Size you wish the canoe, or as large as the Skin will allow to cover, two of those hoops are made one for the top or brim and the other for the bottom the deabth you wish the Canoe, then sticks of the same size are Crossed at right angles and fastened with a throng to each hoop and also where each Stick Crosses each other. Then the Skin when green is drawn tight over this fraim and fastened with throngs to the brim or outer hoop So as to form a perfect bason. One of those canoes will carry 6 or 8 men and their loads." On the return trip Lewis and his detachment also made bull boats to ferry their bags and food across the Missouri near the Great Falls, "the one we made after the mandan fassion with a single skin in the form of a bason and the other we constructed of two skins on a plan of our own." At five the next day, "we transported our baggage and meat to the opposite shore in our canoes which we found answered even beyond our expectations." Among the Welsh people a similar kind of watercraft is used, which is sometimes cited as proof the Mandan are descended from a tribe of lost Welshmen.

Reference: Moulton, vols. 3, 8

Burning glass: Looking or sun glass; a lens used for magnifying the rays of the sun so as to quickly start a fire. While outfitting the expedition in Philadelphia, Lewis bought eight dozen and lists them in the summary of purchases under "Indian Presents." On August 19, 1804, Clark wrote, "a fine morning wind from the S E. I prepd. a present from the Chiefs & Warriers, the main Chief Brack fast with us naked; & beged for a Sun glass." Lewis used burning glasses on August 11, 1805, as part of a package of trinkets to entice the Shoshone to remain in the area of the Beaverhead Rock rather than to flee the oncoming strangers. He tied the trinkets to the end of a pole that "they might from this token discover that we were friendly and white persons." Clark used a sun glass to pay for an Indian to accompany him "as a pilot" when he explored the Multnomah or Willamette River. At Fort Clatsop, Ordway recorded, "a Great nomber of the Savages visited us brought corn & beans to Trade with us they wanted of us looking Glases Beeds buttens or & other kinds of articles pleasing to the Eye." On May 1, 1806, Ordway described two young men of the Walla Walla tribe who came into camp to return a steel trap, "which was forgot at their village. this is an Instance which we had not any right to expect from Savages. we gave them one a knife the other a Sun glass, &.c., and a little vension."

References: Jackson, Letters; Moulton, vols. 2, 5, 7, 9

C

Cache: A pit shaped like a bottle with a long neck, which was used for storage on the upper Missouri by several tribes and trappers in the 1800s. Noting that the practice of building a cache or "deposit" was familiar to Pierre Cruzatte, Lewis wrote, "on enquiry I found that Cruzatte was well acquainted this business and therefore left the management of it intirely up to him." While the goods they started with added up to some thirty-five hundred pounds, they also added to their baggage as they proceeded on, making deposits or caches a necessary way of dealing with the overload. When they left the Canoe Camp in July of 1805, Lewis commented, "We find it extreemly difficult to keep the baggage of our men within reasonable bounds. . . ." They dug three caches on the Marias River about a mile upriver from the camp of June 3–12, 1805. According to Lewis, "the traders of the Missouri, particularly those engaged in trade with the Siouxs are obliged to have frequent recourse to this method in order to avoid being robed." On June 26, 1805, at the lower portage camp near Great Falls, Lewis lists the articles to be deposited, "my desk which I had left for that purpose and in which I had left some books, my specimens of plants and minerals &c. collected from fort Mandan to that place. also 2 kegs of Pork, ½ Keg of flour 2 blunderbushes, ½ keg of fixed ammunition and some other small articles belonging to the party which could be dispensed with." On July 9, 1805, Lewis admitted defeat and reluctantly cached his iron boat: "but it was now too late to introduce a remidy and I bid a dieu to my boat and her expected services." The boat has never been recovered although efforts are currently under way to determine its exact location. At Camp Fortunate on August 20, 1805, Lewis directed a "centinel" to stand guard as a cache was being made and to fire his weapon if any Indians appeared. The cache included "a small assortment of medicines, together with the specemines of plants, minerals, seeds &c. which I have collected between this place and the falls of the Missouri which I shall deposit here." When the cache was opened on the return journey in July 1806, Lewis assessed the damage done by the rising river, which destroyed his bearskins and "all my specimens of plants also lost. the Chart of the Missouri fortunately escaped. . . . found my papers damp and several articles damp. the stoper had come out of a phial of laudinum and the contents had run into the drawer and distroyed a gret part of my medicine in such a manner that it was past recovery." Another cache unearthed by Clark on the return journey, July 8, 1806, contained canoes and a special treat to the "Chewers of tobacco who became So impatient to be chewing it that they Scercely gave themselves time to take their Saddles off their horses before they were off to the deposit." Clark writes that he found every article safe, though damp. Hugh McNeal had a run-in with a grizzly bear on one of his excursions to unearth a cache at Willow Creek in 1806. The bear treed McNeal and then "waited at the foot of the tree untill late in the evening before he left him, when McNeal ventured down and caught his horse which by this time strayed off to a distance of 2 ms." Among the Arikara, Virginia Bergman Peters notes it was the women who constructed caches over a period of several days by digging a pit and laying an old tent cover near the pit so that one end of the cover hung over the mouth. They would then put braided corn and squash into the cache until it was full and use the skin from the flank of a buffalo to cover it tightly. They covered this with a layer of dried grass and several wood planks. The final step in securing the cache was to pack a layer of earth on top of the planks and scatter ashes over it. Properly constructed caches could store and preserve substantial amounts of grain and vegetables for long periods of time with no effect on taste whatsoever.

References: Peters; Moulton, vols. 4, 5, 8

Camas (*Camassia quamash*): The underground bulbs of this lilylike plant were fire baked by many tribes to provide a pleasant-tasting and nutritious staple. The camas, which grows in moist meadows, is called the single most important food item and also an important trade commodity for tribes in the Northwest. Many trickster stories and myths exist about the gift of the camas to the various tribes. The camas growth area in the Northwest ranges from British Columbia east to southwest Alberta, Montana, Wyoming, and Utah. Shoshone traded it to Nez Percé, Nez Percé traded it to Gros Ventre and Crow, Upper Pend'd Orielle traded it to the Kootenai, and Kootenai to the Blackfeet and so on. The hard work of digging the camas root was made easier by regarding it as part of a seasonal celebration. Women usually gathered camas in the spring. They gathered the roots using elk antler digging sticks or sticks fashioned with horn handles. Camas was cooked in earth ovens before eating or storing. The same method of cooking was used throughout the Northwest. It was considered taboo among many tribes for the men to be near the cooking pits. This may have been simply a method of keeping the men away, as the women enjoyed a time of cooking and socializing together. According to Jeff Hart, to cook camas you first preheated an earthen oven with ponderosa pine. Hot stones were placed in the pit and covered with earth or vegetation. Camas bulbs were laid on top. Sometimes black tree moss was added but most women used Douglas onions called small camas to cook with the camas. Water was poured over the top of the pit, then came a layer of bark, followed by more dirt. A fire was built on top of the pit. The camas was cooked for twelve to seventy hours and required much patience and care to prepare correctly. If dry, camas stores indefinitely. It was usually stored in tree limbs or platforms in trees. On October 21, 1805, near the Columbia, Clark wrote, "One of our party J. Collins presented us with some verry good beer made of the pahicoquarmash bread." According to Gary Moulton, "The term *pasigoo* is the Shoshone designation for the camas and its edible bulb. The word literally means water sego, in reference to the sego lily, a common food in the region. Lewis and Clark wrote this word together with *quamash,* or the Nez Percé term for camas, from which the Latin and English designations derive." As the first white men to encounter and sample camas, at Weippe Prairie, one of the major camas collecting grounds in the interior Pacific Northwest, the famished captains appreciated its flavor if not its aftereffects. "Captain Lewis and myself eate a Supper of roots boiled, which filled us both so full of wind that we were scarcely able to breathe all night felt the effects of it." Later at Camp Chopunnish, on June 11, 1806, Lewis wrote, "this root is palatable but disagrees with me in every shape I have ever used it." Elliott Coues comments in his history of the journals, "Taken in sufficient quantity camas is both emetic and purgative to those unaccustomed to eat it." The captains (and Sergeant Gass, who wrote, "the Indian provisions did not agree with us") correctly reasoned that the combination of dried salmon and camas roots caused the symptoms of gastroenteritis they experienced at Weippe Prairie. The men used the remedies they had on hand: salts, Rush's pills, Jalap, and tartar emetic and eventually recovered by eating something easier on their stomachs: dog meat. Camas is a popular place-name in Idaho, where there are five different streams named Camas Creek, a Camas Slough, three Camas Prairies, two Camas meadows, and a Camas Flat. Lab analysis has shown camas is rich in protein and is also a good source of fiber, calcium, phosphorus, and iron. When cooked in the traditional way, the root produces fructose, a highly digestible form of sugar. According to Hart the name was borrowed from Chinook trade jargon, a form of the Nootka word *chamas*, meaning "sweet." Gass remarked, "The Com-mas grows in great abundance on this plain; and at this time looks beautiful being in full bloom with flowers of a pale blue colour." In Peale's *Memorandum of Specimens and Artifacts*, it is listed under Bread. "This is called Passhequo-qua-mash being only a varied preparation of the quawmas bulb." On September 23, 1805, Gass commented, "The provisions which we got consisted of roots which they call comas, and which resemble onions in shape, but are of a sweet taste. The bread is manufactured by steaming, pounding, and baking the roots on a kiln they have for the purpose." Lewis wrote on the return trip, May 10, 1806, "the noise of their women pounding the cows root reminds me of a nail factory." There is a further description in Thwaites, *Original Journals*, vol. 3.

References: *Hart; Moulton, vols. 5, 8; Coues,* History of the Expedition, *vol. 2; MacGregor; Thwaites,* Original Journals, *vol. 3*

Cameahwait (Too-ite-coon, He Never Walks, Musket Owner): Shoshone chief and brother or cousin to Sacagawea. Lewis, McNeal, Drouillard, and Shields first encountered this man on August 13, 1805, near the Beaverhead Rock after alarming some women who were out gathering roots. At this meeting Cameahwait began a "long cerimony of the pipe when we were requested to take of our mockersons, the Chief having previously taken off his as well as all the warriors present." This was an auspicious moment for both peoples; Cameahwait made sure the strangers recognized the fact by performing the pipe ritual in a sacred manner. This band of Shoshone also showed their respect and sincerity by embracing the strangers and repeating "ah he i" (I am much pleased). Despite having only berries to eat, Cameahwait shared with Lewis "some cakes of serviceberries and Choke cherries which had been dryed in the sun; of these I made a hearty meal." From Cameahwait Lewis heard the first Native American mention of "the great lake where white men lived" and that ahead lay territory "impossible for us to pass either by land or water." The fact that Cameahwait's people appeared to own a sizable horse herd reassured Lewis as he proceeded to gather all of the geographical information he could from the chief and an older member of the tribe they called Toby. Cameahwait obligingly drew maps in the sand and used rocks to symbolize mountains. They told Lewis of a tribe of pierced-nose Indians who used a more northern trail over the mountains but warned them "that the road was a very bad one . . . that they had suffered excessively with hunger on the rout being obliged to subsist for many days on berries alone. . . ." Lewis confidently asserted, "I felt perfectly satisfyed, that if the Indians could pass these mountains with their women and Children, that we could also." Cameahwait told Lewis that because they had no guns his people "were obliged to remain in the interior of these mountains at least two thirds of the year where the suffered as we then saw great hardships for the want of food sometimes living for weeks without meat and only a little fish root and berries." This would all change, Cameahwait told Lewis, if they had guns and could live and hunt nearer the buffalo. They were tired of being at the mercy of their enemies, the Minitaris, and they did not want to live and eat like bears. Lewis saw for himself how hungry Cameahwait's people were when they devoured, entrails and all, a deer Drouillard had killed and brought back to camp, "Like a parcel of famished dogs." In an effort to keep the band from heading back into the mountains, Lewis deceived Cameahwait into believing that a note he had left for Clark was instead a note his "brother Chief" had left for him. For further reassurance, the two leaders exchanged hats, and Lewis even surrendered his gun. The gamble paid off, and when Clark and his party reunited with Lewis all were surprised to learn Sacagawea was the chief's long-lost sister. After Lewis struck a deal for the horses, medals and presents were distributed, and the air gun was fired for effect, which the Indians found "perfectly incomprehensible"; shoes were again removed and the pipe smoked: "the cerimony of our council and smoking the pipe was in conformity of the custom of this nation performed bearfoot. on those occasions points of etiquet are quite as much attended to by the Indians as among civilized nations. To keep indians in a good humour you must not fatieque them with too much business at one time." Cameahwait gave Lewis a tippet made of ermine skins he much admired; Lewis wore it when he was painted by Saint-Mémin in 1807. The Shoshone chief also sent an emissary and pilot (as Clark called him), Old Toby, with Lewis and Clark to see them safely over the mountains. Lewis noted that Cameahwait had cut his hair short as had most of the people in his band, "in consequence of the loss of their relations by the Minnetares." See Tippet; Old Toby.

Reference: Moulton, vol. 5

Camera obscura (Crimee): An optical box-shaped machine. With the aid of a lens, light that enters through a hole on one side produces a shadow on the other, which can then be traced. According to the *Dictionary of Arts and Sciences*, which Lewis had in his possession, the machine allowed the viewer to "see the images of objects, in a beautiful manner, on the paper." Meriwether Lewis wished for just such a tool when he first tried to describe the splendor and magnificence of the Great Falls. "after wrighting this imperfect discription I again viewed the falls and was so disgusted with the imperfect idea which it conveyed of the scene that I determined to draw my pen across it and begin agin, but then reflected that I could not perhaps succeed better than pening the first impressions of the mind; I wished for the pencil of Salvator Rosa or the pen of Thompson, that I might be able to give the enlightened world some just idea of this truly magnifficent and sublimely grand object, which has from the commencement of time been concealed from the view of civilized man; but this was fruitless and vain. I most sincerely regreted that I had not brought a crimee (camera) obscura with me by the assistance of which even I could have hoped to have done better but alas this was also out of my reach." In an 1817 Dublin reprint of Biddle's edition of the *Journals of Lewis and Clark*, a view of the "Principal Cascade of the Missouri" appears, which may have been the one commissioned by Lewis when he returned to the United States. In addition Clark mentions "an imperfect drawing of the falls of the Missouri" found among Lewis's papers in Philadelphia. From a receipt found in the Clark papers it is known that, in preparation for the publication of the journals, Lewis engaged the services of an "eccentric Irish engraver," John James Barralett, to provide "two drawings water falls" for forty dollars. Historian Paul Cutright feels "it is highly unlikely that there is any connection between the Dublin drawing and the one located by Clark." (An illustration of a camera obscura appears in *We Proceeded On*, August 1988.)

References: *Society of Gentlemen; Jackson,* Letters*; Biddle; Cutright,* History of the Lewis and Clark Journals

Camp Chopunnish (Long Camp, Camp Kamiah [near present-day Kamiah, Idaho]): The expedition camped here from May 14 to June 10, 1806, on the north bank of the Clearwater River. At the site, they located a circular pit four feet deep and thirty feet in diameter previously used by the natives, which they used for storing baggage. The area became known as Camp Chopunnish after Lewis and Clark passed through, a name given by Elliott Coues, in honor of the name they called the Nez Percé Indians. According to trail historian Roy Appleman, they occupied the Long Camp for a lengthier time than any other site except Forts Mandan and Clatsop and Camp Wood. The forced layover resulted from late snows in the Bitterroot mountain range in the spring of 1806. They waited at Camp Chopunnish for almost a month, having reunited with their horses and the friendly Nez Percé. The men set to work hunting and building a canoe, except for William Bratton, who experimented successfully with sweat-lodge treatments to relieve his extreme lower back pain. While her son Jean Baptiste had a neck infection at the Long Camp, Sacagawea made herself useful by gathering fennel roots for the crew to eat. Lewis observed the wildlife and collected a full one-fourth of the entire herbarium "on the Kooskooskee" (Clearwater). He also tried to determine the distinctions among the many bears they encountered and described in characteristic detail a bird that would later bear his name—Lewis's woodpecker. Clark doctored the two ailing members as best he could and treated the natives, who suffered from a variety of ailments, in exchange for roots. The men competed in races and athletic games with the Nez Percé young men, waited for the salmon to start running, and spent many nights dancing to the tune of Cruzatte's fiddle. Broken Arm, a Nez Percé chief, generously offered the tribe's horses as food for the visitors while they camped together.

Reference: Appleman

Cape Girardeau (Jeradeau): Site of "Lorimer's Red House," a Spanish post visited by Meriwether Lewis on his way up the Mississippi in late 1803. As the commandant of the district military headquarters, the French Canadian Louis Lorimer treated Lewis to a "comfortable and desent" dinner on November 23, 1803. Lorimer had long traded with the local Indian tribes and was married to a Shawnee woman. Their daughter caught Lewis's eye as "an agreeable and affible girl, & much the most descent looking feemale I have seen since I left the settlement in Kentuckey." The commandant had his son escort Lewis via horseback to Old Cape Girardeau: "here I found my boat and people landed for the night. found Capt. Clark unwell." George Drouillard spent his boyhood with his Shawnee mother's nation near Cape Girardeau and returned there briefly following the expedition.

References: Moulton, vol. 2; Large, "Captain Lewis and the Hopeful Cadet"

Car gar no mok she (Raven Man Chief): Chief of the Mandan village Rooptahee, given a medal with several other chiefs during a council at Fort Mandan at the end of October 1804. Clark recorded his speech: "Will you be So good as to go to the Village the Grand Chief will Speek & give Some Corn, if you will let Some men take bags it will be well. I am going with, the Chief of the ricares to Smoke a pipe with that nation." In March 1805, when John Shields was performing smithing duties for the Mandan, Sergeant Ordway noted that the "Savages continue to visit us in Order to git their implements of War made. they bring us pay in corn and beans dryed meat &persim-

blans [summer squashes] &C—" Later the next spring Clark states, "The 2d Chief of the 2d Mandan Village took a miff at our not attending to him perticelarely after being here about ten day and moved back to his village."

Reference: Moulton, vols. 3, 9

Carey, Mathew (1760–1839): Philadelphia publisher who, beginning in 1810, included six woodcut engravings of unknown origin in his three editions of the Patrick Gass journal. As historian Paul Russell Cutright points out, "He was making graphic history of sorts by giving to the world the first illustrated Lewis and Clark journal." Cutright goes on to call the pictures "delightfully preposterous." The Carey editions of Gass's journal are highly prized by rare book collectors.

Reference: Cutright, History of the Lewis and Clark Journals

Carolina parakeets (*Conuropsis carolinensis*): A member of the parrot family, now extinct, but at the time of the expedition found in flocks of hundreds in the eastern United States. Sighted on June 26, 1804, by William Clark, who thereby extended its known range beyond the Mississippi. Near the Kansas River he noted, "emence number of Parrot-quetes," or "I observed a great number of Parrot queets." As with the passenger pigeon, the loss of traditional habitat— forests and swamps—played a significant role in the extinction of the Carolina parakeet. In addition they had to compete with the honeybee for nesting sites. Millinery fashion trends, which used feathers for ornamentation, also figured in their demise as a species. As their numbers decreased the birds became novelty pets. Carolina parakeets were easily domesticated and known to enjoy music. Unfortunately the aviculturalists who kept them did not establish a successful breeding program, and the last Carolina parakeet, "Incas," died at the Cincinnati Zoo in February 1918. His keepers said he died of grief after his mate of thirty-two years, "Lady Jane," died the previous summer. Cutright describes the Carolina parakeet as "a handsome bird, bright green with a yellow head, the size of a mourning dove." A specific kind of mite also became extinct with the Carolina parakeets.

References: Cokinos; Osgood, Field Notes; Moulton, vol. 2; Cutright, Pioneering Naturalists

Carver, Jonathan (1710–1780): Connecticut explorer who served as a lieutenant for Robert Rogers as he searched for a route to the Pacific. Carver wrote the book *Travels through the Interior Parts of North America* (1781) on his exploration of the upper Mississippi valley in the direction of the height of land (core drainage region). Jefferson purchased his book while in Europe and adopted many of Carver's more popular theories. Carver rationalized that the Missouri and the Oregon (Columbia) Rivers had sources in the same area. He speculated on the existence of a Continental Divide and viewed the Rocky Mountains as two distinct mountain chains: north and south. Until they reached Lemhi Pass, Lewis and Clark unquestioningly accepted Carver's theoretical geography. He is the uncredited author of an essay in the apocryphal Lewis and Clark work *The Travels of Capts Lewis and Clarke, from St. Louis.* According to Carver's information the mountains to the west of the St. Pierre River "are called the Shining Mountains, from an infinite number of crystal stones, of an amazing size, with which they are covered, and which, when the sun shines full upon them, sparkle so as to be seen at a very great distance."
Reference: Carver

Cascades of the Columbia (Great Chute, Great Rapids): The last obstacle of the lower Columbia Gorge. A four-mile stretch of furiously churning boulder-strewn water. The party spent two days exploring the chasm during which time Clark observed some Indian burial vaults and commented on, but did not disturb, their contents: "Some contained bones for the debth of 4 feet. on the tops and on poles attached to those vaults hung Brass kittles & frying pans pearced thro their bottoms, baskets, bowls of wood, Seal Shels, Skins, bits of Cloth, Hair, bags of Trinkets & Small peices of bone &c . . . This must bee the burrying place for maney ages of the inhabitants of those rapids, the vaults are of the most lasting timber Pine & Cedar." On November 1, 1805, the captains decided to follow the example of the local Indians and portage the Great Chute, "takeing our Small Canoe and all of the baggage by land 940 yards of bad Slippery and rockey way . . . we got all our baggage over the Portage of 940 yards, after which we got the 4 large Canoes over by Slipping them over the rocks on poles placed across from one rock to another, and at Some places along partial Streams of the river. in passing those canoes over the rocks &c. three of them recived injuries which obliged us to delay to have them repared." As Sergeant Gass recorded, "It was the most fatiquing business we have been engaged in for a long time." After passing through the Cascades and proceeding on past Beacon Rock on November 2 Clark noted, for the first time, a changing of the tides.

References: Kirkpatrick, "Stupendious Columbia Gorge"; Moulton, vols. 5, 10

Castorium: A heavily scented oil from the perineal gland of a beaver, used by George Drouillard and other trappers as bait to attract beaver into traps. Lewis noted that "this bate when properly prepared will intice the beaver to visit it as far as he can smell it, and I think it may be safely stated at a mile, their sense of smell being very accute." After taking the castorium from the beaver, "you will add half a nutmeg, a dozen or 15 grains of cloves and thirty grains of cinimon finely pulverized, stir them well together and then add as much ardent sperits to the compostion as will reduce it the consistency mustard prepared for the table; when thus prepared it resembles mustard precisely to all appearance." By itself, Lewis wrote, castorium was "a pure oil of a strong rank disagreeable smell, and not unlike train (whale) oil." Clark called the glands, which produced castor, "bark stones." Castor is a yellow, waxy, pungent material used by the beaver to keep its fur waterproof and perhaps to mark its territory. Trappers usually saved the perineal gland after skinning a beaver because, along with its power as a baiting ingredient, it served several other purposes: as a stimulant, an antispasmodic, and a fixative for perfume. Catlin told of smoking with a chief who used shavings from dried beaver castor mixed with kinnikinnick and then dropped on top of a soupçon of powdered buffalo dung. After lighting the pipe he and Catlin "enjoyed together for a quarter of an hour the most delightful exchange of good feelings, amid clouds of smoke and pantomimic gesticulations."

References: Cutright, Pioneering Naturalists; Catlin, Letters and Notes, vol. 2; Moulton, vol. 6

Catlin, George (1796–1872): Pennsylvania artist specializing in Indian paintings, author, and anthropologist. From childhood, Catlin was fascinated with wilderness and Indians. He originally studied law in Connecticut; at the same time he taught himself how to paint. He chose art as his profession and worked as a Philadelphia portrait painter of politicians and military heroes but always kept an eye out for more inspiring subject matter. In the 1820s in Philadelphia a visiting delegation of Indians from the "Far West" intrigued him. Catlin was particularly impressed with the natives' inherent dignity and attire, suited, he wrote later, "exactly for the painter's palette." The meeting inspired him to "use my art and so much of the labor of my future life as might be required in rescuing from oblivion the looks and customs of the vanishing races of native man in America." This included the Mandan and Hidatsa tribes visited by Lewis and Clark thirty years earlier. With the approval of, and encouragement from, then governor of the Missouri Territory and superintendent of Indian affairs General William Clark, Catlin set out on the steamboat *Yellowstone* in 1832 and spent the next year in the Upper Missouri region. A man of strong constitution, Catlin would spend summers with the Indians and winters selling his art back East. He produced an amazing number of portraits and sketches, often under less than ideal circumstances. His method was to present Indian culture from the natives' viewpoint with an emphasis on telling a story about their way of life. He painted several portraits of events, people, and places first described by Lewis and Clark. One old Minitari chief, Black Moccasin, fondly remembered his friends "Long Knife," Lewis, and "Red Hair," Clark. Catlin painted Floyd's Bluff, the burial site of Sergeant Charles Floyd. The natives felt his paintings represented powerful medicine. On one occasion he was asked to return a portrait of a young girl who had agreed to sit for him. Catlin was nearly out of sight of the Mandan village when he heard someone shouting, "Mi-neek-e-sun-te-ka (the Mink) is dying! The picture you made of her is too much like her— you put so much of her into it, that when your boat took it away from our village, it drew part of her life with it—she is bleeding from the mouth—she is puking up all her blood—you are drawing the strings out of her heart and they will soon break. We must take her picture back and then she will get well again." Noting she was a beautiful girl, Catlin reluctantly handed the painting back to the Mandan, but later learned she died anyway. Catlin maintained a deep respect and appreciation for the religious beliefs and ceremonies of the tribes he painted. His renditions of the buffalo, bear, and scalp dances as performed by the Mandan contribute significantly to the field of ethnology. Catlin also documented the foot races and games of the tribes he visited. In his entries on rivers and streams, Lewis mentions a "red pipe stone river, the country watered by which is remarkable for furnishing a red stone, of which savages make their most esteemed pipes. The Indians of many nations travel vast distances to obtain this stone, and it is ascerted, tho' with what justice I will not pretend to determine, that all nations are at peace with each other while in this district of country, or on the waters of this river." Catlin was the first white man to visit the Sacred Pipestone quarry, located in southern Minnesota, paint it, and personally experience the profound significance it represented to many of the Indians he knew. He described his feelings of wonder and awe at smoking a pipe of peace with his friends in a place so important to their history and mythology. Although he did not, out of respect, go into the quarry, he did bring back some samples of the soft, soapy, red stone. A noted mineralogist who studied the stone found it to be a new mineral compound and named it, in Catlin's honor, Catlinite. Catlin exhibited his paintings in the United States and Europe and wrote several books based on his travels and illustrations. Although art experts debate his skill as an artist and his value as an ethnographer, his paintings consistently attract appreciative collectors and audiences. He painted Comanches and South American Indians in his later years and, in 1861, wrote *Breath of Life* in which he advised keeping one's mouth closed, especially during sleep. While Congress balked at purchasing his collection of more than eight hundred of his works during his lifetime, they are now housed at the National Gallery of Fine Arts, the National Gallery of Art, as well as at the Smithsonian Institution's National Museum of Natural History.

References: Catlin, Letters and Notes, *vol. 2; McCracken; Thwaites,* Original Journals, *vol. 6*

Celilo Falls: Also known as the Dalles and the Great Falls of the Columbia. Lewis and Clark portaged this thirty-eight-foot obstacle in October 1805 and on their way back to the United States, in April 1806, when high water caused the captains to choose an overland route. Clark wrote on October 23, 1805, "We were obliged to let the canoes down by strong ropes of Elk skins which we had for the purpose, one Canoe in passing got loose by the cords breaking, and was cought by the Indians below." Here the party first observed the elaborate salmon-drying process of the Columbia nations, and found the area so infested with fleas "that every man of the party was obliged to Strip Naked dureing the time of takeing over the canoes, that they might have the opportunity of brushing the flees of their legs and bodies." Lewis and Clark found the Columbia River natives not as friendly and cooperative as the Nez Percé; they decided to break up their canoes rather than leave them behind on the Columbia.

Reference: Moulton, vol. 5

Cenas, Blaze: Part of the crowd who met the keelboat near Pittsburgh, this individual wounded a woman as he shot Lewis's air gun. On August 30, 1803, as part of an impromptu demonstration, Lewis first fired seven times, "after which a Mr. Blaze Cenas being unacquainted with the management of the gun suffered her to discharge herself accidently the ball passed through the hat of a woman about 40 yards distanc cuting her temple about the fourth of the diameter of the ball; shee feel instantly and the blood gusing from her temple we were all in the greatest consternation supposed she was dead but in a minute she revived to our enespressable satisfaction, and by examination we found the wound by no means mortal or even dangerous."

Reference: Moulton, vol. 2

Cevallos (Cavallos), Pedro (1764–1840): Minister of foreign affairs in the Spanish government. Alerted to the intention of the United States government to send "travelers" up the Missouri in January of 1803 by his superior, the Spanish minister to the United States, Cevallos communicated this to the commandant general of the Provincias Internas and sent word from the king of Spain that his representatives had royal approval to "detain the expedition of the American Captain Merry Weather directed to reconnoitre the territory which belongs to His Majesty."

Reference: Jackson, Letters

Chaboillez, Charles (1742–1809): North West Company factor, commander of the Assiniboine District who received a letter from Captains Lewis and Clark written from Fort Mandan and dated October 31, 1804, "If, sir, in the course of the winter, you have it in your power to furnish us with any hints in relation to the geography of the country, its productions, either mineral, animal, or vegetable, or any other information which you might conceive of utility to mankind, or which might be serviceable to us in the prosecution of our voyage, we should feel ourselves extremely obliged by your furnishing us with it." Chaboillez replied via a letter delivered by Hugh Heney in mid-December and "expressed a great anxiety to Serve us in any thing in his power." It may have been Chaboillez whom Clark meant when he described Charbonneau as having been "Corupted by the Companeys&c. Some explenation has taken place which Clearly proves to us the fact, we give him to night to reflect and deturmin whether or not he intends to go with us under the regulations Stated."
References: Jackson, Letters; *Moulton, vol. 3*

Chapman, Matilda: Philadelphia seamstress who supplied the expedition with shirts for $142.14 on June 3, 1803.
Reference: Jackson, Letters

Charbonneau, Jean Baptiste (1805–1866): One of two children of French fur trader Toussaint Charbonneau and his Shoshone wife, Sacagawea, he was named for a Christian saint by his father and nicknamed "Pomp" by William Clark, who sometimes called him "my boy Pomp." Some Lemhi Shoshone say *pomp* is a Shoshone word meaning "first born" or "lots of hair." He was known by his middle name of Baptiste. His birth was recorded by Lewis at the Awatixa village on the south side of the Knife River on February 11, 1805, fifty days before the expedition left the Mandans: "about five o clock this evening one of the wives of Charbono was delivered of a fine boy. it is worthy to remark that this was the first child which this woman had boarn and as is common in such cases her labour was tedious and the pain violent; Mr. Jessome informed me that he had freequently administered a small portion of the rattle of the rattle-snake, which he assured me had never failed to produce the desired effect, that of hastening the birth of the child; having the rattle of a snake by me I gave it to him and he administered two rings of it to the woman. . . . she had not taken it more than ten minutes before she brought forth." Baptiste traveled with his parents as they served as interpreters for Lewis and Clark to the Pacific Ocean and back. His presence, along with that of his mother, reassured natives more than once that the Corps of Discovery came in peace. Baptiste nearly drowned with his mother in a flash flood on June 29, 1805: "Shabano had the woman by the hand indeavouring to pull her up the hill but was so much frightened that he remained frequently motionless and but for Capt. C both himself and his woman and child must have perished." At Camp Chopunnish Lewis treated a teething Baptiste for high fever and swelling of the neck and throat. "We gave him a doze of creem of tartar and flour of sulpher and applyed a poltice of boiled onions to his neck as warm as he could bear it." When the child did not improve despite continued treatment Lewis decided to try a clyster, or enema, which finally cured the sick child. Coues believes he may have been suffering from the mumps. Clark, especially, was fond of the boy and named Pomp's Tower (Pompey's Pillar) and nearby Baptiste's Creek near Billings in his honor. The captain mentioned him with sympathy on August 4, 1806: "the child of Shabano has been so much bitten by the musquetors that his face is much puffed up and swelled." When the expedition returned on August 17, 1806, to the Mandan villages, Clark offered to adopt Baptiste and educate him in St. Louis. Three days later he sent a letter downriver to Charbonneau in which he restated the offer and closed with "Wishing you and your family great suckcess & with anxious expectations of seeing my little danceing boy Baptiest I shall remain your Friend, William Clark." Jean Baptiste was baptized, according to his father's wishes, in St. Louis by a Trappist monk in December of 1809. His St. Louis education began in 1811 when, per his parent's request, Clark enrolled him at a Catholic Brothers seminary where he received instruction from a Baptist minister. (Clark formally adopted Baptiste and his sister, Lisette, after their mother's death in 1812.) The subjects Baptiste studied included French, English, Greek, Latin, classical literature, history, science, and mathematics. Baptiste seems to have visited his mother and her people at Fort Mandan in the summers. In June 1823, while living in a trading village at the mouth of the Kansas, the eighteen-year-old Jean Baptiste met Germany's Prince Paul of Württemberg, who invited him, with Clark's permission, to live in Germany and serve as his "Gunstling" (servant). They went to New Orleans and booked passage aboard the *Smyrna*. Delayed by bad weather and a rough crossing, the pair finally arrived in Europe three and a half months later. While in Europe Baptiste lived at the royal household with the prince at his castle near Stuttgart, Germany, and traveled with him to France, England, and northern Africa. In 1829 he returned with the prince to the United States and ascended the Missouri to visit with Indian agents and work as a trader for the American Fur Company. He spent the next fifteen years as a mountain man, trapping fur from New Mexico to Oregon and picking up several additional Indian languages. Among his associates during these years Baptiste counted several of North America's most famous mountain men: Joe Meek, Jim Bridger, John Fremont, Kit Carson, and William Sublette. In 1840 Baptiste Charbonneau successfully navigated down the Platte River to the Missouri with a boatload of furs. The next spring he accompanied William Clark Kennerly (Clark's nephew) and eighty others under Sir William Drummond Stewart, the Scottish Lord of Grandtully, on a sport and cure-seeking trip to the Rockies via the Oregon Trail. When his father died in 1843, Baptiste inherited 320 acres of land, which he later sold. While on the Arkansas River working for the Bent and St. Vrain Company, an associate, W. M. Boggs, noted he "wore his hair long hung down to his shoulders. It was said that Charbenau was the best man on foot on the plains or in the Rocky Mountains." During the Mexican War, Baptiste helped Cooke's Mormon battalion reach San Diego from Sante Fe in 1846. The following year he accepted an appointment as *alcalde*, or magistrate, of a San Diego mission, a position he resigned in 1848 and one he could not have held if he had not been baptized into the Catholic Church. During the next several years, Jean Baptiste and trapper Jim Beckwourth were in California to prospect for gold. He finally settled in Placer County, California, near present-day Auburn, where he worked as a clerk for the Orleans

Hotel. He died in May of 1866 at a stage stop called the Inskip Ranch near Danner, Oregon. At the time of his death, Baptiste was headed for the gold fields of Montana. Along the way he crossed the chilly Owyhee River and caught pneumonia. According to his July 7, 1866, obituary in the *Auburn Placer Herald*, Charbonneau left California because "the reported discoveries of gold in Montana and the rapid peopling of the territory, excited the imagination of the old trapper and he determined to return to the scenes of his youth." Crossing a river as he had done many times in his mountain-man days proved too much for Sacagawea's son, and "he now sleeps alone by the bright waters of the Owyhee river." Another obituary described him as "of pleasant manners, intelligent, well read in the topics of the day, and was generally esteemed in the community as a good meaning and inoffensive man." Members of the Oregon chapter of the Lewis and Clark Trail Heritage Foundation restored his grave for the bicentennial. See Charbonneau letter.

References: *"Jean Baptiste Charbonneau" in Leroy Hafen,* Mountain Men and the Fur Trade, *vol. 1; Anderson,* Charbonneau Family Portrait; *Furtwangler, "Sacagawea's Son: New Evidence from Germany"; Jackson,* Letters; *Moulton, vols. 3, 4, 7, 8*

Charbonneau, Toussaint (1767–by 1843): Born in Montreal, the short, dark, stocky French trapper for the North West Company hired as interpreter with Lewis and Clark at Fort Mandan in 1804. Most historians agree he was hired so that his Shoshone wife could convey the expedition's need for horses to her people. While Lewis described him as a man of "no peculiar value," Clark evidenced a friendlier attitude toward him, even offering, at the end of the expedition, to assist in finding an employer for Toussaint and to adopt his and Sacagawea's son, Jean Baptiste, so that the boy could attend school in St. Louis. From the beginning of his relationship with Lewis and Clark, Charbonneau seems to have been a bit of an opportunist, refusing at first to follow the regimented life of the expeditionary soldier or contribute in any way (other than that of interpreter) to the success of the corps. Charbonneau could not swim, and Lewis referred to him as "perhaps the most timid waterman in the world." His shortcomings are duly noted in the journals, as when he almost flipped the white pirogue while at the stern: "Cruzatte by repeated threats so far brought Charbono the Sternman to his recollection that he did his duty while two hands bailed the perogue and Cruzatte and two others rowed her on shore were she arrived sarcely above the water." Luckily Sacagawea's quick thinking saved the "papers" and many other articles from floating downriver. In another incident (June 29, 1805) involving near drowning, Charbonneau ignored the maritime law of women and children first and saved himself before thinking of his wife and child in a flash flood. Charbonneau's ability to speak Minitari was vital in the chain of translation. He spoke Minitari with Sacagawea and French to Drouillard, who translated to English for the captains. Among his other duties, Charbonneau often did the horse trading for the corps and served as guard and camp tender. He received $500.33 for his services and use of his tipi, along with the same land grant, 320 acres, as the enlistees.

His relationship with women bordered on the abusive. An early account from Portage la Prairie states that Charbonneau was stabbed with a canoe awl by an irate Indian mother when the Frenchman attempted to rape her daughter. He purchased or won Sacagawea and another Shoshone girl from the Minitari and made them his "wives," something polite society at the time could not accept, referring to him and other white men like him as "squaw men." On August 14, 1805, Captain Clark "severely reprimanded" him for striking Sacagawea at dinner. Yet the tough Frenchman did have a soft side and a dependable talent for cooking. Lewis decreed him "our wrighthand cook" and humorously describes saving the necessary materials from a buffalo cow he killed for what Charbonneau called "boudin blanc." Charbonneau tried Lewis's temper at times. At one point of delicate negotiations with the Shoshone, Charbonneau neglected to tell Lewis of the Indians' plans to leave the area, "and consequently leave me and my baggage on the mountain or thereabouts. I was out of patience with the folly of charbonon who had not sufficient sagacity to the consequencies which would inevitably flow from such a movement of the indians. . . ." Charbonneau declined an offer to travel to the Illinois with the expedition but did eventually take Clark up on his offer, sent by messenger three days later, that they travel to St. Louis and allow Clark to provide an education for his son. He and Sacagawea remained in St. Louis for several years, but after tiring of "civilized life" they returned to the upper Missouri region where Charbonneau went to work for Manuel Lisa as a trader and interpreter for $250 a year. The next year, 1812, trader Luttig lists Sacagawea as dying of putrid fever. According to one of his cohorts, Charbonneau suggested a plan in 1814 to steal women from the Snake (Shoshone) Indians in the Rocky Mountain region and purchase Arapaho women and girl prisoners and sell them to traders working the trading posts on the upper Missouri. On one of his assignments in 1816 (with Chouteau and DeMun), Charbonneau traveled to the southern Rockies and was imprisoned by the Spanish for forty-eight days in Sante Fe. From 1819 to 1838 Charbonneau worked as an interpreter for the Indian Department at the Upper Missouri subagency, no doubt in some measure because of the influence of his old friend William Clark, now the superintendent of Indian affairs. Over the years Toussaint maintained his skills as a camp cook. An early-nineteenth-century traveler, Francis Chardon, writes, "last Night at half past 10 O'Clock we partook of a fine supper Prepared by Old Charbonneau, consisting of Meat pies, bread, fricassied pheasants Boiled tongues, roast beef—and coffee." He also served celebratory meals on the Fourth of July and other holidays. Charbonneau never lost his desire for young women. When his wife died in a smallpox epidemic in 1837, Charbonneau waited a year before he purchased and married a fourteen-year-old Assiniboine woman. According to Chardon's journal: in a state of "spring fret . . . Old Charbonneau, a man of 80, took to himself and others a young Wife, a young Assinneboine of 14, a Prisoner that was taken in the fight of this summer, and bought by me of the Rees, the young Men of the fort, and two rees, gave to the Old Man a splendid Charvieree, the Drums, pans, Kittles &c Beating; guns fireing &c. The Old gentleman gave a feast to the Men, and a glass of grog—and went to bed with his young wife, with the intention of doing his best." It is known he made one more trip to St. Louis in the summer of 1839. A creek in Mountrail County, North Dakota, was named Sharbono's Creek after him on April 14, 1805, because he camped several weeks on it with a hunting party of

Indians. It is now known as Bear Den Creek. He is presumed to have been dead by 1843.

References: *"Toussaint Charbonneau" in Leroy Hafen,* Mountain Men and the Fur Trade, *vol. 1; Cleary; Speck; Luttig; Moulton, vols. 4, 5; Jackson,* Letters; *Brackenridge; Abel,* Chardon's Journal

Charbonneau letter: The following is the text of Clark's letter to Charbonneau:

Charbono   On Board Perogue Near Ricara Village
                                        August 20th 1806

Sir

Your present situation with the Indians givs me some concern. I wish now that I had advised you to come on with me to the Illinois where it most probably would be in my power to put you in some way to do something for your self. I was so engaged after the Big White had concluded to go down with Jessomme as his Interpreter, that I had not time to talk with you as much as I intended to have done. You have been a long time with me and have conducted your Self in Such a manner as to gain my friendship, your woman who accompanied you that long dangerous and fatigueing rout to the Pacific Ocian and back diserved a greater reward for her attention and services on that rout than we had in our power to giver her at the Mandans. As to your little Son (my boy Pomp) you well know my fondness for him and my anxiety to take and raise him as my own child. I once more tell you if you will bring your son Baptiest to me I will educate him and treat him as my own child. I do not forgit the promis which I made to you and shall now repeat them that you may be certain. Charbono, if you wish to live with the white people, and will come to me I will give you a piece of land and furnish you with horses cows & hogs. If you wish to visit your friends in Montrall I will let you have a horse, and your family shall be taken care of untill your return. If you wish to return as an Interpreter for the Menetarras when the troops come up to form the establishment, you will be with me ready and I will precure you the place—or if you wish to return to trade with the indians and will leave your little Son Pomp with me, I will assist you with the merchandize for that purpose from time to time and become my self conserned with you in trade on a Small scale tht is to say not exceeding a perogue load at one time. If you are desposed to accept either of my offers to you and will bring down your Son your famn Janey had best come along with you to take care of the boy untill I get with him. Let me advise you to keep your Bill of Exchange and what furs and pelteries you have in possession, and get as much as you can—and get as maney robes, and big horn and Cabbra Skins as you can collect in the course of this winter and take them down to St. Louis as early as possible in the Spring. When you get to St. Louis enquire of the Governor of that place for a letter which I shall leave with him for you. In the letter which I shall leave with the governor I shall inform you what you had best do with your firs pelteries and robes &c. and derect you where to find me. If you should meet with any misfortune on the river &c. when you get to St. Louis write a letter to me by the post and let me know your situation. If you do not intend to go down either this fall or in the Spring, write a letter to me by the first oppirtunity and inform me what you intend to do that I may know if I may expect you or not. If you ever intend to come down this fall or the next Spring will be the best time. This fall would be best if you could get down before the winter. I shall be found either in St. Louis or in Clarksville at the Falls of the Ohio.

Wishing you and your family great suckcess & with anxious expectations of seeing my little danceing boy Baptiest I shall remain your Friend,

William Clark

Keep this letter and let not more than one or 2 persons see it, and when you write to me seal your letter. I think you best not deturmin which of my offers to accept untill you See me. Come prepared to accept either which you may chuse after you get down.

Mr. Teousant Charbono
Minetarras Village

Reference: Jackson, Letters

Charles (Carlos) IV (1748–1819): King of Spain between 1788 and 1808. He held up the retrocession of the Louisiana Territory to France, thus involving Meriwether Lewis in diplomacy that Lewis had not expected. Although it was not known at the time, later research has proved that Charles himself directed the Spanish intendant at New Orleans, Juan Ventura Morales, to close the Mississippi River in the autumn of 1802. Word of the revocation of the American right of deposit reached Washington, D.C., on November 23, 1802, precipitating a western crisis in the Jefferson administration. It was in part to clarify the American right of deposit in the lower Mississippi that President Jefferson sent James Monroe to France in the spring of 1803. Charles IV held up the transfer of Louisiana to France because he was angry that Napoleon had been dilatory in delivering Tuscany per the provisions of the Treaty of San Ildefonso. The Spanish minister to the United States, Carlos Martinez Yrujo, believed and assured Jefferson that Morales had acted without the crown's authority. In this he was mistaken. By all accounts, Charles was a weak and largely ineffectual king, who preferred hunting and collecting clocks (an Enlightenment obsession!) to governing. Although the Treaty of San Ildefonso had been signed on October 1, 1800, formal transfer of the Louisiana Territory from Spain to France did not take place until March 9, 1804, one day before the territory was transferred forever to the United States.

Chil lar la wil: Chinook chief who received a flag and a medal from Lewis and Clark during the winter at Fort Clatsop. In exchange for a sea otter robe, Chil lar la wil accepted Sacagawea's blue belt, which the captains appropriated in order to purchase the robe.

Chinook olives: On October 21, 1805, among the Chinook, Clark recorded, "we got from those people a fiew pounded roos (roots) fish and Acorns of white oake, those acorns they make use of as food (raw and roasted)." Historians Robert H. Ruby and John A. Brown cite Paul Kane on the Chinook method of roasting acorns: "Acorns were placed with grass and dirt in pits into which the Indians would urinate from time to time. Thus marinated and then cooked in separate cooking pits, the result 'Chinook olives' they considered a delicacy."

References: Moulton, vol. 5; Ruby and Brown, The Chinook Indians

Chokecherry (*Prunus virginiana*): *Chan pa* in the Dakota language. On June 11, 1805, at Grog Spring, on the Missouri River, Lewis found himself with severe stomach pain and running a high fever, unable to march, and forced to make a camp of some willow boughs. He described his remedy: "having brought no medecine with me I resolved to try an experiment with some simples; and the Choke cherry which grew abundanly in the bottom first struck my attention; I directed a parsel of the small twigs to be geathered striped of their leaves, cut into pieces of about 2 inches in length and boiled in water untill a strong black decoction of an astringent tast was produced; at sunset I took point (pint) of this decoction and about an hour after repeated the dze by 10 in the evening I was entirely releived from pain and in fact every symptom of the disorder forsook me; my fever abated, a gentle perspiration was produced and I had a comfortable and refreshing nights rest." The chokecherry is a traditional food and ceremonial ingredient of the Plains Indian tribes; it is used in rituals, songs, myths, and sleight-of-hand performances. The cherry is eaten fresh and dried for use in the winter. At gathering time bands of Indians traveled many miles to assemble in camps along the streams where the cherries grew in abundance. Stone mortars were used in a pounding process, which produced a pulp they then formed into cakes and left in the sun to dry. Pemmican, a favorite treat for the Dakota Indians, included chokecherries as one of the main ingredients. In *Uses of Plants by the Indians of the Missouri River Region*, Melvin Gilmore mentions that the Ponca Indians used a decoction of cherry bark as a treatment for intestinal disorders. A spoonful of the dried fruit crushed into powder and mixed with hot water was likewise used. Trappers washed their traps with cherry bark water to remove the scent of previous captures. Parts of the plant are poisonous to humans if consumed so it must be cooked or dried. See Pemmican.

References: Moulton, vol. 4; Gilmore

Chouteau, Auguste Pierre (1786–1838): Son of Pierre and Pelagie Chouteau of the famous St. Louis entrepreneurial family, young Chouteau secured an appointment to West Point thanks to his old family friend Meriwether Lewis. After a brief military career, during which he served under General Wilkinson, Auguste resigned his position to become a fur trader and eventual partner in William Clark's newly formed Missouri Fur Company. Although his military career was brief, he was known thereafter as Colonel. Lewis engaged the company in 1809 to accompany Ensign Nathaniel Pryor and his charge, Mandan chief Sheheke-shote, to the mouth of the Knife River where Chouteau remained until May 1810. While Chouteau and his partner, Jules DeMun, were pursuing trade with the natives of the upper Arkansas in 1815, Spanish soldiers arrested them and held the two men prisoner for forty-eight days. They lost all of their property, amounting to some thirty thousand dollars, which they later claimed was owed to them by the United States government. Following the Mexican War, a settlement was given to the families of Chouteau and DeMun, but they did not live to see it. Chouteau gave up trading in the mountains and settled near the Verdigris post and at a nearby village, La Saline, where he kept his children and several Osage wives. He maintained a respectful and friendly relationship with several tribes of the area and in 1837 was appointed by the secretary of war as a treaty negotiator with Indian tribes. His influence extended to the newly arrived Creek and Cherokee Indians who were being pushed out of their traditional homeland by United States Indian policy. At one point Chouteau supplied these destitute people with goods, for which he expected to be repaid when they received their annuity checks, but the reimbursement did not occur. Throughout his life financial problems troubled Auguste, and he was often bailed out by one of his more successful brothers. Despite his lack of business savvy, his Indian friends remained constant. According to one account, Auguste was a good trader and a good man. He died near Fort Gibson on Christmas Day, 1838, and was buried there with military honors.

Reference: Janet Lecompte, *"Auguste Pierre Chouteau,"* in Leroy Hafen, French Fur Traders and Voyageurs

Chronometer (Arnolds Watch): An English-made timepiece purchased by Lewis in Philadelphia for $250 plus seventy-five cents for the winding key. The gold-cased watch had a mahogany field case, and Lewis had it cleaned, regulated, and rated before leaving for St. Louis. The chronometer assisted in measuring longitude, distances, and astronomical observations. Although Lewis mentions winding it every day at noon, and regulating it by mean solar time, it eventually ran down. When the corps returned to St. Louis, Congress neglected to set aside funds for preservation or conservation of the scientific instruments used during the expedition, and they were sold at auction for $408.62.

Reference: Bedini, *"Scientific Instruments"*

Claiborne, William Charles Cole (1775–1817): Governor of the Louisiana Territory; Virginian educated at the Richmond Academy and William and Mary College. As a youth Claiborne rose rapidly in the ranks of the legal profession. After starting out as a law clerk, he advanced to become a member of the Tennessee constitutional convention and served on the Tennessee Supreme Court. President Jefferson appointed him governor of the Mississippi Territory in 1803 and listened to his advice concerning the advantages of the United States securing navigational rights on the Mississippi. Jefferson sent Claiborne to the Louisiana Territory to serve as a commissioner with General James Wilkinson where he was soon promoted to governor. In 1803 Governor Claiborne received an unusual shipment of "curiosities" sent from Fort Mandan by Captain Meriwether Lewis, which he was directed to send on to President Jefferson. As he described them in a letter to Jefferson, the shipment contained "Trunks and Boxes directed to you, one Cage with four Birds, and a small Animal somewhat resembling our common Grey Squirrel. They were sent by Captain Lewis and Mr. Chanteau of St. Louis, and by him transmitted to me." Although he feared the "little Animal" would not survive, the trunks, boxes, and assorted other cargo, including skeletons, horns, and furs, were carefully examined, dried out, repacked, and sent on their way to New Orleans. These creatures endured four thousand miles of travel from the plains of Dakota to the ports of St. Louis, New Orleans, then around Florida, up the East Coast to the Chesapeake Bay, and finally to Jefferson in Washington. Three of the four magpies died, but one bird and one prairie dog survived to become popular attractions in Charles Willson Peale's museum in Independence Hall. The magpie would eventually become the subject of a drawing for Alexander Wilson's multivolume study on North American birds.

References: Jackson, Letters; *Cutright,* Pioneering Naturalists

Clamons (clemel, clemons, cuirasses): Shieldlike article of clothing made from elk skins by the Chinook and Clatsop Indians and used for protection in battle and in hunting. Chinook tribal historians Robert Ruby and John Brown describe the clamon as a highly prized trade item, especially with the Indians of the upper northwest coast near the Queen Charlotte and Vancouver Islands. Clamons were traded with the crew of the *Lydia* and were sometimes used by British and American traders to buy native slaves, which they would in turn exchange for sea otter pelts.

Reference: Ruby and Brown, The Chinook Indians

Clark, Frances (1773–1825): Clark's younger sister. He named an island in the Columbia in her honor: "after dinner we proceeded on and passed an Elegant and extensive bottom on the South side and an island near it's upper point which we called Fanny's island and bottom." The name did not stick and "Fanny's bottom" became known as Grim's or Crim's island. William Clark gave Fanny one of the bighorn sheep horns he brought back, which was used as a doorstop in her home for many years. It is currently housed at the Filson Historical Society.

References: Holmberg, Dear Brother; *Moulton, vol. 7*

Clark, George Rogers (1752–1818): Older brother of William Clark. As a young man George scouted the country around West

Virginia and developed a keen interest in nature and in surveying western lands. While he proved successful as a military leader and Indian fighter in the (Old) Northwest campaigns, he could not persuade the Virginia government or the confederation to honor debts incurred as a result of those "wilderness" campaigns. He served as Indian commissioner and eventually became involved in failed attempts by the Spanish and French to found colonies in the Mississippi Valley; trading ventures proved unsuccessful for Clark as well. Throughout his life George was plagued by financial disasters and allegations of fraud in land deals. His faithful brother William did everything in his power to make life easier for him, but his only relief came from alcohol. In 1783 Thomas Jefferson approached him about leading an expedition "from the Missisip to California" in order to head off similar efforts by the British. The next year Clark declined, citing financial concerns. He did suggest, "Large parties will never answer the purpose. They will allarm the Indian Nations they pass through. Three or four young Men well qualified for the Task might perhaps compleat your wishes at a very Trifiling Expence." In a letter to Jefferson at the end of 1802, Clark recommended his younger brother William as "well quallified almost for any business. If it should be in your power to confur on him any post of Honor and profit, in this Countrey in which we live, it will exceedingly gratify me." As a young man William felt pride in, and a particularly close attachment for, George and emulated his interest in geography and in the creatures of the West. (Unlike his older brothers George and Jonathan, William did not receive as much formal education because the family moved to the Kentucky wilderness.) George may have assisted his brother in picking the location for Camp Dubois and in recruiting men from around Forts Massac and Kaskaskia as he was familiar with both areas from his earlier campaigns. The keelboat used by the Corps of Discovery was a modification of the craft George had used previously. Pierre Dorian, the frontiersman who helped the captains council with the Arikara, was an acquaintance of the elder Clark. The father of Charles Floyd, named Robert, served with George Rogers Clark.

References: Jackson, Letters; *Bakeless; Holmberg,* Dear Brother

Clark, Harriet Kennerly Radford (1788–1831): William Clark's second wife, cousin to his first wife, Judith. They were married in 1821, a year after Judith's death. Together she and William had two sons whom they raised with the children of Clark's first marriage and three children from Harriet's first union. Family lore indicates Clark met Judith and Harriet, then both in their early teens, on the same day, as they were riding an obstinate horse in Virginia. After ten years of marriage to William, Harriet died on Christmas Day in 1831.

References: Jackson, Among the Sleeping Giants*; Steffen*

Clark, Judith Hancock (1791–1820): Cousin and first wife of Captain William Clark. Often referred to as Julia, which she preferred, or Judy by family, friends, and descendants. Her father, Colonel George Hancock, was a Revolutionary War soldier, congressman, and prominent lawyer in Fincastle, Virginia. His residence, Santillane, was the site of Clark's collaboration with Nicholas Biddle on his 1814 edition of the journals. According to family lore, Clark met young Judith in Virginia while she was riding with her cousin Harriet Kennerly. When Judith's horse balked, Clark provided assistance. A year and a half after he returned from the Pacific, Clark married the sixteen-year-old Judith on January 5, 1808, at Santillane, followed by a honeymoon trip to St. Louis. As a wedding present Meriwether Lewis sent the couple a complete set of Shakespeare. William and Judith had five children: Meriwether Lewis Clark, William Preston Clark, George Rogers Hancock Clark, John Julius Clark, and Mary Margaret Clark. Three of these children survived to adulthood. President James Madison appointed William Clark governor of the Missouri Territory in 1813. During his seven-year term, the governor and Mrs. Clark enjoyed the company of friends and supporters and hosted many elegant balls and receptions at their home. In 1816 Judith Clark's health deteriorated. Despite consulting the best physicians of the day and enduring tar-fume therapy, Judith died at home in Virginia on June 27, 1820. Sadly for Clark, their daughter, Mary, died a few months later. Sometime after his return, between 1806 and 1810, Clark formally named the Judith River in present-day Montana in honor of his first wife; the river was originally called Big Horn by the captains. In December of

1810, Clark commissioned the first engraving of a map with the name "Judith's River." Lewis described it in his journal entry for May 29, 1805, as a "handsome river." He continues, "Cap. C who assended this R. much higher than I did has (thought it proper to) call it Judieth's River." Today the Judith River formation represents one of the most diversified dinosaur-remains sites on earth.

Reference: Moulton, vol. 4

Clark, William (1770–1838): Indian agent, diplomat, territorial official, and co-leader of the Lewis and Clark Expedition. William Clark was born in Caroline County, Virginia, on August 1, 1770. He was the ninth child and sixth son of John and Ann (Rogers) Clark. He was the youngest brother of George Rogers Clark, who played a heroic role in the American Revolution. Little is known of Clark's childhood. It might be characterized as typical of the Virginia planter gentry of the eighteenth century except for the fact that his formative years coincided with the American Revolution and the political struggle for American independence, to which his family was deeply committed. At an early age Clark was assigned a slave and body servant by the name of York. The lives of York and Clark—nearly identical in age—were intertwined at least until 1810 (for at least thirty years), and York was the only African American to participate in the Lewis and Clark Expedition. When Clark was fourteen, the family moved from Virginia to Beargrass Creek above the falls of the Ohio River. In 1789 Clark joined the Kentucky militia. In 1792 he joined the regular army as a lieutenant, his commission signed by President Washington. He participated in John Hardin's, Charles Scott's, and eventually Anthony Wayne's campaigns against the Indians north of the Ohio River. The Indians were resisting encroachments on their homelands. The whites were attempting to pacify lands they intended to settle and develop. The result was a bloody war, which ended for all practical purposes with the Battle of Fallen Timbers (August 20, 1794) and the Treaty of Greenville (1795). Although William Clark was a junior officer in these campaigns, he exhibited both courage and resourcefulness. (This experience would be useful when the Lewis and Clark Expedition reached the Teton Sioux in today's South Dakota, especially as Lewis had never been involved in battle, though he had spent ample time in the same districts.) During this period, Clark was twice sent on military missions into country controlled by the Spanish. For a few months, in late 1795 and early 1796, Meriwether Lewis served under William Clark in the Chosen Rifle Company. Lewis had been transferred to the rifle company after he was acquitted in a court-martial (November 6–11, 1795) in General Anthony Wayne's Fourth Sub-Legion. Clark would later write, "Captain Lewis was appointed Ensign and arraigned to the company which I commanded a few months before I resigned." In 1796 Clark resigned from the army. He was somewhat disillusioned with army life, his health was none too good, he had pressing family concerns, and he was interested in making his own way as a frontier businessman. Between 1796 and 1803 Clark spent much of his time attempting to sort out the tangled financial and legal affairs of his brother George Rogers Clark. He reported that he had traveled at least three thousand miles to meet with creditors, dispose of lands, fight off lawsuits, and restore his brother's affairs to something like order. A letter to his brother Edmund in 1794 makes clear that William Clark also intended to become a trader-merchant either on the Ohio or the Mississippi. "I think there is a great opportunity for an extension of the Mississippi trade in that river could a man form valuable connections in New Orleans which I make no doubt could be accomplished," he wrote. Thomas Jefferson knew the Clark family well. His respect for George Rogers Clark was at times nearly worshipful. He may have felt partly responsible for Virginia's shabby treatment of George Rogers Clark after the Revolutionary War. He was, at any rate, intensely loyal to his friends and protégés, and he preferred to employ trusted friends in all serious enterprises. George Rogers Clark wrote a letter of solicitation on behalf of his brother to President Jefferson on December 12, 1802. With a directness of appeal unusual in that age of decorum, he spoke of his younger brother William as "well quallified almost for any business . . . of Honor and profit, in this Countrey. . . . I am sure it gives you pleasure to have it in your power to do me a Service. . . ."

Whether Jefferson recommended Clark to Lewis or Lewis initiated the idea of the partnership is unknown. On June 19, 1803, Meriwether Lewis wrote to William Clark inviting him to join him in exploring the American West. After outlining his plan Lewis wrote, "If therefore there is anything under those circumstances, in this enterprise, which would induce you to participate with me in it's fategues, it's dangers and it's honors, believe me there is no man on earth whom I should feel equal pleasure in sharing them as with yourself." Lewis also assured Clark that President Jefferson "expresses an anxious wish that you would consent to join me in this enterprise," and that Jefferson "has authorized me to say that in the event of your accepting this proposition he will grant you a Captain's commission. . . ." In writing this, Lewis either misunderstood the president's intention, or (more likely) the quintessentially civilian Jefferson failed to anticipate the elaborate protocols of the War Department. William Clark was in fact denied his captaincy—an awkward outcome that angered Meriwether Lewis and created a fair amount of bitterness in William Clark. Secretary of War Henry Dearborn wrote Lewis on March 26, 1804, to report that Clark's rank could be no greater than that of lieutenant in the Corps of Artillerists. With characteristic passion, Lewis wrote to Clark, "I think it will be best to let none of our party or any other persons know any thing about the grade, you will observe that the grade has no effect upon your compensation, which by G–d shall be equal to my own." Meriwether Lewis arrived at the Falls of the Ohio on October 14, 1803. In practical terms the partnership of Lewis and Clark may be said to have begun during a thirteen-day interlude before they set out on October 26. Lewis brought with him at least two permanent members of the expedition, likely George Shannon and John Colter. Clark, meanwhile, had been recruiting Kentucky frontiersmen. Lewis's two, plus Clark's Nathaniel Pryor, George Gibson, John Shields, Joseph and Reubin Field, William Bratton, and Charles Floyd would make their mark as the nucleus of the Corps of Discovery, the so-called nine young men from Kentucky.

During the winter of 1803–04 at Camp Dubois opposite the mouth of the Missouri River, Clark did most of the work of turning the disparate crew they had assembled (some army men, some frontiersmen, some permanent members of the expedition, some temporary French river runners) into an integrated corps. Lewis spent much of his time in St. Louis gathering information and supplies for the expedition. Although Lewis and Clark are often presented as virtually interchangeable leaders, they actually played quite different roles in the expedition. Clark was the principal cartographer, Lewis the botanist and zoologist. Lewis provided the most detailed ethnographic notes about the Indians they encountered, but Clark seems to have been a more adroit handler of the diplomatic relations. Lewis seems to have been happiest when he was alone on shore with his gun, his notebook, and his dog, Seaman. Clark was apparently the better boatman and a more skillful manager of the expedition's personnel. Lewis's somewhat odd sense of humor is more often evident in the journals, but Clark seems to have been the more relaxed and playful man. Clark's journal entries are intensely practical. He is not afraid to complain when conditions beyond his control have made him miserable. Lewis never complains, but he frequently lapses into somewhat pessimistic philosophical reflections about the fragility of his mission. Lewis has a propensity for the grandiose and the literary flourish. Clark is an abysmal speller, but his prose is always direct and to the point. Lewis likes to strike out ahead to discover things yet unknown to civilized people. Clark seems more dedicated to getting the expedition across the continent and back again with as little loss as possible. It is perhaps no great exaggeration to say that William Clark managed the day-to-day business of the expedition, and Meriwether Lewis was a kind of scientist, philosopher, and geopolitical commentator-in-residence. Without intending to, Clark came to play an important role in the publication history of the expedition. It seems to have been clear from the beginning that Meriwether Lewis would write the official account of the expedition. Clark would be an important journal keeper, perhaps the most important journal keeper, but Lewis would produce the master narrative in his own words. Lewis's unaccountable silences, and his sudden death in 1809, left a hole in the expedition's records that has never been filled.

The baseline of narrative belongs much more to William Clark than to Meriwether Lewis. For reasons that are still not entirely clear, Lewis was silent for long periods of the journey. Clark's journal is virtually continuous. He fails to make a journal entry for just one ten-day stretch, and with his characteristic sense of responsibility, he summarizes those experiences on the eleventh day. This was the period between February 3 and 12, 1805, at Fort Mandan. Clark led a hunting party south and west of Fort Mandan during a period of bitter cold on the northern plains. That he did not keep a daily log during this strenuous interlude is understandable. That he summarized those days once he was back at Fort Mandan is indicative of his discipline and his lifelong attention to duty. Much of what we know about the basic story of the expedition comes from the pen of William Clark. Lewis was almost completely silent from May 14, 1804, to April 7, 1805. It is Clark's journal that provides the narrative of the death of Charles Floyd, of the expedition's encounters with the Oto, Missouri, Yanktonai, Arikara, Mandan, and—most important—the Teton Sioux. Clark reports the expedition's side trip to the Spirit Mound on August 25, 1804. Clark provides the details of the critical diplomatic exchanges with the Mandan and Hidatsa Indians. It is Clark, not Lewis, to whom we owe our basic understanding of the descent of the Clearwater, Snake, and Columbia Rivers in the autumn of 1805. It is Clark who provides the narrative of the return of the expedition in August and September 1806, following the wounding of Meriwether Lewis by Pierre Cruzatte on August 11, 1806. Lewis's sudden death in 1809 put Clark in a very difficult position. To his brother Jonathan, Clark wrote, "I do not know what I shall do about publication of the Book." Before he went to Philadelphia to get the publication project back on track, Clark wrote himself a memorandum which reveals that Lewis had not informed him about which artists, scientists, and men of letters he had hired to work on the project. Clark's intention was to persuade someone in Philadelphia to accompany him back to St. Louis "to write the journal." Clark soon discovered that, in spite of whatever assurances Lewis had been making about the progress of his book, he had never provided the publishers C. and A. Conrad of Philadelphia a single page of manuscript.

Clark visited Monticello late in 1809 to confer with the retired president about what to do next. When it became clear that Jefferson was not willing to prepare the journals for publication, Clark determined to seek editorial assistance in Philadelphia. Jefferson's friend Charles Willson Peale wrote, "I would rather Clark had undertaken to have wrote the whole himself and then have put it into the hands of some person of talents to brush it up, but I found that the General was too different of his abilities." Eventually, Clark engaged a twenty-six-year-old man of letters named Nicholas Biddle to prepare the journals for the press. Although Biddle had never been west of the Allegheny Mountains, he wrote a masterful paraphrase of the expedition's travels. Clark dutifully cooperated in every possible way with Biddle. Biddle visited Clark in Fincastle, Virginia, to confer about the publication, and he sent Clark a series of letters in which he sought clarification of events and notations in the journals. Moreover, Clark dispatched George Shannon, the youngest member of the expedition, to Philadelphia to serve as a consultant to Biddle as he worked his way through the expedition's journals. With this help, and some later assistance from journalist Paul Allen, Biddle published his *History of the Expedition under the Command of Captains Lewis and Clark* in 1814. Not only did Clark never receive any royalties for the publication, but as of 1815 he had not even received a copy of the published book.

If the journals are an accurate indication, Meriwether Lewis was largely indifferent to, and at times dismissive of, Sacagawea. Clark was much more friendly and respectful. When the expedition party split up, the Charbonneau family was much more frequently with Clark than with Lewis. Sacagawea did a series of small favors for Clark, including bringing him edible plants from along the trail, giving him a small piece of bread she had been hoarding, and giving him a gift of two dozen weasel's tails for Christmas at Fort Clatsop. Clark, in turn, wrote respectfully of Sacagawea, and he rebuked Charbonneau for striking her in his presence. As the expedition raced downstream from Fort Mandan in late August 1806, Clark wrote a letter to Charbonneau in which he lamented that the expedition had been unable to reward Sacagawea properly for her services. Clark offered to sponsor the Charbonneau family if they moved to St. Louis, to raise the son, Jean Baptiste Charbonneau, in white civilization, and to help Toussaint Charbonneau establish a business. The success of the expedition set William Clark up for the rest of his life. Like Lewis, he received a land warrant of sixteen hundred acres, plus double pay for his time of service. This came to $1,228. Lewis had insisted to Secretary of War Dearborn that Clark's compensation package be identical to his own. President Jefferson appointed Clark brigadier general of the militia and superintendent of Indian affairs for the Territory of Louisiana. On January 5, 1808, Clark married Julia Hancock of Fincastle, Virginia.

Clark was thirty-seven, Ms. Hancock sixteen. He was briefly acquainted with her (he named a river for her in Montana), but he had spent comparatively little time in her presence. He understood that her father was a Federalist. In a jocular letter to Lewis, Clark promised to give his father-in-law the gift of Republican grandchildren. Clark had been so busy courting Miss Hancock after the expedition's return that he had missed the official Washington, D.C., celebration banquet on January 14, 1807, which had been several times postponed in the hope that Clark would arrive in time to enjoy it. The Clarks moved to St. Louis in June 1808. At first the newlyweds lived with Meriwether Lewis in a house Lewis had selected on the corner of Spruce and South Main Streets. A few months later Lewis found other sleeping quarters, but he continued to take meals with the Clarks. On March 9, 1807, Secretary of War Henry Dearborn had authorized Clark to issue to appropriate St. Louis traders a two-year license monopoly to trade with Indians along the Missouri River and to return the Mandan chief Sheheke-shote to his earth lodge village. The first attempt (September 1807) to return Sheheke-shote, under the command of expedition veteran Nathaniel Pryor, failed.

In 1808 Clark was involved (with Lewis and others) in creating the St. Louis Missouri Fur Company. Its purpose was to make money in the fur trade, but it also sought to contract with the U.S. government to return Sheheke-shote to his home on the upper Missouri. The second attempt (1809) succeeded, but not before Meriwether Lewis was rebuked by the War Department for undertaking unauthorized expenditures in his efforts to effect Sheheke-shote's return. The stinging rebuff Lewis received from William Eustis on July 15, 1809, precipitated the emergency journey to Washington (and presumably Monticello) that ended in Lewis's death on October 11, 1809. Clark spent a difficult day with his friend Meriwether Lewis a few weeks before the governor's death. He wrote an account of his last hours with Lewis to his brother Jonathan. "I have not Spent Such a day as yesterday for maney years. . . . I took my leave of Govr. Lewis who Set out to Philadelphia to write our Book (but more perticularly to explain Some Matter between him and the Govt.) Several of his Bills have been protested, and his Crediters all flocking in near the time of his Setting out distressed him much, which he expressed to me in Such terms as to Cause a Cempothy which is not yet off—I do not beleve there was ever an honester man in Louisiana nor one who had pureor motives than Govr. Lewis. if his mind had been at ease I should have parted Cherefully. . . ." Clark learned of Lewis's suicide from the public newspapers on October 28, 1809. He immediately wrote to his brother Jonathan. "I fear this report has too much truth. . . . I fear O' I fear the weight of his mind has overcome him, what will be the Consequence?" Clark asked his brother to find and preserve a letter Lewis had written to him (William Clark) from New Madrid in mid-September. This letter, Clark suggests, helps to explain Lewis's suicide. Unfortunately, the letter—perhaps the closest thing to a suicide note—has disappeared. In 1813 Clark was named territorial governor (a post Lewis had held briefly). Clark held this post as governor until 1820, when he was defeated in his halfhearted bid to be elected first governor of the new state of Missouri. After his defeat in the gubernatorial election of 1820, until his death in 1838, Clark devoted himself to Indian affairs. In 1822 he was appointed superintendent of Indian affairs at St. Louis (a post created by Congress in the wake of Missouri statehood). Clark worked assiduously to keep peace with the Indian tribes of the lower Missouri River, to facilitate orderly land cessions, and to carry out (as humanely as possible) the Jefferson-Jackson policy of Indian removal from the east to the west side of the Mississippi River. Clark was respected by the Indians he dealt with, and he is usually considered one of the finest Indian agents in American history. In his capacity as superintendent of Indian affairs, William Clark was an agent for Indian removal. He supervised and signed scores of treaties that dispossessed Indians of their lands and brought about their removal from lands desired by white pioneers and speculators. Clark was the primary federal agent responsible for keeping peace with more than one hundred thousand Indians over a vast region. If Clark felt ambivalence about his role as imperial agent of the U.S. government, he kept his concerns to himself. He expressed real regret over one treaty only, the 1808 treaty with the Osage that ceded fifty thousand square miles to the United States. In all of these Indian affairs, Clark treated native peoples with respect and forthrightness. He sometimes expressed sympathy toward the Indians he was dispossessing and repositioning, but he never questioned the wisdom of official American Indian policy.

A great deal has been made of the postexpeditionary tensions between Clark and his slave York. While these quarrels clearly put Clark in an unfortunate light, they were not untypical in the age of slavery. When their interests as slave owners were threatened, otherwise enlightened men like Thomas Jefferson and William Clark were capable of cruelty and ruthlessness. In May 1809 Clark wrote, "he [York] is here but of very little Service to me, insolent and sukly [*sic*], I gave him a Severe trouncing the other Day and he has much mended." At some point Clark freed York, and helped him to establish a freight-hauling business in Kentucky and Tennessee. York's business eventually failed. In 1832 Clark claimed to the visiting writer Washington Irving that York had come to regret having been manumitted. Julia Hancock Clark died on June 27, 1820. Clark married her cousin Harriet Radford one year later. She in turn died on Christmas Day 1831. Altogether Clark had seven children, five by Julia Hancock and two by Harriet Radford. William Clark died on September 1, 1838. He was sixty-eight years old. His funeral was the biggest in St. Louis history. More than one thousand people attended, and the procession was more than a mile long. He was buried on the family's St. Louis estate, but his body was later reinterred in Bellefontaine Cemetery in Missouri. Clark's biographer Jerome O. Steffen argues that "throughout Clark's life on the frontier there are strong indications that he never really considered himself a part of its heritage, preferring instead to look upon himself as an appointed official manning a government outpost." In other words, Clark lived in St. Louis, but his heart always remained in Virginia and Kentucky. See Charbonneau letter.

References: Steffen; Jackson, Letters; *Holmberg,* Dear Brother

Clark's nutcracker (*Nucifraga columbiana*): Lewis first described this bird near Tendoy, Idaho, on August 22, 1805: "I saw today a speceis of woodpecker which fed on the seeds of the pine. its beak and tail were white, it's wings were black, and every other part of a dark brown, it was about the size of a robin." He later described it in more detail when they were camped at Camp Chopunnish: "The beak of this bird is 1½ inches long, is proportionally large, black and of the form which characterizes this genus. . . . The feet and legs are black and imbricated with wide scales. The nails are black and remarkably long and sharp, also much curved. It has four toes on each foot of which one is in the rear and three in front. The toes are long particularly that in the rear." According to historian Paul Cutright, Clark's nutcracker is one of three birds in the Lewis and Clark Collection of Peale's museum described, drawn, and named by naturalist Alexander Wilson. In his book *American Ornithology* (1811), Wilson gave the bird the Latin binomial *Nucifraga columbiana*, and the common name Clark's nutcracker. Elliott Coues called it Clark's crow. The *National Audubon Society Field Guide to North American Birds* lists it as ranging from southern British Columbia and Alberta south throughout pine-clad western mountains to California and Colorado. "The periodic irruptions of Clark's nutcrackers, which may bring the birds all the way to the Pacific Coast are related to failures of the pine nut crop. Near camps and picnic sites this erratic winter wanderer begs and steals food scraps. It can hold several nuts in a special cheek pouch under the tongue in addition to those it holds in the beak." Wilson's original drawings of the bird that appeared in *American Ornithology* are now in Philadelphia's Academy of Natural Sciences. The bird is sometimes confused with the "camp robber," or Oregon jay.

References: Moulton, vols. 5, 7; Wilson, American Ornithology; Udvarty

Cokalahishkit River (River of the Road to the Buffalo, Blackfoot River, Buffalo Road River): Nez Percé name for a tributary of the Clark Fork River in present-day Missoula County, Montana. According to Roberta Cheney's *Names on the Face of Montana*, "Before the white man came, there was a trail along the Blackfoot where the road now runs which was used for the annual buffalo hunt; it was called Coakahlerisk kit, or 'River of the Road to the Buffalo.' Nez Perce, Shoshone, and Flatheads headed east on it each year, hoping to avoid their Blackfeet enemies. White men recorded the river as the Big Blackfoot Fork on an 1865 map." After separating from Clark, his "worthy friend and companion," to explore the Marias in July 1806, Lewis headed for the confluence of the Blackfoot and Clark Fork Rivers, and then proceeded up the Blackfoot to a gap, now called

Lewis and Clark Pass, then on toward the Dearborn River, the Great Falls, and finally to the Marias River. According to the Nez Percé Indians, who guided him to the Cokalahishkit River, "the road was a well beaten track we could not now miss our way and as they were affraid of meeting with their enemies the Minnetares they could not think of continuing with us any longer."

References: Cheney; Moulton, vol. 8

Collins (Colin, Colins), John (d. 1823): Private. Not to be confused with engagé Joseph Collin. Collins hailed from Frederick County, Maryland. He was possibly transferred from Captain Russell Bissell's company when he entered in service to the Lewis and Clark Expedition on January 1, 1804. Clark called him a "black gard" while they were camped on the Dubois River presumably because he was sent out to hunt grouse and instead found a pig hanging in the woods, which he brought in and told Clark was bear meat. Early on, Private Collins was flogged for stealing whiskey from the barrel he was supposed to be guarding. According to Clark the men were "always found very ready to punish Such Crimes." He was mentioned as "drunk" with several other men on December 31, 1803. Collins was court-martialed in May 1804 and sentenced to fifty lashes for, according to Clark, "being absent without leave, for behaveing in an unbecomming manner at the ball last night and for Speaking in a languguage after his return to camp tending to bring disrespect the orders of the Commanding officer." He was a skilled hunter and performed his duties well enough to secure his spot in the permanent party and to earn his land warrant for 320 acres, which he sold to George Drouillard for $300 in September 1806. Collins may have settled in Missouri. While working as a fur trader with William Ashley he was killed by the Arikara Indians on June 2, 1823. Collins Creek (Nahwah River or Lolo Fork), a tributary stream of the Kooskooskee, was named in his honor.

Reference: Moulton, vol. 2

Colt Killed Creek (White Sand Creek, Idaho): Eastern tributary of the Lochsa River. Crossing the Bitterroots in mid-September 1805, the corps faced the most grueling part of their journey and the genuine prospect of starvation. According to Clark, "I have been wet and as cold in every part as I ever was in my life." They ended up killing and eating two colts. After the first one was killed Clark wrote, "here we wer compelled to kill a Colt for our men & selves to eat for the want of meat & we named the South fork Colt killed Creek." After killing the second one, Clark recorded, "men all wet cold and hungary. Killed a Second Colt which we all Suped hartily on and thought it fine meat." Lalia Boone's *Idaho Place Names: A Geographical Dictionary* argues that the original name should be restored in recognition of the extreme hardship the expedition endured while crossing these mountains.

References: Moulton, vol. 5; Boone

Colter, John (1774–1813): Private. One of the "nine young men from Kentucky," he is considered by some to be the first "mountain man." He was the first or second man recruited near Maysville, Kentucky, on October 15, 1803. The leaders of the expedition thought well of him. Near the end of the journey, William Clark said they were disposed to accommodate the wishes of "any one of our party who had perfomed their duty as well as Colter had done." Even so, Colter had a rough beginning in the Corps of Discovery. With three others Colter was confined to camp at Camp Wood for ten days in the spring of 1803 for having visited a nearby "whiskey shop" while pretending to be out hunting. On March 29, 1803, Colter and John Shields were court-martialed for having threatened to shoot Sergeant John Ordway while the captains were away from Camp Wood. Both men "asked the forgiveness &c & promised to doe better in future." He sat on the court-martial that found John Collins and Hugh Hall guilty of an unauthorized incursion into the expedition's whiskey supply. Collins received a hundred lashes for being drunk while on guard duty, and Hall received fifty lashes for joining Collins in the crime. Colter was sent out to find the lost George Shannon in early September 1804, but—for all his skills in the wilderness—he came back empty-handed. Colter was the first of the expedition victimized by the Teton Sioux. On September 24, 1804, he reported that his horse, bridle, and some salt were stolen from him by the Indians. On August

26, 1805, he was sent by William Clark with a note to Lewis declaring that the Salmon River could not be navigated and that the expedition would have to make its way through the Bitterroot Mountains by land. It was Colter, on September 10, 1805, who made first contact with the Flathead Indians near Traveler's Rest. On October 8, 1805, a creek was named for him in the Clearwater River watershed. Today it is known by the name Potlatch Creek. Colter was one of the men sent by Lewis and Clark in a canoe to float down the Columbia past Point Ellice on November 13, 1805, to see if some less miserable campsite could be located near the shores of the Pacific Ocean. Colter was involved in a dispute during the expedition. Captain Lewis ordered Colter and Drouillard to lead an unbroken horse that was to serve as the corps's dinner. All we learn from the journals is that "in performing this duty a quarrel ensued between Drewyer and Colter." In the commotion, the horse escaped, "much to the chagrine of all who recollected the keenness of their appetites last evening," Lewis wrote. On the return journey in 1806, between the mouths of the Yellowstone and Little Missouri Rivers, the expedition encountered a pair of trappers named Joseph Dickson and Forrest Hancock. On August 15, 1806, William Clark reported that "Colter one of our men expressed a desire to join Some trappers who offered to become Shearers with and furnish traps &c," and that the captains had agreed to discharge him provided that no other member of the expedition asked for similar release. "they all agreed that they wished Colter every Suckcess," Clark wrote. "we gave Jo Colter Some Small articles which we did not want and Some powder & lead. the party also gave him Several articles which will be usefull to him on his expedition—." Colter left the expedition with Hancock and Dickson on Saturday, August 17, 1806, at the Mandan and Hidatsa villages. Colter's fame rests chiefly from his activities after the expedition. He spent the years 1806–1810 trapping beaver on the upper Missouri, sometimes as an employee of Manuel Lisa's Missouri Fur Company. In the course of his wanderings, he happened upon the geysers, mud pots, and hot springs of what is now Yellowstone National Park. Perhaps because some listeners believed he was inventing tall tales about these wonders, Yellowstone was called "Colter's Hell" for many years. The name first appeared in print in Washington Irving's *The Rocky Mountains* and later in *The Adventures of Captain Bonneville*. In the course of Colter's Yellowstone travels, he left a large pine tree marked with his blaze and initials near a place that came to be called, for a short time, Coulter's Creek. Park employees cut down the tree and the signature section was removed in 1889 or 1890, but it could not be relocated and was never placed in the park's museum as intended. Another relic said to be connected with John Colter is a stone carved out of rhyolite in the shape of a human profile with the words *John Colter* on one side and the date *1808* on the other. It was found in 1931 and is known as the Colter Stone but is considered by park historian Aubrey Haines to be the "campfire doodling" of young men working for the U.S. Geological Survey of Ferdinand V. Hayden in 1841 and 1842. In 1808 Colter and another expedition member, John Potts, were trapping on the Jefferson River when they encountered a hostile group of Blackfeet Indians. Potts was killed immediately, but Colter was stripped naked, given a head start, and permitted to run for his life. He managed to kill the lead warrior with a spear he somehow snatched from the warrior's arms, then hid under a logjam, while the remaining Blackfeet scoured the area. After the Blackfeet finally gave up the search, Colter walked naked and barefoot some 250 miles to Manuel Lisa's trading post at the mouth of the Bighorn River. Over the next two years, Colter would again tangle with the Blackfeet at the junction of the Madison and Jefferson Rivers near Fort Henry. This time his near- death experience prompted him to swear he would leave the country forever if his God would allow it. His departure from the land of beaver was a swift one; he paddled the two thousand miles to St. Louis in thirty days. Colter settled in Charette at the mouth of the Big Boeuf Creek near Daniel Boone. He married a woman named Sally sometime between 1810 and 1811; they had a son named Hiram. John Colter provided information for William Clark's masterpiece, the 1814 map of the American West that accompanied the first edition of the journals of Lewis and Clark. He died of jaundice in 1812 or 1813. Because he left the expedition early, Colter was not paid with the other members of the party. Meriwether Lewis held Colter's pay in his own accounts with the intention of paying him when he next appeared in St. Louis. Lewis's premature death in 1809, coupled with his insolvency at the time of his death, made it difficult for Colter to

While the artist exaggerated some details in this depiction, it is a highly evocative image of the party bartering with the nations of the Northwest coast. Lewis and Clark on the Lower Columbia *by Charles M. Russell. Watercolor, gouache, and graphite on paper, 1905. No. 1961.195, Amon Carter Museum, Fort Worth, Texas.*

collect from the estate. Colter believed that he was owed $599. On May 28, 1811, a St. Louis court awarded him a settlement of $377.60.

References: *Moulton, vols. 7, 8; Colter-Frick; Irving,* Rocky Mountains *and* Adventures of Captain Bonneville; *Aubrey Haines, "John Colter," in Leroy Hafen,* Mountain Men and the Fur Trade

Comcomly (d. 1830): Chinook head chief. Comcomly was said to have owned as many as three hundred slaves. An early practitioner in the linguistic art of Chinook jargon (an Esperanto of the western Indians), Comcomly married off numerous slaves, wives, and daughters for profit and to gain access to white traders.

The Chinook Indians would canoe out and meet the trading vessels to sell their women, and because they quickly traded clamons, sea otter pelts, and conical hats for small articles, the Chinook developed a more questionable reputation than the Clatsop, who did not paddle out to meet the ships. Lewis and Clark commented on this reputation frequently during their stay at Fort Clatsop. On January 9, 1806, Clark noted of the Chinook, "they do not hold the virtue of their womin in high estimation, and will even prostitute their wives and Daughters for a fishing hook or a Stran of beeds. . . . notwithstanding the Survile manner in which they treat their womin they pay much more respect to their judgement and oppinion in maney respects than most indian nations; their womin are permitted to Speak freely before them, and Sometimes appear to command with a tone of authority; they generally consult them in their traffic and act conformably to their opinions."

As a successful entrepreneur Comcomly inspired jealousy among some of the Clatsop, a neighboring rival nation, but he managed, through intimidation, to maintain his power. Years after the expedition departed, Comcomly tried to prevent other tribes from trading at the mouth of the Columbia because he wanted to protect his authority and access to the Astorians, as the employees of the J. J. Astor Fur Company were known. He died of smallpox in 1830. Comcomly's burial took place in a canoe according to Chinook tradition, but his head was removed by a trader who sold it as a curiosity in Edinburgh, Scotland.

References: *Ruby and Brown,* The Chinook Indians*; Moulton, vol. 6*

Comowool (Coboway, Comawool, Conia, Commowell, Connyau): First chief of the Clatsops, his name is variously spelled due to the fluidity of the Clatsop language. He lived at the principal Clatsop village on Point Adams (Hammond). On December 12, 1805, Lewis gave him a medal and made him a chief. While hunkered down at Fort Clatsop, the overlanders received many visits from Comowool and his people, usually with gifts of roots and fish for which they expected some kind of payment or trade. On January 3, 1806, in return for some whale blubber, berries, and the meat of three dogs, Lewis gave him a "pare of sattin breechies with which he appeared much pleased." Ordway referred to him as "our old Clotsop chief," and Lewis wrote of him, "At 11 a.m. we were visited by Commwoll and his two boys Sons of his. he presented us with Some Anchovies which had been well cured in their manner, we found them excellent. they were very acceptable perticularly at this moment. we gave the old man's Sones a twisted wire to ware about his neck, and I gave him a par of old glovs which he was much pleased with. this we have found much the most friendly and decent Indian that we have met with in this neighbourhood." On March 22 Lewis praised Comowool for his kindness and hospitality and left all of the furniture and the buildings at Fort Clatsop to him. The chief occupied the fort for a few hunting seasons, and it remained standing in 1836.

Reference: Moulton, vol. 6

Conical hat (basket hats, pagoda hats, knob tops, onion-dome hats): Woven from fine strips of white spruce bark, beargrass, white cedar, and sometimes fur and hide, and worn by the Chinook and Clatsop Indians, conical hats were purchased by the captains during the wet and miserable winter on the coast. Clark described and drew the hats in his entry for January 29, 1806: "Many of the nativs of the Columbia were hats & most commonly of a conic figure without a brim confined on the head by means of a String which passes under the chin and is attached to the two opposit Sides of a Secondary rim within the hat—the hat at the top termonates in a pointed knob of conic form or in this shape (drawing) these hats are made of the bark of Cedar and beargrass wrought with fingers So closely that it casts the rain most effectually in the Shape which they give them for their own use or that just discribed, on these hats they work various figures of different colours, but most commonly only black and white are employed. these figures are faint representations of the whales, the Canoes, and the harpooners Strikeing them. Sometimes Square dimonds triangle &ct." On February 22, 1806, Lewis wrote, "We were visited today by two Clatsop women and two boys who brought a parsel of excellent hats made of Cedar bark and ornamented with beargrass. two of these hats had been made by measures which Captain Clark and myself had given one of the women some time since with a request to make each of us a hat; they fit us very well, and are in the form we desired them. we purchased all their hats and distributed them among the party. the woodwork and sculpture of these people as well as these hats and their waterproof baskets evince an ingenuity by no means common among the Aborigenes of America." The Clatsop tried to sell hats to the corps on several occasions, and most members of the party eventually received their own hats. George Gibson still had a "Chinook hat" as late as 1806. One of the hats ended up in Peale's collection and is now housed in the Peabody Museum. Emory and Ruth Strong point out, "Basket hats with the whale motif were not made on the Columbia but were endemic to the Northwest Coast from Cape Flattery northward" and traded all along the Northwest coast. The double cone hat described by Clark on December 29, 1805, belonged to a chief, as only chiefs were allowed to wear hats with more than one cone. Several cones adorning one's hat symbolized wealth and the social status of the wearer.

References: Moulton, vols. 6, 8; Strong and Strong; Peabody Museum website, "Ethnography of Lewis and Clark," www.peabody.harvard.edu/Lewis_and_Clark

Cordelle (toe coard): According to Win Blevins's *Dictionary of the American West*, a cordelle was "the rope men used to pull keelboats upstream. The verb form means to heave a boat upstream with a cordelle. A cordeller was a fellow who did the heaving. In the early days of travel on the Missouri, before the coming of the steamboat, keelboats were poled or cordelled upriver, and that could be brutal, back-breaking, grunting along the shore or through the shallows." Lewis and Clark employed this method many times during the expedition, perhaps most memorably approaching the Great Falls as Clark recorded on June 15, 1805, "the men in the water from morning untill night hauling the Cord & boats walking on Sharp rocks and round Sliperery Stones which alternately cut their feet & throw them down, not with Standing all this dificuelty they go with great chearfulness, aded to those dificuelties the rattle Snakes inumerable & require great caution to prevent being bitten."

References: Blevins; Moulton, vol. 4

Corps of Volunteers for North Western Discovery: First used by Meriwether Lewis on August 26, 1804, after the death of Sergeant Charles Floyd: "The commanding officers have thought it proper to appoint Patric Gass, a Sergeant in the corps of volunteers for North Western Discovery, he is therefore to be obeyed and respected accordingly." It was shortened to Corps of Discovery in David McKeehan's prospectus for Patrick Gass's journal, which appeared in the *Pittsburgh Gazette* in March of 1807.

References: *Rasmussen; Moulton, vol. 3*

Cottonwood tree (broad or plains, *Populus*; narrow leafed, *Populus angustifolia*; black, *Populus trichocarpa*): First scientifically described by Lewis on June 12, 1805. Paul Cutright notes that of all the western trees, the cottonwood proved to be the most useful for the expedition. On September 13, 1804, Lewis noted cottonwoods as a food source for porcupines: "Killed a porcupine in a Cottonwood tree near the river on the lard. shore the leaves of the Cottonwood were much destroyed as were those of the Cottonwood trees in its neighborhood." Clark described the Mandan Indians feeding it to their horses during the winter: "I observed also numbers of cotton trees fallen for the purpose of feeding their horses on the Bark of limbs of those trees which is Said to be excellent food for the horses." The captains used cottonwood in the construction of Fort Mandan because it was the only timber they had. In February 1805 Lewis observed that horses "prefered the bark of the cottonwood which forms the principall article of food usually given them by their Indian masters in the winter season; for this purpose they cause the trees to be felled by their women and the horses feed on the boughs and bark of their tender branches." In his *Fort Mandan Miscellany*, Lewis wrote the cottonwood was "a soft white wood, by no means durable, and of which it is extreemly difficult to make plank or scantling." He did appreciate the wood for providing shade, windbreaks, and a break in the scenery. Describing a river bottom he wrote, it was "filled with a number of small and handsome Islands covered with cottonwood some timber also in the bottoms, the land again fertile. These appearances were quite reviving after the drairy country through which we had been passing." He also collected the cottonwood seed for his specimen collection: "No. 4 Was taken at a small Village North side of the Missouri called Sharett, on the 25th of May 1804. this is the last settlement on the Missouri; and consists of ten or twelve families

Two twenty-eight-foot cottonwood canoes were constructed and lashed together by Clark and his party to travel down the Yellowstone River (eastern Montana) in July 1806. Courtesy of Charles Fritz Fine Art.

mostly hunters. this specimine is the seed of the Cottonwood which is so abundant in this country, it has now arrived at maturity and the wind when blowing strong drives it through the air to a great distance being supported by a parrishoot of this cottonlike substance which gives name to the tree in some seasons it is so abundant as to be troublesome to the traveler—this tree arrives at great sise, grows extremly quick, the wood is of a white colour, soft, spungey and light, perogues are most usually made of these trees, the wood is not the most durable nor do I know any othe valuable purpose which it can answer except that just mentioned." He would find another purpose for the wood in June 1805, when they were portaging the Great Falls and were lucky to locate "one cotton-wood tree just below the entrance of Portage Creek that was large enough to make our carrage wheels about 22 inches in diameter." Lewis adds they were fortunate because there was not another one of similar size within twenty miles. The wood's softness proved unsuitable as "carrage" parts in the long run and broke down several times along the way. When the iron boat failed near the Great Falls, Clark and several men went ahead to make canoes from the cottonwood trees. In July of 1805 Lewis observed a medicine lodge in Piegan territory constructed of sixteen large cottonwood poles arranged in a circular manner. The cottonwood ranges west to the base of the Rocky Mountains and can be found growing along river bottoms sometimes to heights of eighty to ninety feet. Cutright writes that it survives in arid land because its roots run deep, thirty to forty feet, and that its survival "is a marvel of adaptation." Oglala Sioux spiritual leader Black Elk says that "the cottonwood taught us to make our tipis, for the leaf of the tree is an exact pattern of the tipi and this we learned when some of our old men were watching little children making play houses from these leaves . . . also if you cut an upper limb of this tree crosswise, there you will see in the grain a perfect five pointed star which, to us, represents the presence of the Great Spirit. Also perhaps you have noticed that even in the lightest breeze you can hear the voice of the cottonwood tree; this we understand is its prayer to the Great Spirit, for not only men, but all things and all beings pray to Him continually in differing ways."

References: Moulton, vols. 3, 4; Cutright, Pioneering Naturalists; *Black Elk*

Coues, Elliott (1842–1899): Pronounced "Cowes." Washington, D.C., naturalist, ornithologist, frontier historian, and editor. He displayed an early interest in birds and natural history and was sent to Labrador by the Smithsonian to study birds. Coues worked as a secretary and naturalist to the geological and geographic survey under F. V. Hayden and served as an army surgeon in Arizona. In June of 1892 Harper Publishing approached Coues to edit a reissue of the Biddle version of the Lewis and Clark journals. Coues had previously authored books on ornithology and animals as well as edited a *Century Dictionary*. Harper wanted Coues to produce a bibliography on the expedition as well as to add explanatory and historical notes to the Biddle version. While researching documents for the task Coues "discovered" the original journals in Philadelphia at the American Philosophical Society where they had been stored for some three-quarters of a century. Coues used the knowledge he gained from working for the U.S. Boundary commission and his own firsthand experience of following the trail to certify the accuracy of the geographical references in the journals. In the beginning Coues planned to do a verbatim version of the journals but soon changed his mind and began to "put in the necessary touches" he rationalized readers would prefer. His alterations to the original journals, including removing clamps, as well as his clandestine commission of a copy, do not follow methods and standards of historical research and documentation as practiced among scholars today. Nevertheless Coues is credited with ordering the journals by codex and placing pagination numbers on the documents. His version of the journals, as published in three volumes by Harper, included an index, maps, and portraits of the captains, and represents an important brick in the foundation of Lewis and Clark scholarship. Despite his editors' objections, Coues's annotations and valuable ethnological footnotes nearly outran the journals themselves. Although the Philosophical Society approved of Coues's treatment of the originals, members did not realize he crossed out whole passages and words and substituted his own. They certainly did not know about the copies he commissioned and kept in his possession. Coues was the first to recognize William Clark as the mapmaker of the enterprise, and he was the first of many to demand that the names given by Lewis and Clark be used, in accordance with geographical tradition. He recognized the importance of their discoveries and gave them deserved credit. Coues provided the name Camp Chopunnish for the site on the Clearwater River where the expedition waited in spring 1806 for the snow to melt in the Bitterroot Mountains. From the years 1876 to 1892, Coues edited the unpublished journals and diaries of many explorers, including Zebulon Pike, Alexander Henry, David Thompson, Jacob Fowler, Charles Larpenteur, and François Garces. He was familiar with the territory traversed by these explorers as he traveled many of their trails himself and was able to authenticate specific sites with a high degree of geographical accuracy. He died Christmas Day 1899 after returning from a trip to New Mexico and Arizona.

Reference: Jackson, Letters

Cous (*Lomatium cous*, Biscuitroot): Camped with the Nez Percé in May of 1806, Lewis observed, "among other roots those called by them the Quawmash and Cows are esteemed the most agreeable and valuable as they are also the most abundant. the cows is a knobbed root of an irregularly rounded form not unlike the Gensang in form and consistence. this root they collect, rub of a thin black rhind which covers it and pounding it expose it in cakes to the sun. these cakes ate about an inch and ¼ thick and 6 by 18 in width, when dried they either eat this bread alone without any further preperation, or boil it and make a thick muselage; the latter is most common and much the most agreeable. the flavor of this root is not very unlike the gensang.—this root they collect as early as the snows disappear in the spring and continue to collect it untill the quawmash supplys it's place which happens to be about the latter end of June." Author Jeff Hart notes that if properly dried the biscuitroot is edible for up to two years.

References: Hart; Moulton, vol. 7

Coxe, Daniel (1673–1739): English author. Charles II granted his father an immense tract of land in the lower Mississippi Valley where he traveled extensively from 1702 to 1716 and which he publicized in a promotional tract, *Carolana.* Coxe helped develop and popularize the idea of theoretical symmetrical geography, which held that the river basins on the west side of the Mississippi were equal in size and scope to those on the eastern side. He described large western rivers flowing from the mountains and "passable by Horse, Foot, or Wagon in less than half a day." Coxe's work was an important link in the chain of the geographical thinking of the members (including Peter Jefferson) of the Loyal Land Company, who proposed an expedition to the Missouri to find a passage to the Pacific Ocean. Coxe suggested the possibility of traveling on wagon trails over heights of land and an "easy Communication betwixt the river Meschacebe (Mississippi) and the south sea." Coxe is credited with producing the first English map of the Mississippi Valley, which accurately positioned the Ozark and Appalachian Mountain chain. As they proceeded up the Missouri, Lewis and Clark came to rely more on their own observations and information from local sources than on the theoretical symmetry theories of Coxe and Jefferson.

Reference: Allen, Passage through the Garden

Cramer, Zadoc (1773–1813): Pittsburgh publisher and author of twelve popular editions of *The Navigator; Containing Directions For Nav-*

igating The Monongahela, Allegheny, Ohio and Mississippi Rivers. Cramer published the first edition of *The Journal of Patrick Gass* in 1807 and in subsequent editions of his *Navigator* included an addendum with an abridgment based on information gleaned from Gass's account, including, "On the 15th of Nov. 1805, our adventurers, with much satisfaction, entered the bay into which the Columbia discharges itself, and at length came in sight of the Pacific ocean." Describing the incident at Two Medicine River, Cramer wrote of Captain Lewis, "he therefore found it necessary to hasten to the place of rendezvous, sooner than it was intended."

References: Dahlinger; Cramer

Cruzatte, Pierre (d. 1825 or 1828): Navigator and interpreter, half French and half Omaha Indian. He enlisted with the Corps of Discovery on May 16,1804, and had traded with the tribes on the lower Missouri for the Chouteaus before signing up with Lewis and Clark. He helped facilitate some of the early councils through his knowledge of sign language and frequently played his fiddle at the request of the crew. Cruzatte was the first expedition member to shoot a grizzly bear. His nearsightedness in his one good eye possibly caused the hunting accident on August 11, 1806, when Captain Lewis was wounded by one of Cruzatte's errant shots. The men called him "St. Peter." Clark lists him as killed sometime between 1825 and 1828. See Fiddle.

References: Slosberg, "Pierre Cruzatte"; Clarke

Cumberland Gap: The main trail into Kentucky from the east on the Wilderness Road. Dr. Thomas Walker was the first European to traverse it in 1750, and later used it for the start of his explorations for the Loyal Land Company. Lewis and Clark and members of the expedition, as well as Indian representatives, traveled through it on their way to and from Washington.

Reference: Henley, personal communication

Cut Nose (Neesh-ne-park-ke-ook): The captains called him the Cut Nose for a wound he acquired in battle with the Shoshone. Cut Nose was one of the Nez Percé head chiefs from Colter's Creek near the Clearwater. He resided with Twisted Hair's band (along with Broken

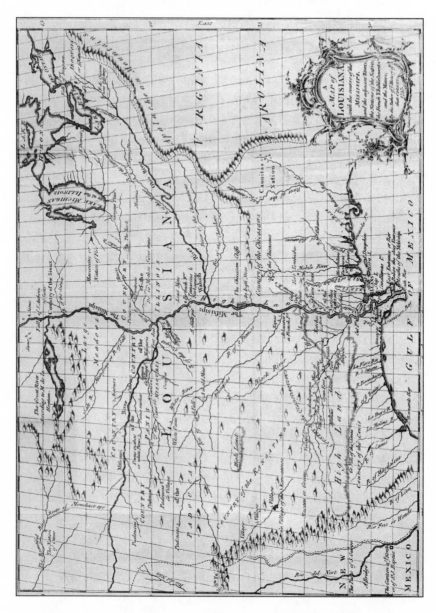

This map from DuPratz's History of Louisiana *accompanied Lewis and Clark on their expedition, and though the map was of little help, the fact that it returned with them and then was given back to its original owner, signed by Meriwether Lewis, makes it, according to Paul Cutright, "unique and priceless." "A Map of Louisiana, with the course of the Mississipi" by Le Page du Pratz, courtesy of the Special Collections department, University of Virginia Library.*

Arm) and was out hunting when the expedition came through the first time and was therefore anxious to meet them when they returned. He was involved in a heated argument with Twisted Hair over the latter's mistreatment of Lewis and Clark's horses while the expedition was at Fort Clatsop. He agreed to a friendship treaty with the captains and received a small medal from them. Cut Nose was one of the principal chiefs who met with Methodist missionary Jason Lee at a trading rendezvous in 1834 on Ham's Fork of the Green River. His nation was one of the most helpful and friendly toward the expedition, and he later asked the missionaries to settle among the Nez Percé and Flathead peoples. The captains describe him trapping an immature gray eagle to raise for its feathers. He is also mentioned as in mourning for a wife in whose honor he sacrificed twenty-five horses.

References: Ronda, Lewis and Clark among the Indians*; Swayne; Moulton, vol. 7*

Cutright, Paul Russell (1897–1988): Teacher, biologist, and author. Recognized as a foremost authority on the scientific discoveries of Lewis and Clark. His works on the Corps of Discovery include "Meriwether Lewis, Naturalist"; *Lewis and Clark: Pioneering Naturalists*; *A History of the Lewis and Clark Journals*; and a biography of journals' editor Elliott Coues. He also penned several books on Theodore Roosevelt.

Reference: Cutright

D

Dame, John (1784–18??): Private. Native of New Hampshire, enlisted in 1801 and recruited by Lewis and Clark from Amos Stoddard's company at Kaskaskia. Dame is mentioned on August 8, 1804, for killing a young "Pilacon," or pelican, near the Little Sioux River, not far from an island the captains named "Pelican Island." In May 1805 Dame returned with Corporal Warfington's party to St. Louis as was probably intended from the start of the expedition. Osgood puts Dame as one of the four enlisted men who served under Warfington's command.

Reference: Osgood, Field Notes

D'Eglise, Jacques (Santiago de la Iglesia) (d. 1806): French trader who worked in St. Louis in the late 1780s. He obtained permission from the Spanish to hunt on the Missouri in 1790 and was among the first whites to visit the Mandan in 1792. Like the Americans, the Spanish wanted to use agents and countrymen to stake a claim to the Upper Missouri country, establish trade relations with the Indian nations, and find a passable route to the Pacific. Toward that end, Governor Carondolet offered a prize of three thousand dollars to the first person to reach the Pacific. D'Eglise tried, independent of the Missouri Company, to set up a trading post at the Mandans in 1793 but made it only as far as the Arikara. He may have partnered with James Mackay on his trip up the Missouri in 1803 or 1804. Ultimately, D'Eglise was murdered in New Mexico in 1806. Carlos Dehault Delassus wrote in August 1804 of "the one named Jacques D'Eglise who for many years has been going on discovery trips without gain because of being an absolutely ignorant man."

Reference: Nasatir, "Jacques D'Eglise," in Leroy Hafen, Mountain Men and the Fur Trade

De Voto, Bernard (1897–1955): Pulitzer Prize–winning historian. Taught at Harvard and Northwestern Universities. Novelist. The *New Encyclopedia of the American West* calls him "a prophet without honor in his own country" because he was unjustly dismissed by literary critics as too much of a historian and by historians as not serious enough, and too popular with the general public, for the field. Among his many publications, he authored an account of the Rocky Mountain fur trade, *Across the Wide Missouri,* in 1947, and his edition of *The Journals of Lewis and Clark* remains among the best single-volume accounts of the expedition. His work *The Course of Empire* also includes chapters on Lewis and Clark. De Voto did not believe in romanticizing the West or clouding it in mythological sentimentality; he eventually embraced conservation as the solution to the woes of western "progress." De Voto was honored with the dedication of a memorial grove of cedars on Crooked Creek, five miles east of the Powell Ranger Station on Idaho's U.S. 12.

Reference: De Voto

Dearborn, Henry (1751–1829): American general. Served as Jefferson's secretary of war from 1801 to 1809. It was with Dearborn's authority that Lewis was able to raid the ranks of Captains Bissell and Stoddard for officers and enlistees. If a man wanted to go to the upper Missouri but his commanding officer was reluctant to send him, Lewis had Dearborn's permission to make the final decision. He offered advice to President Jefferson on the composition of the corps, concluding that a party of twelve men and one interpreter would be sufficient to reach the Pacific. When the expedition returned, Dearborn issued the land grants and wages to each of the men including the captains. Perhaps reflecting his earlier service in the Revolutionary War, Dearborn refused to recognize a co-captaincy and allowed Clark only the rank of lieutenant. Adding insult to injury, he signed the appointment almost a year after Clark had already served. In January 1807 Dearborn offered his opinion regarding the size of the land grant to be issued to Lewis and Clark, and mentioned that "in a conversation with Captain Lewis, he observed that whatever grant of land Congress might think proper to make, to himself and Lieutenant Clarke, it was his wish there should be no distinction of rank so

noticed as to make a difference in the quantity granted to each." Yet in the same letter, Dearborn personally recommended one thousand acres for Clark and fifteen hundred for Lewis. With regard to his appointment to captain, Clark later told Nicholas Biddle, "I did not think myself very well treated," and preferred no mention of the commission appear when the journals were published. Clark was finally granted his captaincy by President William Jefferson Clinton in January 2001. Dearborn served as a major general in the War of 1812 but was relieved of command the following year after a series of tactical misjudgments. From 1822 to 1824 he served as minister to Portugal.
Reference: Jackson, Letters

Delashelwilt: Chinook chief who visited Fort Clatsop several times over the winter of 1805–06 with his wife and six of their daughters and nieces. Upon first encountering the group in late November 1805, Clark surmised they came "for the purpose for gratifying the passions of the men of our party and receiving (small articles) for those indulgiences. . . . Those people appear to view Sensuality as a Necessary evel, and do not appear to abhor it as a Crime in the unmarried State." In March the men received another visit; this time Lewis refers to the chief as an "old baud." He adds, "This was the same party that had communicated the venerial to so many of our party in November last, and of which they have finally recovered. I therefore gave the men a particular charge with rispect to them which they promised to observe." On March 17, 1806, Lewis commented, "Old Delashelwilt and his women still remain they have formed a camp near the fort and seem determined to lay close sege to us but I believe notwithstanding every effort of their wining graces, the men have preserved their constancy to the vow of celibacy which they made on this occasion to Capt. C and myself." Finally, on the last day at Fort Clatsop, Lewis records, "this morning we gave Delashelwilt a certificate of his good deportment &c. and also a list of our names, after which we dispatched him to his village with his female band."
Reference: Moulton, vol. 6

Delassus, Carlos Dehault (1767–1843): Spanish official from Flanders, who served as lieutenant governor of Louisiana and alerted his government to the American intention to send a party to the head-waters of the Missouri. Lewis asked for his permission to proceed up the river in 1803 but was politely declined and advised to remain in Cahokia until the following spring. The Spanish government observed the corps throughout the winter and later made several halfhearted attempts at intercepting the expedition, but they were unable to find the man they called "Captain Merry." Delassus represented Spain at the St. Louis ceremony transferring upper Louisiana to the United States in 1804. He was assigned for a time to Florida's Louisiana Regiment. He resigned from the Spanish army in 1811, lived in St. Louis until 1826, and died in New Orleans in 1843.

References: Jackson, Letters

Dentalium dentalia: A small tusklike tubular shell representing the principal medium of trade on the Northwest Coast. Without any modification dentalia could be strung up as beads or ornamentation immediately. It is found in the waters off Vancouver Island as well as off Alaska and other islands to the north. Dentalium is collected in bunches of forty shells to a fathom, or the length of a man's arm. In fact, according to adornment authority Lois Sherr Dubin, "size was often measured against marks tattoed on the inside of a man's forearm. Tattoed men became known as Indian bankers." Dentalium shells come in shades of white and green and measure up to three inches long. The shells were sometimes engraved by the natives and many tribes, including ones far inland, used them for beads. Lewis observed, of the Kathlamet [*sic*] Indians, "All of [them] have pierced noses and the men when Dressed ware a long taper'd piece of shell or beed put through the nose." Later he described this bead, "This shell is of a conic form somewhat curved, about the size of a raven's quill at the base and tapering to a point which is sufficiently large to permit to hollow through which a small thred passes; it is from one to 1½ inches in length, white, smooth, hard and thin. These are woarn in the same manner in which the beads are; and furnich the men with their favorite ornament for the nose. One of these shells is passed horizontally through the cartilage of the nose and serves frequently as a kind of ring to prevent the string which suspends other ornaments at the same time from chafing and freting the flesh." According to author

Robert Ruby, methods of dentalium gathering included raking the ocean floor and scattering meat for the shells to latch on to. Both Chinooks and Clatsops used them for adornment and to pay for the services of a shaman. In his book *Lewis and Clark: Pioneering Naturalists* Paul Cutright quotes the Reverend Samuel Parker, who wrote that he had seen Indians with dentalium shells extending through the slits in their septums. Another witness said the effect was to render the Indian more hideous than the compression of his skull.

References: Dubin; Thwaites, Original Journals, *vol. 4; Cutright,* Pioneering Naturalists

Dickson, Joseph (1775–1844): Trapper, farmer, preacher. Among the first nonnatives encountered by William Clark and Meriwether Lewis as they returned to St. Louis. According to his great-great-grandson Frank H. Dickson, Joseph was of Scottish-Irish descent. He married Susan in 1798 and decided to purchase land in Tennessee. Eventually they settled in Cahokia, Illinois, at a place called Turkey Hill. Dickson set out with a friend to cut lumber, and together they made money and hunted deer. At a camp in La Charette, Dickson met Forrest Hancock who had come to the area with Daniel Boone in 1799. His aim was to "make a fortune" trapping furs on the Missouri. Dickson and his friend Hancock embarked in August and, because they feared ambushes, likely spent the winter near Sioux City, Iowa, where Charles Floyd, the only member of the expedition to have died, was buried. In the spring of 1805 they found their cache emptied, and their furs gone, so they decided to spend the winter with Canadian fur trapper Charles Courtin in Teton Sioux country, where they were attacked by Indians several times and Dickson sustained an injury to his leg. On August 11, 1806, at Little Knife Creek, they met William Clark, who mentioned in his journal: "at Meridian I set out and had not proceeded more than 2 miles before I observed a Canoe near the shore. I derected the canoes to land here I found two men from illinoies Jos. Dixon and Handcock. Those men are on a trapping expedition up the River Rochejhone. They inform me they left the Illinois in the Summer 1804. the last winter they spent with the Tetons in company with a Mr. Coartong (Courtin) who brought up goods to trade. The tetons robed him of the greater part of his goods and wounded this Dixon in the leg with a hard wad." Dickson went on to tell Clark the Mandans and Minitaris were at war with the Ricaras and had killed two of the latter. Next day they met the wounded Captain Lewis, and relayed information about Clark's whereabouts. They also met John Colter and John Collins. Although intending to go upstream, the pair decided to go back down with Lewis perhaps because of his account of the near catastrophe at Two Medicine. Ordway's journal says Dickson and Hancock "intend to go to Mandan and git a Frenchman or Some body to go with him to the head of the river." Colter offered to secure leftover supplies from the captains in return for a chance to trap with Dickson and Hancock. On August 17 the three set out in a single canoe. For some reason the partnership dissolved, and Dickson decided to remain in the wilderness, hibernating like a bear for the winter. Blinded by the snow, Dickson thought he was dying and, although previously not a believer, experienced a revelation. He made a pledge to God to be a "faithful Christian the rest of his life" if he survived the winter. Eventually he recovered his sight and returned to civilization with more than one thousand pounds of beaver pelts, which earned him several thousand dollars. Joseph Dickson went home to Turkey Hill, where he fulfilled a pledge to name his next child "Missouri," in honor of his revelation on the river. Dickson fathered nine children and moved around Illinois settling farms and building churches. He served as a judge of elections in 1836 and remained politically active until he died in Franklin, Illinois, in 1844. See Hancock, Forrest.

References: Dickson; Moulton, vols. 8, 9

Dog: A frequent source of protein for the men of the expedition who purchased 193 dogs for their own consumption. As Lewis commented at Fort Clatsop, "our party from necessaty having been obliged to subsist some length of time on dogs have now become extreemly fond of their flesh; it is worthy of remark that while we lived principally on the flesh of this anamal we were much more healthy strong and more fleshey than we had been since we left the Buffaloe country. for my own part I have become so perfectly reconciled to the dog that I think it an agreeable food and would prefer it vastly to lean Venison or Elk."

Captain Clark was the only man who did not appreciate the taste of dog, stating, "I have not become reconsiled to the taste of this animal yet." In a revealing incident among the Nez Percé tribe, Lewis felt insulted because a young man threw a dog at him as an indication of that tribe's distaste for men eating dog. "while at dinner an indian fellow verry impertinently threw a poor half starved puppy nearly into my plait by way of derision for our eating dogs and laughed very heartily at his own impertinence; I was so provoked at his insolence that I caught the puppy and threw it with great violence at him and struk him in the breast and face, seized my tomahawk and shewed him by signs if he repeated his insolence I would tommahawk him, the fellow withdrew apparently much mortifyed and I continued my repast on dog without further molestation." According to anthropologist Carling Malouf, the Shoshone avoided consuming dog meat because they recognized dogs as relatives of one of their prominent mythological figures, the coyote.

References: Moulton, vols. 6, 7; Burroughs; Malouf

Dorian, Pierre: Canadian-born interpreter for the expedition when they traveled through the Yankton Sioux country in present-day South Dakota. Dorian had lived with the Sioux for twenty years at the time he met Lewis and Clark and proved extremely useful in setting up councils between the captains and the Yankton Sioux. Through Dorian, Lewis and Clark collected information regarding the various bands of the tribe, their language, and conflicts with other nations. They gave the Sioux medals, clothing, and other presents, which they appreciated; the English and Spanish had given them only medals. During the council one Yankton chief, Half Man, warned the party about the Teton Sioux farther upriver. "I feel those nations above will not open their ears, and you cannot, I fear, open them." He added, "I think our old friend Mr. Dorian can open the ears of the other bands of Sioux." Despite this warning Lewis decided to leave Dorian behind, "with instructions to bring about peace with the Sioux, Mahars, Panies, Poncaries, Otoes, Missouries and to employ any trader to take chiefs, particularly Sioux Chiefs, to Washington in the spring." Two hundred and sixty miles later the captains would sorely regret the decision. Clark notes the interpreter "do not speak the language well," and "we feel much at a loss for the want of an interpreter, the one we have can speek but little." The absence of a good interpreter proved such a hindrance during the meetings with the Teton Sioux, Lewis was forced to "curtail" his council speech. Historian Ron Laycock refers to this as Lewis and Clark's first big mistake. He maintains that without Dorian's assistance the council with the Teton Sioux was a dismal failure; peace and trade did not result, and armed confrontation was only narrowly avoided. Rather than stopping at the next village and attempting to council the chiefs there, Clark records on September 30, 1804, "as we had been treated badly by Some of the band below, after Staying 2 days for them, we could not delay any time, & refured them to Mr. Duron for a full account of us and to here our talk Sent by him to the Tetons."

References: Laycock; Moulton, vol. 3

Drouillard, George (d. 1810): Interpreter, hunter, trapper, half Shawnee Indian and half French, born in Canada. Son of George Rogers Clark's interpreter, Pierre Drouillard. Drouillard, or "Drewyer," as he was referred to in the journals, transferred out of Fort Massac to the Lewis and Clark Expedition despite his value to his commander as a specialist in sign language. During his service under Lewis and Clark, Drouillard proved perhaps the most useful member of the corps because of his ability to communicate in sign and his talents as a hunter. He was frequently chosen by Meriwether Lewis to accompany him when he walked on shore or left the security of the main unit. The captain summed up his contribution on January 15, 1807, in a letter to Secretary of War Henry Dearborn: "George Drulyard Interpreter—A man of much merit; he has been of peculiarly useful from his knowledge of the common language of gesticulation, and his uncommon skill as a hunter and a woodsman; those several duties he performed in good faith, and with an ardor which deserves the highest commendation. It was his fate also to have encountered, on various occasions, with either Captain Clarke or myself, all of the most dangerous and trying scenes of the voyage, in which he uniformly acquitted himself with honor." For his service to the United States Drouillard received twenty-five dollars a month. He later lived for a time in Cape Girardeau, Missouri, then traveled back to the Rockies and helped Clark fill in his map of the northwestern United States. Partnered with Manuel Lisa, he was acquitted of murder charges in St. Louis. Drouillard died a grisly death at the hands of Blackfeet warriors on the Jefferson River, near the Three Forks. He had stubbornly refused to give in to the tribe, despite their repeated harassment of trapping ventures in their territory. He reportedly fought ferociously for his life, so much so that the warriors actually ingested parts of his vital organs in hopes of capturing some of his "medicine." According to Alexander Henry, "From the description the Bloods gave of the dress and behavior of one whom they murdered, he must have been an officer or trader; they said he killed two Bloods before he fell. This exasperated them, and I have reason to suppose they butchered him in a horrible manner and then ate him partly raw, and partly boiled. They said his skin was exceedingly white and tatooed from the hips to the feet."

References: Thwaites, Original Journals, *vol. 8; Chittenden,* American Fur Trade, *vol. 1*

Drycard mariner's compass (pocket surveying compass): Purchased by Lewis with extra needles for $23.50, a scientific instrument used to measure the traverse of the river and the magnetic azimuth of the sun. Carried by Captain Clark who used it to chart the Missouri River and once lost it in a flash flood but recovered it the next day. The compass is owned by the Smithsonian and is currently on display at Monticello.

Reference: Benson

Dunbar, William: Scottish naturalist who had been living in Natchez since 1792; he began corresponding with Thomas Jefferson in 1800. Dunbar was the first person to inform him about the nature of Indian sign language, and they shared a fascination with the remains of prehistoric quadrupeds. In the spring of 1804, Jefferson asked Dunbar to supervise—and perhaps lead—an exploring party along the Arkansas and Red Rivers. Dunbar made a preliminary reconnaissance of the Ouichita River as far as the hot springs before turning back. In 1806, after months of intense planning, Dunbar sent a larger party to ascend the Red River to its source. This expedition was commanded by Thomas Freeman; and for the first time a professional scientist, Peter Custis, was engaged. The Freeman Expedition failed. Spanish officials, jealous of American claims to the southwest, intercepted the expedition at the point where the present states of Texas, Oklahoma, and Arkansas come together. Thus Freeman never got to the headwaters of the Red River, and the professional scientist Custis, if the truth be known, was not nearly so good an observer of nature as his amateur counterpart Meriwether Lewis.

DuPratz, Antoine Simor Le Page (1695?–1775): French author and engineer who explored the lower Mississippi from 1718 to 1734 and, after returning to his homeland, wrote the *History of Louisiana or of the Western Parts of Virginia and Carolina*, which was translated into English in 1763 and 1774. Dr. Benjamin S. Barton gave Meriwether Lewis a copy of this book when Lewis visited the doctor in June of 1803. When he returned to the United States following his own exploration of Louisiana, Lewis returned the book with the following inscription, "Dr. Benjamin Smith Barton was so obliging as to lend me this copy of Mons. Du Pratz's history of Louisiana in June 1803. it has been since conveyed by me to the Pacific Ocean through the interior of the Continent of North America on my late tour thither and is now returned to its proprietor by his Friend and Obt. Servt. Meriwether Lewis Philadelphia, May 9th 1807." According to historian Paul Cutright, "the DuPratz history proved of scant value to Lewis and Clark" but because of its provenance "it is a unique and priceless volume, deeply imbued with the colors of American history." It is owned by the Library Company of Philadelphia.

Reference: Cutright, "Lewis and Clark and Du Pratz"

Dye, Eva Emory (1855–1947): Suffragist, historical novelist, Chautauqua Society founding member. Dye's 1902 novel *The Conquest* is largely responsible for establishing Sacagawea's mistaken reputation as principal guide for the Lewis and Clark Expedition. Eva and her husband, Charles, funded the statue of Sacagawea in Washington Park, Portland, Oregon, erected in 1905, as part of the celebration of the Lewis and Clark Centennial Exposition. See Sacagawea.

E

Earth lodges: Structures built and owned by the Mandan women and used as living quarters in at least seven separate villages in the upper Missouri region. The lodges were built in a domed, circular shape as large as twenty to seventy feet across, using a foundation of heavy posts, covered with willow branches, grass, and finally topped with earth. The lodges could stand for approximately ten to fifteen years, at which time a village would abandon them and move upriver. A hole in the center let the smoke out, and a bull boat was used to cover the hole if it rained. The lodges were strong enough to support people standing on top. Usually several families lived in one of the lodges in a village of up to one hundred lodges. The Mandan, whose name means Those Who Live along the Bank of a River, were an agricultural people; the women grew nine kinds of corn, five kinds of beans, along with squash and sunflowers. Using the surplus the tribe was able to trade for other foods and goods necessary for survival. The men traditionally did the hunting in addition to fighting enemies and engaging in religious ceremonies performed in a very large earth lodge erected specifically for that purpose. Lewis and Clark located their winter quarters in 1804–05 across the Missouri River and upstream from the Mandan and Hidatsa villages (on the Knife River) and built a fort they named after their neighbors. The captains noted that, in the winter, horses were frequently brought inside the earth lodges and fed cottonwood branches.
Reference: Peters

Elk (*Cervus elaphus*): A British term for moose; the animal is also known as *Wapati*, a Shawnee Indian word meaning "light rump." The second largest ungulate encountered by the expedition, the meat of this animal sustained the party and its skins provided not only ropes, harnesses, clothes, and moccasins but also the lining for Lewis's doomed iron boat experiment. According to wildlife biologist Ken Walcheck, the corps killed 396 elk during their journey. Walcheck attributes the concentration of elk in the area between the Missouri and Yellowstone Rivers to the fact that those areas were part of a huge "war zone" of competing Indian tribes. He cites Clark's August 29, 1806, journal entry as evidence the captains were aware of this phenomenon. "I have observed that in the country between the nations which are at war with each other the greatest numbers of wild animals are to be found." It would also account for several of the journal entries that comment on the "gentle" and unalarmed state of the animals in that region since the elk were not hunted during the tribal conflicts. Walcheck further theorizes that the elk populations observed by the corps were not as high in mountain valley terrain due to seasonal patterns of migration. Male elk are known for their "bugle," which is a call "of domination to cows," according to the Audubon guide, and "the vocalization begins as a bellow, changes almost immediately to a loud shrill whistle or scream, and ends with a series of grunts." It is one of the most astounding sounds of the northern plains. The guide goes on to name the bull elk as "the most polygamous deer in America and perhaps the world, [as it] assembles a harem of up to 60 cows." The elk of Lewis and Clark's era lived on the plains and in the mountain forests and ate a large variety of vegetation, which, thanks to nineteenth-century conservation measures, they continue to do today. The corps noted six species of elk as they proceeded on, including the Roosevelt elk, named later in honor of Theodore Roosevelt, who established the National Elk Refuge. Although nearly wiped out in the 1800s, elk herds now number nearly one million ungulates, spread out in suitable habitats throughout the western United States.

References: Walcheck, "Wapati"; Moulton, vol. 8

Ellicott, Andrew (1754–1820): Lancaster, Pennsylvania, astronomer, mathematician, member of the American Philosophical Society, surveyor of the District of Columbia, and one of several instructors of Meriwether Lewis in April of 1803. In three weeks Ellicott taught Lewis how to fix longitude by using a sextant, artificial horizon, and chronometer. Ellicott was one of the scientists who advised Lewis against bringing the cumbersome equatorial theodolite on the expedition.

Reference: Jackson, Letters

Embarras: French term for a dangerous log obstruction in the Missouri. See Sawyer.

Engagé: Contracted to hunt or serve as a boatman, usually with several specific conditions, including length of service and duties to be performed. Several of these men were hired by George Drouillard in river settlements around Camp Dubois in May of 1804. Pierre Chouteau supplied Lewis with seven engagés who would only go as far as Fort Mandan. Lewis wrote Clark, "they will not agree to go further, and I found it impossible to reduce them to any other engagement than that usually made with those people." Engagés were treated differently than the enlisted men. Many were known by their dit or nicknames, which sometimes substituted for their real names. They were listed as follows: Baptiste Dechamps, Etienne Mabbuef, Paul Primaut, Baptist La Jeunesse, Peter Roi, François Rivet, E. Cann, Joseph La Bartee, Peter Pinuat, and Charles Caugee. They are mentioned by Clark as "French higherlins" who "Complain for the want of provisions, Saying they are accustomed to eat 5 & 6 times a day, they are roughly rebuked for their presumption." For the most part they were a tough and hearty lot who did their jobs and received the going rate for it. Several returned with Warfington to St. Louis; some proceeded on with the expedition. Pierre Cruzatte and François Labiche remained with the permanent party and a third former voyageur, Jean Baptiste Lepage, signed on at Fort Mandan. See Lepage, Jean Baptiste.

References: JoAnn Brown; Jackson, Letters; *Moulton, vol. 2*

Equatorial theodolite: Scientific instrument favored by Thomas Jefferson for measuring lunar distances and longitude; it was most accurate in measuring horizontal angles. Jefferson owned the telescopic sight and pedestal and assumed it would be useful on the expedition even without the timepiece the inventor Jesse Ramsden, recommended. Following consultation with members of the American Philosophical Society, Jefferson allowed Lewis to substitute a chronometer for the theodolite, which several doctors told him would be too fragile an instrument to carry to the Pacific.

Ermine skins: Used by the Shoshone Indians for ornamentation and trade. Thwaites writes of two kinds of ermine, stoat or weasel. The type the journals described he refers to as weasel (*Putorius long-icuanda*). In her book *North American Indian Jewelry and Adornment from Prehistory to the Present*, Lois Sherr Dubin writes that among the Piegan Blackfeet "the Ermine was acknowledged as a fierce fighter and source of good war medicine." Lewis admired the Shoshone tippet (cloak) festooned with ermine tails as "the most eligant peice of Indian dress I ever saw . . . they attach from one to two hundred and fifty little roles of Ermin skin formed in the following manner; . . . the collar is confined arond the neck and the little roles of Ermin skin about the size of a large quill covers the solders and body nearly to the waist and has the appearance of a short cloak and is really handsome. these they esteem very highly, and give or dispose of only on important occasions. the ermin whic is known to the traiders of the N.W. by the name of white weasel is the genuine ermine, and might no doubt be turned to great advantage by those people if they would encourage the Indians to take them. they are no doubt extreemly plenty and readily taken, from the number of these tippets which I have seen among these people and the great number of skins employed in the construction of each timppet. scarcely any of them have employed less than one hundred of these skins in their formation." The Shoshone were receptive to Lewis's ideas of supplying white men with otter and ermine furs in exchange for guns and said "that we might rest assured of their friendship and that they would do whatever we wished them." The journals mention that Sacagawea gave Captain Clark "two Dozen white weazils tails" for a Christmas present at Fort Clatsop.

References: Thwaites, Original Journals, *vol. 2; Dubin; Moulton, vols. 5, 6*

Espontoon: Half pike commonly carried by an eighteenth-century infantry officer. Espontoons were six feet one and a quarter inches long, with a foot-long iron tip at the top. According to historian Robert Hunt both Lewis and Clark served under General Anthony Wayne, who advocated the use of the espontoon in the Revolutionary War. George Washington referred to them in his general orders at Valley Forge. Espontoons were used as both an offensive and a defensive weapon. The journals first mention them at Fort Mandan, February 5, 1805, when describing a type of battle-ax used by the Mandan as "somewhat in the form of an espantoon." Many of Lewis's experiences with wild animals involved the espontoon. On May 12, 1805, he writes of the confidence of carrying a big stick, "I walked on shore this morning for the benefit of exercize which I much wanted, and also to examine the country and it's productions, in these excurtions I most generally went alone armed with my rifle and espontoon; thus equipped I feel myself more than an equal match for a brown bear provided I get him in the open woods or near the water." On May 26, 1805, he writes, ". . . and on my return to camp I trod within five inches of a rattle snake but being in motion I passed before he could probably put himself in striking attitude and fortunately escaped his bite, I struck about at random with my espontoon being directed in some measure by his nois until I killed him." Clark wrote on May 29, 1805, "Great numbers of wolves were about this place and verry gentle I killed one of them with my spear." On June 7, 1805, Lewis credited the weapon with saving his life as he hiked on the bluffs above the Missouri: "In passing along the face of one of these bluffs today I sliped at a narrow pass of about 30 yards in length and but for a quick and fortunate recovery by means of my espontoon I should been precipitated into the river down a craggy precipice of about ninety feet." On June 14, 1805, Lewis again relied on the espontoon for protection, this time as he lost his presence of mind while witnessing the dramatic death of a buffalo he had wounded. Faced with a charging grizzly bear, Lewis reached for his rifle and remembered, to his horror, he had not reloaded it and there was no time to do it then. Being alone and in the open, Lewis did the only thing he felt he could do. He ran into the water at such a depth as the bear would have to swim and he would be able to kill it with his espontoon, "accordingly I ran hastily into the water about waist deep and faced about and presented the point of my espontoon, at this instant he arrived at the edge of the water within about 20 feet of me; the moment I put myself in this attitude of defence he sudonly wheeld about as if frightened, declined the combat on such unequal grounds, and retreated with quite as great precipitation as he had just before pursued me." Lewis vowed never again to be caught without his gun properly loaded for refire. No further reference is made to espontoons after June 1805. Hunt writes the espontoons could have been cached in Great Falls. He notes the "pike blade and part of the handle" found in Lewis's effects on the Natchez Trace may have been part of the espontoon Lewis carried with him to the Pacific.

References: *Hunt, "The Espontoon"; Moulton, vols. 3, 4*

Eulachon (*Thaleichthys pacificus*): Native American name for the Columbia River smelt. According to Dan Landeen and Allen Pinkham, "Eulachon are characterized by having cycloid scales, an adipose fin, and no axillary processes at the base of the pelvic fins. They are blue-brown above, have small black specks in back, shading to silver white below and a silver stripe along the side. . . . Eulachon are small, anadromous fish, not reaching more than a foot in length." Landeen and Pinkham note that most eulachon die after spawning in their third or fourth year, but some live to five years. They range from California's Klamath River to the Bering Sea. Among their spawning tributaries are the Cowlitz, Kalama, Lewis, Sandy, and Nooksack Rivers. Eulachon are a favorite food of white sturgeon, dogfish, salmon, Pacific halibut, Pacific cod, gulls, seabirds, and marine mammals. Their diet includes phytoplankton, copepods, mysids, barnacle larvae, and other crustaceans. Eulachon taste oily and have a mild flavor. On February 24, 1806, at Fort Clatsop, Lewis described the taste: "I find them best when cooked Indian stile, which is by roasting a number of them together on a wooden spit without any previous preparation whatever. They are so fat they require no additional sauce, and I think them superior to any fish I ever tasted even more delicate and lussious than the white fish of the lakes which have heretofore formed my standart of excellence among fishes. I have heard the fresh anchovy much extolled but I hope I shall be pardoned for believing this quite as good. The bones are so soft and fine that they form no obstruction in eating the fish." Today, the Columbia's annual commercial catch of the fish ranges between one and six million pounds. Many lower Columbia tribes used the fatty fish as candles by drying them and drawing a wick through them. Coues writes they were unknown to science until discovered by Lewis and Clark. The *Oregon Historical Quarterly* published an essay by Scott Byram and David G. Lewis that describes the "vast indigenous trading network" based on "grease trails," which meandered from the Pacific Coast east to the Rockies as early as the 1760s. The prized grease, which changed hands throughout the network, was eulachon, or "ooligan," "oolichan," "hooligan" oil (and may be the origin of the term *Oregon*), and was an ingredient in special feast dishes served during potlatch celebrations. The fish itself was not technically described until 1836 when Sir John Richardson mislabeled it as a member of the salmon family. At Fort Clatsop, Clark drew an illustration of the fish in his journal entry for February 25, 1806: "I purchased of the Clatsops this morning about half a bushel of small fish which they had caught about 40 miles up the Columbia in their scooping nets. As this was an uncommon fish to me and one which no one of the party has ever seen . . . I have drawn the likeness of them as large as life; its as perfect as I can make it with my pen and will serve to give the general idea of the fish."

References: *Landeen and Pinkham; Byram and Lewis; Thwaites,* Original Journals, *vol. 4; Moulton, vol. 6*

Evans, John Thomas (1770–1799): Native of Waunfawr, Wales; son of a Methodist minister. His belief in the mythical Welsh Prince Madoc og Gwmned and his descendants, the fair-skinned Indians of the upper Missouri, brought Evans to the United States in 1792. The myth became popular in Wales at that time, when the London publication *Gentleman's Quarterly* ran a series of articles and poems on the lost tribe of "Welch." In St. Louis, Evans met Scotsman James Mackay and served under him as a representative for the Missouri Company, a Spanish mercantile outfit. The company ordered them to resupply an earlier detail up the Missouri River led by teacher Jean Baptiste Truteau. Mackay, also interested in the Welsh Indians, hired Evans in part for his ability to speak and write Welsh. The Spanish government wanted Mackay, Evans, Truteau, and other members of the Missouri Company to "ascertain the discovery of the Pacific Sea" and establish a claim for Spain by building forts and encouraging trade with the local tribes. Mackay set out with thirty men, four pirogues, and merchandise worth more than fifty thousand dollars to distribute to the natives as they moved upriver. Each man would earn one thousand dollars with an additional three thousand dollars for those who did not return in a year. The group spent the winter at a fort they constructed south of Sioux City, Iowa, and named Fort Charles. During this period Mackay tried to secure passage from a contentious Maha (Omaha) chief, Black Bird, exchanging many gifts and trinkets in the hope of moving upriver in the spring. Lack of food forced Mackay to send his lieutenant, John Evans, out buffalo hunting with the Mahas for twenty-five days. When delays with Black Bird caused a change in plans, Mackay sent Evans ahead to obtain information about the Mandan and Hidatsa camps. His instructions share charac- teristics with Jefferson's instructions to Meriwether Lewis. Evans was to discover a passage from the sources of the Missouri to the Pacific Ocean. He was also to keep a journal and mark notches on trees or engrave stones with the day, month, year, and the names of Charles IV, king of Spain, and Missouri Company in large letters. He was also to be on the lookout for Russians and persuade the natives that King Charles represented their "Great Father." Evans's group proceeded three hundred miles to the mouth of the White River in south-central South Dakota before the Sioux forced them back to Fort Charles. On his next attempt, on June 8, 1796, Evans kept a journal and made a "chart" of the country he passed through. After being detained by the Arikara, Evans finally was allowed to proceed and advanced to the Mandan villages in September 1796. Upon arrival Evans quickly dis- lodged the Canadians who worked for the British Northwest Com- pany and renamed their fort after Mackay. The lieutenant lived with the Mandan for six months and absorbed much of their culture and geographical knowledge but never located a single Welsh Indian. He managed to anger British traders by forbidding them from trading with the Mandan; his desire for a monopoly angered local trader René Jesseaume into what Evans perceived as attempted murder. Evans's situation did not improve during that winter, which he spent in soli- tude and misery, while Mackay retired and the Missouri Company went bankrupt. Evans left the Mandan, promising Black Cat and the other chiefs that he would return with guns and ammunition. Seven years later, in November of 1804, Black Cat reminded his people of Evans's unfulfilled promises, and cast doubts on the words of Cap- tains Lewis and Clark by hinting they might do the same. It took Evans only sixty-eight days to return to St. Louis and, on July 14,

1797, he wrote a letter to one of his original sponsors admitting that Welsh Indians did not exist. Some Madoc believers felt Evans did not go far enough into the North American frontier, but another expedition (in 1819) also failed to find the mythical descendants of Madoc. Artist George Catlin recorded seven Mandan words he thought resembled Welsh. Evans secured a job to survey Cape Girardeau, south of St. Louis, for the Spanish. In 1798 thieves robbed him of everything he owned. Somehow Evans managed to recover his paper case, his flute, and his chart. He traveled to Louisiana where Lieutenant Governor Trudeau promised him land, and went to work for the new governor of New Orleans, Don Manuel Gayoso de Lemos. Soon after, however, he fell ill. John Thomas Evans died in May of 1799 and is buried in an unmarked grave in New Orleans. A copy of his chart was given by William Henry Harrison, governor of the Indiana Territory, to Thomas Jefferson who passed it on to Lewis and Clark. They made some twelve additions to Evans's map as they traversed the seven-hundred-mile swath of country it described. On October 18, 1804, Clark mentions, "I walked on Shore in the evening with a view to See Some of those remarkable places mentioned by evens, none of which I could find." On the twentieth he wrote, "after brackfast I walked out on the L. Side to see those remarkable places pointed out by Evins. . . . Came to about 1½ miles above off the mouth of a Small river about 70 yards wide Called by Mr. Evins the Little Mississou (Missouri) River." Moulton explains this is not the Little Missouri of North Dakota and that the "remarkable sights" may have been the remnants of native villages seen by Evans. According to Raymond Wood, Rueben Thwaites published the six-part map in his edition of the journals of Lewis and Clark believing that the map was a Clark original of the Missouri River beginning at St. Charles, Missouri. In fact the map begins at Fort Charles, the fort Mackay and Evans built near Sioux City, Iowa. In 1946 Aubrey Diller's paper "Maps of the Missouri River before Lewis and Clark" corrected the mistake. Wood writes that "the Evans map rendered all earlier maps of the area obsolete." All of the major tributaries of the Missouri are named, alternating between English and French. Wood feels Mackay may have made additions to the map on one of his visits to Lewis and Clark while they were at Camp Dubois. Although Evans's map was some three hundred miles off and placed the headwaters of the Missouri much too far south, it served as the base map for parts of at least ten secondary English, French, and Spanish maps until the publication of Clark's map in 1814. Clark used it when he drew his map at Fort Mandan. John Logan Allen writes that "the Yellowstone River and the Great Falls of the Missouri were fixed by their (Mackay-Evans) reports as critical landmarks of the country west of the Mandans. Their journals and maps are part of a short list of geographical materials that can be definitely established as being in Lewis and Clark's possession prior to their departure to the Pacific." See Mackay, James.

References: David Williams; Allen, Passage through the Garden; Wood, "John Thomas Evans and William Clark: Two Early Western Explorers' Maps Re-examined"; "The John Evans 1796–97 Map"; and "John Thomas Evans"; Diller; Nasatir, Before Lewis and Clark, vol. 1; Moulton, vol. 3

Eye water: A combination of white vitriol (zinc sulfate) and sugar of lead (lead acetate), purchased in Philadelphia, diluted with water and applied to sore eyes. Clark used it to treat the Walla Walla Indians in April 1806. According to Lewis, "we gave them some eye-water which I beleive will render them more essential service than any other article in the medical way which we had it in our power to bestoe on them. soar eyes seem to be a universal complaint amonge these people; I have no doubt but the fine sand of these plains and river contribute much to this disorder." Dr. E. G. Chuinard attributes the afflictions to several possible causes: glaucoma, trachoma, gonorrhea, and nearsightedness. By providing medical services to the natives, Clark was able to secure their help and trade for food. The captains gave the ingredients and instructions on how to make eye water to the Walla Walla and left a "phiol of eye water" with Broken Arm, chief of the Nez Percé, and told him they would replenish it. Lewis noted the importance of the eye water even if it treated only symptoms and not the diseases themselves. "my friend Capt. C. is their favorite phisician and has already received many applications. in our present situation I think it pardonable to continue this deseption for they will not give us any provision without compensation in merchandize and our stock is now reduced to a mere handfull. we take care to give them no article which can possibly oinjure them." The eye wash did provide temporary relief, according to Clark: "those two cures (soap and eye wash) has raised my reputation and given those nativs an exolted oppinion of my Skill as a phician." On May 23, 1806, Lewis wrote, "our skill as phisicans and the virture of our medecines have been spread it seems to a great distance. I sincerely wish it was in our power to give relief to these poor afficted wretches." On June 2, 1806, the corps used eye water as one of the last items available to trade for food needed to cross the Rocky Mountains. "Our traders, McNeal and York are furnished with the buttons which Capt L— and my Self Cut off of our Coats, Some eye water and Basilicon which we made for that purpose and Some phials of eye water and Some tin boxes which Capt. L had brought from Philadelphia. in the evening they returned with about 3 bushels of roots and Some bread haveing made a Suckcessfull voyage, not much less pleasing to us than the return of a good Cargo to an East Indian merchant."

References: *Chuinard,* Only One Man Died*; Moulton, vol. 7*

F

Fairfong (Faufon, Farfong, Faufonn): A Frenchman who lived with the Missouri and Oto Indians and interpreted for Lewis and Clark while they passed through and counciled with these nations. According to Donald Jackson he may have been the trader who relayed information about the corps to Thomas Jefferson in November 1804. Jackson also refers to the spelling of his name as "one of Clark's ingenious phonetic atrocities." On August 2, 1804, Clark relates "at sunset 6 chiefs and their warries of the Ottos and Missouries with a frenchman by the name of Farfonge we spoke shook hands and gave them some tobacco and provisions, they sent us some water millions," and "from this place I am told by Mr. Faufong the interpreter that it would take a man 25 days to go to St. a fee pass, the head of the Arkansas, round the Kansas head, across Some mountains from the top of which the city may be Seen." This information could have originated with a Pedro Vial, a Frenchman working for Spain, who crossed from Sante Fe to St. Louis and estimated it would have taken him 25 days if not for Indian problems. Part of Lewis's instructions from Thomas Jefferson involved gathering information concerning trade with Sante Fe. In 1803 Lewis proposed a side trip to explore the southern country but Jefferson decided against it. Fairfong was given a few presents on August 20, 1804, for his interpreting services.
References: Jackson, Letters; *Moulton, vol. 2*

Falls of the Ohio: Extending across the river between Louisville and Clarksville, Indiana, the home of George Rogers Clark, the only obstruction to navigation on the Ohio River, and the site where Clark and Lewis joined forces. George Rogers Clark established the first English-speaking settlement in Louisville in 1778 and founded the town of Clarksville, where he and his brother William lived, on the north or Indiana side. Clark recruited nine men from the surrounding area, who later, thanks to Nicholas Biddle, became known as the "nine young men from Kentucky." After joining forces at Clarksville, Captains Lewis and Clark set forth from the falls on October 26, 1803, on their two-year journey to the Pacific and back. The falls required skill to pass; they presented navigators with the only major obstruction on the Ohio River. At the falls the river descends some twenty-four feet over a three-mile stretch, flowing over a series of limestone ledges, or Devonian fossil beds, which contain more than six hundred species of fossils. The falls are known to be an excellent bird habitat; more than 270 species have been observed in the vicinity and ornithologist John James Audubon produced more than two hundred sketches of birds when he lived nearby. The site is preserved in a sixty-eight-acre park, established in 1990, which features an interpretive center with exhibits on the geology, history, and cultural development of the falls. A reproduction of the George Rogers Clark cabin sits near the original site of his home.

Feathers, The (Ac Ko Mo Ki): Piegan Indian who supplied Hudson's Bay surveyor Peter Fidler with geographical information about the headwaters of the Missouri. Much of this information made it onto a map drawn by British cartographer Aaron Arrowsmith in 1802. It suggested the geography of the Rockies was similar to the Blue Ridge Mountains. Like many of the early charts of the Rocky Mountains, Arrowsmith's map implied that the traverse over the mountains would not be difficult and that the Pacific Ocean could be reached in as little as eight days.
Reference: Benson

Fiddle: Both George Gibson and Pierre Cruzatte took violins, or fiddles, on the journey. The fiddle is frequently referred to at the end of a day's entry. It became an indispensable tool for engaging with the natives and for keeping morale high during the two-year expedition. Lewis writes, in a typical reference to the instrument, "after I had completed my observations in the evening I walked down and joined the party at their encampment on the point of land formed by the junction of the rivers; found them all in good health, and much pleased at having arrived at this long wished for spot (junction of the Yellowstone and Missouri), and in order to add in some measure to the general pleasure which seemed to pervade our little community, we ordered a dram to be issued to each person; this soon produced the fiddle, and they spent the evening with much hilarity, singing & dancing, and seemed as perfectly to forget their past toils, as they appeared regardless of those to come." Along with producing "cheerful" feelings and occasions of "dancing merrily all night," the fiddle intrigued many of the Native American Indians who heard it. Clark wrote that the Walla Walla Indians were "pleased and astonished" and "delighted" by the music of the fiddle or violin. The Wishram-Wasco Chinooks "shewed every civility towards us" after hearing Cruzatte play the fiddle, which according to an earlier observation by Lewis he accomplished "extreemely well." Some tribes even requested Cruzatte and his violin and showed the men their traditional "Prophet" dances in return. Whitehouse indicates perhaps the most important repercussion of having the fiddle: "the party amused themselves dancing all the evening untill about 10 oClock in a Sivel & jovil manner." Some representative fiddle tunes of the day were "Fisher's Hornpipe," "The Flowers of Edinburgh," "Haste to the Wedding," "La Belle Catherine," and "Alouette."

References: Slosberg, *"Pierre Cruzatte"*; Hunt, *"Merry to the Fiddle"*; Moulton, *vols. 4, 7, 9*

Fidler, Peter (1769–1822): Hudson's Bay Company surveyor whose charts supplied the geographical information for the Arrowsmith-King map that Lewis and Clark used as a guide. On June 8, 1805, they began to question Fidler's map. As Lewis wrote, "I now began more than ever to suspect the veracity of Mr. Fidler or the correctness of his instruments." Fidler's map was based on faulty information because he had not traveled below the forty-seventh parallel; he had misjudged some of the distances relayed to him by the Piegan Blackfeet Indian known as The Feathers and placed the Rockies farther south than they actually were.

References: Allen, Passage through the Garden; Moulton, vol. 4

Field (Fields), Joseph (1774–by 1828): Private. Born in Culpeper County, Virginia, but raised in Jefferson County, Kentucky, and considered one of the "nine young men from Kentucky." He and his brother Reubin enlisted on August 1, 1803. The Field brothers served as woodsmen, hunters, and trustworthy members of the corps. On July 4, 1804, a rattlesnake bit Joseph causing his foot to swell; the captains treated him with a poultice of bark and gunpowder. Near the Great Falls on June 4, 1805, Field nearly lost a battle with a grizzly bear but managed to escape with only a scratch. He and George Drouillard later purposefully attracted a huge male grizzly and killed the enraged beast. As a mark of his worthiness, Field was often used as a messenger between the captains when they needed to travel in separate parties. Field was one of the three crafters selected to construct a leather boat after the failure of Lewis's iron boat. Joseph Field killed the first buffalo on August 23, 1804. On May 4 he had to be treated with Glauber's salts and laudanum for what Lewis called dysentery and a high fever. Historians speculate Field discovered the sulphur spring Lewis prescribed for Sacagawea's treatment on June 16, 1805, which cured her of a life-threatening illness. He accompanied Clark, Potts, and York when they went around the Gates of the Mountains in search of the Shoshone. Clark chose Field to lead an auxiliary exploration of the lower Yellowstone, and the Field brothers were with Lewis when he encountered the Piegan Blackfeet on the Marias, July 27, 1806. Joseph Field was one of the men who expressed a desire to see more of the ocean than could be viewed from Fort Clatsop; together with Bratton and Gibson he also served as a salt maker. Clark mentions Joseph "hued" a writing desk for each captain, which he gave them on Christmas Eve 1805. He received a warrant for 320 acres of land in Franklin County, Missouri. Clark lists him as having died sometime in the period 1825–1828. There is a gulch in the Gates of the Mountains named Fields Gulch in honor of the brothers.

References: *Clarke; Lange, "The Expedition's Brothers"; Ella Mae Howard; Holmberg,* Dear Brother, *Appleman*

Field (Fields), Reubin (1772–1822 or 1823): Private; born in Culpeper County, Virginia, but raised in Jefferson County, Kentucky, and considered one of the "nine young men from Kentucky." He and his brother Joseph enlisted on August 1, 1803. The Field brothers served as woodsmen, hunters, and trustworthy members of the corps. On March 3, 1804, Reubin Field is mentioned in the orderly book for disorderly conduct for refusing to do his shift of guard duty. Clark mentions he killed a "Vultur" in November of 1805, otherwise known as the California condor. He has the dubious distinction (on July 27, 1806, at the Two Medicine River) of stabbing a Piegan Indian "to the heart with his knife the fellow ran about 15 steps and fell dead." After returning to Missouri, Clark recommended him for a lieutenant's position in the army, indicating he may have been the older of the two Field brothers. Received a land grant for 320 acres in Missouri but chose to settle in Kentucky. He married Mary Myrtle in Indiana in 1808. Rueben Field died in Jefferson County, Kentucky, near the end of 1822 or early 1823.

References: Clarke; Moulton, vols. 6, 8

Filson Historical Society: Located in Louisville, Kentucky, the society was established in 1884 from the private library of Kentucky pioneer and author Rueben T. Durrett. The historical society now functions as a library and museum with a collection of manuscripts, photographs, prints, and artifacts related to the history of Kentucky, the Ohio Valley, and the upper South. Items related to the Lewis and Clark Expedition include one bighorn sheep horn given to the society in 1929 by the grandson of Clark's sister Fanny, Rogers Clark Ballard Thurston. It is probably one of the horns listed by Clark in a memorandum of articles he forwarded to Louisville in 1806. It is believed Clark gave the horn to his sister and her husband sometime in early November 1806. In addition to housing one of the only animal artifacts brought back by the expedition, the Filson Club Historical Society owns six of Clark's letters and one of Lewis's written during their journey to the Pacific. Other related documents include letters from William Clark to his brother Jonathan indicating harsh treatment of York, account books, and diaries of persons who came into contact with the captains. Portraits of Clark, his brother George Rogers, and the infamous James Wilkinson (traitor to the U.S. government) may also be viewed at the society.

Reference: Holmberg, personal communication

Fincastle, Virginia: Home of George Hancock, friend of William Clark's brother George Rogers Clark and father of his future bride Judith "Julia" Hancock. Lewis and Clark visited this place before the expedition and Clark returned there soon after. The Hancocks resided in several different homes in Fincastle: Santillane (1 and 2) and Forthingay. The citizens of Fincastle welcomed William Clark upon the expedition's return. In a flattering address Pat Lockhart, chairman of the Citizens of Fincastle Committee, stated, "Sentiments of esteem and gratitude induce us to offer you our sincere congratulations, upon your safe return to the bosom of your country. . . . Your fame will be as pure and unsullied, as that great man to whom Europe is indebted for a knowledge of our continent; the extent and importance of which, it has been reserved for you to disclose to the world. We conceive it to be a signal proof of the wisdom and attention with which you have conducted the expedition, that but one man was lost to your country. This fact will afford future travellers the most salutary instruction. It will teach them, that, discoveries (apparently the most difficult) may be effected without the effusion of human blood. . . ." Clark graciously replied that "to respect the rights of humanity has and ever will be the leading principal of my life, and no reflection is more pleasing to me than that of effecting the objects we had in view with the effusion of so small a portion of human blood. Gentlemen we ought to assign the general safty of the party to a singular interposition of providence, and not to the wisdom of those who commanded the expedition. . . . The friendly attention manifested towards us by many of our fellow citizens is highly flattering, but the distinquished attention shewn to me by the Citizens of Fincastle & it's vicinity produces those emmotions which I am unable to discribe. . . ." Although his father-in-law hoped he would remain in Fincastle, and gave him land to settle on, Clark accepted President Jefferson's appointment as the superintendent of Indian affairs in 1807, which necessitated a move to St. Louis. He returned to Fincastle for his wedding to the sixteen-year-old Judith, then took her back to St. Louis, where they had five children together. Captain Clark became governor of the Missouri Territory in 1813. After the sudden death of Meriwether Lewis, Clark invited the scholar Nicholas Biddle to the Hancock home in Fincastle in 1810, "where I have my Books & memorandoms and stay with me a week or two & read over and make yourself thirily acquainted with every thing which may not be explained in the Journals." Biddle eventually complied with Clark's request, and their efforts produced the *History of the Expedition under the Command of Captains Lewis and Clark* (1814). For health reasons, Judith returned to Fincastle, and died there in 1820. Her father died less than a month later. A double funeral was held and the two are buried together in the family mausoleum at Forthingay.

References: Dorothy Kessler; Jackson, Letters

Flintlock rifle (model 1795): The U.S. Army regulation musket of 1803. According to author Carl P. Russell the rifle carried a ball heavy enough to kill a deer or an elk, but "because of its poor accuracy beyond 50 or 60 yards the musket loaded with ball was not the favorite meat-getter." Hugh McNeal once used his musket to fight off an enraged grizzly bear (July 15, 1806). See McNeal, Hugh.

Reference: Russell

Floyd, Charles (1782–1804): Sergeant; one of the "nine young men from Kentucky." Floyd died near present-day Sioux City, Iowa, on August 20, 1804, just three months into the expedition. He was appointed one of the three expedition sergeants no later than April 1, 1804, and was one of seven journalists. His brief journal consists of fifty-six numbered pages of text. It is altogether unremarkable. On July 31, 1804, Floyd writes, "I am verry Sick and Has ben for Somtime but have Recovered my helth again." Actually, Clark had reported the illness one day previously. "Serjt. Floyd verry unwell a bad Cold %c." Floyd's orthography is even worse than Clark's. On Sunday, June 10, 1804, for example, he writes "we imbarked at the yousel ouer." On August 19, Clark reports the collapse of Floyd's constitution. "Sergeant Floyd is taken verry bad all at onc with Beliose Chorlick. we attempt to relieve him without Success as yet, he gets wordse and we are muc alarmed at his Situation, all attention to him." And again on August 20: "I am Dull and heavy been up the greater Part of last night with Serjt. Floyd who is a bad as he can be to live. the motion of his bowels having changed &c. &c. is the Cause of his violent attack &c." Later the same day Captain Clark recorded, "we

Came to make a warm bath for Sergt. Floyd hopeing it would brace him a little, before we could get him in to this bath he expired, with a great deel of composure, having Said to me before his death that he was going away and wished me to write a letter—we Buried him to the top of a high round hill over looking the river & Countrey for a great distance Situated just below a Small river without a name to which we name & call Floyds River, the Bluff Sergts Floyds Bluff—we buried him with all the honors of War, and fixed a Ceeder post at his head with his name title & Day of month and year. Capt Lewis read the funeral Service over him he had at All times given us proofs of his impariality Sincurity to ourselves and good will to Serve his Countrey we returned to the Boat & proceeded to the Mouth of the little river 30 yd. wide & Camped a butifull evening." On the return journey in 1806, the expedition stopped to pay respects at Floyd's grave. On September 4, Clark writes, "we came too Floyd's Bluff below the Enterance of Floyd's river and assended the hill, with Capt Lewis and Several men, found the grave had been opened by the natives and left half Covered. we had this grave Completely filled up, and returned to the Canoes. . . ." Clark later told Biddle that a Sioux chief had buried his son in Floyd's grave "for the purpose of accompanying him to the other world believing the white man's future state was happier than that of the Savages." Floyd's last journal entry was made on August 18, 1804. In it he announced that Moses Reed had been returned by the posse dispatched by Captains Lewis and Clark, and that an Oto delegation had arrived at the camp.

Reference: Moulton, vol. 9

Football: Clark wrote, "The women have a kind of game which they play with a Soft ball with their foot." According to Prince Maximilian, who wintered with the Mandan in 1833, "The women are expert in playing with a large leathern ball which they let fall alternately on their foot and knee, again throwing it up and catching it, thus keeping it in motion for a length of time without letting it fall to the ground. Prizes are given, and they often play high. The ball is often very neat and curiously covered with dyed porcupine quills."

References: Moulton, vol. 3; Culin

Fort Clatsop: A fifty-foot-square structure with three and four huts on each side connected by palisades, surrounding a forty-eight- by twenty-foot inner parade ground. The palisade walls were erected in four days under the direction of Sergeant Patrick Gass, which kept the expedition dry, if not comfortable, during the winter of 1805–06. The decision was made (by vote) to locate the fort on the heavily timbered south side of the Columbia because it would be closer to elk and potas roots, and offered access to places where a salt camp could be established. In addition Lewis and Clark hoped a trading vessel would arrive during the winter and provide them with trade goods they required for the way home. They named the fort in honor of a nearby nation who supplemented their meager fare with fish, berries, and roots. The captains used the time at Fort Clatsop wisely; Lewis described ten new plant species. He scientifically depicted many trees and animals unknown in the United States and made valuable ethnological observations on the neighboring Indian tribes. Clark also worked throughout the winter on the map of their route, which they used to formulate a plan for the return journey. In addition to establishing a salt camp, the men hunted (131 elk and 20 deer) and made 358 pairs of moccasins. Although Christmas at Fort Clatsop proved gloomy, members of the party consoled themselves that the next Christmas would be spent with family and friends; they exchanged gifts, sang, and fired volleys in celebration. As Captain Clark recorded on March 23, 1806, the expedition "left Fort Clatsop on our homeward bound journey. at this place we had wintered and remained from the 7th of Dec. 1805 to this day and have lived as well as we had any right to expect, and we can say that we were never one day without 3 meals of some kind a day either pore Elk meat or roots, notwithstanding the repeeted fall of rain which has fallen almost Constantly. . . ." Clatsop chief Comowool received the fort and all its furnishings in a gesture of goodwill from the captains, but within five years the forest had reclaimed it. Efforts are currently under way to determine its exact location. A replica of the fort is maintained today on a 125-acre national memorial established by Congress in 1958 and offers interpretive programs and other educational opportunities for students of the expedition.

Reference: Moulton, vol. 7

Fort Mandan: Lewis and Clark spent the winter of 1804–05 among the three villages of Hidatsa and two of Mandan Indians. They built their second winter quarters of the expedition a few miles below the mouth of the Knife River, on the east bank of the Missouri River. The nearest village was Matootonha. Construction began on November 3, 1804. Most of the party moved into the fort on November 19, 1804. The two captains moved in on November 20. In addition to housing the men of the expedition, the fort housed a blacksmith shop and a meat storehouse. Among other things, Clark worked on his map of the Missouri within the walls of Fort Mandan, and Meriwether Lewis compiled statistics of rivers and Indian tribes for President Jefferson. It is not clear whether Sacagawea gave birth to her son, Jean Baptiste, within the walls of the fort, or nearby at what Lewis and Clark sometimes call the interpreters' hut. Security at the fort was relatively lax until February 7, 1805, when Lewis, in Clark's absence, noticed that the interpreters' wives were opening the gates of the fort at night to let in their visitors. Lewis ordered a lock installed on the gate. A re-creation of Fort Mandan was built in 1972. The re-creation is inauthentic in a number of ways and nobody pretends that it is on the actual site of Fort Mandan. GPS places its location at 101°14'631" W, 47°26'282" N in present-day McLean County, North Dakota, 1,600 miles upriver from St. Louis.

Reference: Moulton, vol. 3

Fort Massac: Also called Fort Massacre; located on the north bank of the Ohio River above present-day Metropolis, Illinois. The original French owners ceded it to the British in 1763. It languished until 1794 when it was rebuilt by Americans under orders from General Anthony Wayne. On November 11, 1803, Lewis wrote, "Arrived at Massac engaged George Drewyer (Drouillard) in the public service as an Indian Interpretter, contracted to pay him 25 dollars pr. month for his services." Joseph Whitehouse and John Newman also joined the expedition at Fort Massac. See Whitehouse, Joseph; Newman, John.

Reference: Moulton, vol. 2

Frazier (Frazer), Robert (17??–1837): Arlen Large lists *Frazer* as the accepted spelling. Private; Virginian; fencing master. Frazier originally served as one of the five men under Warfington. He joined the expedition at Camp Wood, and transferred to the permanent party in the spring of 1805 to fill the spot left when Moses Reed was discharged for desertion. Frazier has the distinction of being the first man to be bled by Captain Lewis, on July 7, 1804, in his case to treat sunstroke. He was also given niter, which seemed to revive him by the next day. On August 25, 1805, while hunting, Frazier's shot nearly hit Captain Lewis. "This morning while passing through the Shoshone cove Frazier fired his musquet at some ducks in a little pond at the distance of about 60 yards from me; the ball rebounded from the water and pased within a very few feet of me." In early January of 1806, on the way to recover whale meat, Frazier, according to Clark, "behaved very badly and mutonous—he also lost his (big) large Knife." Frazier escaped punishment for the infraction perhaps because of the miserable conditions on this segment of the trip. On June 2, 1806, Frazier is mentioned by Gass for trading an Indian one of his old razors for two Spanish dollars. "They [Chopunnish] said they got the dollars from about a Snake Indian's neck, they had killed some time ago." Gass also comments that Frazier was very fond of conversing with them and of learning their language. In June of 1806 Frazier received a horse from Hohots Ilppilp in exchange for a pair of "Canadian shoes," or snow shoes. In October of the same year, he was the first member of the corps to issue a prospectus on his intention to publish his journal, with Lewis's permission. The publication did not occur although Jackson quotes Frazier's friend John R. McBride commenting on the journal decades later as "in many respects more interesting than that of his commanders." It is presumed lost. A map of the Northwest he intended to include with the journal is at the Library of Congress. Frazier accompanied Captain Lewis to Washington and Virginia after the expedition and then returned to St. Louis. He received a land bond and payment of $166.66 on October 6, 1806, and later served with the Louisiana militia and testified against Aaron Burr and his cohorts in St. Louis and New Orleans. Frazier lived in Missouri on the Gasconade River from 1825 to 1829 and died in Franklin County, Missouri, in 1837.

References: *MacGregor,* Journals of Patrick Gass; *Jackson,* Letters; *Moulton, vols. 5, 6*

Fusil (fuzee): Musket carried by an officer. Usually privately pur-chased and a bit fancier than the enlisted men's muskets. On June 29, 1805, after nearly drowning in a downpour, Clark recorded, "I lost at the river in the torrent the large Compas, an elegant fusee, a Toma-hawk, Humbrallo (umbrella), Shot pouh and horn with powder and mockersons. . . ."

Reference: Moulton, vol. 4

G

Gallatin, Albert (1761–1849): Swiss-born secretary of the treasury in the Jefferson administration. As a member of Jefferson's cabinet, Gallatin had an opportunity to review the president's instructions to Meriwether Lewis. (Only Gallatin and Attorney General Levi Lincoln made suggestions when Jefferson circulated a draft of his instructions.) Jefferson had planned to mention a Missouri River expedition in his annual message to Congress in December 1802. It was Gallatin who proposed that Jefferson submit a secret message, fearing that a public announcement would anger foreign courts. Gallatin's principal contribution to the history of the American West was his study and classification of Indian languages. Lewis and Clark named one of the three forks of the Missouri River for Gallatin; it retains the distinguished name today.

Game of chance: On December 9, 1805, at Fort Clatsop, Clark observed that, in addition to the hand game, the Clatsop Indians played "one other game which a man attempted to Show me, I do not properly understand it, they make use of maney peces about the Shape and size of Backgammon Pices which they role through between two pins Stuck up at certain distancies." This game was also described as "something like the play of ninepins. Two pins are placed on the floor, about the distance of a foot from each other, and a small hole is made behind them. The players then go about ten feet from the hole, into which they try to roll a small piece resembling the men used at draughts; if the piece rolls between the pins, but does not go in the hole, nothing is won or lost; but the wager is wholly lost if the checker rolls outside of the pins. Entire days are wasted at these games, which are often continued through the night round the blaze of the fires, till the last article of clothing or even the last blue bead is won from the desperate adventurer." Lewis and Clark attributed the gambling and trading proficiency of the Clatsops to that tribe's proximity to the great trading center on the Columbia River.

References: *Moulton, vol. 6; Coues,* History of the Expedition, *vol. 2*

Garreau, Joseph: Spanish or French interpreter and trader who accompanied Jacques D'Eglise's 1793 expedition to the Arikaras and settled with them, operating as an interpreter for that tribe as well as for the Mandan people. According to historian Gary Moulton, "He has been called the first white settler in South Dakota" and was sometimes described in unflattering terms. On March 16, 1805, Lewis gave a detailed account of Garreau's lesson on the process of making glass beads in the Arikara and Mandan way: "the discovery of this art these nations are said to have derived from the Snake Indians who have been taken prisoners by the Ricaras. the art is kept a secret by the Indians among themselves and is yet known to but a few of them . . . The Indians are extreemly fond of the large beads formed by this process. they use them as pendants to their years, or hair and sometimes wear them about their necks."

Reference: *Moulton, vol. 3*

Gass, Patrick (1771–1870): Sergeant. Born in Falling Springs, Pennsylvania, of Scottish descent, the largely self-educated Gass joined the militia in 1792, traveled to Cuba in 1793, and apprenticed as a carpenter from 1794 until 1799. He served in the army under General Alexander Hamilton, Major Jonathan Cass on the Ohio River, and Captain Russell Bissell. Although Bissell was reluctant to release Gass because of his valuable carpentry skills, Gass prevailed upon Lewis to secure the necessary permission for him to sign on with the expedition from Fort Kaskaskia as a private (one of the oldest members of the corps except for Captain Clark and John Shields). During the winter of 1803, Gass helped to build the structures at Camp Dubois. Upon the unexpected death of Charles Floyd, Gass was elected by the rest of the men to assume the position of sergeant. Part of his duties included keeping a daily journal as six other members of the expedition tried to do. From the beginning, his unquestioned authority among the men was well established; he was a part of the court during the court-martial and corporal punishment of Hugh Hall and Alexander

Expert carpenter and longest surviving member of the corps, Sergeant Patrick Gass was the first to publish his journal (1807) and was one of only two members to be photographed. He married at age fifty-nine and fathered six children. Montana Historical Society, Helena.

Willard. Throughout his journal, Gass's observations indicate a keen and inquisitive mind, particularly in relation to different kinds of wood, methods of constructing earth lodges, forts, and canoes, and the Indian variations of canoe-making methods. Gass's description of a Nez Percé bear-cooking recipe does not leave out a single step, and his biographer refers to his entry on the building of Fort Mandan as the best description given of its construction. He was fair-minded enough to admit, "The natives of this country [the Skilloots] ought to have the credit of making the finest canoes, perhaps in the world, both as to service and beauty; and are no less expert in working them when made." His creative skills and adaptability helped the expedition numerous times during their trip to the Pacific. In spite of his best woodworking efforts and engineering, Gass could not get the iron boat, or Experiment, to float, but he was able to help construct canoes on the Clearwater River, using the faster and easier Nez Percé Indian method of burning out the wood. Like the rest of the men, Gass could hunt and handle horses but it was his ability to manufacture and fix necessary items such as saddles and canoe masts that made him nearly indispensable to the enterprise. In recognition of his leadership qualities, Gass was left in charge at the Great Falls while Lewis explored the Marias River in 1806. After the expedition he settled in West Virginia and set about getting a publisher for his journal. It was the first account of the expedition to be published (1807), a fact that annoyed Meriwether Lewis considerably. Gass received no real compensation for his journal other than one hundred copies; not one of his descendants owns a copy. According to one of his journal's editors, Carol Lynn MacGregor, Gass was speculating in lead ore around the time of the War of 1812. He lost his left eye and was awarded a pension sometime after his discharge in 1815. Gass married sixteen-year-old Maria Hamilton in 1831, when he was fifty-nine. The former sergeant fathered six children and outlived every other member of the expedition. According to his daughter, he walked eight miles every day before noon nearly until the day he died. He is buried in Wellsburg, Virginia. See McKeehan, David.

References: *MacGregor,* Journals of Patrick Gass*; Smith and Smith; Forrest*

Gates of the Rocky Mountains: Landmark on the Missouri River seen on July 19, 1805, when the corps had split into two groups, one of which consisted of Clark, Joseph Field, John Potts, and York, who explored overland looking for signs of the Shoshone; and the second of Lewis and the rest of the party, who proceeded upriver through "remarkable clifts," which Lewis named "The Gates of the Rocky Mountains." These cliffs, formed of Madison limestone and towering to heights of twelve hundred feet, extended through a canyon some five and three-quarter miles long. Lewis and his men found the terrain inhospitable and struggled to find a place large enough to accommodate their party for the night. "This evening we entered much the most remarkable clifts that we have yet seen . . . it happens fortunately that altho' the current is strong it is not so much so but what it may be overcome with the oars for there is hear no possibility of using either the cord or Setting pole. it was late in the evening before I entered this place and was obliged to continue my rout untill sometime after dark before I found a place sufficiently large to encamp my small party; at length such an one occurred on the lard. side where we found plenty of lightwood and pichpine. . . . from the singular appearance of this place I called it the gates of the rocky mountains." The party would soon reach land familiar to Sacagawea, and meet her people, who would supply the expedition with the horses necessary to cross the Bitterroot Mountains. The Missouri is dammed in this area by the Holter and Hauser Dams, which have raised the level of the water and slowed its speed. Now known as the Gates of the Mountains Wilderness Area, it attracts recreationists and tourists (thirty-two thousand a year) during the summer months when tour boat operators conduct daily trips through the canyon to the Meriwether picnic grounds.

Reference: Moulton, vol. 4

Gauntlet: Form of military punishment used for discipline in addition to whippings. Moses Reed ran the gauntlet for desertion. Clark estimated Reed received 1,500 lashes. Two lines of men would face the convicted, whose back was bare, and thrash him with switches as he ran through the gauntlet the prescribed number of times. An Arikara chief who witnessed the whipping on October 14, 1804, questioned the procedure, and cried aloud. When Clark explained the reason for the punishment, the chief agreed, "He thought examples were also necessary, & he himself had made them by Death, his nation never whiped even their Children from their burth." William Bratton's descendants say that he told them that, instead of switches, the men used the ramrods from their guns when they formed the gauntlet.

Reference: Moulton, vol. 3

Giant Springs ("Large Fountain" on Clark's map): One of the largest freshwater springs in the world. Discovered just above Rainbow Falls by Clark on June 18, 1805: "we proceeded on up the river a little more than a mile to the largest fountain or Spring I ever saw, and doubt if it is not the largest in America Known, this water boils up from under the rocks near the edge of the river and falls immediately into the river 8 feet and keeps its Colour for ½ a mile which is emencely Clear and of a bluish Cast." On June 27, 1805, Ordway notes, ". . . went on until I came to the Spring which was the finest tasted water I ever Saw and the largest fountain which comes up through a ledge of rocks near the River and forces its way up about 10 feet for some distance around them forms a fall in to the River. It is clear as a crystal. I could have seen to the bottom of the fountain to pick up a pin. The water cold and pure. the Rocks green which the water run over." Two days later Lewis commented, "I continued my rout to the fountain which I found as much as Capt. C; had described & think it may well be retained on the list of prodigies of this neighbourhood towards which nature seems to have dealt with a liberal hand, for I have scarcely experienced a day since my first arrival in this quarter without experiencing some novel occurrence among the party or witnessing the appearance of some uncommon object. I think this fountain is the largest I ever beheld, and the hadsome cascade which it affords over some steep and irregular rocks in its passage to the river adds not a little to it's beauty. It is about 25 yds. From the river, situated in a pretty little level plain, and has a suddon decent of about 6 feet in one part of it's course. The water of this fountain is extremely transparent and cold; nor is it impregnated with lime or any other extranious matter which I can discover, but is very pure and pleasant. It's waters marke their passage as Capt. Clark observes for a considerable distance down the Missouri notwithstanding it's rapidity and force. The water of the fountain boil up with such force near it's center that it's surface in that part seems even higher than the surrounding earth which is a firm handsom terf of fine green grass." According to author Julie Fanselow, "Giant Springs produces eight million gallons per hour. The water comes from the Madison limestone formations lying beneath most of eastern and central Montana. Rainfall and melted snow soak into the limestone where it is exposed on the slopes of the Little Belt Mountains. The water drains downward and then flows through openings in the limestone where it flows upward about 700 feet through the fractures before being pushed out at Giant Springs. The 38 mile trip takes hundreds of years, but the water gains momentum as it travels, until it is pumped out at Giant Springs with a force of about 300 pounds per square inch, discharging some 134,000 gallons of water per minute (213,000,000 gallons a day). The spring also forms the world's shortest river, the Roe River, just 201 feet long." The water contains high quantities of calcium, magnesium, bicarbonate, and sulfate and is quite tasty.

References: Fanselow; Moulton, vols. 4, 9

Gibson, George (d. 1809): Private. Although Pennsylvania-born, he enlisted at the Falls of the Ohio in October 1803 and was considered one of the "nine young men from Kentucky." A talented hunter who also assisted in boat-making chores, Gibson was once assigned to gather rosin for the canoes with Sergeants Pryor and Gass and Private Joseph Field, three of the most trustworthy and reliable men of the expedition. When nominations were made for the replacement of Sergeant Floyd, Gibson was one of three men chosen. Although he was nearly injured in a boating accident on June 9, 1804, the men's efforts to hoist the boat free drew appreciation from Captain Clark: "I can Say with Confidence that our party is not inferior to any that was ever on the waters of the Missoppie." Gibson was armed with the usual talents of a Kentucky hunter, for the journals note that he wounded a bear and killed a buffalo. In late May 1805 Whitehouse mentions, "Gibson one of the hunters putt one of his Shoulders out of place to day but got it in again." Author and physician E. G. Chuinard speculates the shoulder was subluxated, or partially dislocated, so that the men were easily able to set it back in place. When Gibson and others fell ill at the Salt Camp, Sergeant Pryor and several men were dispatched to retrieve them. Gibson was so seriously ill he had to be carried back to the fort on a blanket or litter. He is mentioned as entertaining the natives with a "violin" on October 19, 1805. While on the Columbia, Gibson, Bratton, and Willard bravely attempted to go around a point in "Indian Canoes" but were forced back. On July 18, 1806, Gibson punctured his thigh with a stick while mounting his horse; thanks to the captains' attention he healed well. In August 1806, at the village of Black Cat, Gibson's knife was stolen by a young Mandan man who was supposed to accompany the Americans back to Washington, D.C. Captain Clark demanded its return and "reproached those people for wishing to Send Such a man to See and hear the words of So great a man as their great father; they hung their heads and Said nothing for Some time when the Cheif Spoke and Said that they were afraid to Send any one for fear of their being killed by the Sieux." Married following the expedition, Gibson died three years after returning to St. Louis. Goodrich, McNeal, and Gibson were the only men specifically mentioned as having been treated with mercury for "Louis veneri." Clarke speculates Gibson may have been with Sergeant Pryor's party when they attempted to return Sheheke-shote to his village in 1807, and may have been wounded by the Arikara. On May 14, 1804, the expedition passed a creek they named Gibson's Creek, now Sutherland Creek in Valley County, Montana.

References: Moulton, vols. 2, 6, 8, 11; Chuinard, Only One Man Died; Clarke

Gill: Pronounced "jill"; equivalent to four ounces of whiskey or spirits. The unit of measurement used for the daily whiskey ration given to the enlisted men during the expedition. The supply of whiskey ran out on July 4, 1804, at the Great Falls, although there may have been some additional alcohol in reserve for medicinal purposes.

Reference: Hunt, "Gills and Drams of Consolation"

Gillaspay and Strong: George Gillaspay and Joseph Strong, Philadelphia doctors and pharmacists who supplied Lewis and Clark with $90.69 in medicines for the expedition. Jackson's *Letters of the Lewis and Clark Expedition* contains the list of these medicines with a footnote stating, "It is less extensive than the standard list of medicines issued to military posts of the period but contains most of the drugs commonly used for the ailments to be expected among young, healthy soldiers." Regarding the pharmacy, E. G. Chuinard states, "There are no known records remaining from its operation."

References: Jackson, Letters; Chuinard, Only One Man Died

Goforth, William: Cincinnati physician who discovered the remains of an elephant and a mammoth's head near Big Bone Lick, Boone County, Kentucky, in June 1803. Lewis visited the excavation site as he traveled down the Ohio River. Dr. Goforth "obligingly" let Lewis examine his find and gave him "two handsome specimens," which Lewis forwarded on to Jefferson with the promise of more to come. Knowing of the president's intense interest in mammoths, Lewis wrote him a letter describing the fossils in great detail. The specimens were indeed remarkable; one tooth weighed more than twenty pounds. Unfortunately, the boat carrying Lewis's carefully collected specimens sank at the landing in Natchez and so the specimens did not reach their final destination of Monticello. Jefferson remained intrigued by the site, however, and later commissioned Clark to outfit an excavation of Big Bone Lick when he was on his way to St. Louis in 1807 to become chief Indian agent. See Mammoth.

Reference: Jackson, Letters

Goodrich (Guthrich), Silas (d. 1825? 28?): Private; born in Massachusetts. Goodrich transferred to the command of Lewis and Clark in January 1804. Dubbed the "Izaak Walton" of the corps by Paul Cutright, Goodrich's skill as a fisherman provided the expedition with a welcome change in diet and added to the list of discoveries attributed to Lewis and Clark. One evening in late July 1804, Clark observed that Goodrich caught a white catfish, "its eyes Small & tale much like that of a Dolfin." Lewis called him "remarkably fond of fishing" and carefully described and compared the fish Goodrich caught with fish he observed in the Potomac. One new species discovered in the Marias River on June 11, 1805, was the sauger fish. Two days later Goodrich presented the captains with some "fine trout," which turned out to be cutthroat trout, a species new to science and named *Salmo clarki* in honor of William Clark. For Christmas 1805 Clark lists the presents he received and from whom, including "a Small Indian basket of Guterich." Also at Fort Clatsop, Lewis wrote in his journal entry for January 27, 1806, that Goodrich had engaged in "amorous contact with a Chinook damsel I cured him as I did Gibson last winter by the uce of murcury." The mercury treatment of syphilis was unreliable, as the method of administration (topical mercury ointment and oral calomel) was probably incomplete. In addition the terrible side effects of loose teeth, intestinal irritation, death of oral mucosal tissue, and kidney toxicity made this treatment a very sharp, double-edged sword. Goodrich reenlisted in the army after returning to St. Louis. Clark lists him as dead, perhaps of mercury poisoning, sometime between 1825 and 1828. Lewis and Clark named an island after Goodrich in present-day Fergus County, Montana, now known as Dry Island.

References: Moulton, vols. 2, 6; Peck, personal communication

Gratiot, Charles (1754–1817): A member of the Chouteau inner circle, Gratiot was married to Pierre and Auguste's sister Victoire and traded with the Indian tribes in Illinois from 1774 until he moved to St. Louis in 1781. Gratiot signed the articles of cession with Lewis and served as the first presiding justice at the new St. Louis Court of Quarter Sessions. He served as American representative and translator of the speech of Amos Stoddard to the Spanish crowd at the ceremony transferring the Louisiana Territory to the United States. As the number of Americans interested in the fur trade grew and many opportunities for political and economic advancement in St. Louis became apparent, Gratiot obligingly assisted with the needs of the expedition while camped at the Dubois River in winter 1804. Gratiot offered the captains horses, and he was present when Clark and Lewis reunited at St. Charles. In March of 1804 he traveled with Lewis, Clark, and Chouteau to stop a conflict between the Kickapoo and the Osage Indians.

Gravelines, Joseph: Merchant trapper, trader of French colonial descent, associated with Regis Loisel and Pierre Antoine Tabeau. By 1806 he had lived with the Arikara for twenty years and had mastered their difficult language. He traded with the Arikara and other tribes bordering their homeland in the north-central Dakotas. According to Clark, Gravelines was a man "well versed in the language of this nation . . . gave us some information relative to the Country, nation, etc." John Logan Allen writes that Gravelines was one of a handful of men who "would prove important when the captains fleshed out their views of the trans-Missouri region." Gravelines served as diplomat, river guide, and barge pilot for Colonel Warfington on his unit's return trip from Fort Mandan to St. Louis. According to Lewis's April 7, 1805, entry, "One of the Frenchman by the Name of Graveline an honest discrete man and an excellent boat-man is imployed to conduct the barge as pilot." In addition the captains hired him "to conduct a few of the Ricara chiefs to the seat of government who have promised us to decend in the barge to St. Liwis with that view." The captains asked him to "interseed in preventing hostilities" between the Arikara and the Sioux. On February 28, 1805, Gravelines helped persuade Mandan and Minitari (also known as Hidatsa) delegations to council for peace with the Arikara. He informed the captains, "the sisetoons and the three upper bands of the Tetons, with the Yanktons of the North intend to come to war in a short time against the nations in the quarter and will kill every white man they see." Gravelines accompanied and interpreted for Arikara chief Arketarnarshar when he visited Washington, D.C., in 1805. When the chief died en route, it fell to Gravelines to deliver the bad news to the tribe. Gravelines encountered the expedition again on September 12, 1806, when he and Pierre Dorian were on their way back to the Arikaras with presents of muskets and a letter of condolence from the president. They remained "discreetly silent and the tribe were as friendly as ever when Lewis and Clark arrived." Gravelines received a salary of $1.50 a day as an agent to the Arikaras in 1806.

References: Gravelines; Bakeless; Chouteau letter in Nasatir, Before Lewis and Clark; *Thwaites,* Original Journals, *vol. 1; Allen,* Passage through the Garden

Gray, Robert (1755–1806): American captain of the trading ship *Columbia.* In May of 1792, while on a trading voyage along the Pacific Coast, he discovered the great river of the west, which was named after his ship. Previously he had sailed to China with a load of sea otter skins to trade for tea; he was the first American to circumnavigate the globe. His discovery and entrance into the mouth of the Columbia River came to the world's attention with the publication of George Vancouver's journals and established an American claim to the Oregon Territory.

Great Falls of the Missouri: When the expedition reached this landmark they were relieved to learn they had followed the correct fork when the river split in two at the Marias River. In order to determine if the Marias could be the Missouri, the corps divided into two parties. Lewis and his men, going overland, were the first to reach the falls, actually a series of five waterfalls, the highest measuring eighty-seven feet, which they had heard about from the Mandan Indians. The Indians also described a large eagle's nest in a lone cottonwood tree at the falls, noted by the captain, which would be further proof they were on the right river. On June 13, 1805, Lewis attempted to describe the "majestically grand senery" but "after wrighting this imperfect discription I again viewed the falls and was so disgusted with the imperfect idea which it conveyed of the scene that I determined to draw my pen across it and begin agin, but then reflected that I could not perhaps succeed better than pening the first impressions of the mind; I wished for the pencil of Salvator Rosa or the pen of Thompson, that I might be enabled to give the enlightened world some just idea of this truly magnifficent and sublimely grand object, which has from the commencement of time been concealed from the view of civilized man. . . ." The next day he described one cascade as "pleasingly beautifull" and the other as "sublimely grand." At the falls, Lewis first encountered what he described as a "tyger cat" (probably a wolverine) and farther on nearly wrangled with an angry grizzly bear. He ended the day in a face-off with three charging buffalo bulls. Reflecting in his journal that night, Lewis observed, "it now seemed to me that all the beasts of the neighbourhood had made a league to distroy me, or that some fortune was disposed to amuse herself at my expence." In order to pass the falls, the men pitched a portage camp near the mouth of Belt Creek and spent ten laborious days constructing "carriages" to haul their boats and belongings seventeen miles while grizzly bears menacingly disputed the territory with the men. During this period the expedition was pounded by a severe hailstorm, and Clark, Sacagawea, and Charbonneau were nearly drowned in a flash flood. Sacagawea became afflicted with flulike symptoms during the portage and recovered only after drinking water from a nearby sulphur spring. Another local spring, called "Large Fountain" by Clark, amazed the men with its purity and clarity. At the Great Falls, the iron boat experiment failed to pass the test and was cached at White Bear Islands. Two caches were made in the vicinity of the falls, one near the lower Portage Creek site and the other on White Bear Islands; the latter contained Lewis's plant specimens from Fort Mandan and was subsequently destroyed by water. The city of Great Falls, county seat of Cascade, takes its name from Lewis and Clark's journals. In the 1890s the city operated a grist mill powered by a dam, which evolved into a hydroelectric source a few years after. Great Falls is also called the Electric City. See Giant Springs; Sulphur Spring.

References: Cheney, Names on the Face of Montana; *Moulton, vol. 4*

Grey Eyes (*Les Yeux Gris*): Arikara chief whom Clark described as "A stout jolley fellow of about 35 years of age whome the Ricaras call Grey Eyes." Met with Lewis and Clark in August 1806, and promised he would listen to their council and blamed any trouble on the Sioux. He would not go to Washington because, according to Clark, "he wished to see the Chief who went down last summer return first, he expressed some aprehention as to the safety of that Chiefs in passing the Sieoux. the Grey Eyes chief of the ricaras made a very animated speech in which he mentioned his williness of following the councels which we had given them that they had Some bad young men who would not listen to the Councels but would join the Seioux." Historian James Ronda writes, "Grey Eyes certainly wished that the Sioux might be less troublesome at market times, but he was not about to alienate so strong and important a customer in order to please untested whites." Nathaniel Pryor gave Grey Eyes a large government peace medal in 1807 after the unsuccessful attempt to return Sheheke-shote to his people. In 1811 Grey Eyes traded with the Astorians and Manuel Lisa. His son died in a skirmish with Missouri Fur Company traders in 1823. Grey Eyes died at his village after being shelled by Colonel Henry Leavenworth's artillery in August of 1823 in retaliation for his involvement in an attack on American traders and soldiers.

References: Moulton, vol. 8; Abel, Tabeau's Narrative; *Thwaites,* Early Western Travels, *vol. 5; Nye*

Grinder's Stand: An inn, or stand, located on the Natchez Trace in Tennessee, owned and operated by local farmer Robert Grinder (or Griner) and his wife. They had operated the inn for approximately a year when Meriwether Lewis stopped to spend the night on October 10, 1809 on his way to Washington, D.C., to defend his financial status. The stand was composed of two log structures and a nearby barn. On the night of Lewis's visit, Mrs. Grinder, accompanied by her two children and two servants, was the innkeeper on duty. She allowed

Lewis to spend the night in the house while his servants stayed in the barn. Sometime during the night, according to the story Mrs. Grinder told ornithologist Alexander Wilson, Lewis attempted to shoot himself in the head and body. The wounds did not kill Lewis, and for the rest of the night he pleaded with Mrs. Grinder and the others assembled to finish the job. Theories on what happened the night of Lewis's death abound, but most historians believe he killed himself and that, despite local gossip implicating the Grinders in his death, it is most likely Mrs. Grinder simply witnessed the events of that night and did not in any way participate in Lewis's untimely demise.

Grizzly bear (*Ursus arctos horribilis*, hoh-host): Of all the creatures encountered by the explorers this one seems to have captured the attention of the men more than any other. They knew they should expect to see the "turrible-looking animal" thanks to information obtained at Fort Mandan. Lewis and Clark were likely not the first whites to observe grizzlies; the bears lived out on the plains, and French trappers and traders had been familiar with them for years. In the early 1800s they roamed from west of the Mississippi to the California coast and numbered some 100,000 bears. During the course of their voyage, the party mentions seeing approximately sixty-two grizzly bears, as opposed to *Ursus americanus*, or the black bear, mostly in the areas around the Great Falls and Yellowstone River. As they grew more experienced with the "white bear," as they often referred to the grizzly, their change in attitude regarding the animal is apparent: "it is a much more furious and formidable anamal, and will frequently pursue the hunter when wounded. it is asstonishing to see the wounds they will bear before they are put to death. the Indians may well fear this anamal equiped as they generally are with their bows and arrows or indifferent fuzees, but in the hands of skillful riflemen they are by no means as formidable or dangerous as they have been represented." After a particularly alarming encounter with what later trappers called "Old Ephraim," though, Lewis and the men changed their minds: "I find that the curiossity of our party is pretty well satisfyed with rispect to this anamal, the formidable appearance of the male bear killed on the 5th added to the difficulty with which they die when even shot through the vital parts, has staggered the resolution of several of them,

John F. Clymer's "Hasty Retreat" depicts the typical interaction between man and "white bear" near the Great Falls, July 1805. According to Lewis, "the curiossity of our party is pretty well satisyed with rispect to this anamal." Courtesy of Mrs. John F. Clymer and the Clymer Museum of Art.

others however seem keen for action with the bear; I expect these gentlemen will give us some amusement shotly as they soon begin now to coppulate." Another frequently quoted passage that bears repeating here illustrates the next stage in the relationship of the men toward the grizzly: "Bratton had shot him through the center of the lungs, notwithstanding which he had pursued him near half a mile and had returned more than double that distance and with his tallons had prepared himself a bed in the earth of about 2 feet deep and five long and was perfectly alive when we found him which could not have been less than 2 hours after he received the wound; these bear being so hard to die reather intimidates us all; I must confess that I do not like the gentleman and had reather fight two Indians than one bear." Finally, on May 31, 1806, Lewis gives his summation on the variety of bear species he had personally observed and the ones he heard about from the Nez Percé. "I am disposed to adopt the Indian distinction with respect to these bear and consider them two distinct species [the grizzly or hoh-host and the yack-kah or black bear]." Lewis recognizes this yack-kah of the Nez Percé country as somewhere between the bear he was most familiar with, the eastern black bear, and the grizzly, or as he wanted to call it the "variegated bear" because of its many fur shades. Author Paul Schullery calls this one of Lewis's few mistakes as there are in fact only two species of bear in the lower forty-eight states. The captain was also mistaken on some matters of the grizzly anatomy, but compared with the total amount of information provided by the expedition on the grizzly bear, these errors are trivial. Nevertheless it is appropriate to acknowledge that the way the Corps of Discovery regarded the grizzly says more about themselves than it does about the grizzly. As author Paul Schullery reminds us in his outstanding book *Lewis and Clark among the Grizzlies*, "Lewis and Clark brought west with them their own idea of the bear"; they overstated the aggressiveness of grizzly bears and as such, Schullery says, contributed to a national misunderstanding of grizzlies that is still with us today. The stories of confrontations with grizzly bears related in the journals were embellished and exaggerated in popular forms of literature of the early nineteenth century. Schullery does not blame the captains for this; they factually stated what they observed: "They provided a sound outline of other aspects of grizzly bear natural history, including quite a few preferred foods and foraging behavior, mating season, and a surprising number of details about the relationship between grizzly bears and Indians. These last included such obvious things as the popularity and importance of bear claw necklaces and the beliefs attached to hunting grizzly bears (the cultural richness of the claw necklaces, other bear ornaments, and the hunting rituals appears to have been largely lost on the captains). But they also included various other Indian uses of bear skins and oils and methods for cooking bear meat." The problem came with later writers who cast grizzly bears as "demoniacal beasts" and the general public's willingness to believe in monsters in the woods. Among other misconceptions, Schullery addresses the idea that the grizzlies were forced into the mountains they now primarily inhabit by settlement. He cites forester Elers Koch on the issue: "The plains animals were killed off, not driven back in the mountains, and the rough mountain country continued to give some refuge to the animals that were already there." As directed by Jefferson, Lewis and Clark noted the varieties of species they came into contact with. This contact, however, especially in the case of the grizzly bear, was limited. Schullery maintains Lewis and Clark observed a long narrow corridor of land, not a broad eco region. Their observations must be taken in that context. According to the Sierra

Club, grizzlies now number fewer than one thousand in the lower forty-eight states, and the federal government is considering removing them from the endangered species list.

References: *Moulton, vols. 4, 7; Schullery*

Grog: A drink composed of equal parts water and rum used medicinally or for celebration. As the 120 gallons of whiskey carried out from Camp Dubois was consumed, the captains probably diluted the supply, thus the more frequent references to "grog" instead of whiskey. They also refer to "tafia," a rum made from coarse molasses considered inferior and distributed on special occasions like Christmas or New Year's (at the time the official War Department ration for enlisted men was one-half a gill a day). Following a particularly nerve-racking incident involving the near capsizing of the pirogue on May 14, 1805, Lewis wrote, "We thought it proper to console ourselves and cheer the sperits of our men and accordingly took a drink of grog and gave each man a gill [four ounces] of sperits." During the reconnaissance of the Marias River, about eight miles above the confluence, Patrick Gass observed a "beautiful spring where we refreshed ourselves with a good drink of grog." When they decided to investigate the Marias and the Missouri to find out which one was the main tributary, Lewis wrote, "we agreed to go up those rivers one day and a halfs march or further if it should appear necessary to satisfy us more fully of the point in question. . . . we took a drink of grog this evening and gave the men a dram [two thimblefuls or $\frac{1}{32}$ of a gill]." On June 7, 1805, after determining the Marias River was not the main river and naming it in honor of his cousin Miss Maria Wood, Lewis "gave myself this evening to rest from my labours, took a drink of grog and gave the men who had accompanyed me each a dram." Near the portage of the Great Falls on June 27, 1805, "the wormest day we have had this year," Lewis wrote, "I refresh the men with a drink of grog." The site is now called Grog Spring. Noted Lewis and Clark scholar Paul Cutright ranks the shortage of liquor and the deficient amount of blue beads they carried as among the most serious of Lewis's oversights.

References: *Hunt, "Gills and Drams of Consolation"; MacGregor,* Journals of Patrick Gass; *Moulton, vol. 4; Cutright,* Pioneering Naturalists

Ground bean (*Amphicarpa bracteata*, hog peanut): Clark noted among the Arikaras in October 1804, "Those people gave us to eate bread made of Corn & beens, also Corn & Beans boild. a large Been, which they rob the mice of the Prairie which is rich & verry nurrishing also. Squashes &c. all Tranquillity." Cutright states that this bean is a member of the pea family, and that "they are dug up by a species of meadow mouse which stores them in secluded spots in quantities of a pint or more. Because they were nutritious and tasty, the Indian women eagerly sought them. It is said however that they would never rob the mice without leaving some other food in its place."

References: Moulton, vol. 3; Cutright, Pioneering Naturalists

Gumbo: Referring to the sticky, slippery consistency of the clay derived from glacial till and Claggett shale encountered by the expedition in central Montana in June of 1805. Lewis wrote, "in its present state it is precisely like walking over frozan grownd which is thawed to small debth and slips equally as bad. this clay not only appears to require more water to saturate it as I before observed than any earth I ever observed but when saturated it appears on the other hand to yeald it's moisture with equal difficulty." Lewis had several narrow escapes caused by slipping on the gumbo, once nearly plunging ninety feet down a cliff to almost certain death. Windsor also came close to slipping to his death but was saved by the reassuring demeanor and timely assistance of Captain Lewis. See Espontoon; Windsor, Richard.

Reference: Moulton, vol. 4

H

Hadley's quadrant: Also called an octant and predecessor of the sextant, the device was a distance-measuring instrument used by the captains and was included in Lewis's list of requirements for the mathematical instruments needed for provisioning the expedition. On June 30, 1803, he purchased the quadrant in Philadelphia for $22.00, including a tangent screw. On July 22, 1804, Lewis described the instrument, "A common Octant of 14 Inches radius, graduated to 20' which by means of the nonius was devisible to 1' half of this sum, or 30" was perceptible by means of a micrometer this instrument was prepared for both the fore and back observation; her error in the fore observation is 2 degrees+, &   and in the back observation 2 degrees II' 40.3" +." By the time the corps had reached the Pacific and spent several months at Fort Clatsop, Lewis had, by several trials, figured out the exact margin of error in the quadrant's measurements.
Reference: Moulton, vols. 2, 6

Haley, Captain: Haley is presumed to be Samuel Hill of Boston, captain of the *Lydia*. The Clatsop Indians told Lewis and Clark about a three- or four-masted ship captained by a trader named Haley that had recently been among the Quinaults. The Chinook referred to him as a friend and said he had given them an iron bow. He is mentioned by Clark in the journals of November 6, 1805, and again by Clark on January 1, 1806, as "one who visits them in a ship & they expect him back to trade with them in 3 Moons. He is the favourite of the Indians (from the number of Presents he givs) and has the trade principaly with all the tribes." The natives also pointed out a woman in their party whom Captain Haley liked. Baker Bay, east of Cape Disappointment in Pacific County, was renamed Haley's Bay by Clark in honor of the trader they heard mentioned most frequently by the natives. On March 14, 1806, Haley was named as one of three other traders whom the Quinnachart Indians described as presently being in their country some six days' march to the northwest.

Reference: Moulton, vols. 6, 7

Half Man (Aweawechache): Yankton Sioux; spoke at a council in August 1804. A modest man, who, on being called a brave warrior, once said, "I am no warrior I am only half a man." He told the captains, "what you said is well but you have not given (me a paper) anything to the attendants of the Great Chiefs." This council was one of the early encounters with natives for Lewis and Clark, and ended in a disappointment as the chiefs did not seem to care whose flag flew over their lands as long as the trade goods pleased them.

References: Thwaites, Original Journals, vol. 1; Moulton, vol. 3

Hall, Hugh (b. 1772): Private; born in Carlisle, Pennsylvania. Hall enlisted on December 13, 1798, at twenty-six years of age. He reenlisted October 1, 1803, and was detailed (November 24, 1803) to the expedition from Captain John Campbell's company of the Second Infantry Regiment, stationed at South West Point, Tennessee. Clark noted on December 31, 1803, "prohibited a Certain Ramey from Selling Liquor to the Party, Several things killed today. Colter, Willard, Leakens Hall & Collins drunk." On one list Clark has the word *drink* next to Hall's name. He served as a private in the first squad under Sergeant Nathaniel Pryor. Ordway writes on May 17, 1804, "court martial on behalf of the Capt. to hear and determine the evidences aduced against William Warner & Hugh Hall for being absent last night without leave." As Clark recorded on May 17, 1804, "after being duly Sworn the court proceded to the trial of William Warner and Hugh Hall on the following Charges Viz: for being absent without leave last night contrary to orders, to this charge the Prisoners plead Guilty. The Court of one oppinion that the prisoners Warner and Hall are both guilty of being absent from camp without leave it being a breach of the Rules and articles of war and do Sentence them Each to receive twenty-five lashes on their naked back, but the Court recommend them from their former Good conduct, to the mercy of the commanding officer . . . the punishment ordered to be inflicted on William Warner & Hugh Hall, is remitted under the assurance arriveing from a confidence which the

Commanding officer has of the Sincerity of the recommendation from the Court." John Collins and Hugh Hall were charged with stealing whiskey from the expedition's supply after Collins had been assigned to guard the spirits. On June 29, 1804, Hall pled guilty and received fifty lashes on his bare back. Hall was in the St. Louis area on April 11, 1809. Jackson notes Lewis loaned him two dollars. Clark lists him as deceased in the mid-1820s.

References: Moulton, vol. 2; Jackson, Letters

Hammond, John Henry (d. 1890): General who served in the Civil War under Sherman, and later worked as an inspector of agencies for the Indian Bureau. As part of his duties General Hammond was sent to Lawrence, Kansas, in 1878 to close down the Indian office and to make an inventory of the papers he found there and send them on to Washington. Included in these papers was a packet of sixty-seven pages of former superintendent of Indian affairs William Clark's writings and maps wrapped in an 1805 copy of the Washington, D.C., newspaper the *National Intelligencer.* Whether on purpose or by accident, the papers ended up in Hammond's desk in a St. Paul attic, where they were discovered by his granddaughter in 1953. Upon close examination these papers proved to be the field notes of William Clark from 1803 to 1805, including the notes for his journal from Camp Dubois and the second part of the papers known as the River Journal. The Minnesota Historical Society felt they had a claim to the papers as they had been invited to take the Hammond papers by the general's granddaughter. Other interested parties disputed their claim, including the United States government, which argued that the papers were government property. The case was settled in 1959 in favor of Hammond's heirs. They sold the field notes to Frederick Beinecke, who then gave them to Yale University. Historian Ernest Osgood edited the notes for publication in 1964.

Reference: Osgood, Field Notes

Hancock, Forrest: Trapper. Hancock was raised in Boonesborough, Kentucky. He later lived in Maysville and traveled with Daniel Boone in 1799 where he settled near him in Boone's Lick, Missouri. He decided to join in a trapping venture with Joseph Dickson up the Missouri River in the summer of 1804. The following spring they teamed up with the Charles Courtin party for protection from the Teton Sioux, who nevertheless robbed them of all their furs. Dickson's serious wounds forced them to spend the winter of 1805 with the Mandan. While trapping on the Missouri the following summer, they encountered Clark on his way downriver. On August 11, 1806, Clark wrote, "the two men Dixon and Handcock the two men we had met above came down intending to proceed on down with us to the Mandans . . . We proceded on all together having left the 2 leather Canoes on the bank." The trappers persuaded Colter to join them working their way back up the Missouri. They trapped together for the next six weeks when the partnership turned sour because of a dispute. Dickson struck out on his own and Hancock and Colter returned to winter with the Mandan. Manuel Lisa hired Hancock the next year to work for his trapping operation. Records show Lisa paid him in advance several times. Hancock went back to Boone's Lick and visited Colter's old neighborhood in 1832.

   References: Colter-Frick; Clarke; Moulton, vol. 8

Hand game: Observed by Lewis and Clark among the Nez Percé at Camp Chopunnish in May of 1806 and among the Shoshone the previous month. The name refers to the fact that an object is held in the hand during play. Lewis commented, "The indians formed themselves this evening into two large parties and began to gamble for their beads and other ornaments. the game at which they played was that of hiding a stick in their hands which they frequently changed acompanying their operations with a song. this game seems common to all the nations in this country, and dose not differ from that described of the Shoshonees on the S. E. branch of Lewis's river." Although the name of the game varied, eighty-one tribes in the United States played it for entertainment. It was accompanied by a song or chant, during which the group split into two and a small piece of wood, or other palm-sized object that could be hidden in the hand, was passed among the "in-hand" players' group. While they sang the hand game song, the other group tried to guess who had the object and pounded on a log with a set of fifteen sticks in rhythm with the song. The in-hand team passed the object among themselves, or pretended to pass it, as they kept time with the beating of the sticks and the singing of the song. As anthropologist Alice C. Fletcher describes it, "When one on the opposite side thinks he detects the whereabouts of the bead and is willing to risk a guess, he points his drum-stick to the hand he thinks has the bead and cries 'Hi-i' and the hand indicated must be immediately opened so that all may see whether the guess is correct or not." If the guess is correct, the winning team gets to keep the stick; if incorrect, the stick goes to the team that successfully fooled the other. Play continues until one side has won all thirty sticks.

References: Fletcher; Moulton, vol. 7

Harpers Ferry rifle: Recent scholarship indicates that Captain Lewis did not use the U.S. Model 1803 rifle commonly referred to as the "Lewis and Clark Expedition Rifle." Instead, the fifteen rifles he picked up at the Harpers Ferry armory in March 1803 were likely Model 1792 rifles, probably in storage at the armory and made under contract by private gunsmiths. Historian Bob Moore surmises that because Lewis ordered gun slings for the weapons brought on the expedition it is believed they had full stocks, not the partial stocks of the Model 1803 rifles. The 1792 models may sometimes have been referred to as "short rifles" in the journals because they were shorter than the Kentucky or Pennsylvania "long rifles" of the period.

Reference: Bob Moore, personal communication

Hassler, Ferdinand Rudolph (1770–1843): Professor of natural philosophy at Union College, Schenectady, New York. After the return of the expedition, Lewis engaged Hassler to analyze and correct his longitudinal notations. Lewis advanced Hassler $100 on May 3, 1807. The Swiss-born mathematician was thirty-seven years old. Minutes of the American Philosophical Society note that Hassler eventually had "given up the calculations in despair."

Reference: Bedini, Thomas Jefferson: Statesman of Science

Hat Rock: Located in Umatilla County, Oregon, and named on October 19, 1805, by Clark when he noted a "rock on the Lard. Shore resembling a hat a rapid at the lower point of an Island in the middle of a river on which there is 7 Lodges of nativs drying fish." It was near this area that the corps first spotted Mount Adams, although they mistakenly thought it was Mount St. Helens.

Reference: Moulton, vol. 5

Hay, John (1769–1842): Postmaster at Cahokia, Illinois, trader with the North West Company, and clerk of court in St. Clair County. Lewis met him on December 7, 1803. Hay acted as a go-between for the captain when he visited officials of the Spanish government in St. Louis, including Carlos Delassus, governor of the upper Missouri, and Antoine Soulard, surveyor general. As a translator he proved a vital link in persuading the Spanish to allow Lewis to copy three important maps, two drawn by Mackay and one drawn by Soulard, of the country north and west of Cahokia, still officially in Spanish hands. Hay and his partner, Todd, operated a store for trading in the Assiniboine and Red River country. He conveyed other relevant information to the party including Hay's journal of a trip to the Assiniboine River and his translation of Evans and Mackay's journal account of their trip up the Missouri. He also assisted the expedition by showing Clark how to pack the trade goods in separate bundles so that they could be opened one at a time as needed rather than all at once. See Mackay, James; Soulard, Antoine.

References: Osgood, Field Notes; Doerk, personal communication

Heart River: Tributary of the Missouri River, whose waters are entirely contained within the boundaries of North Dakota. The Heart takes its name from the fact that, in the century before Lewis and Clark arrived on the upper Missouri, it was the "heart" of the Mandan Indian world. Sometime around 1780, equally pressed by smallpox and the Sioux, the Mandan had migrated upriver to the area around the mouth of the Knife River. Lewis and Clark record the name as "Chess-che tar," which is their rendering of an Arikara word for "fork (of a river)." At this point in the journey, Lewis and Clark were taking their geographic lessons from an Arikara leader named Arketarnarshar and Joseph Gravelines, who was a trader among the Arikara. The captains were also aware of the name Heart River, which they appear to have accepted as a translation of *chess-che tar*. The expedition reached the mouth of the Heart River on October 21, 1804. Clark noted that the Heart was "about 38 yards wide Containing a good deal of water." Clark understood the source of the Heart to interlock with waters of the Knife River near the Killdeer Mountains (a system of high buttes that Lewis and Clark called Turtle Mountain). Actually, the Heart forks in Stark County, North Dakota, into the Green River, which heads in Dunn County close enough to the Killdeer Mountains to validate Clark's understanding, and the Heart proper, which heads in the "little badlands" in Billings County.

The Heart begins its 270-mile flow at approximately 2,800 feet above sea level and discharges into the Missouri just below Mandan, North Dakota, at 1,615 feet. The drainage area totals 3,340 square miles. The river's flow varies at Mandan between a maximum of 30,500 cubic feet per second and a minimum of zero cubic feet per second. Average flow is 250 cubic feet per second. Clark learned from Gravelines and Arketarnarshar that the Mandan practiced the Sun Dance at a lone oak tree not far from the confluence of the Heart and the Missouri Rivers. The oak tree was revered because it had withstood prairie fires. He also told of an oracular medicine rock somewhere upstream in the Heart drainage. The expedition wounded its first grizzly bear just below the mouth of the Heart River. In the *Fort Mandan Miscellany*, Lewis describes the Heart as "not navigable except in high water, and then but a short distance." The Miscellany is also more precise about the river's source. "It passes through open plains and meadows, generally fertile, and always untimbered." On the return journey, the Mandan leader Sheheke-shote told Clark that he had been born near the mouth of the Heart River, "and at that time his nation inhabited 7 villages as large as that and were full of people."

References: Jackson, Letters; Moulton, vols. 3, 8

Hebert, Charles: Engagé from Canada. Marriage and baptism records show he married Julie Hubert dit La Croix in St. Louis in 1792 and had eleven children. Lewis lists Hebert on the May 26, 1804, roster of engagés. He may also be the "Chalo" Clark wrote on a list of French "Ingishees or Hirelens" (engagés and hirelings). As a hired engagé Hebert would have received cash wages when discharged at Fort Mandan in late 1804.

Reference: Moulton, vol. 2

Heney, Hugh: Trader from Montreal who lived with the Miniconjou on the Missouri River near the mouth of the Cheyenne and worked for the North West Company in 1804. He visited the party twice at Fort Mandan in the winter of 1804–05 and sent them a plant specimen (narrow-leaf purple coneflower, or echinacea) by messenger at the end of February 1805. Lewis described the plant in a letter written to Jefferson from Fort Mandan on March 5, 1805: "Mr. Heney informed me that he had used the root of this plant frequently with the most happy effect in cases of the bite of the mad wolf or dog and also for the bite of a rattlesnake." Clark described Heney as a "Verry intelligent Man from whome we obtained Some Scetches of the Countrey between the Mississippi & Missouri, and Some Sketches from him, which he had obtained from the Indin to the West of this place also the names and charecktors of the Seeaux." On the return journey in July 1806, Lewis wrote a letter appealing to Heney to accompany several Teton Sioux chiefs to Washington, D.C., to visit with President Jefferson and promising to secure employment for him as an Indian agent. The letter was to be delivered by several of the men with Clark on his exploration of the Yellowstone, but the theft of their horses made delivery of the letter impossible and they returned to the Clark party via bull boats. After receiving a note from Clark, Lewis wrote, "This I fear puts an end to our prospects of obtaining the Sioux Cheifs to accompany us as we have not now the leasure to send and engage Mr. Heney on this service."

References: Jackson, Letters; Thwaites, Original Journals, vols. 1, 5

Hennepin, Louis (1640–1701?): Catholic priest, recollet, and historian of LaSalle's first expedition to Mississippi. His accounts became "core segments," according to geographer John Logan Allen, in the geographical lore of the trans-Missouri west, which greatly informed Jefferson, Lewis, and Clark's concept of the land, specifically that beyond the Missouri and the mountains lay a great river that would allow for easier trade with China and India. This notion, combined with the accounts of Antoine DuPratz and Louis Lahontan, led Americans to imagine and embrace the idea of the Northwest as one vast and fertile garden, ideal for occupation and settlement. See DuPratz, Antoine; Lahontan, Louis.

Reference: Allen, Passage through the Garden

Henry, Andrew (1775?–1833): "Major Henry" of Louisiana. In the spring of 1810, he led a party of thirty-two men with John Colter to the Three Forks and built "Henry's Fort" for their Missouri Fur Company operations between the Madison and Jefferson Rivers, right in the heart of Blackfeet hunting grounds. This was the first post on the western side of the Continental Divide built by an American. Among the other stockholders in the company were Rueben Lewis and William Clark. They gathered local information from the friendly Indians, which, along with their loyalty, would be useful in future dealings with the British soldiers. The Blackfeet defended their lands against white intrusion; their constant harassment caused the fort to be abandoned in the summer of 1810. Although they collected thirty beaver packs, it came at too high a cost; twenty men, including corps member George Drouillard, lost their lives to the Blackfeet warriors. Later, Henry partnered in lead mining with William Ashley during the War of 1812 to sell munitions to the government. He was still working with Ashley in 1822 in trading ventures out west, and still harassed by the Blackfeet. Henry retired from the fur trade in 1825 and was replaced by Jedediah Smith.

Hohots Ilppilp or Hohotsillppilp or Hohatsillpilp (Many Wounds, Red Grizzly Bear, The Bloody Chief, Yellow Grizzly): Chopunnish or Nez Percé chief. On May 13, 1806, Lewis wrote, "I observed a tippit woarn by Hohastillpilp which was formed of human scalps and ornamented with the thumbs and fingers of several men which he had slain in battle." According to Nez Percé historian Alvin Josephy, "He carried the scars of many wounds," hence one of his names, Many Wounds. His other name honored either his *Wyakin* or his skill in fighting bears. In the early 1800s the Nez Percé tribe was one of the most numerous and powerful tribes in the Northwest and numbered between four thousand and six thousand souls. The French term *Nez Percé* translated into "pierced noses," because some members of the tribe pierced their noses with a dentalium shell. Lewis and Clark used their term *Chopunnish*. Hohots Ilpilp made a treaty with Lewis and Clark on behalf of his people at Lapwai, Idaho, on May 11 and 12, 1806. The captains presented him with a medal and ranked him as fourth among four powerful chiefs of the Chopunnish. His father indicated he understood the time was right for peace, as the blood of some deceased friends had been properly revenged. Hohots Ilppilp's father pledged to Lewis and Clark on behalf of his tribe that "the whitemen might be assured of their warmest attachment and that they would alwas give them every assistance in their power; that they were poor but their hearts were good." According to historian James Ronda, "There may have been plenty of 'good hearts' in evidence but what the Nez Perces really wanted was guns." Contact with the Chopunnish revolved around trade, medicine, sport, and sex. Nez Percé tradition holds that Clark fathered a child, Halahtookit (by Hohots Ilppilp's sister), who was with Chief Joseph when he surrendered in the Bear Paw Mountains. Photographer W. H. Jackson took a picture of this individual, which now resides at the Montana Historical Society. During the layover at Camp Chopunnish, when the men waited to proceed over the Bitterroot Mountains, they grew increasingly friendly with the people of Hohots Ilppilp's tribe. On one occasion, after smoking with Hohots Ilppilp and some of his men, Lewis reported, "Hohastillpilp with much cerimony presented me with a very eligant grey gelding which he had brought for that purpose. I gave him in return a handkerchief 200 balls and 4lbs of powder." He also gave Hohots Ilppilp the claws of a bear Collins had killed. Hohots Ilppilp prevailed upon some of his countrymen to return two stolen tomahawks to Drouillard, one of which belonged to Sergeant Floyd, and Lewis wrote, "we prized most as it was the private property of the late Sergt. Floyd and Capt. C. was desireous of returning it to his friends." In exchange for a pair of "Canadian shoes" (snow shoes), Frazier received a horse from Hohots Ilppilp. The tribe's friendliness toward the white men prompted Lewis to comment that "they appear to be cheerfull but not gay," and he praised them as "expert marksmen and good riders." On May 27, 1806, Lewis praised their generosity in offering their horses for meat: "this is a piece of liberality which would do honour to such as bost of civilization; indeed I doubt whether there are not a great number of our countrymen who would see us fast as many days before their compassion would excite them to a similar act of liberallity." Clark added that they seemed "much more clenly in their persons and habitations than any nation we have Seen Sence we left the Illinois." Gass mentions them as "the most friendly, honest, and ingenuous of the tribes we have seen in the course of our voyage and travels." The Nez Percé kept their promise of peace with neighboring tribes and friendly relations with the white men until forced to surrender to General Nelson Miles in the Battle of the Bear Paw in 1877. At a council in December 1842, administered by Elijah White, subagent to the Oregon tribes, the ninety-year-old Hohots Ilppilp spoke of his earlier contact with Lewis and Clark: "I am the oldest chief of the tribe, was the high chief when your great brothers Lewis and Clark, visited this country; they honored me with their friendship and council. I showed them my numerous wounds received in bloody battles with the Snakes; they told me it was not good, it was better to be at peace; they gave me a flag of truce; I held it up high; we met and talked but never fought again. Clark pointed to this day, to you, to this occasion; we have long waited in expectation; sent three of our sons to Red river school to prepare for it; two of them now sleep with their fathers; the other is here, and can be ears, mouth and pen for us. . . . I am glad to live to see you and this day, but I shall soon be still and quiet in death." His grandson Ellice, the ears, mouth, and pen Hohots Ilppilp referred to, was later chosen head chief for the Nez Percé. See *Wyakin.*

References: *Josephy; Ronda,* Lewis and Clark among the Indians; *Moulton, vol. 7; MacGregor,* Journals of Patrick Gass

Hooke (Hook), Moses (b. 1779): Succeeded Amos Stoddard in commanding Fort Fayette and also served as the assistant military agent. Ordered by Henry Dearborn to give every aid in his power to Captain Lewis as he prepared to depart on his journey to the Pacific. In 1801 he served with Captain Daniel Bissell's company. Lewis wrote to Jefferson from Pittsburgh in July 1803 that he had not received an answer from Clark to his offer of co-captaincy of the expedition. "in the event of Mr. Clark's declining to accompany me Lieut. Hooke of this place has engaged to do so, if permitted; and I think from his disposition and qualifications that I might safely calculate on being as ably assisted by him in the execution of the objects of my mission, as I could wish, or would be, by any other officer in the Army. Lieut. Hooke is about 26 years of age, endowed with a good constitution, possessing a sensible well informed mind, is industrious, prudent and preservering and withall intrepid and enterprising; he has acted as Military Agent at this place for a few months past, and of course will have some public accounts to adjust, tho' he tells me that he can settle those accounts, deliver the public stores to the person who may be directed to take charge of them, and prepare to go with me, at any time, within the course of a day or two." Clark's letter of acceptance arrived just in time three days later.

Reference: Jackson, Letters

Horned Weasel (Maw-pah'-pir-re-cos-sa too [the large one who wears horns]): Hidatsa chief of the Menetarra village and according to Clark a "verry Considerable man" whom Lewis desired to meet, but was rebuffed: "the Indians in all the towns & Camps treated Capt Lewis & the party with Great respect except one of the principal Cheifs Mar par pa pra ra pas a too or (Horned Weasel) who did not Chuse to be Seen by the Capt.& left word that he was not at home &." As Lewis told Charles McKenzie, who recorded the words in his own narrative, "this conduct surprised me, it being common only among your English Lords not to be 'at home' when they did not wish to see strangers. But as I had felt no inclination of entering any house after being told the Landlord would not be at home, I looked out for another lodging which I readily found." Under President Jefferson's directive, Lewis sought to establish peace among the tribes and to form a village alliance on the upper Missouri. The tribal leaders Lewis counciled with were unimpressed with his trinkets (some even going so far as to reject them) and expressed skepticism with regard to the motives of the expedition. As they told McKenzie, "had these Whites come amongst us with charitable views they would have loaded their 'Great Boat' with necessaries. It is true they have ammunition but they prefer throwing it idly away than sparing a shot of it to a poor Mandan." To display American firepower Lewis shot off his air gun, but a Gros Ventres chief made it known to McKenzie: "Had I these White warriors in the upper plains, my young men on horseback would soon do for them, as they would do for so many wolves . . . there are only two sensible men among them—the worker of Iron and the mender of Guns."

References: Moulton, vol. 3; Wood and Thiessen

Horse: Perhaps the single most important animal to the expedition. Horses meant survival for the party when they crossed the Bitterroot Mountains, not only in terms of transporting baggage but also because the meat of the five horses they resorted to killing gave the men the sustenance they needed to stay alive. According to historian and author Robert R. Hunt, the expedition's progress astride horses consisted of "at least four to five hundred miles on a westward lineal course, plus at least a thousand miles easterly, widely scattered over strikingly varied terrain—with horses ranging in number from two to three at a time up to 65." Hunt points out that the Corps of Discovery essentially evolved into a cavalry unit for at least six of the twenty-eight months of the expedition. The challenges of managing a traveling herd of horses is evident throughout the journals; horses ran off, were stolen, and often fell or became injured as they proceeded on. As Hunt reminds us, neither Jefferson nor Lewis seemed to consider horsemanship as a qualification for the corps. They reasoned that the crossing of the Continental Divide would be a short and easy one so no extra allowance for handling horses was necessary. By the time of departure from Fort Mandan, however, thanks to information from the Mandan and Hidatsa nations, Lewis began to see they would likely need horses to get over the mountains. In an April 7, 1805, letter to Jefferson, Lewis remarked, "The circumstances of the Snake (Shoshone) Indians possessing large quantities of horses, is much in our favour, as by means of horses, the transportation of our baggage will be rendered easy and expeditious overland, from the Missouri to the Columbia river." Lewis relied on the translating skills of Sacagawea to convince her people of their need to trade for horses; in August, near Sacagawea's homeland, Lewis grew concerned they would not locate any Indians and would therefore "be obliged to leave a great part of our stores, of which it appears to me that we have a stock already sufficiently small for the length of the voyage before us." During the course of their journey the captains would bargain nearly everything they had to obtain horses. In recognition of the Nez Percé's superior gelding method, Lewis wrote, "I am convinced that those cut by the indians will get well much soonest and they do not swell nor appear to suffer as much as those cut in the common way." He also observed that the Nez Percé were "expert marksmen and good riders." Historian Alvin Josephy states the Nez Percé were able to combine their horse herd with Mexican horses and selectively breed them so that they were what Lewis called "of an excellent race; they are lofty eligantly formed; active and durable in Short maney of them look like the fine English coursers and would make a figure in any country. Some of those horses in pided with large spots of white irrigularly scattered and intermixed with black, brown, Bey or Some other dark colour, but much the larger portion are of a uniform Colour with Stars, snips, and white feet, or in this respect marked much like our best blooded horses in the U. States, which they resemble as well in fleetness and bottom as in form and Colour." While they were distinctly marked, Josephy maintains there is no proof these were the Appaloosa breed. At several points the captains were given horses by influential members of the native nations, as a sign of respect and friendship, which Lewis and Clark noted and appreciated.

References: Hunt, "Hoofbeats & Nightmares"; Jackson, Letters; Moulton, vols. 5, 6, 7

Howard, Thomas Procter (b. 1779): Private; Massachusetts native; joined the expedition from Captain John Campbell's Second Infantry Company in January 1804. In a list of names of members of the party, Clark wrote next to Howard's name "never Drinks water." Lewis had him court-martialed at Fort Mandan for scaling the fort's walls and according to Sergeant Ordway for "Setting Such a pernicious example to the Savages . . . the court martial came out the prisoner was Sentenced 50 lashes & laid to the mercy of the commanding officer who was pleased to forgive him the punishment awarded by the court." No further formal disciplinary actions are recorded in the journals. The captains named a creek after Howard on the line between present-day Broadwater and Gallatin Counties, Montana, now called Sixteen Mile Creek. Howard served for several years at Fort Adams after the expedition and later married Genevieve Roy in St. Louis. Their son, Joseph, worked in the fur trade with Ashley in 1827.

References: *Clarke; Moulton, vol. 9*

Humboldt, Alexander von (1769–1859): Prussian. Gentleman traveler, scientist, and author who began his career as a mine inspector and was consulted by Jefferson on matters of measuring longitude without a clock. After receiving an inheritance, Humboldt journeyed on a five-year exploration of Venezuela in 1799. He gathered, measured, observed, and collected information accompanied by a French botanist, Aime Bonpland. William Clark used data from Humboldt's maps to fill in the southwestern portions of his own maps. An honorary foreign member of the American Philosophical Society, Humboldt visited with Jefferson in May and June of 1804 and heard about the Corps of Discovery. Among his accomplishments, he climbed the Andean volcano Chimborazo, along with several other peaks, setting an altitude record that held for thirty years. Like Jefferson, he was a generalist and could knowledgeably discuss many subjects in several languages. A writer of exhaustive studies on geography, volcanism, astronomy, botany, animal life, and Native American customs, Humboldt is mentioned in one of Jefferson's letters concerning the determination of longitude. During his visit to Washington, D.C., Humboldt let Americans copy his map and supplied them, according to historian Arlen Large, "with a detailed memorandum on the population, economy, roads, mines and military strength of the region." Later, Zebulon Pike would copy Humboldt's map without permission. Humboldt does not lack for geographical namesakes: Humboldt Bay, Humboldt River, Humboldt Peak, Humboldt Range, Mare Humboldtian (on the moon), and the Humboldt Current. Humboldt wrote a five-volume *Cosmos* on the workings of nature. Although he never returned to the United States, Humboldt traveled extensively in Europe, and in 1829 toured Siberia as a guest of the czar. He remained friends with Albert Gallatin when Gallatin was U.S. ambassador to France in 1816. Humboldt lamented the slow release of the journals, which prompted a response from Thomas Jefferson, "My dear friend and Baron, You will find it inconceivable that Lewis's journey to the Pacific should not yet have appeared; nor is it in my power to tell you the reason." Through his map of New Spain, Humboldt's confusion passed from Pike to Lewis and Clark, causing them some misunderstanding about the Southwest and the location of the Great Salt Lake.

References: Large, "The Humboldt Connection"; Jackson, Letters

Image Canoe Island: Now Tomahawk or Hayden Islands. Located on the east side of the confluence with the Willamette River. On November 4, 1805, Clark's tomahawk was stolen by natives near this spot, and here the party completely missed the Willamette River entering the Columbia, later, in April 1806, realizing "it has 3 small islands which conceal the river from the view of those who pass with the stream of the Columbia." At Image Canoe Island Clark used what Lewis termed a "farcical seen" involving sleight of hand and the aid of a portfire match, compass, and magnet to frighten the natives into bargaining for wapato roots. According to Clark "this measure alarmed them So much that the womin and children took Shelter in their beads and behind the men, all this time a very old blind man was Speaking with great vehemunce, appearently imploreing his gode. I lit my pipe and gave them Smoke & gave the womin the full amount of the roots which they had put at my feet. they appeared Some what passified and I left them and proceeded on on the South Side of Image Canoe Island which I found to be two Islands hid from the opposit Side by one near the Center of the river."
Reference: Moulton, vol. 7

Iron boat (leather boat, the Experiment): Carefully crafted at the armory in Harpers Ferry under Meriwether Lewis's personal supervision; an iron frame canoe, which would be lined with hides to carry up to eight thousand pounds on the Missouri after the portage. In his letter to Jefferson from Fort Mandan dated April 7, 1805, Lewis mentions it as a "perogue of skins, the frame of which was prepared at Harper's Ferry" and which cost some three extra weeks in preparation. Lewis told Jefferson that they intended to leave the other pirogues at the "falls of the Missouri, from whence we intend continuing our voyage." The iron boat was tested on the Potomac and then disassembled and hauled by wagon from Harpers Ferry to Pittsburgh, where it was loaded along with other supplies onto a keelboat destined for the Falls of the Ohio River and a rendezvous with Clark and his party. From there the iron boat traveled, as part of the keelboat's baggage, to the Mississippi and up the Missouri to Great Falls. At the portage, the captain decided to leave the white pirogue and substitute it with the iron boat. As they assembled the iron boat, their careful packing paid off; Lewis noted it lacked only one screw, "which the ingenuity of Shields can readily replace." Archaeologist Donald W. Rose surmises the iron sections must have been bolted together. On June 21, 1805, Lewis sent it in the first load of baggage to be transported over the portage route, and for the next seventeen days the journals repeatedly relay the iron boat's labor-intensive reassembly. Historian Paul Cutright notes it required twenty-eight elk skins and four buffalo hides to line the iron frame canoe. Under Sergeant Gass's direction, they used a concoction of charcoal, beeswax, and tallow for the sealant. Finally on July 8, Gass wrote, "We finished the boat, having covered her with tallow and coal dust. We called her the Experiment, and expect she will answer our purpose." No amount of optimism on the sergeant's part would keep it afloat, however, as Lewis noted the next day: "we launched the boat; she lay like a perfect cork on the water . . . I now directed seats to be fixed in her and oars to be fitted . . . just at this moment a violent wind commenced . . . the wind continued violent untill late in the evening, by which time we discovered that a greater part of the composition had separated from the skins and left the seams of the boat exposed to the water and she leaked in such a manner that she would not answer. I need not add that this circumstance mortifyed me not a little . . . but to make further experiments in our present situation seemed to me madness. . . . I therefore relinquished all further hope of my favorite boat and ordered her to be sunk in the water, that the skins might become soft in order the better to take her in peices tomorrow and deposite the iron fraim at this place as it could probably be of no further service to us. had I only singed my Elk skins in stead of shaving them I beleive the composition would have remained and the boat would have answered; at least untill we could have reached the pine country which must be in advance of us from the pine which is brought down by the water and which is probably at no great distance where we might have supplyed ourselves with the necessary pich or gum but it was now too late to introduce a remedy and I bid adieu to my boat and her expected services." A lack of trees to supply the necessary pitch, along with the large-size holes they made in stitching the hides, probably caused the vessel to fail. The frame was cached along with some other articles, and then Lewis wrote, "having little to do I amused myself in fishing and caught a few small fish." Rose and historian Robert Lange are in agreement that the fishing trip gave Lewis time to let off steam, and that Lewis was lucky to have a sympathetic co-captain who did not dwell on the failure of the iron boat in his journal nor in his actions. After calmly recalling the incident in his journal, Clark went straight to work on finding the trees necessary for the construction of the dugout canoes and did not waste time complaining about its feasibility in the first place. The boat was never recovered, and has become something of a holy grail to Lewis and Clark scholars and enthusiasts.

References: *Rose; Cutright,* Pioneering Naturalists*; MacGregor,* Journals of Patrick Gass*; Lange, quoted in Rose; Moulton, vol. 4; Jackson,* Letters

J

Jackson, Donald (1919–1987): Author, teacher, editor. Preeminent historian of the West, he is the editor of *Letters of the Lewis and Clark Expedition, with Related Documents, 1783–1854,* and author of *Thomas Jefferson and the Stony Mountains* and *Among the Sleeping Giants,* along with works on Washington, Pike, and Frémont. Cutright notes that Jackson's footnotes in the *Letters* collection average approximately two per item, some of them exhaustive in length. According to Cutright, Jackson's *Letters* "stands fair to be the most important contribution to Lewis and Clark literature in the twentieth century excepting the Original journals." Jackson shared his enthusiasm for his subjects with his friends, family, students, and the members of the Lewis and Clark Trail Heritage Foundation. His name is still spoken with reverence and respect among these groups. Friend and fellow Lewis and Clark scholar James Ronda said of Jackson, in his eulogy, "Don gave his friendship unstintingly, openly, gladly, without reservation. He spent his life shepherding us, nurturing us, teaching us. He invited us into his spacious mind and called us friends."

References: Cutright, History of the Lewis and Clark Journals; *Ronda, "In Memoriam"; Jackson,* Letters

Jalap: A strong laxative made from the Mexican morning glory plant. Used in Rush's bilious pills. Lewis purchased one-half pound of it in Philadelphia.

Reference: Peck, Or Perish in the Attempt

Jarrot, Nicholas: Frenchman living in Cahokia who encountered the expedition in December of 1803. Jarrot worked as a trader operating on the Mississippi as far as Prairie du Chien. He served with John Hay as a translator between Meriwether Lewis and officials of the Spanish government when Lewis visited them in St. Louis prior to departing into country that still officially belonged to the Spanish government. See Hay, John.

Reference: Osgood, Field Notes

Jefferson, Thomas (1743–1826): It is impossible to make sense of the Lewis and Clark Expedition without reference to Thomas Jefferson. What lifts the expedition out of the context of the other exploration projects of its time—Pike's two western journeys, the Freeman and Dunbar missions, among others—was Jefferson's direct involvement at every level. It was the realization of what Jefferson might have joined Lewis in calling "one of those great objects on which my mind has been unalterably fixed for many years." Monticello faced west. John Dos Passos once called it a "portico on the wilderness." Jefferson was born sometime between April 2 and April 13, 1743, on the Virginia frontier. His father, Peter Jefferson, his son remembered, "was the third or fourth settler, about the year 1737, of the part of the country in which I live." Peter Jefferson was a surveyor and a cartographer. He made a number of journeys into the wilderness west of Virginia's plantation settlements. With Joshua Fry, professor of mathematics at the College of William and Mary, Peter Jefferson surveyed the boundary line between Virginia and North Carolina, and crafted the first systematic map of Virginia. One of Jefferson's early tutors, the Reverend James Maury, was an ardent advocate of western exploration and expansion, and an active speculator in western lands. After attending the College of William and Mary, Jefferson read law with George Wythe, a classicist and one of the great legal scholars of the day. Jefferson began his public career at the age of twenty-six in 1769 when he was elected to a seat in the Virginia House of Burgesses. He went on to hold virtually every office available to an American statesman of his time. He was the wartime governor of Virginia (1779–81), a national congressman (1783–84), the American minister to France (1785–89), the first secretary of state (1790–93), the vice president (1797–1801), and then, for two terms, the president of the United States (1801–09). He was the author of the Declaration of Independence (1776), the Virginia Statute for Religious Liberty (1786), and the founder of the University of Virginia (chartered 1819). Jefferson had played a key role in creating the public domain of the United

States. He helped to persuade Virginia to cede her vast claims to land between the Appalachians and the Mississippi River (and possibly farther) to the United States government in 1784. While serving as a Virginia congressman under the Articles of Confederation he presented a committee report (March 1, 1784) that helped to define the relationship the original thirteen states would have with new states carved out of the West. New states would be republican in form, they would enter the union on an equal footing after the shortest possible probationary period, and they would adopt the rectangular survey grid system to bring order to western development. At that time Jefferson also tried to prevent slavery from spreading into the American West, but the provision of the 1784 land ordinance that would have achieved that goal was defeated by a single vote in the Congress. Prior to Lewis and Clark, Jefferson had attempted on at least three previous occasions to send an exploration party into the West. Just after the war, he approached George Rogers Clark (brother of William Clark) with a modest proposal: "Some of us have been talking here in a feeble way of making the attempt to search that country. But I doubt whether we have enough of that kind of spirit to raise the money. How would you like to lead such a party?" Jefferson had heard rumors that the British were contemplating an exploration of the interior, and he could not stomach the idea that the British might preempt American entry into the region. George Rogers Clark expressed interest in Jefferson's plan, but made it clear that he would not undertake any further missions on behalf of the United States or Virginia without significant compensation. Nothing came of the scheme. In 1786, while serving as the American minister to the court of Louis XVI in France, Jefferson met a Connecticut Yankee named John Ledyard. Ledyard was a footloose adventurer. He had sailed with Captain James Cook on his third voyage. Together Jefferson and Ledyard concocted a scheme whereby Ledyard would walk from Paris to Moscow, from Moscow to the Bering Strait, cross in a skiff, and then walk down the mountain spine of North America. Eventually he would make his way on foot to Philadelphia, after essentially circumambulating the earth. Chimerical though this sounds, Jefferson sought a passport for Ledyard from Catherine the Great, and Ledyard ventured to within a few hundred miles of the Bering Strait before Catherine had him arrested as a security risk. Thus ended the most whimsical hike in human history. In 1793 the American Philosophical Society took up a subscription to send a competent scientist into the West. A French botanist named André Michaux was selected to make the journey. He actually ventured into the interior as far as Kentucky, but he became embroiled in the political maneuvering (then called filibustering) by the French minister to the United States, Edmund Genet, and he had to be recalled. Meriwether Lewis, then nineteen, had learned of the American Philosophical Society's project, and he had, according to Jefferson, applied to be a part of the mission. There is some reason to doubt whether Jefferson was remembering these events accurately, but on Lewis's birthday in 1813, he wrote, "Capt. Lewis being then stationed at Charlottesville on the recruiting service, warmly solicited me to obtain for him the execution of that object. I told him it was proposed that the person engaged should be attended by a single companion only, to avoid exciting alarm among the Indians. . . . This did not deter him," Jefferson wrote, but Lewis was not chosen to be a part of the mission. Finally, when he became the third president of the United States, Jefferson was in a position to realize his long-standing dream. He hired Meriwether Lewis to serve as his private correspondence secretary and aide-de-camp. Lewis would be paid five hundred dollars per year, and live with Jefferson in the president's mansion as "one of my family." Historian Donald Jackson has argued, probably correctly, that Jefferson did not necessarily hire Lewis with western exploration in mind. At the time of his inauguration, in the spring of 1801, Jefferson was chiefly interested in reducing the size of the American armed forces, and he wanted a friend, a fellow Virginian, and a good Republican to advise him on which officers were both competent and politically reliable and which to retire to private life. Still, when the moment came, Jefferson had an able lieutenant close at hand, one indeed who had long declared his interest in exploring the Missouri country. Events outside of the president's control also propelled him to take action in the West. In the secret treaty of San Ildefonso (October 1800), Spain was coerced by Napoleon into retroceding the province of Louisiana to France. By April 1802 Jefferson was writing, "Every eye in the U.S. is now fixed on this affair of Louisiana. Perhaps nothing since the revolutionary war has produced more uneasy sensations through the body of the nation." Then, on October 18, 1802, the Spanish intendant at New Orleans, Juan de Dios Morales, suspended America's right of deposit at New Orleans. The right of deposit enabled Americans to transfer goods, without tariff, from bateaux and rafts to trading ships and vice versa in New Orleans. In other words, by international agreement, the lower Mississippi had been declared a duty-free zone for U.S. citizens. Morales was required by treaty to provide an alternative port of deposit in the lower Mississippi, but he refused to do so. When the United States launched a stiff protest, Jefferson and his secretary of state, James Madison, were informed that Morales had closed the port of New Orleans to American shippers without authority, but this, of course, did not solve the immediate problem, and it pointed to America's economic vulnerability in the lower Mississippi. Jefferson, a remarkably patient and subtle diplomat, who was normally disposed to take the long view in questions of this sort, realized that he had to take decisive action. The Federalists were questioning Jefferson's leadership—and his manhood. His secretary of state and closest friend, Madison, had written of the anxiety of the westerners, "The Mississippi is to them everything. It is the Hudson, the Delaware, the Potomac and all the navigable rivers of the Atlantic States formed into one stream." On January 13, 1803, Jefferson wrote to his friend and protégé James Monroe to persuade him to go to France to help the American minister Robert Livingston sort things out with Napoleon's foreign ministers. "The fever into which the western mind is thrown by the affair at New Orleans stimulated by the mercantile, and generally the federal [i.e., Federalist] interest threatens to overbear our peace," Jefferson wrote to Monroe. Jefferson sent Monroe's appointment to the U.S. Senate on January 11, 1803. Monroe set sail on March 9, 1803. By May 2, 1803, Monroe and Livingston (chiefly Livingston) had managed to solve the problem in a manner extremely favorable to American interests. On April 10, 1803, Napoleon had impulsively instructed his foreign minister, Talleyrand, to offer the entire Louisiana province to the Americans. Suddenly the United States' rights in the lower Mississippi were unrestricted, and 828,000 square miles of territory had been added to the republic for approximately three cents per acre. It is characteristic of Jefferson that, so far from taking credit for the greatest land sale in human history, he fussed over whether the purchase had actually been constitutional. Even before diplomatic events took this advantageous course, however, Jefferson had launched what became the Lewis and Clark Expedition. On January 18, 1803, he sent a secret message to Congress in which, among other things, he wrote, "The river Missouri, & the Indians inhabiting it, are not as well known as is rendered desirable by their connection with the Mississippi, & consequently with us. . . . An intelligent officer with ten or twelve chosen men . . . might explore the whole line, even to the Western ocean, have conferences with the natives on the subject of commercial intercourse, get admission among them for our traders as others are admitted, agree on convenient deposits for an interchange of articles, and return with the information acquired in the course of two summers." Congress approved the project on February 28, 1803. Jefferson made arrangements for Lewis to visit key figures in the American Enlightenment in Pennsylvania before embarking on his tour. The president made sure that Lewis had brief but critically important training sessions with Benjamin Rush and Benjamin Smith Barton in Philadelphia, and Andrew Ellicott in Lancaster, Pennsylvania. Undoubtedly Jefferson played a significant role in the planning and outfitting of the expedition, though the available records are frustratingly scant. Though it is impossible to prove, one feels the hand of Jefferson in Lewis's iron-framed boat, the so-called Experiment, in the combination canisters that held gunpowder and became lead balls, and in the selection of trade goods to offer Indians as hospitality gifts and tokens of future trade. Jefferson may also have trained Lewis personally to make celestial observations. Jefferson admitted wistfully that Lewis was "not regularly educated," but he knew that survival and safe return would be the most important indication of Lewis's success, and he knew, too, that Lewis had unusually keen powers of observation and—what was still more important—"he possesses a great mass of accurate observation on all the subjects of nature which present themselves here [i.e., on the Atlantic side of the Appalachians], & will therefore readily select those only in his new route which shall be new." Jefferson's famous instructions, dated June 20, 1803, must have challenged even Meriwether Lewis's undaunted courage. The president instructed Lewis to find "the most direct and practicable water route across this continent," to ascertain the latitude and longitude of every key geographical feature on his route, to inventory the plants, animals, minerals, soil types, and climate he encountered, and much more. With respect to the Indians of the West, Jefferson's instructions were no less daunting. Lewis was to inform the tribes he met of the legal transfer of sovereignty from France to the United States; to encourage a continental peace policy among the tribes; to engage in extensive ethnographical studies of the Indians he met; to make arrangements for trade between Indians and American merchants and to determine where the Indians wished trade forts to be located; to invite Indian leaders to visit Washington, D.C.; and to invite Indians to send their children to civilization to be educated by white teachers. It was an extremely comprehensive and exacting set of instructions. Two things seem clear. First, the ideal man for this expedition would have been an individual of great learning, scientific sophistication, extraordinary precision and discipline, boundless curiosity, and indefatigable energy—in short Jefferson himself, in buckskins. Second, no single man could have achieved all of this. In fact, no two men were able to fulfill Jefferson's expectations in full measure. Jefferson continued to play a role in the expedition right up to its departure on May 14, 1804. He sent Lewis a steady stream of maps, journal excerpts, and reports. He intervened in Lewis's decision making just once. When Lewis wrote to announce that he was thinking of making a horseback journey to Santa Fe over the course of the winter of 1803–04 with a view to proving to Congress that it was getting its money's worth from the Corps of Discovery, the president responded immediately (as quickly as nineteenth-century postal logistics allowed) and unambiguously: "The object of your mission is single, the direct water communication from sea to sea formed by the bed of the Missouri & perhaps the Oregon." Jefferson's last communication from Lewis arrived on July 13, 1805. It was Lewis's letter, sent from Fort Mandan, summarizing the expedition's first year of travel, and detailing plans for the push to the Pacific Ocean. After that, the Corps of Discovery went silent. Eighteen months passed before Lewis initiated further communication with the president. Many had concluded that the expedition had come to grief somewhere in the far West. Jefferson retained his famous optimism, but even he was filled with apprehension. When at last he received word of Lewis's successful return to St. Louis, Jefferson wrote on October 26, 1806, "I received, my dear Sir, with unspeakable joy your letter of Sep. 23 announcing the return of yourself, Capt. Clarke & your party in good health to St. Louis. The unknown scenes in which you were engaged, & the length of time without hearing of you had begun to be felt awfully." Lewis arrived at Washington, D.C., on December 28, 1806. Jefferson did not attend the official ball organized by the Washington, D.C., social establishment on January 14, 1807, to celebrate the Corps of Discovery's return. His absence did not signify any displeasure; the president had long since established the habit of not attending Washington social functions at night. He was not an extrovert. One of the great mysteries of the Lewis and Clark Expedition is how, and if, the president debriefed his friend and expedition leader. We know that on at least one occasion the two men spread expedition maps on the floor of the East Room of the White House. Beyond that, we have little evidence of systematic debriefing. Jefferson wrote a handful of letters in response to the expedition, but these represent only a fraction of what they communicated. Three Indian delegations visited Jefferson in Washington as a direct result of the Lewis and Clark Expedition. Jefferson's speeches to each of these delegations are extant. They are masterpieces of their genre, and highly characteristic of Jefferson in their attempt to address Native Americans in what the president took to be their cadences and metaphors. In 1813 Jefferson was asked by the editor of the journals, Paul Allen, to write a biographical sketch of Meriwether Lewis. Jefferson did so with his usual facility. Among other things, Jefferson let it be known to the world that he believed that Meriwether Lewis had committed suicide. There is no ambiguity, no hesitancy in Jefferson's conclusion: "About 3. oclock in the night [at Grinder's Stand] he did the deed which plunged his friends into affliction and deprived his country of one of her most valued citizens. . . ." Jefferson's Indian policy, no matter how benevolent his rhetoric, was really only a kinder, gentler version of the policies that would be adopted by President Andrew Jackson. For all of his love of the American Indian, and his deep fascination with some elements of Indian culture, Jefferson could not contemplate letting Indian rights and sovereignty get in the way of the Euro-American settlement of the continent. He sought, in his terms, to extinguish Indian rights to the lands of the American West, peace-fully if possible, bloodily if the Indians proved recalcitrant. Jefferson urged the carrot rather than the stick. He spoke of "bribing them into peace, and keeping them in peace with perpetual bribes." He urged his agents in the West to extend generous credit to tribal chiefs in the hope that they could seduce them deeply into debt and then convince them to "lope." To Governor William Henry Harrison, on February 27, 1803, Jefferson wrote: "To promote this disposition to exchange lands, which they have to spare and we want, for necessaries, which we have to spare and they want, we shall push our trading uses, and be glad to see the good and influential individuals among them run in debt, because we observe that when these debts get beyond what the individuals can pay, they become willing to lop them off by a cession of lands." Jefferson's benevolence prevailed only so long as the Indi-ans were cooperative. To Alexander von Humboldt in 1813 Jefferson could write that "the cruel massacres they have committed on the women and children of our frontiers taken by surprise, will oblige us now to pursue them to extermination, or drive them to new seats beyond our reach." Extermination was not really Jefferson's plan. The West of his imagination was so large—bordering on infinite in size—that he continued to believe that there was land enough in the trans-Mississippi region to absorb as many Indian tribes as he could persuade (or force) to relocate.

Reference: Jackson, Letters

Jenkinson, Robert Banks, Lord Hawkesbury (1770–1828): British secretary of state for foreign affairs from 1801 to 1804. Jenkinson received updates on the progress and return of the Corps of Discovery and presumably kept Her Majesty informed.

Reference: Jackson, Letters

Jesseaume, René: Canadian free trader (or tenant trader, so called due to his living with the Mandan / Hidatsa and having access to trade goods) who was one of the first white men to live in and become part of the Knife River village. The captains engaged him as interpreter during their time with the Mandan and Hidatsa tribes, and he, his Mandan wife, and children moved into Fort Mandan in the winter of

1804–05. He continued in his capacity as an interpreter, accompanied by his family, when he and Nathaniel Pryor escorted Mandan chief and invited guest Sheheke-shote to visit his "great father," Thomas Jefferson, in Washington, D.C. During their return journey the party was hampered, and Jesseaume wounded, by attacks from the Arikara. As a free trader Jesseaume did not endear himself to his fellow residenters or tenant traders. One complained about "old sneaking cheat Monsr. Jussaume, whose character is more despicable than the worst of the natives." Before the Lewis and Clark Expedition, Jesseaume guided and interpreted for David Thompson on his trip up the Missouri in 1797 and once had a violent confrontation with the Spanish agent John Evans, who wanted to take over "Jesseaume's Fort," an establishment Jesseaume built between the Mandan and Hidatsa villages for the North West Company. It was Jesseaume who suggested the local cure of rattlesnake powder as a treatment for Sacagawea's prolonged labor. Although Lewis remained skeptical, he had to admit the unorthodox remedy worked. Jean Baptiste Charbonneau was brought forth less than ten minutes later. René Jesseaume returned to the Mandan villages in 1809 with Manuel Lisa's party.

Reference: Wood and Thiessen

K

Kakawissassa (Lighting Raven, Crow Going Across): Arikara chief. One of three chiefs who counciled with Lewis and Clark in October 1804 near their villages on the Grand River. Clark states that although they detected "some jealousy exists as to the chiefs to be made . . . we made three one for each village." The captains chose Kakawissassa as first or grand chief and gave him more gifts than the two lesser chiefs. They issued their usual diplomatic speeches and gestures aimed at securing a place in the trade system of the Mandan and other tribes on the upper Missouri while at the same time isolating the Teton Sioux economically. Afterward Clark commented that the Indians were amazed by the air gun and that "the Inds. much astonished at my black Servent, who made him Self more turrible in thier view than I wished him to Doe as I am told telling them that before I coght him he was wild and lived upon people, young children was verry good eating." Although they were offered whiskey, the Arikara made a point of telling the captains they were surprised that "their father would present to them a liquor which would make them fools." On October 11, 1804, Clark recorded these remarks by Kakawissassa, "My Fathers—! My heart is glader than it ever was before to See my fathers. If you want the road open no one Can provent it it will always be open for you. Can you think any one Dare put their hands on your rope of your boat. No! not one dar When you Get to the mandans we wish you to Speak good words with that Nation for us. we wish to be at peace with them. It gives us pain that we do not Know how to work the Beaver, we will make Buffalow roabs the best we Can. when you return if I am living you will See me again the same man The Indian in the prarie know me and listen to my words when you come they will meet to See you. We Shall look at the river with impatienc for your return." In her book *Women of the Earth Lodges,* Virginia Bergman Peters notes that many early visitors to the Mandan and Arikara country, including Lewis and

Clark, were not aware of the underlying complexities of these cultures and their interrelationships.

References: Coues, History of the Expedition, *vol. 1; Peters; Moulton, vol. 3*

Kane, Lucille: Curator of manuscripts at the Minnesota Historical Society who was presented, in 1953, with papers from the attic of St. Paul resident John Henry Hammond, general in the Civil War and inspector for the Indian Bureau. When she examined the papers, Miss Kane realized one packet contained the rough journal or field notes of William Clark from 1803 to 1805. After a protracted battle over legal ownership, the papers are now housed at Yale University and were edited and published by Ernest S. Osgood and the Yale University Press in 1964. The papers represent an extremely valuable portion of the documents of the Lewis and Clark Expedition as they contain Clark's "Dubois Journal" from December 13, 1803, to May 14, 1804, and his "River Journal" from May 14, 1804, to April 3, 1805.

References: Osgood, Field Notes; *Holbrook*

Keelboat: Used as the main mode of river transportation on the Missouri and Ohio Rivers in the early 1800s, and by Lewis and Clark on their journey to Fort Mandan. It was propelled against the current by a combination of sailing, rowing, poling, or cordelling. The journals indicate the keelboat was fifty-five feet in length, about eight feet in width, with a three-foot draft and a thirty-two-foot mast. It could carry twelve to fourteen tons of men and freight and was controlled by a tiller or rudder and an anchor. The anchor was a casualty of the encounter with the Teton Sioux in September of 1804 when, according to Clark, "we were on our Guard all night, the misfortune of the loss of our Anchor obliged us to Lay under a falling bank much exposd to the accomplishment of their hostile intentions." During the first winter at Wood River, the keelboat was modified to include an awning, catwalks, lockers for stowed baggage, and lids, cannon, blunderbusses, and eleven benches for twenty-two oarsmen. It endured the trip to Fort Mandan and back to St. Louis under the command of Corporal Richard Warfington, where it delivered the precious cargo collected by the expedition, including a live prairie dog and four live magpies. The keelboat was likely auctioned off in St. Louis.

References: *Moulton, vol. 3; Willie Johnson, "Keelboats and Pirogues"*

Kentucky rifle: Rifles carried by Lewis, Clark, and Drouillard, and perhaps several other enlisted men during the expedition. The letters *U.S.* were stamped on the rifles, which were probably issued by the previous companies of the enlisted men. Clark referred to it as his small gun; it shot balls of a size of a hundred to a pound.

References: *Russell; Carrick, personal communication*

King, Nicholas (1771–1812): Cartographer from Philadelphia who came to America from England in 1794. He served as surveyor for the city of Washington from 1803 to 1812 and would have had frequent contact with Secretary of the Treasury Albert Gallatin and President Thomas Jefferson. While in Philadelphia Lewis copied the Vancouver survey and had King fit his sketches into a master map made for the expedition. The map affirmed the pyramidal-height-of-land notion and integrated up-to-date geographical information from the maps of Ellicott, Cook, Vancouver, Arrowsmith, Mackenzie, Thompson, Mitchell, Anville, and de L'Isle. When it came time for Clark to fix the longitude of the mouth of the Columbia, he could rely with certainty on the King/Vancouver reading. King made two copies of the map Clark drew during the winter of 1804–05. His map hardly showed the central Rockies and indicated the Yellowstone flowed to Sante Fe. He wrote the word *Conjectural* across the upper Missouri region.

References: *Allen*, Passage through the Garden; *Jackson*, Letters; *Large*, *"Vancouver's Legacy to Lewis and Clark"*

Kinnikinnick (Algonquian term, *bois roule* in French): A rolled wood that was mixed with scrapings from other woods, including sumac, cornel, red osier, and the bearberry plant, also called kinnikinnick, to form a tobacco mixture smoked by Native American Indians for thousands of years. The Teton Sioux Indians stored their kinnikinnick in a dried skunk or polecat skin. It is said to relieve headaches and have a mild sedative effect on respiratory ailments. Lewis and Clark mention its use among the Teton Sioux on September 26, 1804: "the men wear a robe & each a polecats Skin, for to hold ther Bawe roley for Smoking."

References: Coues, History of the Expedition, *vol. 1; Thwaites,* Original Journals, *vol. 1*

L

La Charette: The last white village Lewis and Clark passed on their way up the Missouri River, located about seventy miles upriver from the mouth. They arrived at the village on May 25, 1804. Lewis calls it "the last settlement on the Missouri; and consists of ten or twelve families mostly hunters." Clark counts "five families only." Gass calls it "St. Johns, a small French village situated on the north side." A Spanish fort, San Juan del Misuri, had been established on the site around 1796. Daniel Boone had lived in the vicinity since 1799, but there is no evidence that Lewis and Clark made contact with the famous pathfinder. Boone migrated from Boone's Settlement to La Charette sometime after 1804. The expedition camped just above the village for one night. "The people at this Village is pore," Clark writes, "houses Small, they Sent us milk & eggs to eat." They met Regis Loisel here— he gave them a good deal of information. The expedition passed La Charette on the return journey on September 20, 1806. Clark writes, "we saw cows on the bank which caused a shout to be raised for joy." The men were granted permission to fire a three-round salute. Clark purchased two gallons of whiskey for the men at what he considered a confiscatory price—eight dollars. "two young Scotch gentlemen furnished us with Beef flower and Some pork for our men, and gave us a very agreeable supper." The captains (and perhaps others) "accepted of a bed in one of their tents." The residents of La Charette, including the first white women the men had seen in years, were "much astonished in Seeing us return. they informed us that we were Supposed to have been lost." La Charette no longer exists. The Missouri River swallowed it up later in the nineteenth century.

References: MacGregor, Journals of Patrick Gass; Moulton, vols. 2, 3

La Liberté: French engagé who was sent to find the Oto Indians with a Missouri Indian and deserted, taking a public horse with him. He escaped as he was being returned to camp, but no further effort was made to apprehend him because he was a French hired man. Historian Gary Moulton notes there was a Joseph La Liberté who married in St. Louis in 1835 and a La Liberté was buried there in 1837.

References: Moulton, vol. 2; Osgood, Field Notes

La Verendrye brothers: Sons of Pierre Gaultier de Varennes Sieur de La Verendrye, Canadian fur trader and commandant of several French Canadian trading posts, including Fort Charles and Fort La Reine. In 1738 Pierre was one of the first white visitors to reach the Mandan villages on the Missouri, from Hudson's Bay, looking for furs and access to the western sea. He kept a journal of his travels and is considered the earliest known recorder and observer of Indians in North Dakota. His son Pierre followed him upriver in 1741. The following year two other Verendrye sons, François and Louis-Joseph, visited the villages in search of "horse Indians" and explored south and west of the area, spending the winter with the Arikara, reaching the Black Hills of South Dakota, and most likely sighting the Big Horn or "Stony" Mountains. Their journey west ended when the Indians they were with refused to go any farther. The Verendryes were the first white men to travel on the Assiniboine, Red, and Missouri Rivers. Their explorations and burial of a lead plate near the mouth of the Bad River in South Dakota established a French claim to the western Louisiana territory of North America. The plate, which can be viewed at the South Dakota State Historical Society in Pierre, reads: "in the 26th year of the reign of Louis XV, the most illustrious Lord, the Lord Marquis of Beauharnois, 1741, Pierre Gaultier De La Verendrye placed this." The back reads: "Placed by the Chevalier Verendrye (his brother) Louis (and) Londette and Al Miotte. 30 March 1743." One hundred and seventy years later, in February of 1913, the plate was discovered by two high school students. The State Historical Society later purchased the plate for seven hundred dollars.

References: Wood and Thiessen; Jackson, Thomas Jefferson and the Stony Mountains

Labiche, François: An experienced trader and skilled boatman of mixed blood. Labiche joined the expedition after enlisting in the army at Fort Kaskaskia; later he used his knowledge of French and English to complete the translation chain among the captains, Charbonneau, his Shoshonion-speaking wife, Sacagawea, a young Shoshone prisoner, and finally to the Flathead tribe. From October 1806 until January 1807 Labiche worked as an assistant to Lewis, as well as an interpreter and pack horseman for the Washington, D.C., visit of the Indian delegation headed by Sheheke. In his list of the men who accompanied them to the Pacific Ocean, Lewis wrote, "He has received the pay only of a private, though, besides the duties he performed as such, he has rendered me very essential services as a French and English interpreter; therefore, I should think it only just that some small addition to his pay, as a private, should be added, tho' no such addition has at any time been promised by me." In his list of expedition members, 1825–28, Clark has "F. Labeiche" living in St. Louis, where he may be the "Labuche" who married a Genevieve and baptized seven children.

References: *Jackson,* Letters; *Rogers,* Lewis and Clark in Missouri

Lafrance, Jean Baptiste (d. 1808): Free trader and interpreter for the North West Company who worked with Laroque, Heney, and McKenzie. Lafrance lived with the Mandan perhaps as early as 1793. He is mentioned in the journals, by Clark, on November 26, 1804: "Seven traders arrived from the fort on the Ossinaboin from the N W Companey one of which Lafrances took upon himself to speak unfavourably of our intentions &. the princpal Mr. La Rock, (& Mr. McKensey) was informed of the Conduct of their interpreter & the Consiquinces if they did not put a Stop to unfavourable & ill founded assursions &c. &." Three days later Clark recorded, "Mr. La Rock and one of his men Came to visit us we informed him what we had herd of his intentions of makeing Chiefs &c. and forbid him to give meadels or flags to the Indians he Denied haveing any Such intention." During this period of negotiations with the Hidatsa, the captains chose to blame the "ill founded assursions" of the British hirelings for the difficulties they encountered in their attempts to establish peace between the Mandan and the Hidatsa tribes. As one young warrior asked Lewis, "without war how would we chose our chiefs?" Lafrance died at Fort Mandan of consumption in 1808. See Laroque, François-Antoine.

Reference: Moulton, vol. 3

Lahontan, Baron de Louis Armand de Lom d'Arce (1666–1715?):
One of the early French explorers of Louisiana whose popular and influential 1735 account of his travels, *New Voyages to North America*, was included in Thomas Jefferson's library. Highly critical of the French government and society of Louis XIV's era and of the French missionaries' efforts to convert the natives, Lahontan described tribes of "civilized" Indians he encountered in his nine-year service to the French army in Louisiana. Although he traveled only as far west as Lake Michigan, Lahontan collected stories through sign language from the western Sioux, Pawnees, Crows, Mandans, and from the white traders living among them. In his embellished account, which he finished while in exile from France in Spain, Portugal, and Holland, the Indians he "witnessed" were said to live on the banks of a "Long River" or tributary of the Mississippi, connected to another long river on the other side of the mountains, which flowed to the Pacific Ocean. *New Voyages to North America* became a popular publication in London and Paris, and its use of imaginary characters has invited comparisons to *Gulliver's Travels* (1726).

As historian Marshall Sprague has written, "The baron expressed his views in dialogues suggesting analogies to modern materialism—dialogues between himself and an imaginary Huron friend, Adario, who had been to Quebec, Paris, and Versailles and found no merit in them comparable to that of any Huron village on the Great Lakes. When Lahontan mentioned the blessings and comforts brought to mankind by French science and invention, Adario replied, according to the English translation of Lahontan's book:

> The More I reflect upon the lives of the Europeans, the less Wisdom and Happiness I find among 'em. . . . I know that your Prince, your Duke, your Marshal, and your Prelate are far from being happy upon the Comparison with the Hurons, who know no other happiness than that of Liberty and Tranquility of Mind: For your great Lords

hate one another in their Hearts; they forfeit their Sleep, and neglect even Eating and Drinking, in making their Court to the King, and undermining their Enemies; they offer such Violence to Nature in dissembling, disguising and bearing things, that the Torture of their Soul leaves all Expression far behind it.

"Adario went on to blast European food with 'your Pepper, your Salt, and a thousand other Spices . . . to murder your Health.' And European clothes: 'You dawb your Hair with Powder and Essence, and even your Cloaths are sprinkled with the same. . . . How d'ye think it would agree with me to spend two hours in Dressing or Shifting myself, to put on a Blue Sute and Red Stockins, with a Black Hat and a White Feather, besides colour'd Ribbands? Such Rigging would make me look upon myself as a Fool. . . . And pray what harm would it do ye to go Naked in warm Weather? Besides, we are not so stark Naked, but that we are cover'd behind and before. 'Tis better to go Naked than to toil under an everlasting Sweat, and under a load of Cloaths heap'd up one above another.' And Knowledge: 'In your Books which are publish'd every Day, you write lies and impertinent Stories; and yet you would fain have me to Read and Write like the French.' And health: 'We Hurons know no such thing as your Dropsies, Asthmas, Palsy's, Gout and Pox. The Leprosy, the Lethargy, External Swellings, the Suppression of Urine, the Stone and the Gravel, are Distempers that we are not acquainted with.'

"Lahontan planned to keep the readers of his book awake with bawdy allusions. Of French sex life, his Huron philosopher remarked:

I have observ'd that before you pass the Age of thirty or forty, you are Stronger and more Robust than we . . . but after that your Strength dwindles and visibly declines, whereas ours keeps to its wonted pitch till we count fifty five or sixty years of Age. This is a truth that our young Women can vouch for. They tell you that when a young Frenchman obliges 'em six times a night, a young Huron do's not rise to above half the number and with the same Breath they declare that the French are older in that Trade at Thirty-five than the Hurons are at fifty years of Age. . . . This intelligence, I say, led me to think that your Gout, Dropsy, Phthisick, Palsy, Stone and Gravel, and other Distempers above mention'd, are certainly occasion'd not only by the immoderateness of these Pleasures, but by the unseasonableness of the time, and the inconveniency of the way in which you pursue 'em; for when you have but just done eating, or are newly come off a fatiguing bout, you lie with your Women as often as ever you can, and that either upon Chairs or in a Standing Posture, without considering the Damage that accrues from such indiscretion; Witness the common practice of these young Sparks . . . who make their table serve for a Bed. . . . And besides, to make some Compensation for the Nudity of our Boys, our Girls are Modester than yours, for they expose nothing to open view but the Calf of their Leg, whereas yours lay their Breasts open in such a Fashion that our young Men run their Noses into 'em when they bargain about the Beaver Skins with your handsome She-merchants. Is not this a Grievance among the French that wants to be Redress'd?"

Lahontan was a major contributor to the geographical lore concerning the vast unknown territory of the lands in and beyond the Louisiana Purchase.

References: Allen, Passage through the Garden*; Sprague*

Laroque, François-Antoine (1784–1869): Trader employed by the North West Company, who spent part of the winter of 1804–05 in the vicinity of Fort Mandan. Laroque requested permission to accompany the Corps of Discovery when it left Fort Mandan in April 1805, a request that was denied, apparently to protect American interests and geographic discoveries. Rebuffed by Lewis and Clark, Laroque made his own reconnaissance of the Yellowstone watershed as far west as the Bighorn Mountains between June 2 and October 18, 1805. He thus predated William Clark in the Yellowstone River valley by more than a year. Laroque's notes on the Crow Indians are the first written descriptions of that tribe. Laroque was born on August 19,

1784, at Quebec. He studied briefly at the Collège de Montréal. After his father died in 1792, he traveled to the United States to learn English, the language in which he wrote his remarkable journals. Laroque left the West forever in 1806. He became a Montreal businessman, fought on the British side in the War of 1812, helped to found the Bank of Montreal, and retired from business in 1841. He was married in 1818 to Marie-Catherine-Emilie Cotte. In 1855 he entered a religious establishment in Quebec, where he spent the last fourteen years of his life in meditation and prayer. Two of Laroque's journals are extant. The first, usually called the "Missouri Journal," is an account of his November 1804–February 1805 visit to the Mandan and Hidatsa villages near to where Lewis and Clark wintered. The second, known as the "Yellowstone Journal," establishes Laroque's credentials as a serious explorer of what is now Montana. Laroque arrived at the Mandan and Hidatsa villages on November 24, 1804, in the company of Charles McKenzie, Baptiste Lafrance, William Morrison, Joseph Azure, Baptiste Turenne, and Alexis McKay, all employees of the North West Company, stationed at the company's post near the confluence of the Souris and Assiniboine Rivers. The Corps of Discovery first noticed Laroque on November 27, 1804. Warned by Lewis and Clark not to distribute flags, medals, or other symbols of British sovereignty, Laroque protested in his journals, "as I had neither Flags, nor medals, I Ran no Risk of disobeying those orders." Once this diplomatic contretemps had been settled, Laroque and the American commanders settled into mutually respectful relations and even something like friendship. Laroque visited the fort on November 29 and December 16, 1804, and January 18, January 30, March 2, March 22, and April 3, 1805. Clark reports on January 30 that "we gave him an answer respecting the request he made when last here of accompanying us on our Journey &c." The answer was no. Laroque reports that Meriwether Lewis devoted most of the day to repairing his (Laroque's) compass, "the glass being broke, & the needle not pointing due north." Laroque left the Fort Mandan vicinity on February 7, 1805, to return to the Assiniboine River for more trade goods. He was back by February 26. The remarkable speed of his round-trip in the depths of the plains winter (approximately three hundred miles) testifies to his discipline and the fierce competitiveness of

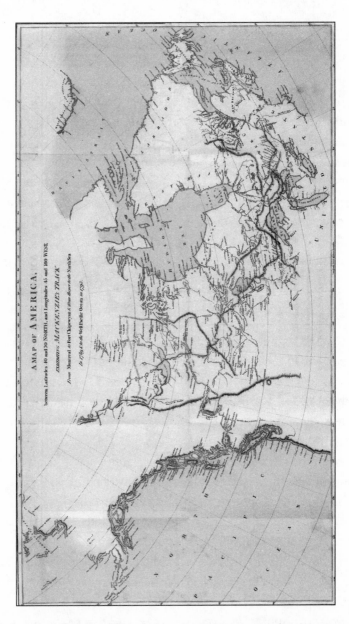

The Lewis and Clark Expedition was in many respects an urgent American answer to Alexander Mackenzie's transcontinental voyage. When Mackenzie signed his name on a rock overlooking the Pacific Ocean in 1793 and later published an account of his travels in 1801, Thomas Jefferson recognized it as a challenge from the British for control of the North American continent. "A Map of America between Latitudes 40 and 70 North, and Longitudes 45 and 180 West, Exhibiting Mackenzie's Track" by Alexander MacKenzie, courtesy of the Special Collections department, University of Virginia Library.

the Mandan Indian trade. On March 2, 1805, shortly after his return from his Assiniboine headquarters, Laroque visited the fort. Among other things, he announced that the X, Y, and North West Companies had merged. Laroque's Missouri Journal provides important details of the Corps of Discovery's stay at Fort Mandan. We learn that Charbonneau, with the captains' permission, continued to provide interpretation services to his British-Canadian trader clients. Indeed, Charbonneau emerges from Laroque's journal a more valuable and respectable man than shown in the writings of Lewis and Clark. Laroque (December 16, 1804) also provides one of the few detailed descriptions of Fort Mandan, the picket of which he says "is made so strong as to be almost Cannon Ball proof." We also learn intriguingly (January 18, 1805) that Lewis and Clark permitted Laroque to borrow a book from the Corps of Discovery's traveling library. Unfortunately, neither Laroque nor the captains records the title. And Laroque informs us (January 20, 1805) that the Hidatsa Indians, thanks to the Corps of Discovery's blacksmith works, "are grown very fond of them (the Americans) although they disliked them at first." See Lafrance, Jean Baptiste.

References: *Masson, vol. 1; Moulton, vol. 3*

Laudanum (laudinum): Tincture of opium, approximately a 10 percent opium solution, first concocted in 1510. Lewis purchased four ounces for fifty cents from the pharmacy of Gillaspay and Strong of Philadelphia. In a letter to his friend Dr. Caspar Wistar, which pretty much sums up the state of medicine in the early 1800s, Thomas Jefferson wrote, "Thus, fulness of the stomach we can relieve by emetic; disease of the bowels, by purgative; inflammation cases, by bleeding; intermittance [fever and chills] by Peruvian bark; syphilis by mercury; watchfulness, by opium." Among the afflictions treated with laudanum: Joseph Field's high fever, thirty drops; Sacagawea's pelvic inflammation, thirty drops. Private Weiser was given "a doze of the essence of peppermint and laudinum" for a "fit of cholic" and was able to ride. William Bratton's back ailment warranted thirty-five drops of laudanum and plentiful sage tea with diluted niter. They also added laudanum to the "volatile linniment" they applied on a poultice to Bratton's sore lower back. Joseph Potts was given a pill of opium by

Captain Clark, "owing to rideing a hard trotting horse"; it soon relieved him. Some laudanum spilled into the cache at the Great Falls and destroyed other contents in the medicine drawer. Lewis probably treated himself frequently with laudanum during the expedition and was believed to be addicted to the powerful narcotic effect of the medicine at the time of his death.

Reference: Chuinard, Only One Man Died

Lawson, Alexander (1773–1846): Scottish artist, who settled in Philadelphia and established himself as an engraver of animal portraits. In addition to completing several engravings based on mammals collected by Lewis and Clark, Lawson worked with his friend and fellow Scot naturalist Alexander Wilson on Wilson's nine-volume *American Ornithology.* Saying he did it "for the honor of the old country," Lawson engraved Wilson's plates for a pittance, but the work launched his career.

References: Johnson and Malone; Wilson, American Ornithology

Le Borgne (Kokookis, the One Eye): Hidatsa chief known for his skills in war, diplomacy, and oration. Blind in one eye and standing over six feet, he counciled with Lewis and Clark in 1804. Le Borgne considered going to Washington to see the Great Father but because of troubles with the Sioux turned down the invitation. The captains recognized him as an important contact and gave him a flag, shirt, and peace medals, along with other trinkets. Le Borgne's curiosity about York's skin prompted him to spit on his finger and try to remove the dark color. He also felt the texture of York's hair in order to be persuaded that he was not a white man. (Artist C. M. Russell immortalized the incident in his 1908 painting *York.*) On the return trip, they gave One Eye the swivel gun to win his favor: "I then a good deel of Ceremony made a preasent of the Swivel to the One Eye Chief and told him when he fired this gun to remember the words of his great father which we had given him. This gun had announced the words of his great father to all the nations which we had Seen &c. &c. after the council was over the gun was fired & delivered, they Chief appeared to be much pleased and conveyed it immediately to his village &c." Traders of the North West Company considered him a reliable informant because he helped them negotiate with the Crow tribe. Le Borgne was killed by a rival chief, Red Shield.

References: Schneider; Coues, History of the Expedition, *vol. 3; Moulton, vol. 8*

Leakens (possibly Seakens), Willard: One of the prospective privates who is listed as drunk by Clark on December 31, 1803, at Camp Dubois. He was discharged, "for theift with a Small Correction," on February 4, 1804.

Reference: Moulton, vol. 2

Leaping Fish (Pop Pank, Jumping Fish): Young Shoshone woman captured with Sacagawea and Otter Woman by the Minitaris at the Three Forks. Leaping Fish (Hunsaker calls her "Naya Nuki") escaped and returned to her people from the Mandan / Hidatsa, which may have been how she acquired her name. She related stories of attempted runs for freedom made by her two friends. Later reunited at Camp Fortunate, the young women expressed sincere emotion, when they recognized each other, as noted by Captain Lewis on August 17, 1805: "the meeting of those people was really affecting, particulary between Sah cah-gar-we-ah and an Indian woman who had been taken prisoner at the same time with her and who had afterwards escaped from the Minnatares and rejoined her nation." According to Clark, "The meeting of these young women had in it something particularly touching, not only from the ardent manner in which their feelings were expressed, but also from the real interest in their situation. They had been companions in childhood, in the war with the Minnataries they had both been taken prisoners in the same battle; they had shared and softened the rigors of their captivity till one of them had escaped from the Minnataries, with scarce a hope of ever meeting her friend relieved from the hands of her enemies."

References: Rees; Frazier; Hunsaker; Coues, History of the Expedition, *vol. 2*

Ledyard, John (1751–1789): Connecticut-born seaman who traveled to London and accompanied James Cook's third voyage in 1776 as corporal of marines. He kept a journal, which was later confiscated by the British. In 1783 he published his recollections of the voyage, including an account of Cook's death. Thomas Jefferson met him in Paris, where he disclosed an ambitious plan; according to Jefferson, he wanted to be the first to attempt to explore the American West. Ledyard, who Jefferson admitted suffered from "too much imagination," was "to go by land to Kamschatka, cross in some of the Russian vessels to Nootka sound, fall down into the latitude of the Missouri, and to and thro' that to the U.S." As historian David Lavender views it, Ledyard masterminded "one of the zaniest ideas in the history of exploration. He would cross Siberia to the Kamchatka Peninsula and embark for Alaska on a Russian fur ship. From there he would walk to the Mississippi, buoyed by two large hunting dogs, an Indian peace pipe, and a hatchet for chopping firewood." Although Jefferson assumed Ledyard had Catherine's permission to remain in her country, he was mistaken. The empress arrested Ledyard and sent him to Poland; after returning to France, he embarked for Cairo on a trip to explore the Nile River. Jefferson notes Ledyard failed in that endeavor as well; he killed himself the day before he was to depart.

References: Lavender, Land of Giants; *Jackson,* Letters

Lepage (Le Page), Jean Baptiste: One of two white men who joined the expedition at Fort Mandan on November 2, 1804 (the other was Charbonneau). He replaced Private John Newman, who was dismissed from the party after his court-martial on October 13, 1804. Lepage accompanied the permanent party to the Pacific Ocean, and back to St. Louis, where he was discharged with the rest of the corps on October 10, 1806. Nothing of certainty is known of Lepage before or after the expedition. According to Bernard De Voto, Lepage had been associated with one of the Hudson's Bay companies. According to William Clark's interlineations in the journals, Lepage had spent time in the Black Hills and found his way to the Mandan villages by way of the Little Missouri River. If this is true, Lepage is almost certainly the first white man to have traversed the Little Missouri country from its source near Devil's Tower to its mouth. It is sometimes alleged that Lepage had therefore ascended the Missouri River farther than any previous white man. This is almost certainly not true, but when the corps passed the mouth of the Little Missouri River on April 14, 1805, it was convinced that it was now entering terra incognita. Lewis writes, "this was the highest point to which any whiteman had ever ascended, except two Frenchmen (one of whom Lepage was now with us) who having lost their way had straggled a few miles farther tho' to what place precisely I could not learn." In the aftermath of the expedition, Lewis concluded (to Henry Dearborn, January 15, 1807) that Lepage was "entitled to no peculiar merit." Lewis paid Lepage only two-thirds of what the other enlisted men received, "as he did not perform the labours incident to the summer of 1804." A river in Oregon was originally named for Lepage; it is now known as the John Day River.

References: Moulton, vol. 4; Jackson, Letters

Lewis, Meriwether (1774–1809): The gifted and mercurial leader of what is now known as the Lewis and Clark Expedition.

Lewis was born on August 18, 1774, in Albemarle County, Virginia, the first son and second child of William and Lucy Meriwether Lewis. He was born within sight of Monticello and lived in the shadow of Thomas Jefferson for most of his life. Like Jefferson he was a Virginia planter. Like Jefferson he was a Republican. Like Jefferson he was a deist, or at least a freethinker. He espoused many of Jefferson's ideas, even adopted Jefferson's idiosyncratic spelling habits. Lewis dutifully attempted to carry Jefferson's vision of the American West into the landscape of the American interior.

Lewis was an Anglophobe, partly because he was an admiring protégé of Thomas Jefferson, but mostly, no doubt, because his father had died (November 1779) while serving the patriot cause in the American Revolution. Lewis was just five years old at the time. Not only did he not therefore really know his father, but his mother, Lucy, soon remarried, uprooted the family from Virginia, and resettled in faraway Georgia. All this, perhaps, Lewis attributed to British tyranny. The Canadian Charles McKenzie, who spent time with Lewis and Clark at Fort Mandan in the winter of 1804–05, wrote, "we lived contentedly and became intimate with the Gentlemen of the American expedition; who on all occasions seemed happy to see us, and always treated us with civility and kindness. It is true Captain

Lewis could not make himself agreeable to us—he could speak fluently and learnedly on all subjects, but his inveterate disposition against the British stained, at least in our eyes, all his eloquence."

Lewis joined the militia during the Whiskey Rebellion in 1794. When that conflict ended without serious bloodshed, he joined the regular U.S. Army and spent six years in the frontier army. He rose to the rank of captain by 1800. He was serving as paymaster of the First Infantry Regiment of the U.S. Army when Jefferson recruited him for service in the White House. He had also served as an army recruiter at Charlottesville, Virginia.

Lewis met William Clark late in 1795, when for a short time he served as an ensign in a rifle company commanded by Clark. Lewis had been court-martialed on November 6, 1795, for an incident, drink-related, involving a fellow officer by the name of Lieutenant Elliott. The formal proceeding charged Lewis with "abruptly, and in an Ungentleman like manner, when intoxicated, entering his [Eliott's] House on the 24th of September last, and without provocation insulting him, and disturbing the peace and harmony of a Company of Officers whom he had invited there." Although he was acquitted, Lewis was quickly reassigned. His new commanding officer was William Clark. Thus the court-martial did not set back Lewis's career as an army officer, and it produced the second most important personal contact of his life (after Jefferson). Clark resigned from the army early in 1796, but the two men maintained a level of contact during the seven years between their parting in the army and their historic meeting at the Falls of the Ohio in October 1803.

When Jefferson was finally confirmed as the third president of the United States on February 17, 1801, he scrambled to assemble his cabinet and staff. One of the first letters he wrote (February 23, 1801) was to Lewis, then in Pittsburgh, to invite him to come to Washington, D.C., to serve as Jefferson's private correspondence secretary. Whether Jefferson already had a voyage of western discovery in mind is impossible to determine, but he did make clear that one of the things that made Lewis an attractive candidate for the position was his "knolege of the Western country, of the army and of all it's interests & relations."

Lewis settled his affairs and made the journey to Washington,

D.C., where he arrived on April 1, 1801. Although the president by then was away at Monticello, Lewis settled in in the East Room of what we now call the White House. The East Room was partitioned to provide Lewis with both an office and personal quarters.

Lewis lived with Jefferson from April 1, 1801, until July 5, 1803. Unfortunately, neither man ever described these twenty-seven months in any detail. Lewis served more as Jefferson's aide-de-camp than his secretary. We know he served as the courier of Jefferson's first Annual Messages (state of the union messages) to Congress. We know that he escorted Jefferson's daughters into the District of Columbia when they visited in the late fall of 1802. We know that Lewis served as Jefferson's negotiator in the affair of honor that the president entered into with James Callendar, the scurrilous journalist who eventually "broke" the Sally Hemings story. We know that Lewis sometimes accompanied Jefferson on his trips to Albemarle County.

We know too that, if Jefferson is a reliable witness, Lewis suffered from depression during this period and ventured too often into the president's wine cabinet. In his famous biographical sketch of Lewis in 1813, Jefferson wrote, "While he lived with me in Washington, I observed at times sensible depressions of mind." In 1810 he had written, "He was much afflicted and habitually so, with hypochondria. This was probably increased by the habit into which he had fallen and the painful reflections that would necessarily produce in a mind like his." The habit, presumably, was excessive drinking.

Even so, Jefferson did not scruple to select Lewis to command the expedition. "I could have no hesitation in confiding the enterprize to him," he wrote. Whenever possible, Jefferson confided important tasks to Virginians and protégés, trusted lieutenants like William Short, James Monroe, James Madison, and Lewis. It was characteristic of Jefferson to prefer a friend and protégé (with whatever faults he had) over a more even-tempered stranger. Jefferson believed that the strenuousness of the expedition would either cure Lewis's melancholia or put it in temporary remission. As he wrote in 1814, "During his Western expedition the constant exertion which that required of all the faculties of body & mind, suspended these distressing affections." How Jefferson knew this is unclear, but it is certain that no evidence has ever been found in any of the journals written by any member of the expedition that Lewis suffered from his "depressions of mind" on his transcontinental journey. If he did, he disguised them sufficiently to prevent them from becoming a matter of concern to his colleagues. Jefferson rightly said that the young Lewis had exhibited "a passion for more dazzling pursuits."

Lewis's preparations for the expedition were masterful. Acknowledging that part of the credit belongs to Jefferson, it is hard to imagine that the Voyage of Discovery could have been better planned. Lewis spent his initial appropriation of $2,500 efficiently, and he managed to carry with him virtually everything (except enough blue beads!) that he could possibly need for a two- to three-year journey. It is true that the expedition ran short of a number of important, though not critical, supplies before it could return to St. Louis in September 1806, but this was inevitable given the length of the journey and the utter impossibility of finding any source of resupply between St. Louis and the Pacific Ocean. The president had provided Lewis with a universal letter of credit for use at the mouth of the Columbia or anywhere else Lewis might encounter white merchants of any nation, but no such encounter occurred. In March 1806 the expedition turned back toward civilization essentially bankrupt but nevertheless undaunted in its commitment to return home as quickly and painlessly as possible.

On the whole, the men recruited for the expedition proved to be precisely what the captains had in mind. The officers handled lapses of discipline with equal doses of fairness and severity, and by the end of the first year of travel the need for court-martials had disappeared. Nobody doubts that the greatest of Lewis's recruitments was his selection of William Clark to serve as his "partner in discovery." Lewis was a somewhat self-important man with a need to consider himself a modern Columbus or Captain Cook, but he recognized the need for a second (equal or nearly equal) leader on so complex and dangerous a mission, and it is quite possible that he was sufficiently self-aware to realize that Clark's even temper and commonsense resourcefulness would be needed to complement his own somewhat eccentric personality.

Lewis was a moody man. He was consumed by a sense of mission and a fear that something would (in his often-repeated words) "defeat the Expedition altogether." He had a propensity to philosophize and to reflect on the geopolitical significance of his mission, while Clark settled for a matter-of-fact description of the day's events. It is clear from his journals that he worried a great deal, and it is hard not to conclude that at times he found the pressures of the journey over-whelming. He appears to have been highly irregular in his habits as a journal keeper, but when words were flowing through his pen he was easily the most interesting, insightful, and articulate journal keeper of the expedition. Lewis had enormous powers of observation and a capacity to commit his experiences to paper in a way that is both sci-entifically precise and dramatic. Nobody who reads the journals of Lewis and Clark fails to wish that he had written much more than he did. He had the best sense of humor of any of the journal keepers, and he is the only one who took time to reflect on the state of his own soul.

Although the journals do not indicate precisely what role each of the leaders played, it is clear that Clark was the cartographer, Lewis the field scientist; Clark the day-to-day leader of the expedition, Lewis a somewhat detached strategist-in-residence; Clark the nuts and bolts negotiator with Indians, Lewis the embodiment of President Jeffer-son's Indian policies; Clark the spokesman of immediate authority, Lewis the holder of final authority; Clark the man of common sense, Lewis the man of reflection; Clark the leader for logistics, Lewis alone on the shore with his gun and his notebook and his Newfoundland dog, Seaman. If the evidence of the journals is correct, Indians seemed to find it easier to befriend Clark than Lewis. So did the Canadians who visited Fort Mandan. So did the Charbonneau family, particu-larly Sacagawea. So, perhaps, did most of the men of the expedition.

Lewis went to great lengths to ensure that Clark was treated as his equal, as co-captain, during and after the expedition, but he also seems to have felt the need to take charge when the great moments of discovery approached. It was Lewis who first reached the confluence of the Yellowstone and Missouri Rivers, "this long wished for spot" (April 25, 1805). It was Lewis who discovered the Great Falls of the Missouri on June 13, 1805. It was Lewis who discovered the source of the "mighty and heretofore deemed endless Missouri River" on August 12, 1805. It was Lewis who made first contact with the criti-cally important Shoshone Indians. And it was Lewis who first stood on the promontory overlooking the Pacific Ocean. Of all the journal keepers of the expedition, Lewis alone spoke of himself in the great tradition of exploration. On April 7, 1805, Lewis, not Clark, wrote: "This little fleet altho' not quite so respectable as those of Columbus or Capt. Cook, were still viewed by us with as much pleasure as those deservedly famed adventurers ever beheld theirs; and I dare say with quite as much anxiety for their safety and preservation."

Even if this pattern of taking the lead at moments of discovery suggests design and not coincidence, the journals indicate a very high level of harmony between Meriwether Lewis and William Clark. Their disagreements are comparatively trivial and they can be enumerated on a single hand. There is no surviving evidence of any disagreement on a serious issue. Lewis insisted that Clark be called captain in spite of his technically lower rank, and because Clark had been a captain in the Kentucky militia. When the expedition was safely home Lewis insisted that Clark be rewarded by Congress equally with himself. Nor is there the slightest evidence that Lewis ever bristled when (as was not infrequently the case) Indians preferred to offer hospitality or gifts to Clark rather than to himself. There is a certain nobility of soul in Meriwether Lewis that is everywhere evident in his writings and his actions.

Although the expedition did not find a Northwest Passage across the continent, and did not fill in every one of Jefferson's many grids with its full complement of data, Jefferson never repented his decision to select Lewis to command the expedition. Eight years after the expedition and five years after Lewis's disturbing death, Jefferson summed up his character:

> Of courage undaunted, possessing a firmness & perseverance of purpose which nothing but impossibilities could divert from it's direction, careful as a father of those committed to his charge, yet steady in the maintenance of order & discipline, intimate with the Indian character, customs & principles, habituated to the hunting life, guarded by exact observation of the vegetables & animals of his own country, against losing time in the description of objects already possessed, honest, disinterested, liberal, of sound understanding and a fidelity to truth so scrupulous that whatever

> he should report would be as certain as if seen by ourselves, with all these qualifications as if selected and implanted by nature in one body, for this express purpose, I could have no hesitation in confiding the enterprize to him.

It is hard to conceive that any endorsement could be more comprehensive and positive than this. Jefferson asserts, in retrospect, knowing that Lewis's governorship had miscarried, knowing that Lewis had not written the promised and critically important book about his travels, knowing that Lewis had probably killed himself in the prime of life, that Lewis had brought so many requisite talents to his command (1803–06) that it was as if nature had created such a man for the express purpose of leading the Voyage of Western Discovery.

Lewis returned to Washington triumphantly on December 28, 1806. Not only had he fulfilled the president's directives with admirable energy and decorum and brought all but one of his men home alive (two if one counts John Colter, who chose to stay in the wilderness), but he had also personally escorted a Mandan Indian delegation to the nation's capital as a capstone to the expedition. Jefferson was thrilled, Congress grateful. The compensation package passed by Congress on February 28, 1807, provided Lewis $1,228 in cash (double pay while on service with the Corps of Discovery) and a warrant for sixteen hundred acres of land. At Jefferson's behest Lewis was appointed governor of the Territory of Upper Louisiana. He was dilatory about taking up that post. He did not arrive in St. Louis until March 8, 1808. Perhaps in part because his long absence had given his lieutenant, a man named Frederick Bates, time to consider himself as the de facto governor, in part because the fur aristocrats of St. Louis were not prepared to conform to the economic and political ideals of the Jefferson administration, and in part because, as Bates put it, "his [Lewis's] habits are altogether military & he never can I think succeed in any other profession," Lewis had an exceedingly frustrating tenure as governor.

On July 15, 1809, Secretary of War William Eustis challenged Governor Lewis's handling of the U.S. government's efforts to return the Mandan Indian leader Sheheke-shote to his tribe in what is now North Dakota. Eustis not only refused to honor Lewis's commitment of $500 for additional gifts to the upriver Indians, over and above the

$7,000 already earmarked for the mission, but rebuked him for not seeking authorization for the extra funds, and hinted that he considered Lewis's handling of the affair a conflict of interest between public and entrepreneurial initiatives on the upper Missouri. Eustis closed his letter by assuring the governor that "the President [James Madison] has been consulted and the observations herein contained have his approval."

This letter, more than anything else, seems to have precipitated the final crisis of Lewis's life. On August 18, 1809, his thirty-fifth birthday, Lewis wrote an agonized and somewhat incoherent letter to Secretary Eustis protesting his innocence, and declaring, "all I wish is a full and fair Investigation." Lewis informed Eustis that the War Department's challenge had "effectually sunk my Credit; brought in all my private debts." And he went to great lengths to assure Secretary Eustis that he was a man of honor who could not be driven to treasonous activity no matter how unfairly he was treated by the U.S. government. "Be assured Sir, that my Country can never make 'A Burr' of me—She may reduce me to Poverty; but she can never sever my Attachment from her."

Lewis decided to travel to Washington (and presumably Monticello) to try to repair his reputation. It was on that journey, on October 11, 1809, that he died of a gunshot wound to the skull, a gunshot wound to the abdomen, and (some witnesses alleged) knife incisions across his flesh. Among his last words were, "I have done the business my good Servant give me some water," and "I am no coward; but I am so strong, [it is] so hard to die." On the night of his death, he was staying at a crude hostelry called Grinder's Stand on the Natchez Trace, approximately seventy miles from Nashville. Eyewitness accounts are somewhat contradictory, but the evidence points to suicide. William Clark and Thomas Jefferson independently concluded that their beloved friend had taken his own life. Clark wrote, "I fear O' I fear the weight of his mind has overcome him, what will be the Consequence?" And five years later Jefferson wrote categorically, "About 3. oclock in the night [October 11, 1809] he did the deed which plunged his friends into affliction and deprived his country of one of her most valued citizens."

Meriwether Lewis never married. After the expedition he courted several women, but without success. To his old friend Mahlon Dickerson, on November 3, 1807, he wrote, "What may be my next adventure, God knows, but on this I am determined, to get a wife." By May 29, 1808, Lewis was describing himself to Clark as "a musty, fusty, rusty old bachelor."

William Clark never ceased to love and respect his former "partner in discovery." Clark named his oldest son Meriwether Lewis Clark. Family tradition holds that in his later years Clark became convinced that Lewis had not committed suicide after all, but had been murdered on the Natchez Trace.

References: Wood and Thiessen; Ambrose; Jackson, Letters; *Holmberg,* Dear Brother; *Moulton, vols. 4, 5*

Lewis's syringa (*Philadelphus lewisii*): Also known as mock orange. State flower of Idaho. It resembles a cultivated plant called the privet. On August 11, 1805, Lewis wrote, "Capt. C observed some bunches of privy near the river." It is one of the specimens collected for the herbarium by Meriwether Lewis on the Clearwater and Blackfoot Rivers in present-day Idaho and Montana in its flowering season of May and July 1806. Along with using the stems of this plant for fashioning arrows, native peoples made combs, knitting needles, basket rims, and cradle hoods from the syringa. Its branches could be boiled for a tea to treat sore chests and as a treatment for eczema and other skin eruptions.

References: Craighead; Moulton, vol. 5; Kershaw

Lewis's wild flax (*Linum lewisii*): Discovered by Meriwether Lewis on July 18, 1805, near the Dearborn River and named by Frederick Pursh in his honor. It is a delicate blue flower with reedlike stems, also known as blue flax or prairie flax, which flowers in June, July, and the first part of August. Lewis collected seeds from this flower on July 23, 1805, near present-day Townsend, Montana, and later specimens of the fully grown plant in July of 1806 along the Sun River. Europeans and Indians used wild flax seeds and oil as a cooking ingredient, in poultices, and as a laxative. The boiled leaves could be taken internally as a treatment for heartburn.

References: Kershaw; Moulton, vol. 12

Lewis's woodpecker (*Melanerpes lewis*): The species was first sighted by Lewis near Helena, Montana, on July 20, 1805: "I saw a black woodpecker today about the size of the lark as black as a crow. I indevoured to get a shoot at it but could not. It is a distinct species of woodpecker; it has a long tail and flys a good deel like a jay bird." Lewis gave a much more detailed description on May 27, 1806, near Kamiah, Idaho: "The black woodpecker which I have frequently mentioned and which is found in most parts of the roky Mountains as well as the Western and S.W. mountains. I had never an opportunity of examining until a few days since when we killed and preserved several of them. This bird is about the size of the lark woodpecker or turtle dove, tho' it's wings are longer than either of those birds. The beak is black, one inch long, rather wide at the base, somewhat curved, and sharply pointed; the chaps are of equal length. Around the base of the beak including the eye and a small part of the throat is of a fine crimson red. The belly and breast is a curious mixture of white and blood reed which has much the appearance of having been artifically painted or stained of that colour. The red reather predominates. The top of the head back, sides upper surface of the wings and tail are black, with a gosey tint of green in a certain exposure to light. The underside of the wings and tail are of a sooty black. It has ten feathers in the tail, sharply pointed, and those in the center reather longest, being 2½ inches in length. The tongue is barbed, pointed, and of elastic cartilaginous substance. The eye is moderately large, purple black and iris of a dark yellowish brown. This bird in it's actions when flying resembles the small redheaded woodpecke common to the Atlantic states; it's note also somewhat resembles that bird. The pointed tail seems to assist it in seting with more eas or retaining it its resting position against the perpendicular side of a tree. The legs and feet are black and covered with wide imbricated scales. It has four toes on each foot of which two are in rear and two in front; the nails are much curved long and remarkably keen or sharply pointed. It feeds on bugs worms and a variety of insects." Lewis also referred to it as the black woodpecker (August 2, 1805) and a lark woodpecker (July 1, 1806). He preserved a "skin" of the bird while at Camp Chopunnish. Naturalist Alexander Wilson, hired by Lewis to "make drawings of such of the feathered tribe as had been preserved and were new," made the first (1811) technical descriptions of the bird and was the first to call this black woodpecker "Lewis's woodpecker." Wilson gave it the Latin name *Asyndesmus lewis*, changed in 1983 to *Melanerpes lewis*. The *National Audubon Society Field Guide to North American Birds* lists Lewis's woodpecker as ranging from southern British Columbia and Alberta south to central California, northern Arizona, and northern New Mexico. It winters from southern British Columbia and Oregon to Colorado and south to northern Mexico; and wanders east to the Great Plains. According to the *Guide*, "Unlike most woodpeckers, Lewis' does not peck at wood for food and is seen more often on top of a fence post than clinging to it vertically. As with the Acorn Woodpecker, its main method of getting food is catching flying insects; both species also store acorns and other nuts for winter, and sometimes damage fruit orchards. Lewis' is the common woodpecker of mountain ranchlands and some ranchers call it the 'crow woodpecker' because of its dark color, large size, and slow flight." Thomas Jefferson gave the specimen Lewis preserved to Charles Willson Peale for his museum. Upon failure to procure national endowment for the museum, Peale gave Lewis's woodpecker to the Boston Museum, along with other species of preserved birds from the expedition. According to naturalist and scholar Paul Cutright, the remains of this collection eventually found a home in the Museum of Comparative Zoology at Harvard University. Cutright writes, "It is the only animal known to exist of all of those collected and brought back by the Expedition."

References: Moulton, vols. 4, 7; Wilson, American Ornithology; Udvarty; Cutright, Pioneering Naturalists

Lisa, Manuel (1772–1820): Fur trader and entrepreneur. Lisa played an important role in the development of St. Louis–based economic activity on the Missouri and Yellowstone Rivers. He managed to prosper under both Spanish and American control of the Louisiana Territory. Born in the Spanish district of the Gulf of Mexico, possibly in Cuba, by 1798 Lisa was living in St. Louis. He had considerable contact with Lewis and Clark during the staging period of the expedition in and near St. Louis. He visited Camp Wood during the winter of 1803–04. This was before he undertook his own career as a

Missouri River trader. In 1807 Lisa established a trading post called Fort Raymond at the mouth of the Bighorn River on the Yellowstone. In 1809 Lisa helped to found the Missouri Fur Company. Although Meriwether Lewis, like many others, found Lisa exasperating, Lewis's brother Rueben and William Clark became his partners in this enterprise. By 1810 he had established a post at the Three Forks of the Missouri. Lisa was as energetic and indispensable as he was disliked. By 1814 he had acquired a post north of present-day Omaha, which came to be called Fort Lisa. He is sometimes credited with being the first white settler in what is now Nebraska. As an Indian subagent for the U.S. government, Lisa proved effective in countering British influence in the region during the War of 1812. In 1818 he married Mary Hampstead Keeney of St. Louis. Lisa died on August 12, 1820, in St. Louis. Several members of the Lewis and Clark Expedition later worked for Manuel Lisa. John Colter was under Lisa's employ when he "discovered" the Yellowstone Basin. George Drouillard was working for Lisa when he was killed by the Blackfeet in 1810.

Reference: Oglesby

Little Ice Age (1400–1850): A climatological event that produced more severe winters and cooler summers than normal. During this period glaciers increased their size and corn agriculture among the Cree Indians of Canada was abandoned. The deep snows encountered by Lewis and Clark in the Bitterroot Mountains may have been a result of this weather phenomenon; it is worth noting that their thermometers were accurate to within five to ten degrees, so the record cold temperature of forty-five degrees below zero observed by William Clark at Fort Mandan in December 1804 is considered reliable.

Reference: Dietrich

Little Thief (Wearrugenor): Oto chief, designated by Lewis and Clark on August 3, 1804, at the Platte River when he agreed that peace would be a benefit for the Otos and Missouri. The meeting ended in disappointment for Lewis and Clark who did not understand the realities of intertribal trade practices on the plains. Little Thief told the captains, "My father always directed me to be friendly with the white people, I have always done so and went often to the french, give

my party pieces of Paper (commissions) & we will be glad." Little
Thief wanted quality trade goods from the white men; he was not
much concerned with their origin.

Reference: Moulton, vol. 2

Livingston, Robert (1746–1813): Thomas Jefferson's minister to
France and the chief negotiator for the United States in securing the
real estate agreement with France known as the Louisiana Purchase,
wherein 828,000 square miles of land known as the Louisiana Territory was bought for $15 million, or 3 cents an acre. This doubled the
size of the United States.

Locust Hill, Ivy, Albemarle County, Virginia: Birthplace of Meriwether Lewis and the land he inherited from his father, William
Lewis. Lewis's widowed mother, Lucy, married Captain John Marks,
and the family moved to Georgia. When Marks died Lewis brought
his family back to Locust Hill. The original house burned after Mrs.
Marks passed away in 1837, but another house was built on the original foundations. It is now a privately owned residence. A descendant
of Jane Meriwether Lewis Anderson, Meriwether's sister, owns a
tract adjacent to Locust Hill, which includes the Lewis family grave-
yard. Meriwether Lewis's mother, sister, brother Rueben, and many
of Rueben's descendants are buried there.

References: Henley, personal communication; M. N. Lewis

Lolo Hot Springs: In present-day Missoula County, Montana, near
the Montana-Idaho border. These seven separate springs were first
visited by the corps on September 13, 1805, when Clark "tasted this
water and found it hot & not bad tasted . . . in further examonation I
found this water nearly boiling hot at the places it Spouted from the
rocks on the Side of the Mountain of the Same texture I put my finger
in the water, at first could not bare it in a Second." According to Gary
Moulton these granitic rocks are "of the Cretaceous-age Idaho
batholith very near the batholith's contact with rocks of the Precam-
brian Belt Group." On the return journey the crew enjoyed the hot
springs again, as Lewis noted on June 29, 1806: "the prinsipal spring
is about the temperature of the warmest baths used at the Hot Springs

in Virginia in this bath which had been prepared by the Indians by stoping the river with stone and gravel, I bathed and remained in 19 minutes [Clark could stand it for only 10] it was with great dificulty I could remain thus long and it caused a profuse sweat. . . . both the men and the indians amused themselves with the use of the bath this evening. I observed that the indians after remaining in the hot bath as long as they could bear it ran and plunged themselves into the creek the water of which is now as cold as ice can make it; after remaining here a few minutes they returned again to the warm bath, repeating this transision several times but always ending in the warm bath." In her book *Names on the Face of Montana*, Roberta Carkeek Cheney writes, "There has been much conjecture concerning the origin of the name Lolo. One idea is that the Indians named it for Lewis, but in their language it came out Lou Lou and finally Lo Lo. Another suggestion is that it was named by early French traders for LeLouis, and that the present form is a corruption. Still another is that lolo is a Nez Perce word meaning muddy water. [In his master's thesis Don] Omundson concluded that it is an Indian rendition of Lawrence, the name of an old French trapper, and that the Flathead Indians unable to sound the *r* replaced it with an *l*." Lolo Hot Springs has operated as a plunge, or resort, on and off since 1885.

References: *Moulton, vols. 5, 8; Omundson study cited in Cheney,* Names on the Face of Montana

Loyal Land Company: A land charter company formed in 1749 by Thomas Jefferson's father, Peter, Dr. Thomas Walker, and several other prominent Albemarle County Virginians to investigate land holdings in the Alleghenies and Mississippi. They were granted 800,000 acres of what were then known as "western" lands. Walker headed expeditions into Kentucky and established which lands were suitable for investment. Along the way Walker and his companions discovered "Cave Gap," later known as the Cumberland Gap. Within three years, inspired by the writings of Daniel Coxe, they proposed an expedition to the source of the Missouri in search of a northwest passage. The men of this company were, like Jefferson himself, highly influenced by the theory of symmetrical geography and the notion of height-of-land. The expedition did not take place.

Lydia: Trading vessel out of Boston sailing under Captain Samuel Hill (known to the Natives as Haley) into the vicinity of the Columbia estuary where they stopped to pick up wood in November 1805 or April 1806. Although the crew of the *Lydia* did not encounter Lewis and Clark, they rescued two white captives from the Vancouver Island Indians. One of them, John Rodgers Jewitt, kept a journal of his imprisonment, which was later embellished and published in 1807 under the title *A Journal Kept at Nootka Sound*. In this account Jewitt recalls seeing the Jefferson medals the Indians received from the explorers who visited a "fortnight before." (No exact date is mentioned and author O. D. Wheeler thinks it was probably later than Jewitt reckoned.) Captain Hill wrote his own account and described the "paper" given to him by the natives who said Lewis gave it to them and which listed the members of the expedition and how they arrived on the coast. The letter later arrived in Philadelphia with Hill of the *Lydia* by way of Canton, China. Several theories exist regarding the lack of contact between the expedition's captains and the crew of the *Lydia*. Even if the dates coincided, they may simply have missed each other. Some speculate the Chinook deliberately did not tell Lewis and Clark about the ship. Perhaps Jewitt made an error in recalling the dates. In any event, none of the men would return by sea as Thomas Jefferson originally proposed in his Letter of Credit. At the time Jefferson's navy was stretched thin, and he could not afford to send any ships for the corps's return or resupply. In *The Way to the Western Sea*, David Lavender writes the ship may have been in the estuary before Lewis and Clark's arrival, which would account for the many references to vessels they heard as they proceeded down the Columbia.

References: Moulton, *vol. 6; Jewitt; Wheeler; Lavender,* Way to the Western Sea*; Coues,* History of the Expedition, *vol. 3*

M

Mackay, James (1759–18??): Scottish trader who explored and lived with the Mandan in the upper Missouri region in the 1780s. He worked for the Spanish enterprise Missouri Company. Mackay's companion, John Evans, whom he sent to the Pacific, went as far as the Mandan villages in search of a mythical lost tribe of "Welsh Indians." According to historian Donald Jackson, "Mackay lived in the St. Charles district while Lewis and Clark were wintering at Wood River; a note by Clark 10 Jan. 1804 mentions that Mackay had just come down the Missouri from a surveying trip." Jackson feels it is most likely the material known as the Mackay-Evans journals was given to the captains personally by James Mackay while they were stationed at Wood River. See Evans, John Thomas.
Reference: Jackson, Letters

Mackenzie, Alexander (1763–1820): Scottish-Canadian explorer who became the first European to cross the North American continent north of Mexico. In 1789 Mackenzie, an employee of the Montreal-based North West Company, became the first European to travel the entire length of the Mackenzie River to the Arctic Ocean. In 1793 he threaded his way across the Canadian Rockies all the way to the Pacific Ocean. He traveled with a fellow Scot, Alexander Mackay, two Indians, and six Canadian voyageurs. Although Mackenzie succeeded in reaching the Pacific, he had traveled much of the way by land, not water, and he considered his voyage something of a failure. His route would certainly not be useful as an artery for the Canadian fur trade. The Lewis and Clark Expedition was, in many respects, an urgent American answer to Mackenzie's transcontinental voyage. On a rock overlooking the Pacific Ocean, Mackenzie had written, "Alexander Mackenzie, from Canada, by land, the twenty-second of July, one thousand seven hundred and ninety-three." Clark, at the Pacific twelve years later, wrote, "Capt William Clark December 3rd

1805. By land. U. States in 1804–1805." It seems unlikely that so tight a verbal echo was accidental. It was the publication of Mackenzie's *Voyages from Montreal, on the River St. Lawrence, Through the Continent of North America, to the Frozen and Pacific Ocean,* late in 1801, that seems to have spurred President Jefferson to action. Among other things, the book proposed a unification of fur trade enterprises in Canada and an aggressive British drive to wrest the fur trade and the lower Columbia River basin from the Americans.

Reference: *Mackenzie; Benson*

Madison, James (1751–1836): Thomas Jefferson's secretary of state, fourth president of the United States, principal author of the Bill of Rights, father of the United States Constitution. Madison was Thomas Jefferson's neighbor, chief political collaborator, and best friend. When Jefferson circulated a draft of his instructions to Captain Lewis among his five-member cabinet, Albert Gallatin (treasurer) and Levi Lincoln (attorney general) made important suggestions, while Madison, who was not only Jefferson's chief collaborator through life but the one person Jefferson trusted to edit his state papers and important private letters, was largely silent. According to Donald Jackson, Secretary Madison made only four minor suggestions. Even so, at the Three Forks of the Missouri, Captain Lewis named one branch the Madison in honor of Jefferson's prime minister. Ironically, Madison may have helped to precipitate Meriwether Lewis's suicide. Thomas Jefferson left Washington, D.C., forever on March 11, 1809. His handpicked successor, James Madison, was less interested in the West than Jefferson, and less willing to protect Meriwether Lewis from bureaucratic scrutiny. The new secretary of war, William Eustis, challenged a number of Lewis's vouchers. The famous rebuke of July 15, 1809, from Eustis to Governor Lewis made it clear that President Madison had been directly consulted on the matter. "The President has been consulted and the observations herein contained have his approval." This, for Meriwether Lewis, may have been the unkindest cut of all. It was this letter, more than anything else, that led to Lewis's final journey. On September 15, 1809, at Fort Pickering, near today's Memphis, Tennessee, Lewis wrote a letter to the president of the United States. It was one of the last letters he ever wrote. Among other things, Lewis apologizes for having communicated so infrequently, and he announces his intention to seek exoneration for his controversial public expenditures. "I bring with me duplicates of my vouchers for public expenditures &C which when fully explained, or reather the general view of the circumstances under which they were made I flatter myself they receive both approbation & sanction." When James Neelly reported Lewis's death to former president Jefferson on October 18, 1809, he wrote, "previous to the Governors death he requested of me in case any accident happened to him, to send his trunks with the papers therein to the President, but I think it very probable he meant to you." Jefferson, with his usual attention to detail and sense of honor, made sure that the trunks were sent on to the current president, Mr. Madison. Equally characteristically, Jefferson sent Madison detailed suggestions about how the trunks' contents should be sorted and distributed. On July 1, 1813, President Madison appointed William Clark as the first governor of the newly created Missouri Territory, an office Clark held until Missouri statehood in 1821. Generally speaking, Madison's western policies were an extension of Jefferson's, though it is clear from both the volume and the content of the Madison administration documents that the fourth president did not regard the West as one of his primary interests.

Reference: Jackson, Letters

Ma-laugh: Chief of the lower Chehalis village on the great chute of the Columbia.

Reference: Moulton, vol. 6

Mammoth: Immense quadruped related to the elephant, the object of great fascination to the scientists of the Enlightenment. Some, like Jefferson, engaged in wishful thinking that the mammoth might still exist somewhere in North America. In fact, all species of mammoth were extinct ten thousand years before Lewis and Clark undertook their expedition. The search for living mammoths in the age of Jefferson is not so naive as it now seems. The idea of extinction offended Enlightenment scientists, who assumed that the universe was purposeful and fundamentally orderly, that all species were simultaneously created at the beginning of the world, and that the extinction of any single species might jeopardize the intricate chain of being that linked mice to mammoths to man through a series of gradations of species sophistication. Jefferson lived a generation before the theory of evolution shattered any notion of the nonextinction of species. Speaking for his age, Jefferson wrote, "I cannot . . . help believing that this animal [the megalonyx], as well as the mammoth, are still existing. The annihilation of any species of existence, is so unexampled in any part of the economy of nature which we see, that we have a right to conclude, as to the parts we do not see, that the probabilities against such annihilation are stronger than those for it. . . . For, if one link in nature's chain might be lost, another and another might be lost, till this whole system of things should vanish by piecemeal." In his instructions to the French scientist André Michaux, in 1793, Jefferson, on behalf of the American Philosophical Society, specifically placed the mammoth on the list of desiderata. "Under the head of Animal history, that of the Mammoth is particularly recommended to your enquiries . . ." (April 30, 1793). Jefferson was a man who stubbornly clung to his favorite ideas, but he was also a rational being. By 1803 it had begun to dawn on him that the quest for a living mammoth might be chimerical. In his instructions to Lewis, Jefferson asked his protégé merely to keep his eye open for "the remains and accounts of any [animals] which may be deemed rare or extinct." During his descent of the Ohio River in August 1803, Meriwether Lewis made a stop at Big Bone Lick on behalf of Jefferson. Lewis collected bones for the president and wrote a detailed account of his investigation. Unfortunately, the shipment was lost at Natchez and never recovered. The only reference to the mammoth in the journals of Lewis and Clark is found in the *Fort Mandan Miscellany*, the interim report that the captains prepared for the U.S. government during the winter encampment in North Dakota, near the mouth of the Knife River. Lewis's summary of rivers and creeks states, "on the South side of this river [the Osage] 30 leagues below the Osage Village, there is a large lick, at which some specimens of the bones of the Mammoth have been found; these bones are said to be in considerable quantities, but those which have been obtained as yet, were in an imperfect state. Mr. Peter Chouteau, a gentleman of St. Louis, mande an attempt some years since to explore this lick, but was compelled to desist from his labour, in consequence of the quantity of water discharged into the lick from a neighbouring spring, which he had not the means or the leasure to divert; since which time, no further attempt has been made. The specimens obtained by Mr. Chouteau were large; but much mutilated." After the Lewis and Clark Expedition, Jefferson pressed William Clark to obtain for him mammoth remains at Big Bone Lick, on the Kentucky side of the Ohio, near Cincinnati. Jefferson paid for Clark's excavations with his own money, but the commission was actually on behalf of the American Philosophical Society, which was attempting to create a comprehensive collection of mammoth remains. The Clark family eventually sent three boxes of Big Bone Lick artifacts to the White House. As president, Jefferson made available a Navy Department pump to further his friend Charles Willson Peale's attempt to extricate a mammoth skeleton at Newburgh in New York State. Jefferson's enthusiasm for the woolly mammoth was the source of much mirth, especially among his Federalist detractors. Mammoths were, in a sense, the "dinosaurs" of Jefferson's world, mysterious creatures, perhaps prehistoric, of enormous stature, raising questions about man's place in the great chain of being, and inspiring virtually unlimited curiosity in devotees of natural wonders. The French scientist Georges Cuvier's (1769–1832) pioneering discovery of true dinosaurs was largely unknown to Jefferson.

References: Moulton, vol. 3; Jackson, Letters

Marias River: Journals editor Nicholas Biddle confused this with the Mandan/Hidatsa Indians' Milk River, the "River which scolds at all others" (Milk). The Marias starts east of present-day Glacier National Park and flows into the Missouri at Loma; it is also known as a miniature Missouri. Lewis and Clark camped near its confluence with the Missouri on June 2, 1805, and debated which fork was the true Missouri: "what astonishes us a little is that the Indians who appeared to be so well acquainted with the geography of this country should not have mentioned this river on wright hand if it be not the Missouri; the river that scolds at all others as they call it if there is in reallity such a one, ought argeeably to their account, to have fallen in a considerable distance below." Historian Bob Doerk theorizes that the Indians did not neglect to describe the Marias, they simply did not know it existed.

Named by Lewis the "Maria's" River in honor of Lewis's cousin Miss Maria Wood, "the hue of the water of this turbulent and troubled stream but illy comport with the pure celestial virtues and amiable qualifications of that lovely fair one." Later historians and mapmakers dropped the apostrophe. Writing on June 8, 1805, Lewis extolled the beauty of the area, "one of the most beautifully picteresque countries I ever beheld, through the wide expanse of which, innumerable herds of living anamals are seen, it's borders garnished with one continued garden of roses while it's lofty and open forrests are the habitation of miriads of the feathered tribes who salute the ear of the passing traveler with their wild and simple, yet sweet and cheerfull melody." Faced with an unexpected fork in the river and the advice of the seasoned crew to take the northern fork, the leaders studied the situation. With their "cogitating facilities" hard at work, the captains scouted both the Marias and the Missouri for several days. The turbidity of each branch, the kind of bottom it flowed over, the Arrowsmith map, and the information received from the Minitaris all came into careful consideration at this juncture. At Fort Mandan the Indians had told the explorers that the water of the Missouri was nearly transparent at the Great Falls; this was the case with the water flowing to the south. After ruminating for a precious seven days, Lewis and Clark decided to take the southern fork. Notably all of the men voted to go with the final verdict of the captains rather than follow their own instincts. Lewis described his interest in the Marias: "it was a noble river, one destined to become in my opinion an object of contention between the two great powers of America and Great Britain with rispect to the adjustment of the Northwesternly boundary of the former; and it will become one of the most interesting branches of the Missouri in a commercial point of view." Lewis knew that if the Marias River extended to fifty degrees north it would establish a northern boundary to the United States, so he determined to return to the Marias on the journey home. On that excursion, accompanied by Drouillard and the Field brothers, he encountered the Piegan Indians, which resulted in the death of He That Looks at the Calf (Side Hill Calf), one of the warriors. Lewis shot the man in self-defense and Reubin Field stabbed another man in the chest.

References: Saindon, *"River Which Scolds All Others"*; Moulton, *vol. 4; Thwaites*, Original Journals, *vol. 2; Doerk, personal communication*

Marks, Lucy Meriwether Lewis (1752–1837): Meriwether Lewis's mother; daughter of Thomas Meriwether of Cloverfields, Virginia. She married a cousin, William Lewis, and bore him three children: Jane, Meriwether, and Rueben. When William died in 1779, Lucy became a widow at the age of twenty-seven and, along with her brothers, took over management of the thousand-acre Lewis estate of Locust Hill. She next married Captain John Marks and migrated to Georgia. Lucy once led a party of settlers and their families to a new settlement in Georgia when her husband was unable to proceed. Upon John Marks's death, the family returned to Locust Hill. Lucy was fondly known as Aunt Marks to family and friends. She counted among her treasured possessions collections of silver and books, which were equally distributed among her children upon her death. As a Yarb doctor, or dispenser of herbal cures, she inspired the habit of careful observation in her sons, and eventually two of them became doctors. Her skill in smoking hams and turkeys earned her a loyal following; neighbor Thomas Jefferson bought smoked meats from her. Family lore indicates she chased off rowdy British soldiers, and on another occasion shot a buck and had it dressed and cooked by the time the hunting party returned. "She was sincere, truthful, industrious, and kind without limit," according to a Georgia neighbor, George Gilmer, who noted her son Meriwether "inherited the energy, courage, activity and good understanding of his admirable mother." After joining the army in 1794, Meriwether wrote Lucy Marks several earnest and sincere letters. "The general idea is that the Army is the school of debauchery but believe me it has ever proven the school of experience and prudence to your affectionate son." Writing to his mother about his new assignment for President Jefferson, Lewis hoped to assuage her fears: "I go with the most perfect preconviction in my own mind of returning safe and hope therefore that you will not suffer yourself to indulge any anxiety for my safety." On March 31, 1805, Lewis wrote his mother a lengthy description of Fort Mandan and before signing off with "devoted filial affection," he wrote, "I request that you will give yourself no uneasiness with respect to my fate, for I assure you that I feel myself perfectly as safe as I should do in Albermarle; the only difference between 3 or 4 thousand miles and 130, is that I cannot have the pleasure of seeing you as often as I did while at

Washington." Lewis had hoped to bring his mother to St. Louis when he was governor of the Louisiana Territory. She died at age eighty-six in 1837 and is buried at Locust Hill. In addition to the Lewis children, she had two others by John Marks: John Hastings Marks and Mary Garland Marks.

References: Bakeless; Jackson, Letters; *M. N. Lewis*

Mat houses: Observed by Lewis and Clark among the Chimnapams and Kokulks (Yakimas and Wanapams), as Clark recorded on October 17, 1805, on the Columbia near the Yakima River: "The Houses or Lodges of the tribes of the main Columbia river is of large mats made of rushes, Those houses are from 15 to 60 feet in length generally of an Oblong Squar form, Suported by poles on forks in the iner Side, Six feet high, the top is covered also with mats leaveing a Seperation in the whole length of about 12–15 inches wide, left for the purpose of admitting light and for the Smok of the fire to pass which is made in the middle of the house.—The roughfs are nearly flat, which proves to me that rains are not common in this open Countrey Those people appear of a mild disposition and friendly disposed—They have in their huts independant of their nets gigs & fishing tackling each bows & large quivers of arrows on which they use flint Spikes. Theire ammusements are Similar to those of the Missouri. they are not beggerley and receive what is given them with much joy."

Reference: Moulton, vol. 5

Matsi: Mandan word for white men, which translates to "pretty people."

Reference: Burroughs, personal communication

McClellan, Robert (1770–1815): Veteran of the Ohio Indian wars who served as an Indian scout or spy under Anthony Wayne. A hunter, trapper, and trader, and old acquaintance of Lewis and Clark, and the leader of one of a dozen trading parties who encountered the expedition on its way back down the Missouri on September 12, 1806. Clark notes he "receved us very politely, and gave us all the news and occurrences which had taken place in the Illinois within his knowledge." Biddle added the note that McClellan was an old acquaintance. Ordway wrote in his entry for the twelfth, "Mr. McLanen informed us that the people in general in the united States were concerned about us as they had heard that we were all killed then again they heard that the Spanyards had us in the mines &C." On the following day, according to Clark, McClellan gave each man a Dram at sunrise. Ordway tells a different story: "Mr. McLanen Gave our party as much whiskey as they would drink and gave our officers three bottles of wine." McClellan tried to establish a trading post at Council Bluffs in 1807, but because of pressure from hostile Sioux Indians he abandoned the plan and instead joined the Astorians, journeyed to the Columbia, and returned with Robert Stuart via the South Pass in Wyoming. His name and feisty character received mention in Washington Irving's *Astoria*. McClellan eventually moved back to St. Louis, where he died and was buried on the Clark farm. The inscription on his tombstone, most likely written by Clark, reads, "To the memory of Capt. Robert McClellan. This stone is erected by a friend who knew him to be brave, honest, and sincere; an intrepid warrior, whose services deserve perpetual rememberance. A.D. 1816."

Reference: Moulton, vols. 8, 9

McCrachan, Hugh: Irish free trader, occasionally employed by the North West Company located at Fort Assiniboine. McCrachan lived part time among the Mandan and Hidatsa people on the upper Missouri in the late 1700s and early 1800s. On October 26, 1804, Clark notes he came through the Mandan village "to trade for horses and Buffalo robes." Previously, in 1797, British explorer David Thompson wrote in his journal, "bled poor Hugh McCrachan, an honest Irishman, he is of the greatest service to me, as by his Information only I guide myself and conduct the March." McCrachan also guided Alexander Henry from Fort Assiniboine to the Mandan villages in 1806. Lewis and Clark sent a letter with McCrachan to the principal agent of the North West Company at Fort Assiniboine, appealing for information and assistance and notifying the company of their presence and passport from the British minister to the United States.

References: Wood and Thiessen; Moulton, vol. 3

McKeehan, David: Bookseller and teacher; lived in Wellsburg, Virginia, and may have met a neighbor, expedition member Patrick Gass. McKeehan operated a "Book and Stationery" business in 1807 in front of the courthouse in Pittsburgh. He is thought to have graduated from Dickenson College in 1787 and been admitted to the Pennsylvania Bar in 1792. McKeehan purchased, edited, and published Gass's journals of the expedition, "with geographical and explanatory notes by the Publisher," in 1807 before Lewis or any other journalist (including Private Robert Frazier, who had issued a prospectus with Lewis's permission) published an account. After seeing the McKeehan prospectus, Lewis wrote a letter to the public, one week before publication, dated March 14, 1807, in the *Philadelphia National Intelligencer*, stating, "I have considered it a duty which I owe the public, as well as myself to put them on their guard with respect to such publications. . . ." Lewis expressed concern that the publication of Gass's journal would "depreciate the worth of the work" he maintained he would produce. McKeehan countered with a scathing public reply, printed in the *Pittsburgh Gazette*. He denied any need for permission and cast doubt on Lewis's honor, suggesting he had already received just compensation for his efforts and was now trying to keep all the profits and glory for himself. He rebuked the captain in an extremely personal way and even went so far as to suggest that Lewis's gunshot wound had not been accidental. To further make his case, in his prospectus for the one-volume work, which would sell for one dollar, McKeehan had already added the testimonal Lewis wrote on behalf of all the men of the corps, including Gass: "As a tribute justly due the merits of the said Patrick Gass, I with chearfulness declare, that the ample support, which he gave me, under every difficulty; the manly firmness, which he evinced on every occasion; and the fortitude with which he bore the fatigues and painful sufferings incident to that long voyage, intitles him to my highest confidence and sincere thanks, while it eminently recommends him to the consideration and respect of his fellow citizens." Some Lewis and Clark scholars accuse McKeehan of heavily editing Gass's journal; however, other than adding thirty footnotes and some flowery language Gass probably did not write, McKeehan's version did not change the content of the journal. The original Gass journal was either destroyed or lost. Subsequent editions were published in London, Paris, Weimar, and in Philadelphia with illustrations by Mathew Carey included.

References: MacGregor, Journals of Patrick Gass; *Moulton, vol. 10; Jackson,* Letters; *Cutright,* History of the Lewis and Clark Journals

McKenzie, Charles (1774–1855): Scottish-born clerk for the North West Fur Company who joined in four trading expeditions to the Mandan and Hidatsa villages on the upper Missouri in 1804–06. He visited with Lewis and Clark in the winter of 1804–05 and later wrote in his journal of Lewis's strong anti-British leanings and recorded a Gros Ventre chief's opinion regarding the party: "only two sensible men among them, the worker of Iron and the mender of guns." After the merger of the North West Fur Company with the Hudson's Bay Company, McKenzie stayed on as clerk but was judged harshly by a governor of the company's Northern Department. George Simpson wrote in his character book of 1832: "McKenzie Charles. A Scotchman about 56 years of Age. 29 years in service. A queer prosing long winded little highland body, who traces his lineage back to Ossian and claims the Laureatship of Albany District now that Chief Factor Kennedy is gone. Never was a bright active or useful man even when there was a greater Dearth of Talent in the country than now, but fancies himself neglected in being still left on the list of Clerks notwithstanding a Servitude of nearly 30 years; his Day is gone by, and I think it would be highly inexpedient to promote such men who have no other claim to advancement than their antiquity." McKenzie did manage to keep a journal of his travels and observations on the Mandan and Hidatsa nations; his eyewitness accounts of these people, decimated by smallpox in 1837–38, authenticates those of other visitors', including Lewis and Clark's. His memoir was eventually published in 1889 and 1890.

References: Wood and Thiessen; Williams

McMahon, Bernard (1775–1816): Prominent gardener, seed merchant, and nursery owner in Philadelphia; a friend of Thomas Jefferson; author of the first book on American gardening. On March 22, 1807, President Jefferson sent McMahon seeds from the expedition and advised him that Meriwether Lewis would provide more. Jefferson was sending some of his own share, he wrote, because he would not get back to Monticello in time to plant them in the present growing season. It was McMahon who convinced Meriwether Lewis to engage German-born Frederick Pursh to make scientific descriptions of the plants collected by the expedition. Pursh, said McMahon, was "better acquainted with plants, in general, than any man I ever conversed with on the subject." After the death of Lewis, McMahon wrote a letter to Thomas Jefferson asking what he wanted done with the plant collections of the expedition. He explained to the former president that Frederick Pursh had undertaken drawings of the preserved plants and would of course expect to be compensated. McMahon was the author of *The American Gardener's Almanac*, which is considered the first book-length study of gardening in the New World. From McMahon, Jefferson obtained expedition seeds for the snowberry (*Symphoricarpos aureum*), Missouri currant (*Ribes odoatum*), and yellow currant (*Ribes oroatum*) and grew them at Monticello.

Reference: Bedini, Thomas Jefferson: Statesman of Science

McNeal, Hugh (d. 1825? 28?): Private. Clarke lists him as from Kentucky and on army muster rolls as of September 1811. William Clark lists him as dead on his list of expedition members 1825–28. McNeal is mentioned in the journals for his hunting skill, and specifically for his encounter with a grizzly bear on the return journey. Lewis immortalized him when he quoted McNeal's words upon reaching (August 12, 1805) the source of the Missouri River: "two miles below McNeal had exultingly stood with a foot on each side of this little rivulet and thanked his god that he had lived to bestride the mighty & heretofore deemed endless Missouri." One of three men (along with Goodrich and Gibson) mentioned as suffering from the effects of "Louis Veneri" at Fort Clatsop during the winter of 1805–06. A creek near present-day Dillon, Montana, was named "McNeal's Creek" by the captains but later became known as Blacktail Deer Creek.

References: Clarke; Moulton, vol. 5

Medicine: The concept in Indian religion of discerning spiritual energy in things that are outside the control or the understanding of the observer. The editors of the *Oxford English Dictionary* (*OED*) argue that

Indian awe over white men's powers was first focused on the drugs and medical equipment of the newcomers and that the word later became generalized to cover all powers, objects, and situations beyond Indian comprehension. Meriwether Lewis provided his most detailed definition of *medicine* on August 17, 1805, while he was observing the habits of the Shoshone Indians: "every article about us appeared to excite astonishment in ther minds; the appearance of the men, their arms, the canoes, our manner of working them, the back man york and the segacity of my dog were equally objects of admiration. I also shot my air-gun which was so perfectly incomprehensible that they immediately denominated it the great medicine. the idea which the indians mean to convey by this appellation is something that eminates from or acts immediately by the influence or power of the great sperit; or that in which the power of god is manifest by it's incomprehensible power of action." Among the medicine items in the kit of Lewis and Clark (if the captains are reading Indian responses correctly) were Meriwether Lewis's air gun, phosphorescent matches, the compass as manipulated by a magnet, the fire-making capacity of a magnifying glass, the "segacity" of Lewis's Newfoundland dog, Seaman, and the blackness of Clark's slave York. Probably the Indian responses to what was exotic in the world of Lewis and Clark was more subtle than the journalists realized. Nor is it certain that all of the Indians they met responded to their gadgetry in the same way. The Canadian trader Charles McKenzie, who witnessed the interplay between the expedition and the earth-lodge villagers near Fort Mandan, quotes the Hidatsa skeptic Le Borgne as declaring, "All white flesh is medicine." Given Le Borgne's general disdain for Lewis and Clark, this seems to mean that white people possess a technological superiority that gives them power beyond their intrinsic merit in Indian country. By European standards, the Indians of America were pantheists. They professed a variety of religious views, but they all seemed to believe that divine energy, or spiritual essences, percolated through the physical universe and that it was possible for humans, under certain circumstances, to gain access to those energies. The Indians were disposed to see medicine in phenomena, which their white counterparts analyzed through the lenses of science and reason. Thus Patrick Gass reports that at a Mandan Indian feast his hosts "presented a bowlful to a buffalo head, saying, *'eat that.'* Their superstitious credulity is so great, that they believe by using the head well the living buffaloe will come and that they will get a supply of meat" (January 20, 1805). Gass, speaking on behalf of the Enlightenment, regarded as "superstitious credulity" what the Mandan considered an essential propitiation to the buffalo.

On the whole the men of the Lewis and Clark Expedition responded to Indian medicine with derision. On August 25, 1804, William Clark reported what he took to be the Indian understanding of uncanny energies at the Spirit Mound near today's Vermillion, South Dakota, then provided an explanation wholly in keeping with his scientific outlook. Large numbers of birds frequent the hill, Clark explained, because prevailing winds drive insects against the side of the hill. "One evidence which the Inds Give for believeing this place to be the residence of Some unusial Spirits is that they frequently discover a large assemblage of Birds about this mound—is in my opinion a Suffient proof to produce in the Savage mind a Confident belief of all the properties which they ascribe it." A few weeks later, as he entered what is now North Dakota with an Arikara leader, Clark nonchalantly wrote, "This Chief tells me of a number of their Treditions about Turtles, Snakes, &c. and the power of a perticiler rock or Cave on the next river which informs of everr thing none of those I think worth while mentioning—" Interestingly enough, it is Meriwether Lewis, who is usually considered less sympathetic to Indian culture than Clark, who seems most open to the possibility that there is medicine in the American West. After a series of mishaps involving one of the expedition's boats, he writes, "it appears that the white perogue, which contains our most valuable stores, is attended by some evil gennii." A few days later (May 31, 1805), he writes, "I fear her evil gennii will play so many pranks with her that she will go to the bottom some of those days." After a day in which he has harrowing encounters with a grizzly bear, charging buffalo, and some kind of burrowing cat, Lewis writes, "I . . . did not think it prudent to remain all night at this place which, really, from the succession of curious adventures wore the impression on my mind of enchantment." The Lewis and Clark Expedition was the expression of the Enlightenment, which coupled a deep fascination about Indian culture with an unrelenting skepticism toward things of the spirit. William Clark's religious views, if any, are hard to ascertain. Meriwether Lewis was clearly a deist like his famous patron. Jefferson, in fact, in an 1820 letter to John Adams, wrote, "When once we quit the basis of sensation all is in the wind. To talk of *immaterial* existences, is to talk of *nothings*." The men of the expedition carried what the historian of ideas Morris Berman has called a "disenchanted" mind-set into a world that was seen by Indians as fully alive with spirit. On the outbound journey, 1804–05, Lewis and Clark came to *understand* the Indian concept of medicine. On the return journey in 1806, bankrupt of trade goods, they *manipulated* the concept as a means of obtaining food, firewood, shelter, and political cooperation. The first recorded use of the word *medicine* in the Indian spiritual sense, according to the *OED*, comes in 1805 in the journals of Zebulon Pike. "This they called their great medicine; or as I understood the word, dance of religion," Pike wrote.

References: MacGregor, Journals of Patrick Gass; *Moulton, vols. 3, 5; Morris Berman; Pike, quoted in OED*

Medicine River: Tributary of the Missouri in Cascade County located near present-day Great Falls, Montana. Lewis noted it on June 14, 1805. A few days later, after hearing a mysterious noise "resembling precisely the discharge of a piece of ordinance of 6 pounds at the distance of 5 or six miles," Clark commented, "it is probable that the large river just above those Great falls which heads in the derection of the noise has taken it's name Medicine River from this unaccountable rumbling Sound, which like all unaccountable thing with the Indians of the Missouri is Called Medicine." Biddle theorized the noise came from an avalanche, but recent speculations include a theory that shifting sands no longer present account for the sound. The river today is called the Sun River, perhaps because the Blackfeet names for medicine and sun resemble each other. Hank and Carol Fischer credit the Blackfeet, who used the term *medicine* because of "unusual mineral deposits along its banks which possessed remarkable medicinal properties. One can only speculate on how the river came to be known as the Sun." Roberta Carkeek Cheney states, "The Indians called this river Natae-osueti which French trappers took to mean Medicine or Sun River."

References: Jackson, Among the Sleeping Giants; *Fischer and Fischer; Cheney,* Names on the Face of Montana; *Moulton, vol. 4*

Menard, Pierre (1766–1844): French-Canadian merchant, business-man, developer. He opened a store at Kaskaskia in 1790 and part-nered with François Valle in business on the Missouri. Active in local politics, Menard married into the prominent St. Louis Chouteau fam-ily after his first wife died. He partnered with Manuel Lisa to trap furs up the Missouri River in 1807 and worked with George Drouillard. He was appointed by Governor Meriwether Lewis to accompany Chief Sheheke on his return upriver in 1809. Menard spent the winter at Fort Raymond and built a fort at Three Forks for the Missouri Fur Company in 1810, but hostile Blackfeet Indian tribes kept profits down. Menard worked on an Illinois legislative council and gradually drew enough support to become lieutenant governor even though technically he had not been a United States citizen long enough to earn that honor. He fathered ten children and gave much of his money to nearby Indian tribes. In 1813 William Clark named him subagent for the Illinois Indians. Menard complained constantly about treat-ment of the Illinois tribes and mediated between the Winnebagos and other tribes for two presidents. In addition he worked to promote the Illinois Central Railroad. There is a county in Illinois named after him. Menard earned the respect of all those who knew him, Indians and non-Indians alike.

References: Leroy Hafen, Mountain Men and the Fur Trade*; Thrapp*

Mercury: "One lb. of Mercurial, 4 oz. of Calomel mercury pills, and ½ lb of Jalap," the powdered plant *Exogonium jalapa*, the Mexican Morning Glory plant, were purchased in Philadelphia from Gillaspay and Strong for medicines "for the use of M. Lewis Esquire, on his tour up the Mississippi river." At the time of the expedition, mercury was commonly used as a cathartic, but because cases of mercury poisoning occurred after prolonged use, its prescription declined. The captains used it as a purgative as prescribed by Dr. Benjamin Rush, who used it as an ingredient in his infamous "Rush's bilious pills." Mercury was a common treatment for syphilis and was believed to be effective because it successfully treated the symptoms. Chuinard indicates Lewis and Clark followed the standard practice of administering mer-cury to the syphilitic patient until he salivated. On January 27, 1806, Lewis wrote, "Goodrich has recovered from the Louis veneri [syphilis] which he contracted from amorous contact with a Chinnook damsel. I cured him as I did Gibson last winter by uce of murcury." McNeal also came down with "the pox" during their stay at Fort Clatsop. Both Gibson and Goodrich developed further symptoms six months later. Long-term mercury poisoning is suspected as the cause of early death in some of the members of the expedition, although it remains a theory.

References: *Moulton, vol. 6; Chuinard,* Only One Man Died

Michaux, André (1746–1802): French botanist working in Canada who alerted the American Philosophical Society of British interest in the headwaters of the Missouri and was originally commissioned by the society to find the shortest and most convenient route of communication between the United States and the Pacific Ocean. According to geographer John Logan Allen, his instructions, from society member Thomas Jefferson, "illustrate the concept of the practicable water communication as Jefferson saw it in 1793, thus providing a preliminary view of his knowledge of western geography; and second they provided a model for the instructions that Jefferson was to give Meriwether Lewis ten years later." Jefferson's instructions to Michaux are printed in Jackson's *Letters of the Lewis and Clark Expedition.* Michaux's expedition was thwarted due to his involvement in the "Citizen Genet conspiracy" between France and the United States.

References: *Allen,* Passage through the Garden; *Jackson,* Letters

Mississippi River: Lewis and Clark spent very little time on the Mississippi River, unless one believes, as Thomas Jefferson did, that the upper Mississippi is the tributary and what we call the Missouri is the true continuation of the river that flows past Memphis and New Orleans. It was the Mississippi that precipitated the foreign relations crisis that led to the Louisiana Purchase in 1803. Alarmed by the retrocession of Louisiana from Spain to France, and the possibility that one or both colonial powers would close the lower Mississippi to American commerce, Jefferson instructed his diplomats Robert Livingston and James Madison to secure New Orleans or some other port of deposit in the lower Mississippi. Jefferson's diplomatic efforts in the spring of 1803 were precipitated by the news, slow in reaching

Washington, D.C., but alarming when it came, that the Spanish intendant at New Orleans had closed the Mississippi River to American
commercial traffic. Jefferson was interested in the Missouri country
and intended for the United States to obtain it in the course of its history, but in the short term he was more interested in keeping the Mississippi open and obtaining the Floridas (today's state of Florida and
the coastal lands adjoining the Gulf of Mexico). The Louisiana Purchase solved the problem of the lower Mississippi. Before the
Louisiana Purchase was consummated, Jefferson instructed Meriwether Lewis to spread the rumor that his expedition intended to
ascend the Mississippi rather than the Missouri River. Jefferson was
afraid of adverse reaction among Spanish colonial authorities. Alone
among foreign powers, Spain had declined to issue Lewis a passport
for his western tour. Lewis and Clark reached the mouth of the Ohio
(at today's Cairo, Illinois) on November 14, 1804. They spent a week
at the confluence of the Ohio and the Mississippi taking celestial
observations, measuring the two great streams, and examining the
countryside. On November 20, 1804, they began their ascent of the
Mississippi proper. By December 10 the expedition had reached St.
Louis, and by December 12 the boats reached the mouth of Wood
River, where the expedition would spend the winter. It is important to
remember that the Lewis and Clark Expedition spent the winter of
1803–04, from December 12, 1803, until May 14, 1804, on the Mississippi River, on the Illinois shore, across from the mouth of the Missouri.

While Lewis and Clark were ascending the Missouri, Lieutenant
Zebulon Pike explored the Mississippi River. He was traveling on
orders from General James Wilkinson, not under the direct instructions of President Jefferson. Pike left St. Louis with twenty soldiers
and a seventy-foot keelboat on April 9, 1805. Pike formed a winter
encampment at today's Little Falls, Minnesota, and proceeded on by
sled to Mille Lacs Lake, which he took (erroneously) to be the source
of the Mississippi River. He had returned to St. Louis by April 30,
1806. Although his expedition was less successful than that of Lewis
and Clark, Pike's journal and map were important documents in the
history of the exploration of the upper Mississippi valley.

On the return journey, the Lewis and Clark Expedition spent just one day in the Mississippi River, September 23, 1806. They had spent the night of September 22 at Cantonment Belle Fontaine on the bank of the Missouri River three miles above its mouth. The Mississippi is also important to the Lewis and Clark story because it was a factor in the establishment of the northern boundary of the United States. Initially President Jefferson believed that the northern boundary should be determined by drawing a line due west of the source of the Mississippi. In 1818, when Secretary of State John Quincy Adams settled the border with Great Britain, the line was drawn not from the source of the Mississippi, at Lake Itasca, but from the Lake of the Woods. That established the forty-ninth parallel as the boundary.

Missouri River: The Lewis and Clark Expedition eased into the mouth of the Missouri River at four P.M. on May 14, 1804. Meriwether Lewis reached what he took to be the source of the Missouri on August 12, 1805. Lewis was wrong. If one discounts the nominal beginning of the Missouri proper at the confluence of the Gallatin, Madison, and Jefferson Rivers, the source of the Missouri is usually said to be the Red Rock Lakes in Beaverhead County, Montana. What Lewis bestrode was Trail Creek, approximately seventy-five miles west and slightly north of the source of the Missouri. Lewis had in fact reached the source of one of the dozens of small capillary feeder streams of the upper Missouri. His assumption that he had now at last triumphed over what he called the "mighty and heretofore deemed endless Missouri River" was perfectly plausible, if technically imprecise. It was, moreover, closer to the path he needed to take to get to navigable waters of the Pacific Ocean than are the Red Rock Lakes. The Missouri River, at 2,464 miles, is the longest river in North America and the principal tributary of the Mississippi River. Its watershed includes 528,000 square miles. Aside from a handful of side excursions on the White, Platte, and Marias Rivers, the expedition seldom strayed from the immediate vicinity of the Missouri. From May 14 until October 26, 1804, the flotilla of three boats ascended from the mouth of the river to earth-lodge villages at the great bend of the Missouri at the mouth of the Knife River. From April 7 to August 26,

A view of Black Eagle Falls before dam construction. It took the expedition a month to portage the five separate falls that make up the Great Falls. Haynes Foundation Collection, Montana Historical Society.

1805, the expedition traveled from what is now central North Dakota to the head of navigation of the Missouri River and its upriver tributaries. On the return journey, subgroups of the expedition resumed navigation of the Missouri (this time downstream) in July 1806, but it wasn't until August 3, 1806, at the confluence of the Missouri and Yellowstone Rivers, that all members of the expedition were again on the Missouri at the same time. Lewis, who by now knew something about the dynamics of rivers, wrote on August 10, 1805, "I do not believe that the world can furnish an example of a river running to the extent which the Missouri and Jefferson rivers do through such a mountainous country and at the same time so navigable as they are." The only obstruction they had come to in more than two thousand miles of travel was the cluster of falls constituting the Great Falls of the Missouri River. Lewis believed that this boded well for the idea of a Northwest Passage, a navigable water route that would link the Atlantic and Pacific Oceans. He would soon discover that the Columbia and its tributaries were not so hospitable to navigation.

The Missouri River proved to be a formidable obstacle. Currents are strong and unpredictable, and before the Corps of Engineers tamed the river in the second half of the twentieth century, the Missouri routinely changed its course, swept sandbars downstream, and destabilized its banks at every bend. The river, particularly above the mouth of the Platte, is beset with sandbars and false channels, and it often spreads out in its valley in a manner that makes its navigation channel dangerously shallow. The immense turbidity of the water made it difficult for boatmen to spot objects in the water. That same turbidity wrought havoc on the digestive systems of the men of the expedition, who were drinking water straight from the river. Logs, snags, and sawyers in the river posed a potentially lethal threat. When the fierce plains winds blow from the right direction, sandstorms in the Missouri valley can be oppressive, and the river can be whipped into waves difficult for bateaux to negotiate. Meriwether Lewis was first able to wade across the Missouri River on August 2, 1805, in the Beaverhead valley in southwestern Montana. "This is the first time I ever dared to wade the river," he wrote, "tho' there are many places between this and the forks where I presume it might be attempted with equal success."

Thomas Jefferson had a keen interest in the Missouri River, though he never was far enough west to witness its flow. He believed that the Missouri was the principal stream, and that the upper Mississippi was a tributary of the main stream. In his only book, *Notes on the State of Virginia*, Jefferson wrote, "The Missouri is, in fact, the principal river, contributing more to the common stream than does the Mississippi, even after its junction with the Illinois." Modern geographers tend to agree, as did Jefferson's contemporary Amos Stoddard, who published *Sketches, Historical and Descriptive of Louisiana* in 1812. In a love letter written in Paris on October 12, 1786, to Maria Cosway,

Jefferson made a Herculean vow: "I hope in God, no circumstance may ever make either [Mrs. Cosway or her husband Richard Cosway] seek an asylum from grief! With what sincere sympathy I would open every cell of my composition, to receive the effusion of their woes! I would pour my tears into their wounds; and if a drop of balm could be found on the top of the Cordilleras, or at the remotest sources of the Missouri, I would go thither myself to seek and to bring it."

References: Moulton, vol. 5; Stoddard; Merrill Peterson

Moccasins: Shoes made out of leather or animal hides. Spring of 1805 found the Corps of Discovery in sore need of shoes. Lewis had not received money for additional supplies despite adding twenty-one people to the roster. As noted by historian Robert R. Hunt, Dr. Benjamin Rush, in his *Rules of Health*, wrote, "Shoes made without heels, by affording equal action to all the muscles of the legs, will enable you to march with less fatigue, than shoes made the ordinary way." The lack of a trained shoemaker did not deter the men of the Corps of Discovery from adopting the natives' style of shoe or "mockerson." They took advantage of the awls and needles Lewis brought to trade with the Indians and became experts at producing and mending their own. While at Fort Clatsop the men fashioned some 358 pairs of moccasins, still not enough to get them all home shod. Although not thick enough to protect against the troublesome prickly pear cactus of the upper Missouri, the moccasin served, for the most part, as adequate foot covering under the harshest of circumstances. A common practice among the tribes of the plains involved "reading moccasins," so that by design and outline a footstep or shoe could be traced to a specific tribe. Sacagawea, herself a former member of the Shoshone or "people of the broken moccasins," practiced the skill. "The Indian woman with us examined the mockersons which we found at these encampments and informed us that they were not of her nation the Snake Indians, but she beleived they were some of the Indians who inhabit the country on this side of Rocky Mountains [Blackfeet]." Hunt calls her, in addition to an interpreter, a "consultant on the mockersons language." The captains frequently mention the various styles of moccasins, or lack thereof, found among the tribes they came into contact with. Clark observed on June 23, 1805, that "the men mended their mockersons with double Soles to Save their feet from the prickley pear." Lewis noted that the Shoshone moccasins were sometimes ornamented with porcupine quills sewn in the shape of various figures: "some of the dressey young men orniment the tops of their mockersons with the skins of polecats [skunks]." The journals note moccasins given to the captains as gifts, and on August 20, 1805, Lewis described the Shoshone making and repairing moccasins for the men. A sample pair of moccasins may have been among the "clothing" included in the Indian collection sent on to Jefferson with Corporal Warfington.

References: Rush, cited in Jackson, Letters; *Hunt, "Mockersons"; Moulton, vols. 4, 5, 6*

Monture Creek (Seaman Creek): This creek flows into the Blackfoot River, west of present-day Ovando, Montana. Lewis and his party followed it on the return trip when they crossed the Continental Divide using the Nez Percé trail to the buffalo country near Great Falls. It derives its present name from a family of fur traders who settled in the area in the early 1800s. When he was researching the place-names of Lewis and Clark in Montana, Donald Jackson found that the original name referred to Meriwether Lewis's Newfoundland dog. Jackson looked closely at the original journals and discovered the name "Seaman" had been misread by editor Milo Quaife and others as "Scannon." Ernest Osgood also used the spelling "Scannon" when he edited William Clark's field notes, and the mistake was not corrected until Jackson's discovery in June 1985.

References: Jackson, "Call Him a Good Old Dog"; Osgood, Field Notes

N

Natchez Trace: The primitive wilderness road, between Nashville, Tennessee, and Natchez, on the Mississippi River, on which Meriwether Lewis was traveling when he died violently in 1809. The Natchez Trace (or Trail) follows old Indian trails for approximately five hundred miles. At the request of the U.S. government, General James Wilkinson negotiated treaties with representatives of the Chickasaw (October 24, 1801) and Choctaw (December 17, 1801) nations to enable non-Indians to cross their territories. Mississippi territory commissioners located the lower sections of the road in 1802. It was not until Congress appropriated six thousand dollars in 1806 that the northern section of the road was developed. The Natchez Trace was never much more than a primitive trail, but it was an important artery for land travel between the lower Mississippi and Tennessee Rivers. It was developed by the United States in part to lessen dependence on the Mississippi as a commercial conduit. Early development predates the Louisiana Purchase by two years. By the time Meriwether Lewis chose it for his trip to Virginia and Washington, D.C., in 1809, the trace supported postal service. Whether the trace was infested by thieves and ruffians in 1809 is a contested issue. It is possible that Meriwether Lewis was murdered by outlaws simply because he was clearly a man of means. When Lewis left St. Louis on September 4, 1809, he was intending to descend to New Orleans and travel the rest of the way to the nation's capital by sea. At Fort Pickering (near today's Memphis), he changed his mind and determined to travel overland to Virginia. He left Fort Pickering on September 29, 1809. He intersected the Natchez Trace near the Chickasaw Agency (today's Houston, Mississippi) and traveled overland approximately two hundred miles before he reached Grinder's Stand (near today's Hohenwald, Tennessee). Most of the stands (or inns) on the Natchez Trace were operated by Indians. On October 10, 1809, Lewis made it clear to his traveling companion, James Neelly, that he would stop for the night at the first stand operated by white entrepreneurs. Lewis's death occurred early on October 11, 1809. He was thirty-five years old. Lewis's body is buried near the junction of the Natchez Trace and Tennessee highway 20. The gravesite was fenced in 1810. A columnar monument was erected on the site in 1848 by the state of Tennessee.

Neelly, James: Major; Indian agent to the Chickasaw nation 1809–12. He was asked by his commanding officer, Gilbert Russell, to accompany Meriwether Lewis on the trail called the Natchez Trace from Chickasaw Bluffs overland through to Nashville and then on to Washington, where Lewis was to face an investigation into his finances. Russell had observed enough odd behavior by Lewis to think him a danger to himself and to forbid him from drinking any hard liquor while he was at Fort Pickering. Neelly left Lewis with his servants while they were en route to Grinder's Stand (an inn) with the intention of meeting there after Neelly caught several missing horses. Before he arrived, however, Lewis had killed himself, although some maintain his cause of death remains unknown. Neelly reported what he learned of Lewis's death on October 11, 1809, in a letter written to Thomas Jefferson on October 17, 1809, based on accounts from Mrs. Grinder. Neelly recalled that Lewis had appeared "at times deranged in mind" several days before the night he "shot himself in the head with one pistol & a little below the Breast with the other." Major Neelly buried Governor Lewis on the side of the trail and sent his belongings, including the journals, on to Jefferson. According to one Lewis biographer, Richard Dillon, who believed Lewis was murdered, the Natchez Trace was a dangerous place, as shown by Major Neelly's reports in 1812 and his requests for more manpower and weaponry to defend against Indian attack. Russell suspected Neelly of foul play in the incident at Grinder's Stand and accused him of getting Lewis drunk and of taking his guns, pocket money, and other articles. Russell himself was a man of dubious distinction who was discharged from the army in 1815.

Reference: Jackson, Letters; *Daniels; Dillon*

Newman, John (d. 1838): Private, discharged; Pennsylvania-born recruit from Captain Bissell's First Infantry Company. On October 13, 1804, near Stone Idol Creek, Captain Clark recorded, "Newmon confined for Mutinous expressions." He was tried by a jury of nine of his peers, sentenced to seventy-five lashes, and discharged from the corps. Among those peers only Ordway mentions the incident. In a letter on his behalf to Secretary Dearborn and the War Department, Lewis wrote, "John Newman was a private in the Infantry of the U'States army who joined me as a volunteer and entered into an enlistment in common with by which he was held and mustered as one of the permanent party. In the course of the expedition, or shortly before we arrived at the Mandan Villages he committed himself by using certain mutinous expressions which caused me to arrest him and to have him tryed by a Court Martial formed of his peers; they finding him guilty sentenced him to receive seventy five lashes and to be discharged from the permanent party, this sentence was enforced by me, and the punishment took place. The conduct of this man previous to this period had been generally correct, and the zeal he afterwards displayed for the benefit of the service was highly meritorious. In the course of the winter while at Fort Mandan, from an ardent wish to attone for the crime which he had committed at an unguarded moment, he exerted himself on every occasion to become usefull. This disposition induced him to expose himself too much to the intense cold of that climate, and on a hunting excurtion he had his hands and feet severely frozen with which he suffered extreme pain for some weeks. Having recovered from this accident by the 1st of April 1805, he asked forgivness for what had passed, and begged that I would permit him to continue with me through the voyage, but deeming it impolitic to relax from the sentence, altho he stood acquited in my mind, I determined to send him back, which was accordingly done. Since my return I have been informed that he was extremely serviceable as a hunter on the voyage to St. Louis and that the boat on several occasions owed her safety in a great measure to his personal exertions, being a man of uncommon activity and bodily strength. If under these circumstances it should be thought proper to give Newman the remaining third which will be deducted from the gratuity awarded Paptiest La Page who occupied his station in the after part of the voyage I should feel myself much gratifyed." According to Clarke, Newman married Olympia Dubreuil of St. Louis in 1832 and spent his remaining years trading on the upper Missouri, where he was killed by the Yankton Sioux in 1838.

References: Osgood, Field Notes; *Charles G. Clarke; Jackson,* Letters

O

Old Sieur Menard (d. 1804): French fur trader or "residenter" tenant trader. Associate of Hugh Heney and René Jesseaume who passed on information to the expedition. Lived with the Mandan and Hidatsa for approximately twenty-five years prior to Lewis and Clark's arrival. Old Menard was the first white man to visit Yellowstone River and trade with the Crow Indians, and he may have traded at the Hudson's Bay Post on the Red River. Old Menard lived at the Awaxawi Hidatsa village of thirty-seven dwellings of Mandans and fifteen of Hidatsa at the time of David Thompson's visit. He was a most valuable asset to all fur companies in the region. In his narrative, Thompson called him "a handsome man with a native woman, fair and graceful, for his wife. They had no children; he was in every respect a native. He was an intelligent man, but completely a Frenchman; brave, gay, and boastful." This final characteristic cost Menard his life; he was killed by Assiniboine enemies for questioning their bravery in comparison to his. His information on the Yellowstone and Crow proved valuable to the Spanish and British traders well before Lewis and Clark. It is believed his reports on the Yellowstone River region prompted Laroque's expedition to the area in 1805. He helped to establish horse trade between the whites and the Mandan Indians. Jean Baptiste Truteau mentions him as providing information on the Crow nation and the Yellowstone. He died in October of 1804, a few days before Lewis and Clark arrived at the Arikara villages.

References: Tyrrell; Saindon, "Old Menard"

Old Toby: A Shoshone elder who consented to guide the corps down the Salmon River to the Clearwater River. Referred to by name only once in Lewis's journal, on May 12, 1806: "we now have six horses out only as our old guide Toby and his son each took a horse of ours when they returned last fall." His band of Shoshone, the Lemhi, included Sacagawea's brother Cameahwait. He "appeared to be a very friendly, intelligent, old man Capt. C. is much pleased with him." Cameahwait told the captains that Toby was well acquainted with the country to the north of the Salmon River. This section of the journey, the Lolo trail, proved to be most troublesome for the men as it is thickly forested and extremely steep and irregular. The scarcity of food and lack of a discernible path made the necessity of a guide obvious to the captains. John Rees, a trader who lived among the Shoshone for fifteen years in the late 1870s, learned many of the nuances of the Shoshonian language. He wrote that the employment of Toby is the only instance of Lewis and Clark hiring a guide. (They later hired two teenage Nez Percé boys for the trip back.) "I once happened to ask a Shoshoni what was meant by 'Toby' without uttering a word he made the sign of one leading another." When Rees inquired how such a name originated in his language, he replied, "Tosa-tive koo-be" (Tobe), meaning "furnished white-white man with brains" distinguishing between the black-white man (York) and the white-white man. Rees goes on to say Toby's real name was "Pi-keek queen-ah," or swooping eagle, because he swooped down on the enemy like an eagle. Some scholars have questioned Rees's etymologies, but his story remains an intriguing one. Fortunately for the Corps of Discovery, Toby's familiarity with the tribes and topography of the region remained relatively intact despite his advanced age. He wandered down the wrong trail for a few miles (Lost Trail Pass), but overall his advice and assistance proved invaluable. Not only did he guide Clark and Private Gass down the Salmon so Clark could be assured it was indeed a "river of no return," he successfully led the expedition to Weippe Prairie and the Nez Percé tribe, who proved to be the most helpful natives the corps encountered. Toby pointed out old buffalo hunting trails, which the captains used on their way back over the mountains. He assisted as an interpreter with the Shoshone and Salish tribes, assuring them the white men meant no harm, and aided the corps by negotiating food trades with the natives. At one point the captains asked Cameahwait for another guide, but "he had no doubt the old man who was with Capt. C would accompany us if we wished him and that he was better informed of the country than any of them." When Toby decided he no longer wanted to guide, he and his son ran off to the mountains, taking two horses with them for their services.

On October 9, 1805, Clark wrote, "We could not account for the cause of his leaveing us at this time, without receiving his pay for the Services he had rendered us, or letting us know anything of his intention. . . . we requested the Chief to Send a horseman after our old guide to come back and receive his pay &tc which he advised us not to do as his nation would take his things from him before he passed their camps." Toby's reluctance to proceed was perhaps because, as Sergeant Gass suspected, "he was afraid of being cast away passing the rapids" after witnessing a close call with the canoe in rough water. Other possible reasons for Toby's quick departure include the threat of winter or the fact he may simply have come to the end of the world as he knew it. His name, as translated by Rees, is a fitting tribute for the service he provided the expedition and the United States.

References: MacGregor, Journals of Patrick Gass; Moulton, vols. 5, 7; Rees

Ord, George (1781–1866): Naturalist, philologist, and biographer of his friend Alexander Wilson. He was an associate of the naturalists who founded the Academy of Natural Sciences of Philadelphia in 1812. According to historian Paul Cutright, Ord worked with the expedition's specimens, given to Charles Willson Peale, and "formally described more animals discovered by Meriwether Lewis than any other individual." When Wilson died before completing *American Ornithology*, Ord finished the eighth volume for him in 1814. Ord's most noteworthy work was *A Sketch of the Life of Alexander Wilson* (1814).

Reference: Cutright, History of the Lewis and Clark Journals

Ordway, John (1775–1817): Sergeant and second in command to the captains. A New Hampshire resident who mustered in to the Corps of Discovery in the winter of 1804 out of Kaskaskia. Ordway kept the Orderly book, or the book of detachment orders, and maintained a journal, which was lost and not discovered for more than a century. (It was finally published in 1916.) His April 8, 1804, letter to his "Honored parence" from Camp Dubois reveals his youthful enthusiasm and tender concern for his parents: "I now embrace this oppertunity of writing to you once more to let you know where I am and where I am going. I am well thank God, and in high Spirits. I am now on an expidition to the westward, with Capt. Lewis and Capt.

Clark, who are appointed by the President of the united States to go on an expidition through the interior parts of North America. We are to ascend the Missouri River with a boat as far as it is navigable and then to go by land, to the western ocean, if nothing prevents &ct. This party consists of 25 picked Men of the armey and country likewise I am So happy as to be one of them pick'd Men from the armey and I and all the party are if we live to Return, to Receive our Discharge when ever we return again to the united States if we chuse it." The sergeant attempted to maintain order in the captains' absence at Camp Dubois; when that failed he served on the jury called to court-martial those accused of infractions. On May 23, 1804, Ordway may have signed his name in Tavern Cave as the letters *ORD* can still be viewed there. The name given to the barking squirrel came from John Ordway, who adopted the French term and called the creatures prairie dogs. The sergeant was the only journalist to describe (on December 15, 1805) the Mandan hoop and pole game, and the only one to note "4 men went over to the prairie near the coast to take a canoe which belongd to the Clotsop Indians as we are in want of it." Like his fellow sergeant Patrick Gass, Ordway appreciated the canoes of the Indians who lived on the Columbia River. "I must give these Savages as well as those on the coast the praise of making the neatest handsomest lightest best formed canoes I ever saw & are the best hands to work them." Among other duties, he kept track of the daily distribution of staples. As with many of the men, Ordway became sick and weak during the winter at Fort Clatsop but was healthy overall, and other than having to retrieve a forgotten ax, and once getting lost with a hunting party, he proved to be a consistently responsible, reliable, and competent leader. After the expedition, the sergeant accompanied Lewis when he went to Washington, D.C., with an Indian delegation to see President Jefferson. He briefly visited his home state, then purchased land in Tywappity Bottom, Missouri, and began fruit farming. He continued to expand his land holdings and eventually owned two plantations. Ordway married a woman named Gracy; they had no children. A creek near the present-day capital of Montana was named Ordway's River in his honor but is now known as Little Prickley Pear Creek.

References: *Jackson,* Letters; *Moulton, vol. 9*

Osage orange (*Maclura pomifera*): Also known as Osage apple or hedge apple and commonly found in Arkansas, Oklahoma, and parts of Texas. Lewis sent cuttings of this plant to Jefferson from St. Louis in late March 1804. The plant can still be found in hedges; early settlers planted them for windbreaks. Indians valued the hardwood for bows and arrows.

References: Moulton, vol. 2; Cutright, Pioneering Naturalists

Osgood, Ernest Staples (1888–1983): Author and history professor trained at the University of Wisconsin who edited *The Field Notes of Captain William Clark* (1964). The notes, which covered the years 1803–05, were found in an attic in St. Paul, Minnesota, in 1953.

Otter Woman (Ponzo-bert): Shoshone woman a few years older than Sacagawea and captured with her at Three Forks by a Hidatsa raiding party around 1798. Otter Woman and Sacagawea were taken to the Hidatsa earth-lodge villages near present-day Stanton, North Dakota. How they became the wives of Toussaint Charbonneau is uncertain. Some accounts stress a gambling incident, others that the two women were a gift of the Hidatsa tribe to Charbonneau. Just how Charbonneau (or others) chose Sacagawea to accompany Lewis and Clark is also uncertain, particularly in view of the fact that she gave birth to her first child, Jean Baptiste, just fifty days before the expedition left Fort Mandan. According to William Clark, two of Charbonneau's wives were scheduled to make the trip. As late as April 1, 1805, Clark still writes of "one French man as an interpreter with his two wives who are L hiatars or Snake Indians of the nations through which we Shall pass, and to act as Interpretess thro him." Just why Otter Woman was left behind is unknown. Sacagawea may have been the more conversant of the two young women. Legend has it that Otter Woman gave birth to a son who died in infancy before the return of her husband. (Some sources indicate she was not a real person, but some kind of mythical character.)

Reference: Moulton, vol. 3

P

Pacific salmon (coho, sockeye, pink, king, chum): A fish of the Columbia River basin that was and is as integral to the society of the coastal tribes as the buffalo was to the plains Indians. Given his first taste of salmon by the Shoshone chief Cameahwait, Lewis expressed some relief: "this was the first salmon I had seen and perfectly convinced me that we were on the waters of the Pacific Ocean." Later the captain described a first-fish-of-the-season ceremony at Celilo Falls, on April 19, 1806: "there was great joy with the natives last night in consequence of the arrival of the salmon; one of those fish was caught; this was the harbinger of good news to them. they informed us that those fish would arrive in great quantities in the course of about 5 days. this fish was dressed and being divided into small peices was given to each child in the village. this custom is founded in a superstitious opinion that it will hasten the arrival of the salmon." According to Dan Landeen and Allen Pinkham, the Nez Percé believed that, if these ceremonies were properly performed, the salmon would return each year and sustain the tribe. As they proceeded through the Columbia basin, the party observed various methods of catching, drying, cooking, and storing salmon, all described in their journals. Fishing areas like the Dalles, where people had gathered for thousands of years to trade and exchange information, bustled with economic activity. It was, perhaps, the busiest place along the entire trail. The taste of salmon did not appeal to the party; they much preferred dog or lean elk meat during their time at Fort Clatsop. Salmon populations at the time of Lewis and Clark numbered somewhere in the vicinity of sixteen million returning fish. According to a recent Sierra Club report that number has dwindled by nearly 98 percent. The Columbia's twenty-nine dams, logging operations, irrigation demands, and pollution have all but ruined the salmon's habitat. Five of the six salmon species are currently listed as endangered or threatened.

References: Landeen and Pinkham; Moulton, vols. 5, 7; Sierra Club

Partisan (Torto-hongar, Bad Fellow, War Leader): Teton Sioux chief. Was among those encountered near present-day Pierre, South Dakota, who failed in an attempt to detain the expedition in their territory, September 1804. Referred to as "vile miscreants" by the captains, who showed them curiosities onboard the pirogue and gave them some whiskey as a gesture of goodwill only to find the chiefs, as Clark recounted in his journal, "Soon began to be troublesom, one the 2nd chief assumeing Drunkness as a Cloake for his rascally intentions I went with those Cheifs to Shore with a view of reconseleing those men to us, as Soon as I landed the Perogue, the Chefs Soldr Huged the mast, and the 2nd chief (the Partisan) was verry insolent both in words & justures were of Such a personal nature I felt my Self compeled to Draw my Sword, at this motion Capt. Lewis ordered all under arms in the boat, those with me also Showed a Disposition to Defend themselves and me, the grand Chief then took hold of the roop & ordered the young warrers away, I felt my Self warm & Spoke in verry positive terms." Clark was prevented from returning to his vessel by the many assembled warriors but he sent the rest of the men back, except for the interpreters, and they soon returned with twelve determined men, according to Clark, "ready for any event. . . . After remaining in this Situation Some time I offered my hand to the 1 and 2 chief who refused to recve it. I turned and went with my men on board the perogue. . . . I call this Island bad humered Island as we were in a bad humer."

After several days of cautious friendliness, during which the men were offered (and declined) women by the Teton Sioux, and the keelboat anchor was lost, the Partisan again attempted to detain the expedition when he held on to a rope and, backed by two hundred of his fiercest warriors, demanded a toll from the Americans of a flag and tobacco. After ordering the visitors off the keelboat, "Capt. L said he would not agree to be forced into anything." Seeing the situation again getting troublesome, Clark stepped in. He knew, through some Omaha prisoners of the Sioux, that they were disguising their true intentions, and so threw a carrot of tobacco to the first chief and "Spoke So as to touch his pride took the port fire from the gunner. [At this point Clark also reminded the Sioux he had on board more medicine than would kill twenty such nations in one day.] the Chief gives the Tobaco to his Soldiers & he jurked the rope from them and handed it to the bows man we then Set out under a Breeze from the S. E. about 2 miles up we observed the 3rd Chief on Shore beckining to (him) us we took him on board he informed us the roap was held by the order of the 2nd chief who was a Double Spoken man. . . ." The Partisan may have counciled with Zebulon Pike at the confluence of the Mississippi and the Minnesota Rivers in September 1805 and was mentioned in attendance at the Portage des Sioux council with the United States government in July 1815. According to historian James Ronda, while the Partisan and his fellows made clear the long-term Sioux interest in being gatekeepers to the flow of goods upriver, in the end, the encounter with the Teton was "more of a tussle between rival head men" than a genuine conflict between the Indians and the American explorers.

References: Ronda, Lewis and Clark among the Indians; *Moulton, vol. 3*

Passenger pigeon (*Ectopistes migratorius*, which means wandering wanderer): First noted in the journals on September 13, 1803: "observid many pigeons passing over us in a south East course." Their feathers were red, blue, and gray, and they resembled a mourning dove in shape. Native American Indians used them for feathers, food, and fat but did not hunt them in great numbers. A contemporary of Lewis and Clark's, the naturalist Alexander Wilson, estimated a flock he observed flying from Kentucky to Indiana to number 2,230,272,000, which covered a distance of a mile wide and 240 miles long. The largest known nesting colony was sited in Wisconsin in 1871; it covered an area of 850 square miles. Though they were once the most abundant land bird on the planet, hunting and habitat destruction reduced their numbers considerably. The passenger pigeon depended on large forests for food and nesting areas; as those forests disappeared, so did the pigeon. They were hunted commercially with very effective nets and used for trap-shooting practice. The term *stool pigeon* refers to the live decoys pigeoners used to attract the flock. One method of calming the stool pigeon involved sewing its eyelids shut. By the fall of 1912 passenger pigeons no longer existed; the last wild one, later nicknamed Buttons, after it was stuffed, for its shoe-button eyes, was killed in March 1900 and is displayed in the

Cincinnati Zoo. During the expedition, the men occasionally resorted to eating passenger pigeons; on July 24, 1806, near the Marias, Lewis wrote, "we have still a little of the bread of cows remaining which we made a kettle of mush which together with a few pigeons that we were fortunate enough to kill served us with food for this day." Cookbooks from the nineteenth century contain many recipes for passenger pigeon, and because of its abundance it became a staple on the frontier.

References: Cokinos; Moulton, vols. 2, 8

Patterson, Robert (1743–1824): University of Pennsylvania professor of mathematics and member of the American Philosophical Society. One of several Philadelphia-based scientific advisers to Thomas Jefferson and Meriwether Lewis in April and May of 1803 as they prepared for the expedition.

Reference: Peck, Or Perish in the Attempt

Patterson, William Ewing: Son of Robert Patterson; scheduled to accompany Lewis when he left Wheeling, Pennsylvania. Patterson had been invited by Lewis to become the official doctor of the expedition, but he was reputed to be a drunk and somehow missed the boat's departure, and Lewis did not wait.

Peace Medal (Jefferson Peace Medal): Following a tradition started by British diplomats in North America, the U.S. Mint produced this particular set of medals for distribution to Native American Indian tribes from 1801 to 1812. They served as tangible tokens of friendship and underscored President Jefferson's plans to embrace the Indian nations of the American West and include them, partially, in his Empire of Liberty. Engraved by Robert Scott, the medals were produced in three sizes, four, three, and two inches in diameter, and showed a bust of Jefferson and the words TH. JEFFERSON PRESIDENT OF THE U.S. A.D. 1801 on one side, and two hands clasped in PEACE AND FRIENDSHIP with a tomahawk and pipe on the other. Lewis and Clark carried and presumably distributed some 235 medals of the three sizes. According to historian Francis Paul Prucha, the medals were hollow shells held together by a silver rim, and "large numbers of Jefferson medals in all three sizes found their way to the West for distribution to the Indians in addition to those given out by Lewis and Clark. It is, therefore, extremely difficult to decide with certainty the exact time of presentation of particular Jefferson medals excavated in the Mississippi and Missouri River valleys or passed down by generations of Indians in those areas." The captains also carried fifty-five medals left over from the Washington administration, which showed three different farm scenes. Attempts are currently under way to locate and inventory all remaining Lewis and Clark–era medals.

References: Prucha; Venso, personal communication

Peale, Charles Willson (1741–1827): Artist, natural scientist/collector, and proprietor of the Philadelphia Museum (or the "Great School of Nature," as he called it). Peale's museum was selected by Jefferson and Lewis to be the repository of most of the zoological and ethnological specimens brought back by the corps. Lewis approached Peale to do some of the drawings for his proposed three-volume account of the expedition. Peale wrote to a friend, "The drawings for Governor Lewis's Journal I mean to draw myself." Four of these drawings survive: Lewis's woodpecker, a mountain quail, "fisher," and horned toad. Today they can be viewed at the American Philosophical Society in Philadelphia. It is known Peale worked on several others, which are no longer extant. Peale also produced portraits and was best known as the painter of George Washington's portrait. In 1805 he cut twelve silhouettes of some visiting Indians and presented the mounted "blockheads," as his children called them, to President Jefferson. Peale produced souvenirs for visitors to his popular museum using the same method. He persuaded Captain Lewis to sit for him for a likeness to be displayed with the portraits of famous men in his museum. Three years later Clark agreed to pose as well. These two portraits, often shown as a set, rank as perhaps the most familiar representations of the captains in existence. Lewis further accommodated the artist by posing for a wax sculpture, which was then adorned with the tippet given to Lewis by Shoshone chief Cameahwait. The figure was supposed to symbolize friendship between Indians and whites. Peale urged Clark to write the narrative of the journals he still planned to illustrate, but in a letter to his son Rembrandt wrote, "I found that the General was too diffident of his abilities. I would rather see a single narrative with such observations as I am sure Clark could have made on the different Nations of Savages & things, which the Notes taken by Capt. Lewis probably passed over unnoticed." The 1814 Biddle version of the journals of Lewis and Clark included none of Peale's illustrations.

Reference: Jackson, Letters

Pemmican: Cree word for manufactured grease; a mixture of dried strips of meat, usually buffalo, pounded with berries, mixed with fat, and finally formed into cakes. It preserved well and was an ideal winter or travel food, easily carried in leather bags or parfleches, and used by Indians and fur traders especially on the Great Plains. The mixture has a high protein content, and it was not unusual for the average voyageur or engagé to consume a pound and a half per day. Pemmican can be stored almost indefinitely; a Manitoba cache of pemmican discovered in 1934 was still edible. On December 3, 1804, Lewis first tasted pemmican when a Mandan man gave him some as part of a present in respect for the captains' offering to avenge the death of his son. He ate it with some potato and pronounced it "good." Dietrich writes it has the consistency of dried dog food, but does not comment on the taste. Later, Captain Lewis would direct his hunters to prepare the mixture in advance of lengthy days on the trail.

References: Moulton, vol. 3; Dietrich

Pernier, John (d. 1810): Free mulatto who served as Meriwether Lewis's servant and valet after the expedition. On November 9, 1808, Lewis borrowed forty-nine dollars from General Clark to pay a physician who treated Pernier. He wrote in his account book he considered the price exorbitant, "but which my situation in life compels me to pay," an indication of the sad state of his financial affairs following the return to St. Louis. Pernier, or Pernia, as Lewis called him, was given the small minute book that contained a list of Lewis's debts as a part of his last will and testament. In it Lewis bequeathed all of his estate to his mother, Lucy Marks. Pernier may have tried to prevent Lewis from getting possession of his powder the night he killed himself. As Pernier prepared Lewis's bearskin and buffalo robes to spread on the floor of his room, Lewis somehow managed to obtain the gunpowder. When two attempts to end his life failed, the captain began to cut himself from head to foot with a razor. Lewis told Pernier, "I have done the business my good Servant give me some water." Mortally wounded but still conscious, Lewis is reported to have said to Pernier and the others assembled at Grinder's Stand, "I am no coward; but I am so strong, [it is] so hard to die." He reportedly said he had tried to kill himself so that his enemies would be deprived of the pleasure and honor of doing so. He then begged his servants to finish the job and told them that they could have all of the money in his trunk if they complied. Lewis succumbed sometime after sunrise on October 11, 1809. Sometime in October or November of 1809, Pernier gave an eyewitness account of Lewis's death to Jefferson. Pernier himself died of self-inflicted laudanum poisoning on April 29, 1810. Conspiracy theorists conjecture Pernier could have been Lewis's murderer. Meriwether Lewis's account book is in the Grace Lewis Miller papers at the Missouri Historical Society.

References: Dillon; Jackson, Letters; *Ambrose*

Peruvian bark: Taken from the cinchona tree, this substance contains quinine (known nowadays to be effective against the malarial parasite) and other alkaloids used for treating high temperatures, aches, and pains. It was known as the aspirin of the day and was used as a tonic and an astringent; it also had an antiseptic effect. One third of the money Lewis spent on medical supplies went for fifteen pounds of this medicine. The captains prescribed it for a variety of ailments to be taken internally and as a poultice.

Reference: Peck, Or Perish in the Attempt

Philanthropy (Ruby) River: The Shoshone call it Passamari, meaning "water of the cottonwood groves." In the vicinity of the Beaverhead Mountains and nearing the Shoshone on August 6, 1805, Lewis wrote, "that which ought of right to bear the name we had given to the lower portion or River Jefferson and called the bold rapid an clear stream Wisdom, and the more mild and placid one which flows in from the S.E. Philanthropy, in commemoration of those two cardinal virtues, which have so eminently marked that deservedly selibrated character through life." The men began to find water travel extremely taxing at this time. Ordway commented that they had to "wade and hall" their canoes at this point. Later settlers called it the Stinkingwater River after a heavy spring flow killed many buffalo. In the spring, runoff brings down rocks from the mountains, including the colorful garnets that give the meandering river its current name.

Reference: Moulton, vols. 5, 9

Piaheto (Eagle's Feather): Arikara chief of the Waho-erha village, near present-day Corson County, South Dakota, who counciled with Lewis and Clark in October 1804. He may be the same person as Ar ke tar na shar or "Chief of the Town," also known as Too ne or whip-poor-will. If so, he was with Lewis and Clark when they went to the Mandan and Hidatsa villages in an attempt to establish peace among the upper Missouri tribes and to form an alliance against the Sioux. Piaheto may have been the individual who died in Washington, D.C., in 1806 while visiting the Great Father. Thomas Jefferson, unsure of the exact name of his guest, wrote a letter of condolence to the Arikara in the hope of salvaging friendly relations. "On his return to this place he was taken sick; every thing we could do to help him was done; but it pleased the Great Spirit to take him from among us. We buried him among our own deceased friends & relatives, we shed many tears over his grave, and now we mingle our afflictions with yours on the loss of this beloved chief. But death must happen to all men; and his time was come."

References: Moulton, vol. 3; Jackson, Letters

Pirogue: French, Spanish, or Dutch term for a flat-bottomed, open-water craft used by the party, sometimes with a small sail, and outfitted with a rudder and modified to include a blunderbuss gun at the bow. The expedition used two of these boats; one smaller white pirogue held six men under the command of Corporal Richard Warfington, the other red "canoe," as Lewis sometimes called it, held seven engagés. Questions remain concerning the origin of the pirogues, and about the sort of wood that was used in their construction. The white one, once referred to as the "poplar perogue" at Fort Mandan, could have been made of one of several kinds of poplar. It was considered unlucky, but usually carried the journals, and was cached at the Great Falls on June 18, 1805. Observations on the white pirogue include the following from Meriwether Lewis: "the toe rope of the white pirogue, the only one indeed of hemp, and that on which we most depended, gave way today at a bad point, the perogue swung and but slightly touched a rock, yet was very near overseting; I fear her evil gennii will play so many pranks with her that she will go to the bottomm some of those days." Once, with Charbonneau at the bow, it nearly sank and was prevented from doing so only by Cruzatte's threat to shoot Charbonneau if he did not take the rudder. On that occasion Sacagawea saved many of the "light articles," perhaps even the journals, when she quickly scooped them up as the boat was going under. During the portage its mast was used for the axletrees on the "carriage." Ordway's party picked up the boat on the way back to St. Louis. What became of it after the expedition is unknown. One of Captain Lewis's biggest disappointments came when the iron boat he planned on using as a replacement for the white pirogue did not float. It meant the remaining boats would be overloaded, and the risk of losing articles would be higher. The red one, cached near the Marias, did not survive its burial; the men salvaged the nails and iron from it on the return journey.

Reference: Moulton, vol. 4

Pocasse (The Straw, Hay): Arikara chief of the Rhtarahe village near present-day Corson County, South Dakota. One of three chiefs who counciled with Lewis and Clark in October 1804. In a speech to the captains, Pocasse said, "you Come here & Derect us to Stay at home & not go to war, we shall do So, we hope you will when you get to the Mandins you will tell them the Same & Cleer the road, no one Dar to Stop you, you go when you please." On October 12, 1804, Clark noted, "this Chief & people gave us about 7 bushels of Corn, Some tobacco of their own make, and Seed Legins & a Robe." Ordway was impressed with the hospitality of the Arikara, who he wrote "have used us in the most friendly manner." Although the Americans considered the meeting a successful one, the complexities of middle Missouri trading and social systems were unknown to President Jefferson and the bearers of his complicated message. Pocasse raised important questions when he spoke to Lewis and Clark; pointedly he asked them to "stop the guns" of the neighboring tribes who would come to make war on them once the expedition moved on. Although they did not fully reassure the chiefs, they accomplished the task of persuading several of them to visit their Great Father in Washington, D.C. Trader Pierre Antoine Tabeau mentions Pocasse's less than hospitable reception of him in 1803. The captains named a creek for Pocasse; it is now known as Hunkpapa Creek and is near the site of John Newman's court-martial. See Tabeau, Pierre Antoine.

References: Abel, Tabeau's Narrative; *Moulton, vols. 3, 9; Thwaites,* Original Journals, *vol. 1*

Poggarmaggon (bgamaagan): Chippewa word for a weapon similar to one used by the Shoshone Indians. Lewis described it as "An instrument with a handle of wood covered with dressed leather about the size of a whip handle and 22 inches long; a round stone of 2 pounds weight is also covered with leather and strongly united to the leather of the handle by a throng of 2 inches long; a loop of leather united to the handle passes arond the wrist a very heavy blow may be given with this instrument."

Reference: Moulton, vol. 5

Pompy's Tower (Pompy's Pillar): Sandstone formation on the Yellowstone River about twenty-eight miles east of present-day Billings, Montana. Named by William Clark on July 25, 1806, in honor of Jean Baptiste Charbonneau, or "Pomp": "at 4 pm arrived at a remarkable rock Situated in an extensive bottom on the Stard. Side of the river & 250 paces from it. this rock I ascended and from it's top had a most extensive view in every direction. This rock which I shall Call Pompy's Tower is 200 feet high and 400 paces in secumphrance and only axcessable on one Side which is from the N. E the other parts of it being a perpendicular Clift of lightish Coloured gritty rock on the top there is a tolerable Soil of about 5 or 6 feet thick Covered with Short grass. The Indians have made 2 piles of Stone on the top of this Tower. The nativs have ingraved on the face of this rock the figures of animals &ct. near which I marked my name and the day of the month

& year." According to cartographers Jon Reiten and Bob Bergentino, the Crow Indians called the rock "where the Mountain Lion lies," and for centuries used it as a lookout. Clark's signature remains preserved behind bullet- and shatter-proof glass and can be viewed by the public. It was thought to be the only remaining physical effect from the

William Clark's carved signature at the sandstone formation that he called Pompy's Tower (Pompy's Pillar today), named for Sacagawea's son. It is thought to be the only physical evidence of the expedition's passing through the area (near present-day Billings, Montana). Montana Historical Society, Helena.

expedition but other items have surfaced, some of questionable provenance. Efforts are under way to construct an interpretive center at
the site.

References: Reiten and Bergentino; Moulton, vol. 8

Pond, Peter (1740–1807): Fur trader for the North West Company;
explorer who presented one of his maps of the Canadian Northwest to
Congress about 1784. Pond's map was amazingly accurate but
showed the headwaters of the Missouri to be in a single mountain
chain running from north to south. It also represented a large river on
the opposite side of the mountains flowing into the Pacific, which he
called the "Naberkistagon," later referred to as the Oregon River or
the Great River of the West: the Columbia. Pond influenced the geographical lore Lewis and Clark would rely on before entering the
Bitterroot Mountains. Some of his information was misinterpreted to
mean the mountains could be crossed in twelve hours when he meant
twelve days.

Reference: Allen, Passage through the Garden

Portable soup (pocket soop, veal glew): Lewis purchased 193
pounds of the substance for $1.50 per pound from Philadelphia cook
François Baillet in preparation for the overland journey. Most likely
the recipe followed the time-honored traditional ingredients favored
in the military of the late 1700s. These included meaty bones, pigs'
feet, onions, carrots, celery, and a variety of spices, especially pepper.
The concoction is boiled at a simmer for at least six hours and then
cooled until firmly set. It becomes of a leatherlike consistency, which
is then dried, rendered portable, and stored in canisters. It came in
handy when the men faced starvation in the Bitterroot in September
of 1805. "we dined and suped on a skant proportion of portable
soupe, a few canesters of which, a little bears oil and about 20lbs of
candles form our stock of provisions. . . ." There is some dispute
among scholars as to whether or not the men actually consumed the
candles. While they certainly could have eaten them, as they were
made of rendered animal fat, it is more likely they ate bear's oil, also
made of rendered animal fat, as sustenance during their starving time
in the Bitterroots. Later they would add horse meat to the soup to

make it more agreeable. Most of the men expressed no enthusiasm for the soup, but it did help sustain them on the Lolo trail. Traditionally, ingredients for portable soup include thirty pounds of very meaty bones, two pigs' feet or a one-pound ham, six large onions, six large carrots, parsley, thyme, hyssop, marjoram (handful of each), tablespoon of mace, twelve cloves, three tablespoons of peppercorns, salt, and water.

Reference: Moulton, vol. 5

Potts, John (1776–1808): Private; born in Germany; worked as a miller. Potts joined the expedition from Captain Purdy's company on November 24, 1803. Along with the usual tasks of a private, Potts served on jury duty in the court-martials of fellow privates Warner, Hall, and Collins and later sat as judge advocate when Collins and Hall were charged with stealing whiskey. After portaging the Great Falls, Potts, York, Joseph Field, and Clark went as far as the Dearborn River and then traveled overland around the Gates of the Mountains searching for signs of the Shoshone Indians. While waiting for the snow to melt at Camp Chopunnish, Potts succeeded, with Charbonneau, in trading knitting awls, pins, and armbands for six bushels of cous root. Potts nearly drowned on the upper Kookooske River when the canoe he was riding in capsized, causing the loss of three blankets, a blanket coat, and various other personal possessions. Lewis called the loss of the blankets a serious one. On June 18, 1806, Potts severely cut himself with a large knife, opening a vein on the inside of his leg. Lewis applied pressure to the wound and with great difficulty stopped the bleeding. Ordway recorded that "Lewis Sowed up the wound and bound it up." By June 22 the leg was painful and inflamed; Lewis applied a poultice of cous root. On June 27 Potts's leg improved thanks to a poultice of pounded roots and wild ginger. In July 1806 Potts was given a pill of opium to ease pain caused by "rideing a hard trotting horse." Upon discharge he was paid and given a 320-acre land grant. He signed up with Manuel Lisa in a trapping venture in 1807 and headed back up the Missouri River. Potts saved Lisa's life when he was nearly killed in an argument with one of his engagés. In July of 1808 Potts and his partners, Peter Weiser and Forrest Hancock, signed a note indicating Lisa advanced them more than $400 in trapping supplies. Trapping with his old friend John Colter, he was attacked by the Blackfeet Indians and suffered arrow wounds and, according to Colter, "made a riddle of." Two years later Colter escaped death by outrunning Blackfeet warriors in his bare feet, and killing one, finally stumbling naked and starving into Fort Lisa seven days and several hundred miles later. Another experience, in 1810, caused Colter to return to civilization and vow never to return to the upper Missouri River country as long as he lived. Today's Spring Creek near the Gates of the Mountains was originally called Potts Creek in honor of John Potts. His estate was sued by Lisa, Menard, and the Missouri Fur Company for one thousand dollars in past debts.

References: Colter-Frick; Moulton, vols. 8, 9; Chuinard, Only One Man Died; Oglesby

Prairie dog (*Cynomys ludovicianus*, black tail, barking squirrel): First encountered by the expedition on September 7, 1804, in present-day Boyd County, Nebraska. The prairie dog is not related to dogs but is a member of the rodent family and is a distant cousin to the more familiar squirrel and chipmunk. When alarmed they emit a bark somewhat similar to what Lewis called "that of the little toy dogs." This shrill cry has been studied and recorded by scientists, who found the prairie dog warning call is able to communicate which one of their natural enemies is in the area and even distinguish between men of different sizes. Their "language" has been called the most sophisticated so far decoded in the animal world. According to Paul Cutright the Indians called them "wishtonish," and Ordway may have been the first to call the animal a "prairie dog." Clark described the animal as a "ground rat," a burrowing squirrel, and using the French term *petite chien* he noted that, although his men dug six feet into a burrow trying to catch one, they realized they had not even gotten "half way to his Lodges" so they spent the better part of a day attempting to drown them out: "we por'd into one of the holes 5 barrels of water without filling it, Those Animals are about the Size of a Small Squrel (shorter) & thicker, the head much resembling a Squirel in every respect, except the ears which is Shorter, his toe nails long, they have fine fur & the longer hair is gray." (A more detailed description is given by Lewis on July 1, 1806.) Although their burrows can be twenty feet deep and more than a hundred feet long, the men did eventually succeed in capturing a live prairie dog, which was sent along with other specimens from Fort Mandan to Thomas Jefferson in Washington, D.C., in April 1805. The circuitous route of these creatures, one "wild dog of the Prairie," four magpies, and a grouse, which did not survive the trip, went from St. Louis to New Orleans to Baltimore by ship and ultimately by land to Washington, D.C. Jefferson then sent some of the specimens including the "burrowing squirrel of the prairies" to Peale for his museum; Peale intended to draw the prairie dog but does not mention it after writing it "stirs but little" on April 5, 1806. At the turn of the century biologists guess the prairie dog population would have numbered five billion. Meriwether Lewis reported seeing them in "infinite numbers," but because of eradication programs, habitat destruction, disease, and sport hunting their numbers have declined dramatically in recent years so that they now live in only about 2 percent of their former rangeland. Recently, scientists recognized prairie dogs as an important part of the prairie ecosystem because they enrich the soil and provide the main food and habitat source for the endangered black-footed ferret.

References: Jackson, Letters; *Moulton, vols. 3, 8; Cutright*, Pioneering Naturalists; *Matchet, personal communication*

Prairie of the Knobs: Knob Plains, also known as Blackfoot or Steven's Prairie, located near the present-day town of Ovando in Powell County, Montana, near the Blackfoot River. After dividing the party and heading west so he could explore the Marias River, Lewis wrote, "these plains I called (the knob plains) the prairie of the knobs from (the) a number of knobs being irregularly scattered through it." In addition he observed, "up this valley and creek a road passes to Dearbourn's river and thence to the Missouri." The road followed a river called Cokahlarishkit or the "river to the road to the buffalo," used by most of the tribes on the western side of the Continental Divide. The young Nez Percé men guiding Lewis at this point told him he could now go ahead on his own: "they alleged that as the road was a well beaten track we could not miss our way and as they were affraid of meeting with their enimies the Minnetares, they could not think of continuing with us any longer." If the expedition had been looking for the shortest passable route to the Pacific without the added chore of locating the source of the Missouri River, this would have been an excellent shortcut.

Reference: Jackson, Among the Sleeping Giants

Prickly pear cactus (*Opuntia polyacantha*, haw): First observed by the party in September of 1805, the prickly pear went on to become one of "our trio of pests," which, Lewis noted, "still invade and obstruct us on all occasions, these are the Musquetoes eyeknats and prickley pears, equal to any three curses that ever Poor Egypt laiboured under except the Mahometant yoke." Usually described in terms of "great abundance" or "immense numbers," Lewis noted on June 4, 1805, that the prickly pear "are extreemly troublesome; as the thorns very readily perce the foot through the Mockerson; they are so numerous that is requires one half of the traveler's attention to avoid them." Out of necessity, the men double-soled their moccasins in an effort to prevent punctured feet. Lewis added buffalo parchment to the bottoms of his moccasins but, walking late one night near Great Falls, admitted he would have thought himself dreaming except that the "prickley pears which pierced my feet very severely once in a while, particularly after it grew dark, convinced me that I was really awake. . . ." Clark, too, endured the insufferable prickly pear: "my feet is verry much brused and cut walking over the flint & constantly Stuck full Prickley pear thorns, I puled out 17 by the light of the fire to night." As troublesome as the cactus proved to be, the captains also noted when they flowered in July 1805: "prickly pear is now in full blume and forms one of the beauties as well as the greatest pests of the plains." They grow in hot, dry localities from Alberta to Arizona. Native Americans often ate the soft red fruit inside the cactus, and the Sioux and Crow Indians used it to fix colors on hides. The stems were sometimes applied topically to injured extremities. The Flathead Indians used a boiled-stem tea for intestinal disorders.

References: Hart; Moulton, vol. 4

Prisoner's base, or base: A game played by the men and the Chopunnish (Nez Percé) Indians during the extended time the expedition spent waiting for the snow in the Bitterroots to melt, from May 15 to June 6, 1806. This camp, which later became known as Camp Chopunnish, was the third longest camp of the journey and was notable for the friendly and sportsmanlike competition between the men and the Nez Percé warriors. The game is mentioned in entries on June 8 and 9, 1806: "Our party exercised themselves running and playing games called base." Lewis wrote, "our party seem much elated with the idea of moving on towards their friends and country, they all seem allirt in their movements today; they have everything in readiness for a move, and notwithstanding the want of provision have been amusing themselves very merrily today in running footraces, pitching quites [flattened rings], prison basse &c."

Reference: Moulton, vols. 7, 9

Pronghorn antelope (*Antilocapra americana*; *koke* in Mandan): This unique ungulate, unrelated to any other species, was first killed by William Clark in Lyman County, South Dakota, on September 14, 1804: "his eyes like a Sheep—he is more like the Antilope or Gazella of Africa than any other species of Goat." According to Sergeant Ordway, "Such an anamil was never yet known in the U. S. States—The Capt had the Skins of the hair & Goat Stuffed in order to Send back to the city of Washington. the bones and all.—" For a time the men called these swift runners goats, then *cabres*, or *cabras*, which means "goat" in Spanish. Lewis consistently referred to it as an antelope, a term that is incorrect but which persists since his time. Pronghorns are capable of reaching speeds of sixty to seventy miles per hour because of a unique oxygen-intake system that enables them to consume three times the oxygen of similar-sized animals. Hunted by Native American Indians as long as thirty thousand years ago, they are considered one of the few living links to the Ice Age. They shed the outer sheaths of their horns annually, can live without water for days, and eat almost any plant. In addition to being a source of meat, pronghorns also supplied hides for clothing. Cutright cites early observers who said they once outnumbered the buffalo. Near present-day Bismarck, North Dakota, the corps witnessed an antelope migration and the subsequent hunting practices of the local Indians. In late April 1805 Lewis observed, "the buffaloe Elk and Antelope are so gentle that we pass near them while feeding, without apearing to excite any alarm among them, and when we attract their attention they frequently approach us more nearly to discover what we are, and in some instances pursue us a considerable distance apparenly with that view." Jefferson gave his antelope mount to Peale, who housed it in the quadruped room of his museum in Philadelphia. Once threatened, pronghorns benefited from conservation programs and are now so numerous some states allow them to be hunted. There is also an Oregon pronghorn, which was sighted on the Columbia just below Celilo Falls in April 1806.

References: Montana Outdoors; *Cutright,* Pioneering Naturalists; *Moulton, vols. 3, 4, 9*

Pryor, Nathaniel Hale (1775–1831): Sergeant; born in Virginia but his family moved to Kentucky; considered one of the "nine young men from Kentucky." Pryor married in 1798, but his wife was deceased at the time of the expedition. He was a distant cousin to Sergeant Charles Floyd and volunteered with him in 1803 at the Falls of the Ohio River. During the expedition Pryor served reliably and without disciplinary incident. Early on he was entrusted to persuade some Yankton Sioux chiefs to attend a council at Calumet Bluff. Pryor permanently injured his shoulder on November 29, 1804: "Sergeant Pryor in takeing down the mast put his Shoulder out of Place, we made four trials before we replaced it." It was dislocated at least twice more during the trip (July 11, 1805, and December 11, 1805). On the return journey Pryor was assigned to take horses overland and give a message to North West Company trader Hugh Heney about accompanying some Teton Sioux to Washington. He was prevented from doing so when Crow warriors stole the horses. Rather than panic the young sergeant ordered his men to skin some buffalo hides and construct two bull boats, which they used to float down the Missouri to its confluence with the Yellowstone. The party arrived there one hour after Clark. Pryor is mentioned as one of the men who chose to go with Clark to see the Pacific Ocean. The sergeant likely kept a journal, but it has never been found. Upon discharge he was paid $250.78 and given a land grant for 320 acres. He served as an ensign with the First U.S. Infantry and was assigned to lead the unit directed to return Mandan chief Sheheke-shote to his homeland in 1807. The mission ended unsuccessfully when the Arikara Indians would not allow the boats to proceed. Four men were killed and nine, including George Shannon, were wounded. After resigning from the army in 1809, Pryor secured a license from Superintendent of Indian Affairs William Clark to trade with the Shawnee Indians near Galena, Illinois. Clark asked him to provide information on the Winnebago chief Tecumseh, setting in motion a chain of events that would eventually cost Pryor all of his goods, his possessions, and very nearly his life. He tried to sue the government for $5,212.25 in losses incurred at the hands of the angry Winnebagos but was never able to collect. He reenlisted in the army and served as a captain under Andrew Jackson at the Battle of New Orleans in 1815. Eventually Pryor became a trader with the Osage Indians of Oklahoma, married an Osage woman, and raised a family with her. He lived peacefully with the Osage tribe and worked voluntarily, without pay, to promote good relations between his adopted people and neighboring tribes as well as with the whites, religious authorities, and the federal government. In 1830, the year before he died, Clark gave him the formal title of sub-agent to the Osage and a salary of five hundred dollars per year. Throughout his career Pryor held the respect and admiration of the people he dealt with no matter what their origin. The city of Pryor, Oklahoma, was named in his honor. There are two Pryor Creeks, one in Oklahoma and one in Montana headed in the Pryor Mountains. Prickly Pear Creek, near today's Helena, was originally named for Pryor. See bull boats.

References: *"Nathaniel Pryor" in Leroy Hafen,* Mountain Men and the Fur Trade; *Shoemaker; Moulton, vol. 3*

Pursh, Frederick (1774–1820): German-born botanist who came to the United States in 1799 and worked as a curator and collector for Dr. Benjamin Smith Barton, botany professor at the University of Pennsylvania. Lewis hired Pursh in 1807 to do the botanical illustrations and assist in arranging the plant collection for his proposed three-volume set on the expedition. Aware of the value of the plants, Lewis gave the specimens to Pursh when he left Philadelphia for Washington and St. Louis. Pursh transferred the collection to gardener Bernard McMahon before he departed from Philadelphia in 1809. Inexplicably, Pursh secreted some of the expedition's plants to the site of his new job in London with the noted plant collector Aylmer Bourke Lambert. Yet it was Pursh's training as a botanist that ensured that Lewis received proper credit for the discovery of more than a hundred new plants, including four named specifically for the captains. Pursh was the first to draw some of the botanical specimens of Lewis and Clark and included many of these illustrations in his book *Flora Americae Septentrionalis . . . the Plants of North America.* The work, according to Gary Moulton, can be considered "the intended botany book of the Expedition. But it was not the book Jefferson wanted, nor was it the kind of book Lewis probably would have written. It is a catalog of specimens without a narrative of the ranges, habitats, or native uses of the plants." Furthermore Pursh misjudged Lewis as having "but little practical knowledge of the Flora of North America." He returned to North America but died penniless in Canada. The plants he removed ended up in the collection of Mr. Lambert, whose estate sale attracted many collectors and botanists, including American Edward Tuckerman, who purchased the so-called small collection of North American plants for a trifle. Tuckerman returned the specimens to the Academy of Natural Sciences in Philadelphia in the spring of 1856.

References: Pursh, vol. 1; Moulton, vol. 12

R

Ramsey, Jack: On the last day of 1805, at Fort Clatsop, Clark wrote, "With a party of Clatsops who visited us last was a man of much lighter Coloured than the nativs are generaly, he was freckled with long duskey red hair, about 25 years of age, and must Certainly be half white at least, this man appeared to understand more of the English language than the others of his party, but did not Speak a word of English, he possessed all the habits of the indians." Sergeant Gass also noted the strange-looking young man: "In the afternoon, 10 of the Clat-sop nation that live on the south side of the river, came over to our camp. These are also naked, except the small robes which hardly cover their shoulders. One of these men had the reddest hair I ever saw, and a fair skin, much freckled." Ramsey was later noted by a member of Astor's company, Ross Cox, who mentioned his fair skin, his height, freckles, normal head, and red hair, along with the fact that a name, presumably his father's, was "punctured on his left arm." His father, according to the Clatsop, was a deserter from an English trading ship who lived with them and married into their nation. Ross Cox states, "Poor Jack was fond of his father's countrymen, and had the decency to wear trousers whenever he came to the fort."

References: Strong and Strong; Cox; Pollard; Moulton, vols. 6, 10

Reed, Moses: Private; deserter along with La Liberté. He was court-martialed in August 1804, according to Captain Clark, after he "Confessed that he 'Deserted & Stold a public Rifle-Shot pouch Powder & Bals' and requested that we would be as favourable with him as we Could consistantly with our Oathes—which we were and only Sentenced him to run the Gantlet four times through the Party & that each man with 9 Swichies Should punish him and for him not to be considered in future as one of the Party—." After witnessing the gauntlet penalty, three Oto chiefs "petitioned" for Reed's pardon. In October 1804 he was confined after John Newman uttered "mutinous expression." He returned, presumably performing the most menial of tasks, to St. Louis with Warfington's party in 1805. Clarke mentions he received extra wages for January through mid-February, 1805.

References: Clarke; Moulton, vol. 2

Rivet, François (1757–1852): French-Canadian hunter from Montreal, roved around the Mississippi River valley until he signed up with Lewis and Clark at St. Louis as an engagé. During the winter at Fort Mandan he "danced on his head" (on his hands). "In the morning we permitted 16 men with their music to go up to the first village, where they delighted the whole tribe with their dances, particularly with the moves of one of the Frenchmen, who danced on his head." Rivet accompanied Colonel Warfington downstream as far as the Arikara village. He met up with Lewis and Clark again when they came downriver. He may have traveled west to join with Manuel Lisa's enterprise. In 1809 a son, Antoine, was born to him at Paradise, Montana. Rivet married the mother of his child, a Flathead woman named Therese Tete Platte, and had a second son, Joseph. From 1813 to 1824 Rivet worked as an interpreter and hunter. In 1823 he was a member of Alexander Ross's Snake River Expedition. Rivet worked for Ross at the Flathead Post as an interpreter until 1829 when he transferred to Fort Colville on the Columbia, where he worked for the Hudson's Bay Company. In 1838 he retired to French Prairie having worked as an interpreter and a "hedge Blacksmith." Also in 1838 his marriage to Therese received formal recognition from the Catholic Church of the Willamette Valley. As a naturalized U.S. citizen, Rivet secured title to a land grant less than three weeks before his death. The *Oregon City Spectator* noted his visit in July 1851: "The oldest resident of Oregon, Monsieur Rivet, was in town yesterday. He came to this country in 1805 and lives in the French settlement some 20-odd miles up the river. Monsieur Rivet is the oldest man in Oregon, save one—he is in his 93rd year. He came to the country with Lewis and Clark—is healthy, robust, and active and bids fair to live out the hundred." François died in September 1852 and is buried in the Old Cemetery at St. Paul.

References: Munnick, "François Rivet," in Leroy Hafen, Mountain Men and the Fur Trade; Thwaites, Original Journals, vol. 1; Coues, History of the Expedition, vol. 1; Moulton, vol. 9

Robinson (Robertson) John (1780–18??): New Hampshire shoe-maker who transferred from Stoddard's Company in October 1803 at Kaskaskia. He was dismissed from the corps on June 12, 1804, and previously had been cited for disorderly conduct while at Camp Dubois. In his detachment orders for March 3, 1804, Lewis wrote, "The abuse of some of the party with respect to the prevelege hereto-fore granted them of going into the country, is not less displeasing; to such as have made hunting or other business a pretext to cover their design of visiting a neighbouring whiskey shop, he cannot for the pres-ent extend this prevelige; and dose therefore most positively direct, that Colter, Bolye, Wiser, and Robinson do not receive permission to leave camp under any pretext whatever for ten days. . . ." He returned to St. Louis and probably went back into Stoddard's Company.
Reference: Moulton, vol. 2

Roche Jhone River: The French term for the Yellowstone River, a tributary of the Missouri, located near today's North Dakota–Montana border. The expedition arrived at the Yellowstone on April 25, 1805. The captains knew of the existence of the river based on information obtained from the Mandan and Minitari Indians. They immediately recognized that the confluence would be strategically and economi-cally important. Sometimes called the Elk River by local Indians, Lewis marveled that "the whol face of the country was covered with herds of Buffaloe, Elk and Antelopes; deer are also abundant, but keep themselves more concealed in the woodland." Clark explored the Yellowstone on the return journey in 1806; at the designated ren-dezvous site he and his party were tormented by swarms of mosqui-toes and moved camp several times in an attempt to find relief.
Reference: Moulton, vol. 4

Rocky Mountain goat (*Oreamnos americanus*): Lewis records that Clark may have first spotted one on August 24, 1805, on the Lemhi River near Shoshone Cove and that he, himself, was "now perfectly convinced that the sheep (mountain goats) as well as the Bighorn exist in these mountains." The captains obtained a hide as a specimen near Strawberry Island on April 10, 1806, from the Clahclellah (or Watlala Chinook) Indians, who gave them the skin to use as a sail in exchange for a knife and two raw elk skins. "I entered one of the houses of those people and was Scercly Seated before they offered me a Sheep Skin for Sale nothing could be more acceptable except the Animal itself in exomoning this skin I found it was a young one, the Skin of the head was Cased So as to fit the head of a man and was esteemed as a great orniment and highly prised by them. we precured this Cased head for a knife and, the Skin we were obliged to give two Raw Elk Skins for. Soon after they offered a large one for Sall. after finding us anxious to purchase they declined silling this Skin. those people informed us that they killed those Animals among the rocks in the mountains under which they live; and that great numbers of those animals inhabit those mountains & that the lamb was killed out of a gange of 36 at short distance from their village. The wool of a full grown Sheep or that on the Skin which we Saw was much Corser than that of the one we purchased, the skin was about the Size of a Common deer." Coues credits Lewis and Clark with the discovery of the mountain goat but it may have been Alexander Mackenzie who first saw the ungulate during his explorations in 1789, calling it the "white buffalo." Naturalist George Ord first scientifically described and named it in 1815. Not a true goat, this quadruped is actually a member of the goat/antelope family and is distinguished from true goats by the shape of its horns. They naturally range in extreme southern Alaska, southern Yukon, British Columbia, southwest Alberta, parts of Washington, northern Idaho, and northwest Montana. Mountain goats have been introduced or planted in several western states, including South Dakota. The animal's life span is approximately thirteen years; some can be as large as three hundred pounds, with horns as long as twelve inches. Bands of mountain goats are usually led by a mature female, her offspring or kid, and a two-year-old, or nearly mature, sibling. During the rut or mating season in November and December, billies, or mature males, will herd up with the nannies, or females. The hoof of a mountain goat is ideally suited to climbing sheer rock faces and cliffs; it has a sharp outer rim for gripping and a rubbery sole for traction on smooth surfaces. They prefer to live at higher elevations with suitable forage of aspen, birch, lichen, and grasses.

Reference: *Moulton, vols. 5, 7*

Rogers, Robert (1731–1795): French and Indian War veteran, who wrote a petition to secure funding from the British Parliament for his dream of an expedition in search of a water passage to the Pacific. Rogers's plan was to head west from the Great Lakes to a "height of land," which he theorized was the source of the Mississippi and the "Ouragan" Rivers, among others. He felt the mountains of the West were, according to geographer John Logan Allen, "situated in the center, and are the highest lands in North America from which rivers flowed in every direction, by those rivers the continent is divided into many departments as if from a center." Although he never received funding, Rogers financed a trip himself, but it too fell through. Among his lieutenants, Jonathan Carver succeeded in reaching the valley of the upper Mississippi and collected enough information from the Indians to suggest the existence of the "pyramidal height of land" much as Rogers had conceived. Carver went on to describe, without giving Rogers credit, the characteristics of the "height of land" in his *Travels through the Interior Parts of North America* (1781). Rogers himself wrote a *Concise Account of North America* (1765), where he described the Mississippi River and the rivers that flow into it. His was the first account to use the term *Ouragan* (Oregon) for the River of the West. See Eulachon.
Reference: Allen, Passage through the Garden

Roloje (Aowa Creek): A creek whose name came to Clark in a dream: "a Creek Coms in above the Bluffs on which there is great quantities of those minerals. This Creek I call roloje a (name given me last night in my Sleep)." Clark later crossed out the reference to the name's source. The creek is located in Dixon County, Nebraska, near Ponca, and is called Aowa Creek.
Reference: Moulton, vol. 2

Rush, Benjamin (1745–1813): Philadelphia physician and adviser on medical matters concerning the expedition. Lewis visited him in May 1803 prior to embarking on his journey and received a two-week crash course on common medicines, military medical practices of the day, and on the specific questions he was to ask the native tribes they would encounter. Rush was a member of the inner circle of the

American Philosophical Society and a friend of Thomas Jefferson. He was educated at Nottingham Academy in Maryland and at Princeton College in New Jersey, where he graduated at the age of fourteen. In 1761 Rush returned to Philadelphia and apprenticed with Dr. John Redmon. At twenty-one Rush traveled to Scotland to study for two years at the University of Edinburgh under the instruction of William Cullen and John Brown. As Dr. David Peck points out, Cullen developed theories on bodily solids being the source of disease, and Brown believed "that disease was caused by variations of nervous excitability." Rush received his degree from the university in 1768. Upon his return to Philadelphia, Rush began an illustrious career of teaching medicine, writing political treatises, and serving as physician general during the Revolutionary War. Rush developed his own medical theories based on the belief that "excited" blood vessels, a condition he termed "hypertension," either contributed to or caused disease. His solution was to bleed patients for any and all ailments. As Peck writes, "his proof of the effectiveness of his theory was that a good bleeding would relax a tense patient." Rush was not adverse to draining a patient of as much as four-fifths of his total blood supply. When Philadelphia was hit by a yellow fever epidemic, Rush refused to leave and insisted on staying in the city to treat the unfortunate victims. As part of the treatment, he bled his patients, including the British minister and his family, and administered his own mixture of drugs to purge their bowels. He called it his depleting therapy and bled patients up to four times a day. Around this time Rush's popularity came into question as his critics began calling him "the bloodletter." Peck notes that the controversy regarding Rush's methods continues to this day among the medical community. As a supporter of progressive political and social ideas, he was one of the signers of the Declaration of Independence. Rush's reluctance to admit his medical theories had some flaws could account for the long-lasting argument over his legacy in medicine. Meriwether Lewis applied Rush's methods throughout the two-and-a-half-year expedition. The captain purchased fifty dozen Rush's pills, also known as Rush's "thunderclappers," to take to the Pacific; as stated in the journals, they never failed to produce the desired effect.

References: Peck, Or Perish in the Attempt*; Jackson,* Letters

Rush's pills (bilious pills): The expedition brought fifty dozen (1,300 doses) of these so-called opening pills or "thunderclappers," known as a powerful purgative and composed of jalap and calomel (mercurous chloride), an inorganic mercury salt composed of two mercury ions and two chloride ions (Hg_2Cl_2). Dr. Benjamin Rush recommended them for almost every illness known to medicine.

Reference: Peck, Or Perish in the Attempt

Russell, Charles M. (1864–1926): Western artist; born in St. Louis. As a young man Russell probably heard stories of Lewis and Clark from his great-grandfather, Silas Bent, who witnessed the expedition's return festivities. Fascinated by tales of the Old West, and steeped in the romance of the Missouri River, Charles persuaded his father to let him work on a sheep ranch in the Judith Basin of Montana. Although he did not succeed as a sheepherder, Russell did learn how to hunt and trap and wrangle cows. He also practiced sketching and would give away his early drawings to friends and saloon owners. He began painting scenes from cattle drives but soon displayed a talent for capturing the Indian people engaged in hunting buffalo. He lived near the Blackfeet in Alberta for five months and became keenly aware of the vanishing culture of the Indian tribes. Russell blamed the changes he witnessed on the arrival of farmers, fences, and plows. In 1888 Russell's work appeared in *Harper's Weekly*; soon his art was reproduced in New York galleries. Luckily for Russell, his wife, Nancy Cooper, recognized and appreciated his talent. She became his representative and saw to it that he spent more time in his studio and less time trading stories at the local Mint Bar in Great Falls. Under her direction Russell was able to charge what he called "dead men's prices" for his art. Over his lifetime Russell would produce some 2,500 paintings, sketches, and sculptures. As his stature as an artist grew, Russell expanded his themes to historical episodes, including illustrations of the Lewis and Clark Expedition. Between 1896 and 1918 he worked on thirteen works of art representing scenes described in their journals. One of his most famous paintings, *York*, shows the Hidatsa chief Le Borgne trying to rub the black off York's skin, an incident that came to light through the Biddle interviews. Another painting, which hangs in the Montana State Capitol, depicts Lewis and Clark meeting the Flathead at Ross's Hole. In order to complete the huge project, Russell had to raise the roof of his studio. Russell has been criticized for historical inaccuracies related to the clothing in some of his paintings, but he remains closely associated with the captains and their trip to the Pacific. His art continues to attract collectors and western art enthusiasts, who readily pay "dead men's prices" to own his work. Upon his death, his hometown of Great Falls gave him a funeral fit for a head of state, and his studio and home are preserved as a historical treasure. The newly remodeled Charles M. Russell Museum sits next to his log cabin studio in Great Falls, Montana.

Reference: Larry Len Peterson

S

Sacagawea (1787?–1812): The woman we call Sacagawea was probably born Shoshone around 1787, the year the United States Constitution was crafted in Philadelphia. Her childhood homeland was thus in the Lemhi Valley in what is now Idaho. Lewis and Clark understood that she had been abducted at about the age of eleven from the Three Forks. Her tormenters were Hidatsa raiders from the Knife River earth-lodge villages in what is now North Dakota. She spent the next five or six years among the Hidatsa, and by the time Lewis and Clark arrived in late October 1804, she was one of the wives of a resident French-Canadian trader named Toussaint Charbonneau. When they arrived at the earth-lodge villages, Lewis and Clark almost immediately hired Charbonneau to serve as their interpreter among the Hidatsa. At some point during the winter, it became clear that the expedition would need horses to cross from the Missouri to the Columbia watersheds by way of the Bitterroot Mountains, and that the Shoshone were said to reside at or near the source of the Missouri. The journals of Lewis and Clark do not explain how the decision to take Charbonneau *and* Sacagawea west along with the permanent party in April 1805 was made, but it is certain that Sacagawea was brought along to interpret among her people, the Shoshone. Her perceived value must have been considerable because the captains (especially Lewis) had already developed a dim view of Charbonneau. In addition Sacagawea was pregnant and complicated the logistics of a military command by giving birth on February 11, 1805, to her first child, Jean Baptiste Charbonneau. When the moment came, Sacagawea did in fact explain the expedition's purposes, needs, and character to the Shoshone. One of the headmen of the tribe, whom Lewis and Clark called Cameahwait, proved to be Sacagawea's brother. Meriwether Lewis reports a tearful reunion in the beleaguered Shoshone's one remaining lodge. In the Shoshone village near Lemhi Pass, Sacagawea was reacquainted with, and released by, a Shoshone man to whom she had been betrothed as a girl. She also met a child-hood playmate who had managed to escape from the Hidatsa raiders at the Three Forks. Undoubtedly Sacagawea helped to establish a trusting relationship between the Corps of Discovery and the Shoshone, but the journal keepers report that the Shoshone continued to be wary, even skittish, in the presence of these exotic strangers. When the expedition said farewell to the Shoshone on August 30, 1805, the entire Charbonneau family continued with Lewis and Clark to the Pacific Ocean. Sacagawea's services to the expedition were not confined to linguistic interpretation and diplomacy. She gathered and dug for prairie edibles, which may have supplemented the expedition's largely meat diet. She did not, as legend has it, guide Lewis and Clark to the Pacific, but she did confirm some of the geographical decisions, particularly when they approached the landscape of her childhood; and on the return journey in 1806, she advised William Clark to cross into the Yellowstone watershed by way of what later became known as Bozeman Pass. On July 13, 1806, William Clark spoke of her as "the indian woman who has been of great Service to me as a pilot through this Country." She seems also to have played a significant symbolic role. On more than one occasion Clark notes that Saca-gawea's presence—with an infant in tow—disarmed potential hostil-ity among Indians who were alarmed by the sudden visitation of more than thirty heavily armed strangers. "The sight of This Indian woman, wife to one of our interprs. confirmed those people of our friendly intentions, as no woman ever accompanies a war party of Indians in this quarter," Clark wrote on October 19, 1805. And it is possible that Sacagawea inspired some civility, perhaps even domesticity, among an overwhelmingly masculine troop. She was, after all, the only woman among thirty-one highly active young men between the ages of eighteen and thirty-five. When Lewis and Clark canvassed the opinions of the company about where to winter between November 1804 and March 1805, Sacagawea and York (Clark's slave) were con-sulted. She cast her "vote" for "a place where there is plenty of Potas [i.e., wappato root]." In the social dynamics of the Corps of Discov-ery, the Charbonneau family soon gravitated to William Clark rather than Meriwether Lewis. Lewis was somewhat contemptuous of Saca-gawea's character. "If she has enough to eat and a few trinkets to wear

I believe she would be perfectly content anywhere," he writes on July 28, 1805. Clark seems to have developed genuine affection for Sacagawea, whom he sometimes called Janey, and especially for her son Jean Baptiste, whom he called "my boy Pomp." Thus the Charbonneau family traveled with Clark in July and August 1806 when the corps split into two exploring parties, one (led by Clark) to reconnoiter the Yellowstone River valley and the other (led by Lewis) to handle the Great Falls portage and determine the source of the Marias River. The Charbonneau family was with Clark (and York) at the Great Falls in July 1805 when a flash flood forced them to scramble up a ravine just ahead of the rising waters. Clark and Sacagawea performed small acts of kindness for each other that have led some to posit a star-crossed romance. Sacagawea gave Clark two dozen white weasels' tails for Christmas 1805 at Fort Clatsop—a gift that is sometimes construed as romantic among the Shoshone. At a critical moment (November 30, 1805), she also gave Clark a small piece of bread that she had been hoarding in her personal kit. On at least one occasion Clark rebuked Charbonneau for striking his wife, and it was Clark who pushed Sacagawea to safety during the flash flood in Montana, while Charbonneau characteristically panicked and prayed. It may be that Clark served as a kind of patron-protector of Sacagawea among a company of young men where she might otherwise have been the object of harassment. The Charbonneau family was discharged from the Corps of Discovery on August 17, 1806, at the Hidatsa villages on the Knife River. Charbonneau was paid $500.33. Thus ended one of the most fascinating—if improbable—cross-cultural alliances in American history. The story does not end along the Knife River, however. On August 20, 1806, just as the Corps of Discovery was leaving the present state of North Dakota, William Clark wrote an extraordinary letter on board the expedition's pirogue. After expressing friendship for Charbonneau and apologizing for not having had time to discuss the future with him in the hurried last days with the Mandan and Hidatsa villagers, Clark wrote, "your woman who accompanied you that long dangerous and fatiguing rout to the Pacific Ocian and back diserved a greater reward for her attention and services on that rout than we had in our power to give her at the Mandans." What an extraordinary sentence from the pen of an army officer, a Kentucky gentleman, and the busy leader of a military reconnaissance. "Charbono, if you wish to live with the white people, and will come to me I will give you a piece of land and furnish you with horses cows & hogs." The Charbonneau family did come to St. Louis—probably in 1810. William Clark made good on his promise to supervise the education of Jean Baptiste, who went on to have a long, colorful life in Europe and the American West. By 1812 Sacagawea and Charbonneau were back upriver, at Fort Manuel just below the North Dakota–South Dakota border. There, on December 20, 1812, the factor at Fort Manuel announced that Sacagawea had died of putrid fever. This seems to accord with William Clark's understanding. In his account book of 1825–28, Clark lists Sacagawea as dead. These are the facts about the life and achievement of the remarkable Sacagawea as most historians understand them, but it must be acknowledged that a cloud of uncertainty hangs over virtually every aspect of her life. She has been claimed—genetically as well as culturally—by the Shoshone, the Hidatsa, the Comanche, and even the Dakota Indians. The pronunciation and spelling of her name have been the subjects of endless speculation and even controversy. Some have argued that she is to be called Sacajawea, a Shoshone word that means "boat launcher." Others, that she is Sacagawea or Sakakawea, a Hidatsa word that means "Bird Woman." This is how Lewis and Clark saw it. Some believe that she died at the age of about twenty-five of putrid fever at Fort Manuel, others, that she lived a very long and busy life, and died at about the age of one hundred on the Wind River Indian Reservation in Wyoming, where indeed a grave marker tells her story. Some (notably James Ronda, a leading authority on Lewis and Clark among native peoples) have granted Sacagawea a severely limited role in the success of the expedition. Others have elevated her to guide, and at times even savior, of the expedition. This much is certain. The Sacagawea of American popular culture and mythology is a larger-than-life figure, and she has in two hundred years eclipsed every other member of the expedition with the possible exceptions of Meriwether Lewis and William Clark themselves. She is by now what is called a cultural construct—a blend of legend, mythology, politics, historical fiction, iconography, fantasy, and multicultural embrace. It is hard, almost impossible, to reconstruct the real Sacagawea who serves as the basis for all of this nonrigorous historical activity. It must always be remembered that everything we know about Sacagawea comes through the lenses of early-nineteenth-century men: Meriwether Lewis, William Clark, John Ordway, Patrick Gass, Joseph Whitehouse, and—thanks to their work on the official narrative of the expedition—Nicholas Biddle and George Shannon. It is inescapable that the "historical" Sacagawea is the product of patriarchal and indeed Eurocentric sensibilities. She wrote nothing herself. She was almost certainly illiterate. The cultures that shaped her were still entirely mediated by oral rather than written traditions. Had Sacagawea recorded her own history, it seems certain that our understanding of her would be significantly, perhaps fundamentally, different. The seven journal keepers—Ordway, Gass, Floyd, Pryor, Frazier, Lewis, and Clark, four of whose journals are extant for the Sacagawea phase of the expedition—did not routinely report her activities. Sacagawea gets noticed when she feeds the expedition, when she gets sick, when she nearly drowns, when her beads are needed for an economic transaction, when she interprets among her people, the Shoshone. Sacagawea is mentioned substantively only a handful of times in the journals. No journal keeper ever pauses to describe her physique, her posture, her clothing, her parenting style, or her location in the daily dynamics of the boats and the camps. Only Lewis appraises her in a general way, and his dismissal of her personality is rarely considered authoritative. We have only one indirect quotation, reported by Meriwether Lewis. When the expedition learned of a whale beached southwest of Fort Clatsop and mounted a team to visit the carcass and scavenge whatever might be useful, Sacagawea and Charbonneau were not originally chosen to make the journey. But Sacagawea mounted a protest. On January 6, 1806, Meriwether Lewis wrote, "the Indian woman was very importunate to be permitted to go, and was therefore indulged; she observed that she had traveled a long way with us to see the great waters, and that now that monstrous fish was also to be seen, she thought it very hard she could not be permitted to see either (she had never yet been to the Ocean)." Oral tradition of Lemhi Shoshone refutes this. There is no adequate biography of Sacagawea. Grace Hebard's *Sacajawea* (1933), Eva Emery Dye's *The Conquest* (1902), and Anna Lee Waldo's *Sacajawea* (1979) are unreliable. The most interesting recent study of Sacagawea, Donna Kessler's *The Making of Sacagawea: A Euro-American Legend* (1996), is the only book that attempts to explore the way in which the biological Sacagawea became the figure of American mythology. The best narrative analysis remains Harold P. Howard's *Sacajawea* (1971). Remarkable oral traditions exist in Hidatsa, Mandan, Dakota, Comanche, and Lemhi Shoshone cultures. Although some of them are mutually exclusive, they are increasingly regarded by historians as possessing cultural validity, even when they challenge existing understandings of Sacagawea's life and achievement.

References: Jackson, Letters; *Donna Kessler; Harold Howard*

Sage grouse (*Centrocercus urophasianus*, cock of the plains, logcock, mountain cock, heath grouse, and pheasant): As seen in Clark's drawing of the cock of the plains for March 2, 1806. First observed by Lewis while reconnoitering the Marias, although it was originally technically and scientifically named *Centrocercus urophasianus* by Charles Lucien Bonaparte in 1827. Lewis wrote that "the flesh of the cock of the Plains is dark, and only tolerable in point of flavor. I do not think it as good as either the Pheasant or the Grouse." Cutright writes that "only rarely have modern ornithologists credited Lewis and Clark with the discovery of a bird," but he adds that Smithsonian scientist Arthur Bent did so with the sage grouse. Lewis first called this bird a "mountain cock," although he changed that when he reached the Columbia by referring to it as the "prairie cock" or "cock of the plains." Burrows lists it as the largest of the North American grouse and one of the few gallinaceous birds recognized by Bent as discovered by Lewis and Clark. According to the *National Audubon Society Field Guide to North American Birds*, "The sage grouse is well named for it is quite dependent on sagebrush. In the fall and winter the leathery leaves of sagebrush are one of its only foods, and during the rest of the year the sagebrush provides it with cover. Each spring the males gather on a traditional display ground called a lek to court the females. Once a female has mated she goes off and raises her family by herself." It ranges from southern Alberta and Saskatchewan south to eastern California, Nevada, Colorado, and South Dakota and has recently declined in numbers.

References: Cutright, Pioneering Naturalists; *Udvarty; Moulton, vol. 6*

Saint-Mémin, Charles Balthazar Julien Fevret (1770–1852): French-born Philadelphia artist. His family emigrated to New York City in 1796, where he sold engravings of landscape sketches and developed his talents for portraiture. Saint-Mémin used a physiogno-trace: a wooden-framed device invented in France that produced a quick and precise life-size profile of the sitter in pencil on red paper. He would then fill in the picture with crayon or watercolor and reduce the drawing by pantograph to a two-inch miniature on a copper engraving plate for which he charged thirty-three dollars for the drawing, plate, and twelve proofs. In 1804 Saint-Mémin produced portraits of the Osage chiefs President Jefferson had Lewis invite to Washington. Three years later Lewis commissioned him to do the Indian portraits for Lewis's proposed three-volume account of the expedition. He produced a famous watercolor of Meriwether Lewis showing the captain wearing an ermine-skin tippet and holding his rifle. In 1816 William Strickland engraved the watercolor. Lewis paid Saint-Mémin $83.50 for his likenesses of the Indians, which included one of a Mandan chief and another of his wife. Five of these portraits survive. He returned to France in 1814.

Reference: Cutright, History of the Lewis and Clark Journals

Salal (*Gaultheria shallon*): First described by Clark on December 9, 1805, when he tasted some syrup made of the salal berry; he noted the Clatsops called it "shele wele." He later commented that it was about the size of a "Chery." Lewis observed, "the natives either eat these berrys when ripe immediately from the bushes or dried in the sun or by means of their sweating kilns; very frequently they pound them and bake then in large loaves of 10 to fifteen pounds; this bread keeps very well during one season and retains the moist jeucies of the fruit much better than any other method of preservation. this bread is broken and sitred in could water until it be sufficiently thick and then eaten; in this

John F. Clymer's "The Saltmakers" shows coastal Indians wearing conical hats as they observe members of the party boiling seawater to manufacture salt. Courtesy of Mrs. John F. Clymer and the Clymer Museum of Art.

way the natives most generally use it." It is described and sketched in detail by Lewis in his entry for February 8, 1806. Salal was sometimes used as an antiseptic agent by the natives, and in a tea for bladder ailments.

Reference: *Moulton, vol. 6*

Salt Camp: Occupied from December 28, 1805, to February 19, 1806, on the Pacific Coast near present-day Seaside, Oregon. The salt-making crew hauled five kettles to a beach fifteen miles southwest of Fort Clatsop where from three to five men kept the fires burning under the kettles in order to extract salt. They managed to collect three bushels, enough to sustain them until they unearthed the salt cached at Camp Fortunate. Privates William Bratton and George Gibson became ill while working at the salt works; Gibson had to be carried back to Fort Clatsop on a litter. The camp was dismantled on February 21, 1806. As Sergeant Ordway recorded, "we Set out eairly with all the Salt and baggage. took an Indian canoe and crossed the River and travelled verry hard. when we got halfway Set in to Storming & rained verry hard & the wind blew So high that we could not cross the creek in a canoe and waided across and got to the Fort about half past 12 o clock. much fatigued and I am at this time verry Sick and wet to my Skins waiding the Slashes and marshes. The day verry disagreeable and Stormey &c." There is a replica of the salt works in Seaside on Lewis and Clark Way.

Reference: Moulton, vol. 9

Saugrain, Antoine François (1763–1820): French physician and scientist, in 1800 a resident of St. Louis. He helped treat malaria in the Ohio Valley and most likely advised Meriwether Lewis on medical matters prior to the expedition. Although no written evidence exists, family tradition indicates Saugrain supplied Lewis and Clark with a medicine chest, thermometers, and matches.

Reference: Chuinard, Only One Man Died

Sawyer: Frequently encountered dangerous obstruction (along with the logjam, snag, and *embarras*) found in the Missouri River. Explorer David Thompson observed, "The sawyer is generally a Tree of large dimention broken about the middle of its length, it's roots are in the mud . . . the strong current bends the tree as much as the play of the roots will permit, the strain of which causes a reaction, and the tree rises with a spring upwards above the water and with such force as will damage or destroy any vessel." According to Elliott Coues, "A sawyer is a snag or timber so fixed in the water that it oscillates up and down under the varying stress of the current, and forms a special danger to navigation. A firmly embedded snag is called a planter." On August 4, 1806, Alexander Willard narrowly escaped drowning because of a sawyer. As Captain Lewis noted, it was fortunate Willard could swim.

References: Lavender, Way to the Western Sea; *Coues,* History of the Expedition, *vol. 1; Moulton, vol. 8*

Seaman (Scannon): Newfoundland dog. Accompanied the Corps of Discovery to the Pacific and believed to have returned with his owner, Meriwether Lewis, to St. Louis. Historian Ernest S. Osgood conjectures Seaman was most likely purchased by Lewis before he left Washington, D.C., for Pittsburgh in 1803. According to his Ohio journal, Lewis paid a substantial sum for the dog whom he "prised much for his docility and qualifications generally for my journey." He rejected a Shawnee Indian's offer of three beaver skins for his pet, writing, "of course there was no bargain. I had given $20.00 for this dogg myself." Indeed Seaman's "qualifications generally" would prove most valuable to the expedition. Intelligent, loyal, and strong, contemporary Newfoundlands are black in color (although nineteenth-century Newfoundlands were sometimes mixed in color), weigh up to 150 pounds, and stand thirty inches in their prime. A Newfoundland's coat is thick and water resistant. Accomplished swimmers, their long tails function as rudders while their webbed feet and massive chests power them through the water. Also known as sea dogs, Newfoundlands rescued men fallen overboard and hauled lines and nets for fishers. Descriptions of Newfoundland standards state, "A good specimen of the breed has dignity and proud head carriage." Some speculate the breed originated in Europe because today's "Newf" (as it is sometimes called) so closely resembles the Great Pyrenees breed. According to Margaret Booth Chern, historian of the breed, the Newfoundland was indigenous to North America and often lived with the Indian tribes along the coast and on the central plains. Ben Franklin and Samuel Adams both owned Newfoundlands. Typical of his breed, Seaman sought above all to protect and please his master. On the Ohio River in September 1803, he and Lewis witnessed a gray squirrel migration swimming across the river. "I made my dog take as many each day as I had occation for, they wer fat and I thought them when fryed a pleasant food—many of these squirrels were black they swim very light on the water and make pretty good speed—my dog was of the Newfoundland breed very active and docile, he would take the squirrel in the water and kill them and swimming bring them in his mouth to the boat." Seaman's skill as a hunter impressed Sergeant Ordway many times. Ordway's journal noted Seaman retrieving geese, deer, and, on April 26, 1805, he witnessed the dog catching, killing, and bringing in an antelope as it swam across the river. More than once Seaman protected the expedition at risk of his life. On May 29, 1805, he saved the crew when a buffalo charged into camp, "and was within 18 inches of the heads of some of the men who lay sleeping before the centinels could alarm him or make him change his course, still more alarmed, he now took his direction immediately towards our lodge, passing between 4 fires and within a few inches of the heads of one range of men as they yet lay sleeping, when he came near the tent, my dog saved us by causing him to change his course a second time, which he did by turning a little to the right, and was quickly out of sight." Many times he protected the party from fierce grizzlies. On June 28, 1805, Lewis observed that "they come close around our camp every night but have never yet ventured to attack us and our dog gives us timely notice of their visits, he keeps constantly padroling all night." Seaman endured every trial the men did, except perhaps homesickness. Commenting on a terrible barbed seed that penetrated their moccasins and leggings Lewis noted, "my poor dog suffers with them excessively, he is constantly binting and scratching himself as if in a rack of pain." The dog played his role in what historian James Ronda calls the traveling "Lewis and Clark medicine show." Lewis did not hesitate to use him at a critical juncture in building up good feelings with the Shoshone. On August 17, 1805, Lewis reported the natives equally admired "the appearance of the men, their arms, the canoes, our manner of working them, the back [sic] man York, and the sagacity of my dog." The dog's inevitable afflictions caused some concern for Lewis. On a trip to the Spirit Mound in August of 1804, Seaman's suffering proved bad enough that Clark noted, "at two miles further our Dog was So Heeted & fatigued we was obliged Send him back to the Creek." Later, Seaman endured a bite on the hind leg from a defensive beaver. Ordway reported on May 19, 1805, "Semon, Captain Lewiss dog got bit by a beaver." Lewis wrote, "It was with great difficulty that I could stop the blood. I fear it will yet prove fatal to him." With regard to fleas, it is safe to assume no one suffered as much as Seaman during the winter at Fort Clatsop. On April 24, 1805, Seaman did what most male dogs do from time to time and disappeared. According to Lewis, "my dog had been absent during the last night and I was fearfull that we had lost him altogether, however, much to my satisfaction he joined us at 8 o clock this morning." That spring the corps encountered immense herds of buffalo along the Missouri River. Lewis mentions Seaman: "Walking along the shore this evening I met with a Buffalo calf which attached itself to me and continued to follow close at my heels until I embarked and left it. It appeared allarmed at my dog which was probably the cause of its attaching itself to me." Sometime during the journey, Seaman became "our dog" as described in the journals of Clark, Ordway, and Gass.

For the readers of the journals, the idea of having a dog along made the story of the Lewis and Clark Expedition take on qualities of an extended camping trip, and his story has been the subject of several books and many articles. Filson Historical Society curator James Holmberg found an interesting entry taken from a dog collar and subsequently noted in Timothy Alden's *Collection of Epitaphs and Inscriptions* (1814). The collar, which Alden found in a museum in Alexandria, Virginia, reads, "The Greatest Traveller of my species. My name is Seaman, the dog of Captain Meriwether Lewis, whom I accompanied to the Pacifick ocean through the interior of the continent of North America." Alden included a note describing the dog's reaction to the sad end of Captain Lewis—apparently he would not leave Lewis's gravesite and died there of dehydration and malnutrition. Holmberg asserts the timing of this evidence, within five years of Lewis's death, provides a credible indication of Seaman's fate. He viewed letters indicating that Clark presented the collar to the Mason's lodge of Alexandria-Washington and their museum in 1812. No trace of this collar remains extant. It is certain Lewis and Seaman shared a strong emotional attachment. When he was nearly stolen by the Wah-cle-lar Indians on the lower Columbia River, it so enraged Lewis he dispatched three men in pursuit with orders to fire upon the thieves if there was any resistance or hesitation in returning the dog. Seaman was last mentioned by Lewis on July 15, 1806: "The musquetoes continue to infest us in such a manner that we can barely exist . . . my dog even howls with the torture he experiences from them." Readers did not learn of the name of Lewis's dog until the publication of Sergeant Ordway's journal in 1916. Milo Quaife, Ordway's editor, transcribed it three ways: Scannon, Semon, and Scamon. Earlier editions of the Lewis and Clark journals did not mention the dog. In his edition of the journals, Coues comments on a creek named Seaman: "A name I believe not found elsewhere in this History and to the personality of which I have no clew." Lewis and Clark scholar Donald Jackson corrected the mistake in 1985 when researching place-names along the trail. According to his wife, Kathy, Jackson reasoned that because Lewis and Clark named so many geographical formations after members of the corps, it seemed logical to assume they would eventually get around to naming one for the dog. Expecting to find "Seaman's creek" was actually "Scannon's Creek," Jackson writes he was mildly startled when he found, upon close inspection of handwriting samples, "the stream was named Seaman's creek because the dog's name was Seaman." Thanks to Jackson's diligence we now know Seaman's Creek was named in honor of Lewis's beloved dog—a fitting honor for such a loyal, devoted, four-legged friend and one that deserves to be restored. The creek today is called Monture Creek. It is located in the picturesque Blackfoot River valley near Ovando, Montana.

References: Chern; Charbonneau; Moulton, vols. 2, 3, 9; Jackson, "Call Him a Good Old Dog"; Holmberg "Seaman's Fate"; Albers

Shannon, George (1785–1836): Private. Youngest and least experienced of the corps, Shannon was born in Pennsylvania but had moved to Ohio around 1800. He probably joined the expedition at the Falls of the Ohio. He is, therefore, considered one of the "nine young men from Kentucky." Perhaps because of his youth and inexperience, Shannon often drew the more menial tasks. He once badly cut his foot with an adze tool. He managed to lose his tomahawk, several horses, and was twice himself lost for several days. On August 29, 1804, Joseph Whitehouse remarked, "colter Sent on with Some provision for to hunt Shannon & the horses &c." The next time Shannon separated from the corps it proved more dangerous; he kept trying to catch up when in fact the boats were behind him. Whitehouse noted, "we came to Shore and found it was Shannon that had been with the horses. he had been absent 16 days and 12 of them he had Eat nothing but Grapes. the reason was his balls ran Short." Clark remarked, "he had been 12 days without any thing to eate but Grapes and one Rabit, which he Killed by shooting a piece of hard Stick in place of a ball—. This man Supposeing the boat to be a head pushed on as long as he Could when he became weak and fiable determined to lay by and waite for a tradeing boat, which is expected Keeping one horse for the last resorse,—thus a man had like to have Starved to death in a land of Plenty for the want of Bulletes or Something to kill his meat." Lewis named a nearby creek in Shannon's honor. After the expedition, Clark hired him to help return Mandan chief Sheheke-shote from his visit to see the Great Father in Washington, D.C. In the first attempt, in 1807, Shannon's leg was wounded when the party, including Nathaniel

Pryor, was attacked by Arikara Indians who were angry because one of their chiefs died while visiting Washington. The wound became infected and the leg was amputated in St. Charles, Missouri. Shannon later received a pension from the U.S. government for the injury. In 1810, at the suggestion of William Clark, Shannon helped Nicholas Biddle edit the journals. Although Clark offered him a partnership in his fur company, Shannon decided to practice law. He married fellow student Ruth Price of Lexington in 1813. He served in the Kentucky House of Representatives (1820 and 1822), practiced law in Missouri, and became a senator from that state. Shannon was arguing a case when he dropped dead in Palmyra, Missouri, at the age of fifty-one.

Reference: Moulton, vols. 3, 11

Sheheke-shote (Le Gros Blanc, Bag of Lies, White Coyote; also known as Sheheke [1760–1815]): Mandan chief of the Metutahanke village at the confluence of the Knife and Missouri Rivers. He encountered Lewis and Clark on October 24, 1804, and shared life with the expedition throughout the winter of 1804–05. The location of Fort Mandan was in close proximity to Sheheke's village. He was a frequent source of information and food for the corps, and he treated the captains with fairness and respect. He pledged to follow their advice and cease hostilities with the Pania, telling Clark, "we kill them like the birds, we do not wish to kill more, we will, make a good Peace." As far as sharing hardship during the brutal winter, Shehekeshote went on to say, "if we eat you Shall eat, if we starve you must Starve also, our village is too far to bring the Corn to you, but we hope you will Call on us as you pass to the place you intend to Stop." At the end of October Clark presented Sheheke with a medal, some flags, cocked hats, and a steel corn mill, which the Mandan promptly dismantled to use for arrows. At the direction of Sheheke-shote, his wife, Yellow Corn, hauled more than one hundred pounds of "very fine meat," buffalo, to the corps. He also invited them to accompany the tribe on a hunt and later to join in the sacred Buffalo Calling Ceremony. As the expedition made plans for departure, Sheheke-shote helped Clark fill in missing details on his western map. In 1806 the captains persuaded Sheheke-shote to travel to Washington for a meeting with the Great Father, President Thomas Jefferson. Traveling with his wife and child and an interpreter, Jesseaume, and his family, Sheheke left along with the expedition on August 17, 1806, for what he assumed would be no more than a few months. The chief visited Jefferson's home to see his collection of Indian relics and went to Philadelphia, where he sat for a portrait painted by the French artist Saint-Mémin. Hostilities with the Arikara delayed his return for three years, at which time former expedition mates Nathaniel Pryor and George Shannon tried unsuccessfully to bring Sheheke home. Shannon lost his leg in the attempt. Sheheke finally returned to his homeland in 1809 with the help of Pierre Chouteau's Missouri Fur Company and at a cost of seven thousand dollars to the U.S. government. Replaced by other tribal leaders, Sheheke lost the respect of his people when he returned, and his stories about Washington were dismissed as lies. He died in 1815 at the hands of Sioux warriors.

References: Moulton, vol. 3; Roger Wendlick, personal communication

Shields, John (1769–1809): Private. Age thirty-four when he enlisted with the expedition on October 19, 1803, Shields was the oldest and possibly the only married member of the enlisted men. He was born in Virginia, but because he was living in Kentucky and enlisted there, he is considered one of the "nine young men from Kentucky." He performed invaluable service for the corps as a blacksmith and gunsmith; he also assisted in boat repair whenever needed. When Shields fixed the main spring on Lewis's air gun, the captain noted, "we have been much indebted to this man on many occasions; without having served any regular apprenticeship to any trade, he makes his own tools principally and works extreemly well in either wood or metal, and in this way has been extreenely servicable to us, as well as being a good hunter and an excellent waterman." Not only did Shields repair tools, he also took the suggestion of one of his Mandan patrons and produced battle-axes and arrow points in addition to scrapers for treating hides. Shields's smithing talents, along with those of Bratton and Willard, ensured a steady supply of corn and other foodstuffs during the winter of 1804–05, with enough left over to cache away for the return journey. Near the Great Falls he fashioned a handmade screw for the iron boat and helped construct a leather boat, June 18, 1805. *We Proceeded On* editor Robert Lange contends

Shields probably formed the expedition's rounds of ammunition by melting the lead from the empty gunpowder canisters. On August 11, 1805, in pursuit of horses and at a crucial juncture with the Shoshone Indians, Shields's failure to halt alarmed the Indians and sent them scurrying away from Lewis's advance party. In no uncertain terms Lewis describes this: "I now felt quite as much mortification and disappointment as I had pleasure and expectation at the first sight of this Indian. I felt soarly chagrined at the conduct of the men particularly Shields to whom I principally atributed this failure in obtaining an introduction to the natives. I now called the men to me and could not forbare abraiding them a little for their want to attention and imprudence on this occasion." Later the usually observant and helpful Shields prescribed the cure for his fellow private William Bratton when he suffered from a debilitating lower back illness. As a last resort the men took Shields's suggestion and watched as "he sunk a circular hole of 3 feet diamiter and four feet deep in the earth. he kindled a large fire in the hole and heated well, after which the fire was taken out a seat placed in the center of the hole for the patient with a board at bottom for his feet to rest on; some hoops of willow poles were bent in an arch crossing each other over the hole, on these several blankets were thrown forming a secure and thick orning of about 3 feet high. the patient being striped naked was seated under this orning in the hole and the blankets well secured on every side. the patient was furnished with a vessell of water which he sprinkles on the bottom and sides of the hole and by that means creates as much steam or vapor as he could possibly bear in this situation he was kept about 20 minutes after which he was taken out and suddonly plunged in cold water twise and was then immediately returned to the sweat hole where he was continued three quarters of an hour longer then taken out covered up in several blankets and suffered to cool gradually. during the time of his being in the sweat hole, he drank copious draughts of a strong tea of horse mint. Shields said that he had previously seen the tea of the Sinneca snake root used in stead of the mint. . . ." Bratton's treatment and recovery show the resourcefulness of John Shields. Although his own rheumatism bothered him at Fort Clatsop, Shields consistently performed his services admirably, so much so that upon his discharge Lewis appealed for extra compensation on his behalf:

"Has received the pay only of a private. Nothing was more peculiarly useful to us, in various situations, than the skill and ingenuity of this man as an artist, in repairing our guns, accoutrements, &c. and should it be thought proper to allow him something as an artificer, he has well deserved it."

The captains named two streams in Shields's honor: one is the present-day Highwood Creek near Great Falls; the other flows into the Yellowstone River near the town of Livingston and retains its rightful name. In addition Shields is credited with the discovery of a "bould spring" near the Yellowstone, significant because of its lack of minerals.

References: Yater and Denton; Jackson, Letters; Moulton, vols. 4, 5, 7

Side Hill Calf (also known as He That Looks at the Calf [d. 1806]): Piegan warrior who encountered Lewis and several of his men on July 27, 1806, near Two Medicine River and tried to steal a gun belonging to Joseph Field. When he was discovered a fight ensued, and Side Hill Calf was mortally wounded, stabbed in the chest by Rueben Field. Following the encounter in which another Piegan was also killed or wounded, Lewis removed the amulets and shields from Side Hill Calf's neck and left a peace medal in their place so, as Lewis put it, "that they might be informed who we were." Lewis's party then fled on horseback at high speed to the rendezvous with the rest of their party about five miles from Grog Spring.

Reference: Moulton, vol. 8

Sign language (Indian or Plains sign language): A gesture method of communication that evolved among Native American Indian tribes and was practiced extensively in the eighteenth and nineteenth centuries so that members of different linguistic groups were able to converse with each other. Accounts describing the use of Indian sign language go as far back as the time of Coronado. Despite some variations the language could be understood across cultures, with certain individuals emerging as experts known as sign talkers. Captain William Philo Clark, not to be confused with William Clark, studied and practiced sign language during his six years of service (1876–82) in the U.S. Army when he commanded scores of Indian scouts including Pawnee, Shoshone, Arapaho, Cheyenne, Crow, and Sioux, in addition to working with members of the Bannock, Assiniboine, Gros Ventre, Mandan, and Arikara tribes. In 1881 his commander, Lieutenant General P. H. Sherman, asked him to produce a study of the Indian sign language including remarks upon the habits, manners, and customs of the Indians, which he submitted in July of 1884. It is a highly readable dictionary and encyclopedia of sign language, with the author's deep respect, understanding, and appreciation obvious throughout. As Clark put it, to become accomplished in sign talking "one must train the mind to think like an Indian." He further theorized that the language would "seem meaningless and contemptible in a land of art and science, but beautiful, graceful, rich, and useful in the realm of nature." Graceful execution of this language, he maintained, "can only result from long practice." Clark found Plains sign language developed because of the lack of a dominant economic or political force on the Great Plains to impose its language on other tribes. In the absence of an imposed method of communication, the natives approached each other as equals; they did not view the use of gestures or signs as evidence of primitive reasoning faculties. Although sign language is not universal, it is much easier to learn than spoken language. Clark wrote that sign language was constantly evolving: "Even in my comparatively short experience with Indians, I have observed the birth, growth, and death of many gestures." Sign language was used by both women and men and within the same language group in addition to their spoken language. Although the natives of the upper Missouri region definitely practiced sign language, the journals do not mention the use of sign until the initial encounter with the Shoshone at the headwaters of the Missouri. Lewis, who was ahead of the main party, attempted to use sign to express his peaceful intentions toward three Shoshone women he found hiding in the bush. Although he did succeed in making friends, thanks to signs he learned from Sacagawea, his limited knowledge of the language was insufficient to guarantee success in bargaining with the Shoshone for horses. For that crucial accomplishment, the captains relied on their highly qualified sign talker, George Drouillard. Drouillard's mother was a Shawnee Indian and his father a French Canadian who served with George Rogers Clark. Drouillard had transferred from Fort Massac to the Lewis and Clark Expedition in November of 1803 to serve as an inter-

preter. Among his many skills as an outdoorsman and a hunter, George Drouillard was also valuable as a sign talker, arguably the most proficient of the entire expedition. In addition, he proved to be an extremely capable horseman, hunter, tracker, boatman, trader, negotiator, and a trustworthy companion for both the captains, but most often for Meriwether Lewis. Drouillard's ability to communicate with the Indians helped secure assistance from the Nez Percé and played a key role in the encounter at Two Medicine River. See Drouillard, George.
Reference: W. P. Clark

Sniggle: Nez Percé term for horsehair balls stuffed with bait and used in fishing; when a fish bites a *sniggle* its teeth became ensnared. One of several (including hook, line, and spear) Nez Percé fishing methods.
Reference: Landeen and Pinkham

Soulard, Antoine (1766–1825): French surveyor residing in St. Louis; appointed the Spanish king's surveyor general of upper Louisiana in 1795. That same year Soulard drew a map of the Mississippi and Missouri Rivers, which was later copied and used as a reference by Lewis and Clark. According to geographer John Logan Allen, "the critical information that came through on the Soulard map was that when the Great Falls were reached, the traveler would have traversed the mountain chain." On the map, the Pacific Ocean appeared very close to that mountain chain. Soulard's map also suggested that the Missouri River flowed almost due east from its source, an accepted part of the geographical lore Lewis and Clark were familiar with. Soulard secured employment as a surveyor for the new American government in St. Louis but was dismissed in 1806 because of questions regarding his impartiality in the land surveys he engaged in. For the rest of his life, Soulard and his wife, Julie, sought to reclaim lands granted to them by the Spanish government. In 1836, eleven years after her husband's death, Julie Soulard won back the land titles, and a section of old St. Louis bears their name to this day.
Reference: Allen, Passage through the Garden

Spirit canoe: Used by the coastal Salish in a curing ceremony during which the participants acted out a search for the lost soul of a family member. Formed of painted wooden planks placed upright in the ground in the shape of a canoe. Not to be confused with the image canoe, which was a carved canoe used for transportation by the coastal tribes.

Reference: Coues, History of the Expedition, *vol. 2*

Spirit Mound (Mountain of Little People or Spirits, Hill of Little Devils): Seventy-foot-high conic mound north of the Missouri River in Clay County, South Dakota, described as being surrounded by an immense prairie. The captains and ten men investigated it on August 25, 1804, after hearing tales of "evel Spirits" from the Maha Indians, who believed the area to be inhabited by little devils: eighteen-inch-high dwarfs with huge heads who skillfully hurled sharp arrows at anyone brave enough to trespass. None of the neighboring tribes, Mahas, Otos, or Sioux, would visit the area. Despite high temperatures and a six-mile hike to reach the mound, Lewis and Clark bravely set out with Ordway, Shields, Joe Field, Colter, Bratton, Cane, Labiche, Warfington, Frazier, York, and Seaman. All suffered from dehydration during the four-hour march, especially the recently mineral-poisoned Lewis and the dog: "our Dog was so Heeted & fatigued we was obliged to send him back to the Creek." They determined the mound did not house spirits of any kind except numerous birds catching flying and biting ants. (Ordway called them Stone piss ants; Moulton calls them harvester ants.) The long hike rewarded the men with a magnificent view of the surrounding plains. "From the top of this Mound we observed Several large gangus of Buffalow & Elk feeding upwards of 800 in number." Native American myths and legends concerning a little people are common among the tribes of the West. There are published accounts of mummified remains of little people found in the mountains of Wyoming and skeletons of pygmies have been found near the Yellowstone River. (Remains of a fossilized human found in Wyoming, proved to be that of a sixty-five-year-old man.) Clark remarked that the large assemblage of birds they observed at the mound was "a Sufficient proof to produce in the Savage mind a Confident belief of all the properties which they ascribe it." A local effort is under way to reestablish prairie grasses and other native plants and remove any objects that obstruct the view so that decades from now the mound will look much the same as when Lewis and Clark first saw it in 1804.

References: *Moulton, vol. 3; Wetmore*

Stil-la-sha: Clatsop chief of a village on the south bank of the great chute of the Columbia.

Stoddard, Amos (1762–1813): Connecticut born, Stoddard served in the American Revolution from 1779 to 1782. He later worked as a clerk of the Massachusetts Supreme Court and studied and practiced law in Maine. Stoddard became a captain of the 1798 artillery in the U.S. Army. In July 1803 Secretary of War Henry Dearborn ordered Captain Stoddard, and the Bissell brothers, then stationed at Kaskaskia, to supply Lewis with "good men who understand rowing a boat to go with Capt. Lewis as far up the River [Missouri] as they can go & return with certainty before the Ice will obstruct the passage of the river." Alexander Willard and the dismissed John Robertson came out of Stoddard's unit of artillerists. He also furnished Lewis with seventy-five pounds of public, or gun, powder "for the use of my command, bound to the western waters." In Lewis's absence Stoddard served as his agent both in terms of paying the engagés and in assisting any Indian chiefs the captain sent downriver. Stoddard wrote Dearborn upon the corps's departure: "Sir: I have the pleasure to inform you that Captain Lewis, with his party, began to ascend the Missouri from the village of St. Charles on the 21st ultimo. I accompanied him to that village and he was also attended by most of the principal gentlemen in this place and vicinity. He began his expedition with a Barge of 18 oars, attended by two large perogues all of which were deeply laden, and well manned. I have heard from him about 60 miles on his route, and it appears that he proceeds about 15 miles per day—a celerity seldom witnessed on the Missouri; and this is the more extraordinary as the time required to ascertain the courses of the river and to make the other necessary observations must considerably retard his progress. His men possess great resolution and they were in good health and spirits." When the Spanish surrendered the city of

St. Louis, Stoddard became the commandant of upper Louisiana. He received a promotion to major in 1807 and served in the War of 1812 as a deputy quartermaster. He died of tetanus in May of 1813 after being wounded at the siege of Fort Meigs, Ohio.

Reference: Jackson, Letters

Sulphur Spring (Sacagawea Spring): On June 16, 1805, near the Great Falls, opposite the mouth of Belt Creek, Lewis returned to camp to find "the Indian woman extreemly ill and much reduced by her indisposition. this gave me some concern as well for the poor object herself, then with the young child in her arms, as from the consideration of her being our only dependence for a friendly negociation with the Snake Indians on whom we depend for horses. . . ." He sent some of the men to collect water from a sulphur spring nearby, which he "now resolved to try on the Indian woman. . . . the water is as transparent as possible strongly impregnated with sulpher, and I suspect Iron also, as the colour of the hills and bluffs in the neighbourhood indicate the existence of that metal. the water to all appearance is precisely similar to that of Bowyer's Sulpher spring in Virginia." The next day Lewis reported, "The Indian woman much better today, I have still continued the same course of medecine; she is free from pain clear of fever, her pulse regular, and eats as heartily as I am willing to permit her of broiled buffaloe well seasoned with pepper and salt and rich soope of the same meat; I think therefore that there is every rational hope of her recovery." Though Lewis guessed her illness "originated principally from an obstruction of the mensis in consequence of taking could" and at first treated her with "cataplasms of barks and laudnumn" and the old cure-all of bleeding the patient, Clark wrote, "if she dies it will be the fault of her husband as I am now convinced" and may have been closer to the truth. According to Chuinard, Sacagawea suffered from chronic pelvic inflammatory disease, a common symptom of gonorrhea, which she probably acquired from her husband, Charbonneau. According to Whitehouse's journal, all of the men drank from the spring "for their healths which had the desired effect." The spring, soon to be accessible to the public, is about two miles downstream from Morony Dam.

Reference: Moulton, vols. 4, 11

Sun dog: An optical illusion produced by the sun reflecting off floating ice crystals in cold temperatures such as those encountered at Fort Mandan and recorded in the journals: "the Sun Shows and reflects two imigies, the ice floating in the atmespear being So thick that the appearance is like a fog Despurceing." Also known as a parhelion, the sun dog was, according to John Logan Allen, "used by plainsmen to predict weather changes."

References: Allen, Passage through the Garden*; Moulton, vol. 3*

Swivel gun: A small two- to three-pound cannon used by the military and fur traders during the time of the expedition and used by the Spanish on the lower Missouri for a decade or more before Lewis and Clark. It operated from a Y-shaped mount, which allowed the gun to swivel, or move, from side to side; and it could be loaded heavily with buckshot or with a single ball if the target was far away. The swivel gun was frequently fired as a signal or in farewells and salutes. It proved an effective threat on September 25, 1804, when the captains faced off with the Teton Sioux and loaded the cannon with sixteen musket balls just in case. During the winter at Fort Mandan, swivel guns were most likely mounted on the walls of the fort for added security. In June of 1805 the one swivel gun and the two blunderbusses (a similar swivel-type weapon, from the Dutch word *donderbus,* meaning "thunder gun") were cached at Great Falls and picked up on the return journey. The swivel gun was presented to the Hidatsa chief Le Borgne on August 16, 1806, in an effort to win his favor.

References: Russell; Rasmussen's website, "Firearms of the Lewis and Clark Expedition"

T

Tabeau, Pierre Antoine: French-Canadian trader from St. Louis who lived with the Arikara when the corps passed through their territory in 1804. Tabeau was an educated man who worked for trader Regis Loisel from 1802 to 1805. He translated for the captains and gave them information on the Arikara: "It is worthy of remark that the recares never use speritous liquors. Mr. Tibeau informed me that on a certain occasion he offered one of their considerate men a dram of sperits, telling him it's virtues—the other replyed that he had been informed of it's effects and did not like to make himself a fool unless he was paid to do so—that if Mr. T. wished to laugh at him & would give him a knife or breech-cloth or something of that kind he would take a glass but not otherwise—." In addition to interpreting for the captains, Tabeau was assigned, through a letter written from Fort Mandan on December 2, 1804, to "interseid in proventing hostilities" between the Arikara and the Sioux. He wrote a narrative of his travels to the upper Missouri, which was published in 1939. The editor, Annie Heloise Abel, summed up his relationship with the Corps of Discovery, "What little the American explorers had to say of Tabeau was good. They entertained him at breakfast on terms of equality; they sought his advice; they trusted him; they took his word as against that of others; and they obtained from him a great deal of information of so valuable a character that they incorporated it, unquestioned, into their own report."

References: Abel, Tabeau's Narrative; *Moulton, vol. 3*

Tah-cum (Stock home): Chinook chief. On February 20, 1806, Lewis recorded, "This forenoon we were visited by Tah-cum a principal Chief of the Chinnooks and 25 men of his nation. we had never seen this chief before he is a good looking man of about 50 years of age reather larger in statue than most of his nation; as he came on a friendly visit we gave himself and party some thing to eat and plyed them plentifully with smoke. we gave this cheif a small medal with which he seemed much gratifyed. in the evening at sunset we desired them to depart as is our custom and closed the gates." Ruby and Brown describe his previous dealings with traders on the coast, as early as 1794.

References: Ruby and Brown, The Chinook Indians*; Moulton, vol. 6*

Tavern Cave: A cave in limestone cliffs near present-day St. Albans, Missouri. It is a local landmark named by the French voyageurs approximately two miles past the Femme Osage River on the Missouri's south side. It is 120 feet wide and forty feet deep, according to Ann Rogers in *Lewis and Clark in Missouri*, and is lined with the names of the trappers and traders who visited there. It also contained "many different immages" observed by Clark, who mentioned "this is a place the Indians & french Pay omage to, many names are wrote up on the rock Mine among others." Sergeant Ordway called it "corn Tavern," which Moulton suggests meant it was used as a cache. Lewis lost his footing while exploring the cliffs and would have fallen nearly three hundred feet had he not, "by the assistance of his Knife, . . . caught at 20 foot," as Clark stoically recorded. Rogers reports the river no longer flows under the cliff at St. Albans, and the cave is now owned privately.

References: Rogers, Lewis and Clark in Missouri*; Moulton, vol. 2*

Tchung-kee: A game observed among the Mandan by Sergeant Ordway and probably the captains in December of 1804: "Although the day was cold & Stormy we Saw Several of the chiefs and warries were out at a play which they call 'hoop and pole game' they had flattish rings made out of clay Stone & two men had Sticks abt. 4 feet long with 2 Short peaces across the fore end of it, and neathing on the other end, in Such a manner that they would Slide Some distance they had a place fixed across their green from the head chiefs house across abt. 50 yds. to the 2 chiefs lodge which was Smothe as a house flour they had a Battery fixed for the rings to Stop against. two men would run at a time with [stick] Each a Stick & one carried a ring. they run abt. half way and then Slide their Sticks after the ring. they had marks made for the Game but I do not understand how they count the game." Artist

George Catlin also observed the game, and noted the name, "tchung-kee." He explained, "This game is a very difficult one to describe, so as to give an exact idea of it, unless one can see it played—it is a game of great beauty and fine bodily exercise, and these people become excessively fascinated with it; often gambling away everything they possess, and even sometimes, when everything else is gone, have been known to stake their liberty upon the issue of these games, offering themselves as slaves to their opponents in case they get beaten."

References: Catlin, North American Indians; Moulton, vol. 9

Tetoharsky: Younger of "our two old chiefs" (the other one was Twisted Hair); Nez Percé (Nimiipu) who guided and interpreted for Lewis and Clark on the Columbia. Twisted Hair and Tetoharsky used sign language to communicate the explorers' "friendly intentions towards all nations." Through the two Nez Percé translators, the captains attempted to make peace between the Chinook and the Sahaptian nations near the Dalles. Also through these translators the explorers could barter for dogs, dried salmon, and horsemeat. The Nez Percé men saw the corps to the Great Falls (Dalles) of the Columbia but did not wish to go beyond that point as they regarded it as a boundary line between their nation and the Chinooks, and the two old chiefs could no longer understand the language. The captains kept the men on alert because of information provided by the chiefs regarding the murderous plans of Indians downriver. Tetoharsky and Twisted Hair postponed their departure for two days at the urging of Lewis and Clark "with a view to make peace with those Indians below as well as to have them with us dureing our Delay with this tribe." Ronda calls their help invaluable. On October 25, 1805, Clark "had a parting smoke with our two faithful friends." The friendship of these two chiefs and their people toward the men of the expedition was a contributing factor in the overall success of the corps. See Twisted Hair.

References: Thwaites, Original Journals, vol. 3; Ronda, Lewis and Clark among the Indians; Moulton, vol. 5

Thompson, David (1770–1857): British explorer, surveyor, fur trader, and mapmaker. Thompson visited the regions of the upper

Missouri seven years before Lewis and Clark; they carried a copy of his map as they traveled upriver to the Mandans. In 1784 Thompson apprenticed at the Hudson's Bay Company; three years later he spent the winter with the Piegan Indians. Later, as an employee for the rival fur company, the North West Company, he crossed the Rockies in 1807 and established a post at the headwaters of the Columbia. Thompson explored several rivers in the Pacific Northwest and eventually charted the entire length of the Columbia River. Somehow officials of the North West Company had acquired a copy of a letter from Lewis detailing his voyage to the Pacific. Thompson made a copy of the letter and used it as a guide for his explorations around the Bitterroot valley and over Lolo Pass. One of the Indians he met was Chief Yellept, who showed him an American flag and the peace medal given to him by Lewis and Clark. After settling in Montreal, Thompson became the chief surveyor and astronomer for the International Boundary Commission. He continued working on maps and wrote an account of his travels, which was not published until after his death. Thompson once suggested the forty-seventh parallel as the British–U.S. border, extending from the Rocky Mountains to the Columbia where the line would run down the center to the Pacific Ocean. According to biologist and author Jack Nisbet, "The Americans held firm in their demands for the entire region and in 1846 the British government ceded its claim to all of the lands south of the 49th parallel. Thompson was outraged, and for the rest of his life he felt that 'blockhead' politicians had given away to the Americans some of the best country he had explored."

Reference: Nisbet

Thompson, John B. (17??–1825? 28?): Private. Former surveyor and Indiana resident who most likely helped the captains with mapping and frequently served as a cook during the expedition.

Reference: Charles G. Clarke

Thwaites, Rueben Gold (1853–1913): Librarian, editor, and author. He studied at Yale and at the University of Wisconsin, where he eventually became the successor to Lyman C. Draper as president of the State Historical Society of Wisconsin. His efforts in support of a joint library for the state historical society and the University of Wisconsin were instrumental in constructing the building that was dedicated on the lower campus in 1900 and where he worked alongside noted historian Frederick Jackson Turner. Among other works, Thwaites edited the eight-volume *Original Journals of the Lewis and Clark Expedition, 1804–1806.* At a memorial address in Thwaites's honor, Turner commented on Thwaites's work on the journals: "He ferreted out from their concealment missing documents necessary to complete the journals; deciphered the difficult handwriting and spelling of these historic frontiersmen . . . mastered the problem of correlating and printing the several journals of the Expedition; drew upon all of his resources of typographic and editorial skill to give an absolutely faithful reproduction of the originals."

References: Thwaites, Original Journals, *vols. 1–8; Cutright,* History of the Lewis and Clark Journals

Tipi (leather lodge): A pole frame covered with buffalo hides and typically used for shelter by the plains Indians. The tipi had a cone shape, which formed a small hole at the top to allow smoke to escape. Lewis and Clark shared Charbonneau and Sacagawea's tipi when they departed from Fort Mandan in the spring of 1805. "Captain Clark and myself the two Interpretters and the woman and child sleep in a tent of dressed skins. this tent is in the Indian stile, formed of a number of dressed Buffaloe skins sewed together with sinues. it is cut in such a manner that when foalded double it forms a quarter of a circle, and it is left open at one side where it may be attatched or loosened at pleasure by strings which are sewed to its sides to the purpose. to erect this tent, a parsel of ten or twelve poles are provided, fore or five of which are attatched together at one end, they are then elivated and their lower extremities are spread in a circular manner to width a proportionate to the demention of the lodge, in the same position orther poles are leant against those, and the leather is then thrown over them forming a conic figure." Later, Clark noted, "The Ossinniboins make use of the Same kind of Lodges which the Sioux and other Indians on this river make use of—Those lodges or tents are made of a number of dressed buffalow Skins <dressed> Sowed together with Sinues and deckerated with the tales, & Porcupine quils." While traveling through Blackfeet country, on July 13, 1805, Lewis observed the remains of a medicine lodge; "I passed a very extraordinary Indian lodge, or at least the fraim of one; it was formed of sixteen large cottonwood poles each about fifty feet long and at their larger end which rested on the ground as thick as a man's body . . . it was 216 feet in circumpherence at the base. it was probably designed for some great feast, or a council house on some great national concern. I never saw a similar one nor do the nations lower down the Missouri construct such." Nez Percé chief Hohots Ilppilp, a courteous host, "had a large conic lodge of leather erected for our reception and a parsel of wood collected and laid at the door after which he invited Capt. C and myself to make that lodge our home while we remained with him." On May 15, 1806, in Nez Percé territory, Lewis mentions their own "leather lodge has become rotten and unfit for use." When the time came to settle with Toussaint Charbonneau for his services as an interpreter, he was paid $500.33, which included the "pric of a horse and Lodge purchased of him for public Service."

Reference: Moulton, vols. 4, 7, 8

Tippet: An ermine-skin shoulder garment given to Meriwether Lewis by Shoshone chief Cameahwait on August 16, 1805: "the Chief with much cerimony put tippets about our necks such as they temselves woar I redily perceived that this was to disguise us." In return Lewis gave Cameahwait his hat and, in desperation to maintain contact with the tribe, his gun. On August 20, 1805, Lewis described the tippet as "the most eligant peice of Indian dress I ever saw, the neck or collar of this is formed of a strip of dressed Otter skin with fur. it is about four or five inches wide and is cut out of the back of the skin the nose and eyes forming one extremity and the tail at the other. begining a little behind the ear of the animal at one edge of this collar and proceeding towards the tail, they attach from one to two hundred and fifty little roles of Ermine skin." On May 13, 1806, Lewis observed a tippet worn by Chopunnish chief Hohots Ilppilp, "which was formed of human scalps and ornamented with the thumbs and fingers of several men which he had slain in battle." Lewis liked the tippet Cameahwait gave him so much he wore it when his portrait was painted by Charles Saint-Mémin in 1807. Later it adorned a wax figure of Lewis at

Meriwether Lewis, the year following his return from the Pacific Ocean, proudly wearing a tippet (ermine skin robe) he received from the Shoshone chief Cameahwait. Lewis described it as "the most eligant peice of Indian dress I ever saw." By Charles B. J. F. Saint-Mémin, 1807. No. 1971.125, collection of the New-York Historical Society.

Peale's museum in Philadelphia, where Peale used it to "give a lesson to the Indians who may visit." The tippet was lost or destroyed after the dissolution of Peale's museum in the 1840s.

References: *Jackson,* Letters; *Moulton, vols. 5, 7*

Tower Rock: A large volcanic feature near Hardy, Montana, first described by Lewis on July 16, 1805, as the party left the plains and entered the mountains: "at this place there is a large rock of 400 feet high wich stands immediately in the gap which the missouri makes on it's passage from the mountains; it is insulated from the neighbouring mountains by a handsome little plain which surrounds it base on 3 sides and the Missouri washes its base on the other, leaving it on the Lard. as it decends. this rock I called the tower. it may be ascended with some difficulty to it's summit, and from there it is a most pleasing view of the country we are now about to leave. from it I saw this evening immence herds of buffaloe in the plains below. near this place we killed a fat elk on which we dined and suped. the Musquetoes are extreemly troublesome this evening and I (have) had left my bier, of course suffered considerably, and promised in my wrath that I will never be guily of a similar peice of negligence while on this voyage." Lewis assumed the rock was granite; in fact, it is pyroclastic in origin. The expedition passed another "Tower" rock on November 25, 1803, near Perry County, Missouri.

Reference: Moulton, vol. 4

Train oil: Oil extracted from whale blubber or any fish or seal. At Fort Clatsop, Lewis lists items purchased from the Clatsop Indians and notes, "we also purchased a small quantity of train oil for a pair of Brass armbands and a hat for some fishinghooks."

References: Strong and Strong; Moulton, vol. 6

Truteau, Jean Baptiste (1748–1827): Indian trader, explorer, and teacher. He was born in Montreal on December 11, 1748, and was educated and worked as a teacher beginning in 1774 in St. Louis. Truteau likely made trading trips out of St. Louis to Indian tribes in Spanish Illinois country. In 1795 he wrote in his journal that he had spent twenty-six years in voyaging and never had an accident. During wartime, when the British attacked St. Louis, he was an enlisted member of the militia, serving as a "rower." Truteau was chosen to lead the first expedition sent out by the Missouri Company in 1794. In defense of the Spanish empire, Truteau, in the first of three expeditions, was to oust the British, capture trade with the Indians, and discover a route to the Pacific. He was to establish an agency among the Mandan, note the rivers falling into the Missouri, and establish friendly relations with the Indians on the east side of the Rockies. Truteau's engagement of three years was to end with a detailed report of what belonged to the company. He was to keep a daily journal and inquire of the Indians information about the existence of minerals, animals, and fruits. He was also to present flags and presents to the tribes he met. His orders were to tell the Mandan that they must trade with the Spaniards only; that the latter could supply them and they would have better results from that trade. After his goods were partially stolen, Truteau decided to cache the remaining portion and spend the winter in Charles Mix County, South Dakota, at a place they called Ponca House in honor of that tribe. The following spring he traveled back up the river as far as the Arikara. In the end the Sioux proved too much of an obstacle for the Missouri Company. Truteau was back in St. Louis by 1796, where he spent the rest of his life as a teacher and respectable citizen. In 1827 Truteau died in poverty at the age of seventy-nine. According to historian A. P. Nasitir, "Although Truteau did not ascend the Missouri much above the Arikara villages, he procured a great deal of valuable geographical information. . . . Accurate knowledge of the Missouri as far as the mouth of the Yellowstone is derived from his 'Description of the Upper Missouri,' which was written in 1795. His journal was sent by Jefferson to Meriwether Lewis." Jefferson wrote Lewis on November 16, 1803, "I inclose you also copies of the Treaties for Louisiana, the act for taking possession, a letter from Dr. Wistar, & some information collected by myself from Truteau's journal." This was followed by "Extracts from 1795 Journal of Truteau the Agent of the Company of haut Missouri estab. at Illinois." Thwaites refers to him as Printeau because of a copyist error.

References: Nasatir, *"Jean Baptiste Truteau," in Leroy Hafen,* Mountain Men; *Thwaites,* Original Journals, *vol. 7; Jackson,* Letters

Tuttle, Ebenezer (1773–18??): Private; born in Connecticut. He enlisted in the corps in 1803, recruited from Amos Stoddard's artillery company. He may be the person who returned to St. Louis in June of 1804. If not, he came back with the Warfington party in 1805.

Twisted Hair (Walammottinin [hair bunched or tied in a knot]): Nez Percé chief, "a Chearfull man with apparant Siencerity." As he smoked with Clark one evening, he drew maps or charts for Clark on whitened deerskin, pointing out the route of the Columbia and estimating it would take the corps five days to reach the mouth of the Columbia where white men lived by a large waterfall. He promised to watch over the horses Lewis and Clark would need to cross back over the Bitterroot on their return trip. Twisted Hair listened to the captains' diplomatic speeches, helped find wood for canoes to go down the Columbia, and instructed them in the Indian method of burning out the center of the trees for the canoes rather than hewing them. Tetoharsky and Twisted Hair acted as guides and interpreters on the way down the Columbia to Celio Falls, where they turned back because of tensions with tribes farther down. See Tetoharsky.

References: Thwaites, Original Journals, *vol. 3; Moulton, vol. 5*

V

Vancouver, George (1757–1798): British sailor who sailed around the world with James Cook. In 1790 he commanded his own ship, the *Discovery,* on a three-year survey of the Pacific Coast. Initially he missed the Columbia River, but five months after Robert Gray discovered and named that river, Vancouver sent one of his lieutenants, William Robert Broughton, exploring up the Columbia in his smaller ship, the *Chatham.* Broughton was able to proceed as far as one hundred miles to a spot he named Vancouver, where he observed, on his eastern side, Mount Hood. The lieutenant measured the Columbia as a quarter of a mile wide and twelve to thirty-six feet deep. He noted that the source must be much farther inland. These accounts, when combined with those of Alexander Mackenzie, implied the reality of water communication across the continent. Secretary of the Treasury Albert Gallatin advised Jefferson to purchase a copy of the Vancouver survey (1798) when he was gathering material in preparation for the Corps of Discovery. Lewis hastily traced the map while in Philadelphia and then had Nicholas King draw a base map using his copies of Vancouver's surveys. Lewis did not carry the original because of its weight and value. The geographical information contained in the map proved reassuring when the expedition neared the coast.

Vermillion: Powdered dye moistened and applied to the cheeks and prized equally with beads in trade negotiations with the natives. Alexander Mackenzie mentions using vermillion mixed with grease to sign his name on a rock at the Pacific Ocean in 1793. A quart of vermillion was included in the purchases made by Lewis in Philadelphia. Captain Lewis used vermillion, which was obtained from grinding minerals into pigment, to convince three wary Shoshone women he meant no harm on August 13, 1805: "I now painted their tawny cheeks with vermillion which with this nation is emblematic of peace," information he had obtained from Sacagawea. On May 12,

1806, the captains gave some vermillion to the Nez Percé men who delivered two horses to them on the Columbia. A half ounce of vermillion was given to the men at Fort Clatsop so that they all might equally share in what was left of the expedition's supplies, "with a view that each should purchase therewith a parsel of roots and bread from the natives as his stores for the rocky mountains . . . slender stock indeed with which to lay in a store of provision for that dreary wilderness. . . ." On June 1, 1806, the valuable trade commodity was destroyed when the horse carrying small articles and "paint" of Lepage fell off a cliff into the river.

References: Appleman; Moulton, vols. 5, 7

Vigonia blanket: Purchased by Meriwether Lewis and presumably made of the llama wool from Peru. A gift for Jefferson, purchased by Lewis during his time in Philadelphia. Lewis wrote him on May 29, 1803, "I have also purchased a Vigogna blanket of which I hope you will approve."

Reference: Thwaites, Original Journals, vol. 7

W

Walker, Thomas (1715–1794): Doctor, self-taught surveyor, and land agent for the Loyal Land Company's 800,000-acre land grant in Kentucky and West Virginia. Walker built the first cabin in Kentucky and was one of the first white men to travel the "Buffalo-Indian Rd," or Wilderness Road, through the Cumberland Gap in March–July 1750. Walker kept a journal and drew maps, which located the gateway into Kentucky. The doctor owned a plantation and a store and had great success in land speculation. He was elected to serve in the Virginia House of Burgesses and also worked as a boundary official in negotiations with local Indian tribes. Walker was a friend of and doctor to Thomas Jefferson's father, Peter, and a guardian, for a time, of young Thomas. It is worth noting that Daniel Boone did not travel through the Cumberland Gap until nineteen years after Walker. One of Walker's daughters married Nicholas Lewis, an uncle of Meriwether Lewis.
Reference: David Burns

Wapato (*Sagittaria latifolia*, wappato, wappaatoe, Indian potato, common arrow head): Once common along the Columbia and Willamette marshlands west of the Cascade Mountains and mentioned in the journals as a preferred food and trade item. On November 4, 1805, near the Willamette River, Clark observed, "it has an agreeable taste and answers very well in the place of bread, we purchased about 4 bushels of this root and divided it to our party." Lewis noted that it was the "principal article of traffic" with the natives and that they would "dispose of their most valuable articles to obtain this root." Clark provided a detailed description of the harvesting method employed by the Indian women, who would hold on to canoes while rooting up the wapato with their feet, sometimes standing up to their necks in the water. On April 2, 1806, Clark performed a "farcical seen" with his compass, a magnet, and a port-fire match (a piece of cord covered with gunpowder) to persuade the reluctant Shahala Indians to offer up some of their wapato roots for trade. To assure them he was not an enemy, he smoked with them and traded fairly for their roots. To cook the wapato, Indians would roast them in hot ashes or pit-steam them. The roots could also be steamed to make a tea for stomach ailments. According to journalist and historian Roy Craft, "The wapato is among the oldest flowering plants on earth and its characteristics have enabled it to survive millions of years of living to adapt itself to harsh growing conditions. According to Indian legend it was an article of food before the salmon came to the Columbia River." Craft attributes the decline of the wapato to several causes, among them the drainage of marshes, land development, and the dumping of raw sewage and industrial waste into the Columbia. Conservation-minded landowners and a Society for the Preservation of Wapato are working together to ensure the survival of this endangered species.

References: Craft; Moulton, vols. 6, 7

Warfington, Richard (b. 1777): Corporal; born in Louisburg, North Carolina. Warfington served under Lewis and Clark from May 1804 until June 1, 1805, when he commanded the return party in the keelboat from Fort Mandan to St. Louis. The return party included Joseph Gravelines, John Dame, John Boley, John Robertson (or Robinson), Ebenezer Tuttle, Issac White, and the expelled John Newman and Moses Reed. Warfington rejoined his original unit after the expedition and was honorably discharged. A Coues footnote cites a letter (in poor condition) from Lewis, which reads, "Richard Warfington was a Corporal in the Infantry of the U' States army, whom I had occasion to take with me on my voyage as far as the Mandan nation. his term of service expired on the 4th of August [1804] within? nearly three months previous to my arrival at that place? nation? and? knowing that it would become necessary for me to send back my boat in the spring of 1805 with a party of soldiers whose terms had not expired; that it was of some importance that the government should receive in safety the dispatches which I was about to transmit from thence; that there was not one of the party destined to be returned from thence in whom I could place the least confidence except himself, and that if he discharged at the moment of his expiration of his term of service that he would necessarily loose his military standing, and thereby lessen the efficiency of his command among the soldiery; I was induced under these considerations to make an arrangement with him by which it was agreed between us that he should not receive his discharge from the military service untill his return to St. Louis, and that he should in the interim retain his rank and receive only for his services the accustomed compendation. accordingly he remained with me during the winter, and was the next spring in conformity to my plan placed in command of the boat and charged with the dispatches to the government. the duties assigned to him on this occasion were performed with a punctuality which uniformly ? characterized ? his conduct while under my command. Taking into view his cheerfulness with which he continued in the service ? after every obligation ceased to exist."

Reference: Coues, History of the Expedition, *vol. 1*

Watkuweis: Nez Percé woman who was captured by Blackfeet or Atsinas during a raid in the Montana buffalo country and taken to Canada. She was sold to another tribe living farther east, perhaps the Assiniboines or plains Crees. Eventually she was purchased by a white man, probably a French Canadian or half blood, and lived for a while among the whites. Watkuweis was the first Nez Percé to see white men and return to tell about them. They treated her with kindness and gave her medicine for conjunctivitis. After giving birth to a child, she ran away and, after several months of wandering, during which her child died, she reached a band of friendly Salish who reunited her with her own people. The Nez Percé call her Watkuweis, which means "gone from home then come back." Her stories of the white men, whom she called So-ya-pos, or Crowned ones, spread among the Nez Percé villages. According to the Nez Percé it was Watkuweis, at the time a dying old woman, whom William Clark saw in Twisted Hair's village on the Clearwater the night after the explorer's arrival in Nez Percé country. On September 21, 1805, Clark wrote, "11o Clock p.m. arrived at a camp of 5 Squars a boy & 2 children those people were glad to See us & gave us some drid Sammon one had formerly been taken by the Minitarries of the north & seen white men." It was at her recommendation that the Indians received the expedition in a friendly manner. "These are the people who helped me," tribal tradition quotes the old woman telling her people, "Do them no hurt."

References: Swayne; Moulton, vol. 5

Wearkkoomt (Apash Wyakaikt, Looking Glass, Flint Necklace): Nez Percé chief who lived on the Snake River above its confluence with the Clearwater. He assisted Lewis and Clark and was "of infinite service to us on several former occasions," and "consoled" them with information concerning provisions farther downriver in May 1806 on the return journey. Lewis exchanged horses with him and presented him with a small flag, "with which he was much gratifyed." Looking Glass's son and grandson, each also named Looking Glass, were Nez Percé leaders in the war of 1877.

References: Josephy; Moulton, vol. 7

Weir: Used by the Nez Percé and other tribes; a wooden fence constructed in a stream to trap fish or force them into a narrow channel where they could be easily netted. Lewis encountered weirs on the Lemhi River and sketched one in his journal entry for August 21, 1805. Describing one form of weir he wrote, "the main channel of the water was conducted into this basket [weir], which was so narrow at it's lower extremity that the fish when once in could not turn itself about, and were taken out by untying the small ends of the longitudinal willows, which formed the hull of the basket." Along the Walla Walla River, about a mile from the Columbia, Lewis discovered the Walla Walla form of weir: "This wear consists of two curtains of small willow switches matted together with four lines of withs of the same materials extening quite across the river, parrallel with eah other and about 6 feet assunder. those are supported by several parsels of poles placed in the manner before discribed of the fishing wears. these curtains of willow are either roled at one end for a few feet to permit the fish to pass or are let down at pleasure. they take their fish which at present are a mullet only of from one to five lbs." He also sketched an illustration of the weir in his entry for April 29, 1806.

Reference: Moulton, vols. 5, 7

Weiser, Peter (1781–1825?): Private; most likely recruited from Bissell's company. Among those disciplined early on at Camp Dubois for making "hunting or other business a pretext to cover their design of visiting a neighboring whiskey shop," according to Lewis, who ordered the men confined to camp for ten days. While portaging the Great Falls of the Missouri, he cut his leg badly with a knife and was unable to work. Camped with the Shoshone in 1805, Weiser had what Lewis termed a "fit of cholic," which he successfully treated with a dose of peppermint and laudanum. Weiser was one of the crew who succumbed to seasickness on the swells of the Columbia. Along with being a camp cook and hunter, he assisted with duties at the Salt Camp and returned to the fort with news of the friendly Clatsop Indians and their willingness to share whale blubber. After the expedition he was one of several expedition members to join Manuel Lisa's 1807 trapping enterprise on the upper Missouri. He revisited the Three Forks and perhaps the Snake River. Clark mentions him "killed" in his list of expedition members of 1825–28. Weiser, Idaho, and nearby Weiser River were named in his honor.
References: Moulton, vol. 2; Boone

Werner, William: Private. According to Charles G. Clarke, Werner was most likely a Kentuckian who enlisted from an unknown unit and served as a cook and as a member of the salt-making party on the Pacific Coast. On March 17, 1805, Werner lost his "tommahawk"; Ordway blamed the Hidatsa Indians for its disappearance. He was court-martialed on May 17, 1805, along with Hugh Hall and John Collins, for being absent without leave. They were each sentenced to twenty-five lashes on their naked backs but were excused because of their "former Good conduct." He worked as an Indian agent under General William Clark, who listed him as in Virginia in 1828. The captains named a creek after Werner near present-day Valley Creek County, Montana.
References: Charles G. Clarke; Moulton, vol. 9; Jackson, Letters

Weucha (La Liberator): Yankton Sioux chief who counciled with Lewis and Clark at Calumet Bluff on making peace with the Missouri and the Oto tribes and on future trading with the whites. Ordway wrote, "they Gave the Grand chief which they call in Indian weucha, La liberator in french, a red laced coat & a fine cocked hat & red feather & an american flag & a white Shirt &C. all of which he was much pleased with, they recd. all their presents verry thankfully and divided them among one another &c—." The meeting at Calumet Bluff proved an early success in diplomacy for Lewis and Clark, notable for the camaraderie they felt at the party that night and the warning of an associate of Weucha who said, "their is one tribe of red men my fathers that have not their ears open, but the old chief (Weucha) & us will do the best we can for you with regard to the punkaws nation & all others as far as in our power lies &C."

Reference: Moulton, vol. 9

Whelan, Israel: Purveyor of public supplies at the Schuylkill arsenal in Philadelphia from 1800 to 1803. Whelan received one thousand dollars from the U.S. Treasury for the purpose of purchasing articles requested by Captain Meriwether Lewis for his journey to the Pacific. See Appendix I.

White, Isaac (b. 1774): Private; born in Massachusetts and enlisted in 1801. He was recruited from Amos Stoddard's artillery company and was not a member of the permanent party. He served under Lewis and Clark until he returned with Warfington to St. Louis in 1805. Moulton mentions the possibility he was the man of Stoddard's company who was sent back in June 1804.

References: Charles G. Clarke; Moulton, vol. 2

White Bear Islands: Campsite and final spot of the portage of the expedition from June 22 until July 13, 1805, and one that none of the men likely forgot. Not only were Willard and Colter chased by a grizzly or "white" bear on these islands, it was also where Lewis had to admit the defeat of his experiment of the iron boat, when it would not float: "I therefore relinquished all further hope of my favorite boat and ordered her to be sunk in the water, that the skins might become soft in order the better to take her in peices tomorrow and deposite the iron fraim at this place as it could probably be of no further service to us."

There were some good times on the island, however; the corps held a fine celebration in honor of the Fourth of July here and in addition to dancing and singing partook of the last of the spirits. According to Ella Mae Howard, of the three islands, "only one is readily distinguishable today. The other two have melded with the river's bank." Archaeologist Ken Karsminski recently led an iron-boat recovery effort near the area. According to Karsminski, finding the iron-frame boat would be roughly equivalent to finding the Holy Grail.

References: Moulton, vol. 4; Ella Mae Howard; Karsminski, personal communication

Whitehouse, Joseph (1775–18??): Private from Kentucky who served under Captain Russell Bissell in Kaskaskia and likely joined the expedition in November of 1803. In April 1804 Clark observed that Whitehouse "wishes to return" but did not elaborate; he was retained as a member of the permanent party. Little is known of him, despite the fact that he kept a journal, which he intended to publish. His main talents lay in curing hides and in sewing clothes for the men. Whitehouse served as part of the court in the court-martial of William Werner and Hugh Hall. Near the Great Falls of the Missouri, Whitehouse recorded, "One of the party was near being bit by a Rattle snake, which he killed, it measured 4 feet 2 inches in length and 5 ½ Inches round." (Gary Moulton says Whitehouse himself was the one nearly bitten.) He almost broke his leg in a canoe accident near the Three Forks on August 6, 1805, and lost "the greater part of my cloathing &ca." Upon return to St. Louis, Whitehouse sold his land grant to George Drouillard and was arrested for debt in 1807. He reenlisted with the army but was demoted from corporal to private in 1813 and, according to Moulton, deserted in February 1817. Clark's list of expedition members does not mention him as alive or dead in 1825–28.

Reference: Moulton, vols. 2, 11

Wilderness Road: This route, along with its northern extension the Great Wagon Road, was the main road through the Shenandoah valley to southwestern Virginia and on to the Cumberland Gap and Kentucky. Both Lewis and Clark and their parties, including some Native

American Indian chiefs, traveled this route when they came to Virginia and Washington in the 1806–07 period and later. Both used it in returning to the West. Lewis was on his way to these roads in 1809 when he stopped at Grinder's Stand and ended his life. The Wilderness Road followed an old Indian trail toward the west from Big Lick (Roanoke), passing through Christiansburg, Wytheville, Abington, and numerous other small communities in Virginia until it reached the Cumberland Gap. There it passed into Kentucky, where one branch went to present-day Lexington and ended at Maysville on the Ohio River. The other branch headed farther west to present-day Louisville. Much of the original road was cleared by men led by Daniel Boone and was a rough trail. As more and more settlers headed to Kentucky before and after the Revolution, the road was improved to be able to handle wagons. It remained the major land route from the east to the Ohio valley for many years.

References: Henley, personal communication; David Burns

Willard, Alexander (1778–1865): Private; born in New Hampshire but lived in Kentucky and served under Captain Amos Stoddard in 1800. Joined the corps on January 1, 1804. His skills as a blacksmith, gunsmith, and hunter aided in the overall success of the expedition. Fashioning battle-axes and other weapons, the three blacksmiths, Willard, Bratton, and Shields, exchanged these items with the natives for much-needed corn. Willard likely kept a journal whose location remains a mystery, but like other pieces in the Lewis and Clark puzzle may yet be found. (Wheeler says it was accidentally destroyed.) In one memorable incident, Willard was court-martialed for, according to Lewis, "Lying down and sleeping on his post whilst a Sentinal on the night of the 11th of July. To this charge the prisoner pleads. Guilty of lying down and not Guilty of Going to Sleep." The captains sentenced him to one hundred lashes on his bare back to be administered over a period of four days. He must have learned his lesson and performed admirably thereafter as he was one of the three men nominated to replace Sergeant Floyd. He and McNeal share the honor of being two of the men nearly caught and killed by a grizzly bear. Near the Beaverhead Rock, Willard had a creek named after him, later renamed Grasshopper Creek. Lewis lost his temper with Willard on

Expedition member Alexander Willard and his wife, Eleanor. He was one of only two members to be photographed. Willard returned to the West by covered wagon in 1852. Montana Historical Society, Helena.

April 19, 1806, because "one of the men Willard was negligent in his attention to his horse and suffered it to ramble off; it was not to be found when I ordered the others to be brought up and confined to picquits. . . . I repremanded him more severly for this peice of negligence than had been usual with me." Willard helped in the salt making on the Pacific Coast and subsequently took ill right before the departure. He married in 1807 and raised, with his wife from Kentucky, Eleanor McDonald, a family of seven sons (one named Lewis and another named Clark) and five daughters. Willard worked as a government blacksmith for the Sauk and Fox Indians and later served in the War of 1812. He moved to California in 1852, where he resumed blacksmithing at a stagecoach stop. Willard died in Sacramento in 1865 at age eighty-seven, the second-to-last surviving member of the expedition and still married to his Kentucky bride. The creek, originally named in his honor, then renamed Grasshopper, is now called Divide Creek, on the Jefferson River. His gravesite is located in a cemetery near Franklin, California.

References: Charles G. Clarke; Moulton, vols. 2, 7; Hoffman; Wheeler

Wilson, Alexander (1766–1813): Wilson emigrated to the United States in 1794. Frustrated in his attempts to earn a living by weaving or poetry, he turned to education and taught for about ten years in small schools in New Jersey and Pennsylvania. In February 1802 he began to teach at a school at Gray's Ferry on the Schuylkill River below Philadelphia. This made him the neighbor of William Bartram, who encouraged Wilson's interest in ornithology and made his library available to him. The first volume of Wilson's *American Ornithology* appeared in 1808. Seven volumes had been published by 1814. When Wilson died in 1813, his friend George Ord completed the series from Wilson's manuscripts. Of Wilson, Elliott Coues wrote, "Perhaps no other work on ornithology of equal extent is equally free from error; and its truthfulness is illumined by a spark of the 'fire divine.' " Among his most important accomplishments was the description, illustration, and designation of three birds: the western tanager (*Piranga ludoviciana*), Clark's nutcracker (*Nucifraga columbiana*), and Lewis's woodpecker (*Melanerpes lewis*). Although described as melancholic and known for playing sad songs on his flute, Wilson was an enthusiastic traveler. He walked from Philadelphia to Niagara Falls in 1804. In 1808 he undertook a book promotion tour that carried him from Portland, Maine, to Savannah, Georgia. In 1809 he visited St. Augustine, Florida. In 1810 he traveled west of the Alleghenies on a journey that took him from Pittsburgh to New Orleans. In 1811, while on a bird-collecting excursion in the West, Wilson visited Grinder's Stand, met Mr. Grinder, and interviewed Mrs. Grinder. Wilson had in fact been planning a walking trip from Philadelphia to St. Louis, with William Bartram, to visit Governor Lewis and collect specimens along the way, when news reached him of Lewis's death. Wilson, who did not doubt that Lewis had committed suicide, records Mrs. Grinder's recollections of Lewis's actual words in the last hours of life. Wilson engaged Mr. Grinder to tend Lewis's grave, for a fee. Wilson wrote that it was "the request and particular wish of Captain Lewis, made to me in person, that I should make drawings of such of the feathered tribes as had been preserved and were new." Lewis also informed Wilson that the passenger pigeon could be observed as far west as the Great Falls of the Missouri, and that the blue jay could be found far up the river. Lewis also arranged for Wilson to meet with Sergeant John Ordway, who supplied Wilson with a number of natural history anecdotes. Wilson wrote to a friend about Lewis, "He lies buried close by the common path with a few loose rails thrown over his grave." He further wrote, "I left this place in a very melancholy mood, which was not much allayed by the prospect of the gloomy and savage wilderness which I was just entering, alone." Near the gravesite, Wilson wept for his friend. Wilson wrote an elegy for Meriwether Lewis.

> *The anguish that his soul assailed,*
> *The dark despair that round him blew,*
> *No eye, save that of Heaven beheld,*
> *None but unfeeling strangers knew.*
>
> *Poor reason perished in the storm*
> *And desperation triumphed here!*
>
> *For hence be each accusing thought,*
> *With him my kindred tears shall flow,*
> *Pale Pity consecrate the spot*
> *Where poor lost Lewis now lies low.*
>
> *Love as these solitudes appear*
> *Wide as this wilderness is spread,*
> *Affection's steps shall linger here,*
> *To breathe her sorrows o'er the dead.*

Like his friend Meriwether Lewis, Wilson exhibited a talent for observation and description. His art, while admired, was critically dismissed and even referred to as "frequently childish and wretched."

His original illustrations are housed at the Academy of Natural Sciences in Philadelphia; the prints were published in plate XX, volume three, of *American Ornithology* (1811).

References: Cokinos; Cutright, Pioneering Naturalists; *Wilson, "Particulars"*

Windshake: Cracks in wood caused by strain from the force of wind, such as those that occurred in the boats of the expedition.

Reference: Criswell

Windsor, Richard: Private; enlisted in Kentucky, probably from the company of Captain Russell Bissell. His service in the Corps of Discovery included a terrifying experience he shared with Captain Lewis on June 7, 1805, while he slogged through "gumbo" on the shores of the Missouri River. First, Lewis slipped and nearly fell ninety feet into the river below: "I had scarcely reached a place on which I could stand with tolerable safety even with the assistance of my espontoon before I heard a voice behind me cry out god god Capt. what shall I do on turning about I found it was Windsor who had sliped and fallen abut the center of this narrow pass and was lying prostrate on his belley, with his one wright hand arm and leg over the precipice while he was holding on with the left arm and foot as well as he could which appeared to be with much difficulty. I discovered his danger and the trepedation which he was in gave me still further concern for I expected every instant to see him loose his strength and slip off; altho' much allarmed at his situation I disguised my feelings and spoke very calmly to him and assured him that he was in no kind of danger, to take the knife out of his belt behind him with his wright hand and dig a hole with it in the face of the bank to receive his wright foot which he did and then raised himself to his knees; I then directed him to take off his mockersons and to come forward on his hands and knees holding the knife in one hand and the gun in the other this he happily effected and escaped." Windsor was a reliable hunter and all-around member of the corps. According to Charles G. Clarke, after the expedition he settled in Missouri and "later re-enlisted in the army where he served until 1819." Perhaps rivers stayed in his blood; he lived on the Sangamon River in Illinois from 1825 to 1829. The captains named a creek after him on May 26, 1805, near present-day Blaine County, Montana. It is now known as Cow Creek.

References: Charles G. Clarke; Moulton, vol. 4

Wirt, William: Richmond attorney who wrote a biography of Patrick Henry and who was suggested to Clark as a possible editor for the journals. Wirt declined the offer, chiefly because he did not have time to make a copy of the journals.

Reference: Cutright, History of the Lewis and Clark Journals

Wistar, Caspar (1761–1818): Philadelphia physician, anatomist, paleontologist, instructor of Lewis in 1803. Wistar was raised a Quaker and educated at the University of Pennsylvania, in Great Britain, and the University of Edinburgh, where he was elected president of the Royal Medical Society and the Edinburgh Natural History Society. According to author and historian Nancy M. Davis, Wistar returned to Philadelphia in 1787 and was affiliated with the American Philosophical Society. He was named to succeed Benjamin Rush at the College of Philadelphia, which merged with the University of Pennsylvania, and became professor of anatomy, midwifery, and surgery. During a yellow fever epidemic, Wistar contracted the disease and began to question the bleeding and purging philosophy of Rush. Wistar distanced himself professionally from Rush but went on to serve as the vice president of the American Philosophical Society for twenty-one years. In 1803 Jefferson wrote Wistar asking him to help with Lewis's preparations for exploration: "What follows is to be perfectly confidential. I have at length succeeded in procuring an essay to be made of exploring the Missouri and whatever river, heading with that, runs into the Western ocean. Congress by secret authority enables me to do it. A party of about 10. chosen men headed by an officer will immediately set out. We cannot in the U.S. find a person who to courage, prudence, habits & health adapted to the woods, & some familiarity with the Indian character, joins a perfect knolege of botany, natural history, mineralogy &astronomy, all of which would be desirable. To the qualifications Capt. Lewis my secretary adds a great mass of accurate observation made on the different subjects of the three kingdoms as existing in these states, not under their scientific forms, but so as that he will readily seize whatever is new in the country he passes thro and give us accounts of new things only: and he has qualified himself for fixing longitude and latitude of the different points in the line he will go over. I have thought it would be useful to confine his attention to those objects only on which information is most deficient & most desirable: & therefore would thank you to make a note on paper of those which occur to you as most desirable for him to attend to. . . . Any advice or hints you can give him will be thankfully received & usefully applied. I presume he will complete his tour there & back in two seasons." Wistar set Jefferson straight on his misidentification of megalonyx—ground sloth bones, which Jefferson thought were the remains of a giant cat. When Jefferson's enemies voiced concern over the Louisiana Purchase, Wistar wrote the president, "I cannot conclude this letter without offering you my most sincere & cordial congratulations on the very happy acquisitions you have made for our Country on the Mississippi. Altho no one here appears to know the extent or price of the cession, it is generally considered as the most important & beneficial transaction which has occurred since the declaration of Independence & next to it, most like to influence or regulate the destinies of our Country. I believe that almost all impartial people here, who take the pains to think for themselves, consider the British reasons for war very slight." In 1808 Wistar secured appointment as the chair of anatomy at the University of Pennsylvania, and founded a society to promote vaccination. He retired in 1810. Caspar Wistar authored *A System of Anatomy for the Use of Students of Medicine* (1811), the first American textbook on anatomy. He served as president of the American Philosophical Society for two years after Jefferson. Wistar was most beloved by the people of Philadelphia, evidenced by the citywide turnout for his funeral. His family donated his anatomical collection to the University of Pennsylvania. Nancy Davis writes, "Wistar's peers regarded him as intellectually strong rather than brilliant and a lover of truth who was patient in uncovering it and generous in sharing it." Botanist and friend Thomas Nuttall named the wisteria vine in his honor.

References: *Jackson, Letters; Davis, "Caspar Wistar"*

Wolf Calf: Piegan (Blackfeet) Indian involved in the altercation of Lewis, his party, and the Piegan Indians at the Two Medicine fight site on the Marias River, which ended with one, and possibly two, of his fellow warriors dead. Interviewed in his old age, Wolf Calf recalled the incident in vivid detail for ethnologist George Bird Grinnell in the early 1900s. According to those interviews, the warriors planned in advance to steal the white men's weapons. As historian James Ronda points out, the notion that the Americans were going to arm and supply the Blackfeet (or Piegan)'s traditional enemies, as Lewis made clear through his interpreter, was the equivalent of dropping a "geo-political bombshell."

Reference: Grinnell, quoted in Ronda, Lewis and Clark among the Indians

Wood, Maria: Meriwether Lewis's cousin and the inspiration for the name given to the Marias River. On June 8, 1805, Lewis wrote, "I determined to give it a name and in honour of Miss Maria W——d, called it Maria's River. it is true that the hue of the waters of this turbulent and troubled stream but illy comport with the pure celestial virtues and amiable qualifications of that lovely fair one; but on the other hand it is a noble river; one destined to become in my opinion an object of contention between the two great powers of America and Great Britin. . . ." Perhaps because his affections for Miss Wood were not reciprocated, Meriwether Lewis later called himself "a perfect widower with respect to love." The name of this river is pronounced locally in the southern form, "Mariahs."

References: Jackson, Letters; *Moulton, vol. 4*

Wyakin **(weyekin, wyekin):** According to Clark's journal entry for October 9, 1805 (with the Nez Percé), "A woman fain(d) madness &c &c Singular acts of this woman in giving small portions all she had & if they were not received (or she had no more to give pitied by Indians she sang) She would scarify herself in a horid manner. &c." Whitehouse observed: "one of their women was taken with the crazey fit by our fire. She set to singing Indian and gave all around hir some roots and all she offered had to take from her. One of our men refused to take them from hir. She then was angry and hove them in the fire, and took a sharp flint from hir husband and cut hir arms in Sundry places

So that the blood gushed out. She wiped up the blood and eat it. Then tore off some beads and peaces of copper& which hung about hir and gave out to them that were around hir a little to each one. Still kept hir singing and making a hishing noise. She then ran around went to the water. Some of her kindred went after hir and brought hir back. She then fell into a fit and continued stiff and speechless some time they pored water on hir face until she came to. Capt. Clark gave her some small things which pleased her." The incident also impressed Sergeant Gass: "At dark one of the Squaws, who kept about us, took a crazey fit, and cut her arms from the wrists to the shoulders with a flint; and the natives had great trouble and difficulty in getting her pacified." Ordway noted: "She scraped the blood in her hand and eat it and so continued (for) in this way for about a half an hour then fainted or went in to a fit. . . ." According to historian James Ronda, "What Clark and Ordway recorded as a seizure was perhaps the woman's Wyakin or guardian spirit at work." The *Encyclopedia of Native American Healing* defines *weyekin* as a Nez Percé term meaning "both the Shaman's healing spirit and the ability derived from such a spirit through vision quest, inheritance, or an unsolicited visitation from a power bearing spirit." Historian and author Alvin Josephy wrote that *wyakins* represented "supernatural guardian forms . . . the Wyakin belief reflected a Nez Perce universe filled with individual spirits that existed in dreams and in real life, and to which Nez Perce could appeal for assistance: Thunder, lightning, a soaring eagle, a grizzly bear and so forth. Each spirit could harm or protect a man according to its powers and inclination. Each man (or woman) had a personal Wyakin, warning him, protecting him, and assisting him through his life on earth." *Wyakins* made themselves known to individuals during a vision quest exercise involving fasting and meditation.

References: *Thwaites,* Original Journals, *vol. 3; Lyon; Josephy; MacGregor,* Journals of Patrick Gass; *Ronda,* Lewis and Clark among the Indians; *Moulton, vol. 11*

Y

Yampah, Gairdners (*Perideridia gairdneri*): With the Shoshone in late August 1805 as the expedition was about to go over Lolo Pass, Lewis wrote, "I observe the indian women collecting the root of a species of fennel which grows in the moist grounds and feeding their poor starved children; it is really distressing to witness the situation of those poor wretches." Later, in mid-May of 1806, "Sahcargarmeah geathered a quantity of the roots of a species of fennel which we found very agreeable food, the flavor of this root is not unlike annis seed, and they dispell the wind which the roots called Cows and quawmash are apt to create particularly that of the latter." He collected and pressed a specimen of yampah on April 25, 1806. In her book *Edible and Medicinal Plants of the Rockies* Linda Kershaw states that these roots were a favorite of many tribes and eaten in a variety of forms. It was also used for a medicinal tea and to give quick energy to horses. She warns, however, that eating roots from the carrot family is like playing "herbal roulette" because there are many poisonous species in this family.

    References: Kershaw; Moulton, vols. 5, 7

Yellept (became Tamtappam after Lewis and Clark treated him for rheumatism): Walla Walla chief on the Columbia. When he met the explorers for the first time he gave them firewood and three roasted mullets as a welcome gift. He presented Clark with a white horse, in part as a gesture to place himself and his people within the American trade system and in the hope of obtaining a "kittle" (kettle). Yellept persuaded the captains to spend an extra day with him and the Yakima tribe before crossing the Columbia. He was also friendly with David Thompson. On October 19, 1805, Clark described him as "a bold handsom Indian with a dignified countenance about 35 years of age, about 5 feet 8 inces high and well perportiond." The captains gave Yellept a medal, a handkerchief, and a string of wampum beads.

His medal was later found on an island at the mouth of the Walla Walla. In return for the gift of the "very eligant white horse," Clark gave him his sword, one hundred balls, some powder, and other small articles of which "he appeared perfectly satisfied."

References: Coues, History of the Expedition, *vol. 3; Moulton, vols. 5, 7*

Yellowstone River: Principal upriver tributary of the Missouri. The Yellowstone flows from its source at Yellowstone Lake a distance of 670 miles before it enters the Missouri River in northwestern North Dakota. Clark estimated the length of the river from today's Livingston, Montana, to its mouth at 837 miles. With an advance party, Meriwether Lewis reached the confluence of the Missouri and the Yellowstone on April 25, 1805. He had known of the existence of the Yellowstone as far back as St. Louis. In the last years of the eighteenth century, John Evans and James Mackay had noted the Yellowstone and the Great Falls as principal landmarks on the upper Missouri, though they had never been to either place. At Fort Mandan, William Clark had estimated that the mouth of the Yellowstone would be found 250 miles upriver from the Mandan and Hidatsa villages on the Knife River. Upon arrival, Lewis called the confluence of the two rivers "this long wished for spot." On April 26, Captain Lewis ordered Joseph Field to ascend the Yellowstone as far as he could and still return the same day. At noon on April 26, William Clark arrived with the main party in six dugout canoes and the expedition's two pirogues. Meriwether Lewis was ecstatic: "found them all in good health, and much pleased at having arrived at this long wished for spot, and in order to add in some measure to the general pleasure which seemed to pervade our little community, we ordered a dram to be issued to each person; this soon produced the fiddle, and they spent the evening with much hilarity, singing & dancing, and seemed as perfectly to forget their past toils, as they appeared regardless of those to come." Aware of the geographic and strategic importance of the confluence, Clark took measurements of the rivers, and Lewis attempted to ascertain latitude and longitude. Both leaders immediately realized that the confluence would be an ideal location for a trade fort. "This low plain is not Subject to over flow, appear to be a few inches above

An early photograph taken from the top of the sandstone formation that Clark named Pompy's Tower, looking down the Yellowstone River. Montana Historical Society, Helena.

high water mark and affords a butifull commanding Situation for a fort," Clark wrote. On the return journey, two groups descended the Yellowstone River. With twelve others Clark made his way by horse to a place between today's Laurel and Columbus, Montana, where the trees were adequate to make canoes. Then, on July 24, 1806, Clark, with the Charbonneau family, York, and four others, descended the Yellowstone in two narrow cottonwood dugouts (lashed together), arriving at the confluence of the Yellowstone and Missouri on August 3, 1806. Sergeant Nathaniel Pryor and three others (Shannon, Windsor, and Hall) followed behind the Clark party in two bull boats. Pryor had been dispatched on July 23 to take the expedition's remaining horses overland first to Fort Mandan, and then on to the Assiniboine River in search of the Canadian trader Hugh Heney, whom the expedition intended to recruit for a Sioux Indian peace initiative. When Indians (presumably Crow) stole his horses, Pryor intelligently retreated to the Yellowstone and fashioned watercraft that could be constructed without much by way of tools, and quickly enough to give him a chance to catch up with the main Clark party. These two Yellowstone River strands came back together on August 8, 1806, in the

Missouri River a short distance below the confluence of the Missouri and the Yellowstone. Clark's Yellowstone journey was notable chiefly for the stupendous abundance of game the party encountered. Clark's journal notes on the wild herds in the Yellowstone valley are characterized by awe. On July 24, he wrote with some exasperation, "for me to mention or given an estimate of the different Spcies of wild animals on this river particularly Buffalow, Elk Antelopes & Wolves would be increditable. I shall therefore be silent on the Subject further." But he cannot be silent. On July 27, Clark wrote: "The Buffalow and Elk is estonishingly noumerous on the banks of the river on each Side." And on July 28: "The Elk on the banks of the river were So abundant that we have not been out of Sight of them to day." On August 1, the party had to lay by for an hour to permit a gigantic herd of buffalo to ford the Yellowstone River. Members of the party could hardly sleep at night in the midst of so many bellowing buffalo: "emence herds of Buffalow about our as it is now running time with those animals the bulls keep Such a grunting nois which is very loud and disagreeable Soun that we are compelled to Scear them away before we can Sleep" (July 25). On July 16, 1806, Clark wrote, "no other alternative for me but to proceed on down until I can find a tree Sufficently large &c. to make a Canoe.—" Clark arrived at the mouth of the Bighorn River on July 26, Rosebud Creek (which he named the Little Big Horn) on July 28, the Tongue River on July 29, and O'Fallon Creek on July 31. Clark hoped to make contact with the Crow Indians in the Yellowstone valley. He even wrote a peace, sovereignty, and trade speech, which is extant, though the party never encountered an Indian of any nation on its descent of the Yellowstone. Clark's closest brush with the Crow came on July 18. He wrote, "The Country back from the river on each Side is generally open wavering plains. Some pine is to be See in every direction in those plains on the Sides of hills &c." Clark's party began to make canoes on July 20, 1806. On July 25, Clark reached a lone sandstone rock pillar near the Yellowstone, which he climbed, carved his name on, and named Pompy's Tower in honor of the child Jean Baptiste Charbonneau. See Evans, John Thomas; Mackay, James.

Reference: Moulton, vols. 4, 8

York (1772?–1822?): Clark's slave. By most accounts, York is considered the only African American of the Lewis and Clark Expedition. Because York wrote nothing, at least nothing that has been preserved, what we know about him comes from the writings of white men, chiefly William Clark. It is not clear that what we learn of York from such sources can be considered completely objective. York's biographer, Robert B. Betts, believes that York was probably born a few years before William Clark, that is, a few years before 1770. If Betts is right, this would make York one of the oldest members of the Lewis and Clark Expedition. From an early age, apparently, York was assigned to Clark as a body servant. William Clark legally inherited York from his father in 1799. There is no way of knowing just how much of the time York accompanied Clark during the years Clark spent in the army or traveling on behalf of his older brother George Rogers Clark. Like most slave body servants, he was probably more often with Clark than elsewhere. It was not unusual in that era for slaves to accompany their masters into military service. York was a dark-skinned man. Pierre Antoine Tabeau, who was a trader among the Arikara Indians, had the opportunity to observe York in the fall of 1804 near today's North Dakota–South Dakota border. He described York as "black as a bear." The will of John Clark indicates that both of York's parents were African Americans. York was apparently a man of considerable bulk. The journals refer to his unusual size on several occasions. The most famous of these was at the Spirit Mound (near today's Vermillion, South Dakota) on August 25, 1804. After a hike of at least eighteen miles, "we returned to the boat at Sunset," Clark wrote, "my Servent nearly existed with heat thurst and fatigue, he being fat and unaccustomed to walk as fast as I went was the Cause—." Historians have been uncertain just what "fat" means here. Clark makes it clear that it was an exceptionally hot day. The dog, Seaman (certainly not fat), became so overheated that he had to be sent back to the Missouri River before the reconnaissance party reached the Spirit Mound. Even Captain Lewis found the heat virtually unbearable that day. The Mandan Indians invited members of the expedition to come to a dance on January 1, 1805, "by as they Said the particular request of the Chiefs of that village." York was one of the sixteen men who visited the lower Mandan village that day. Clark wrote, "I found them much pleased at the Dancing of our men, I ordered my black Servent to Dance which amused the Croud verry much, and Some what astonished them, that So large a man Should be active &c. &." When Clark gave orders to York, it was not as his commanding officer but as his owner and master. York's principal contribution to the expedition had more to do with the color of his skin than the quality of his character. Most of the Indians Lewis and Clark met had never seen an African American before, and some frankly doubted that such a being could exist. The skeptical Hidatsa leader Le Borgne famously challenged York's blackness by spitting on his fingers and trying to wash off what he took to be paint. In the words of Nicholas Biddle, "Le Borgne was very much surprised at his appearance, examined him closely, and spit on his finger and rubbed the skin in order to wash off the paint; nor was it until the negro uncovered his head and showed his short hair, that Le Borgne could be persuaded that he was not a painted white man." This indelible scene inspired a famous painting, Charles M. Russell's *York*. York is infrequently mentioned in the journals, where routine matters go unmentioned and only extraordinary occurrences find their way onto paper. If much of York's life is shrouded in mystery, this does not make him different from most of the other members of the expedition, whose lives before and after (and in some cases during) their time with Lewis and Clark are obscure. For two centuries York was considered less an individual than a projection of salacious racist stereotypes. Even scholars as fair-minded as James Ronda and Stephen Ambrose have perpetuated the stereotype of York as buffoon and sexual prodigy. Recent attention to York has focused on his significance as an individual and the multicultural light he brings to the adventure. After April 7, 1805, York was one of the seven people who slept in a tipi obtained from the Mandan and Hidatsa Indians. Meriwether Lewis, William Clark, George Drouillard, Toussaint Charbonneau, Sacagawea, Jean Baptiste Charbonneau, and York occupied the lodge, while the rest of the men slept on the open ground. What might have seemed to others (and to us) as privileged access to the inner circle of authority was perhaps for York a reminder of his status as Clark's personal servant. York probably shaved—and he may have

helped dress—William Clark. A great deal of nonsense has been written about York's supposed sexual prowess. Aside from one reference
in the paraphrase of Nicholas Biddle, the actual journals of the members of the Lewis and Clark Expedition contain not a single reference
to York and sexual activity. In 1810, four years after the expedition,
William Clark told Nicholas Biddle that an Arikara husband invited
York into his earth lodge, offered him his wife, and then stood watch
at the lodge door while York had sexual contact with her. The Arikara
man even apparently sent away one of York's colleagues who came in
search of him. Biddle's 1814 paraphrase narrative read, "such was
their [the Arikara's] desire to oblige us that two very handsome young
squaws were sent on board this evening, and persecuted us with civil-
ities. The black man York participated largely in these favors; for,
instead of inspiring any prejudice, his color seemed to procure him
additional advantages from the Indians, who desired to preserve
among them some memorial of this wonderful stranger." On December 8, 1804, Clark reported that, after a hunting excursion with the
temperature at twelve degrees below zero, "my Servents feet also
frosted & and his P___s a little." This, the only penis reference in all of
the journals of the expedition, has inspired endless silly commentary,
some of it in the form of racial stereotyping. Robert B. Betts rightly
insists that there are two Yorks, the York of history and the York of
American myth. Betts writes, "Writers have taken liberties with him
they would not have dreamed of taking had his skin been white." In
fact much of the York legend stems from the brief Arikara interlude
October 8–12, 1804. The Arikara Indians were the first to call York
"the big medicine." Clark wrote, "the Indians much astonished at my
Black Servent and Call him the big medison, this nation never Saw a
black man before." On October 10, Clark reports, "the Inds. much
astonished at my black Servent, who made him Self more terrible in
their view than I wished him to Doe as I am told telling them that
before I cought him he was wild & lived upon people, young children
was verry good eating Showed them his Strength &c. &c.—" It is
worth noting that Clark did not witness this scene. He was told by others of York's comedic performance. Whether this indicates that York
was a practical joker or merely that he had developed an elaborate
coping mechanism for his enslavement is not clear. Nor is it clear just

why Clark objected to York's foolery. Clark's tone seems to indicate that he did not wish to alarm the Arikara with tales of cannibalism, or possibly that he did not want to give his Indian hosts a distorted image of African-American character. On October 15, 1804, Clark writes of the Arikara, "Those people are much pleased with my black Servent—" A moment later he writes, "Their womin verry fond of caressing our men. &c." It is not at all clear that these two statements are related. On June 5, 1804, York swam to a sandbar in the lower Missouri to collect greens for the expedition's dinner. He most likely cooked the captain's dinner. On June 20, 1804, York was the victim of either a practical joke or a hazing incident. Clark wrote, "My Servent York nearly loseing an Eye by a man throwing Sand into it." None of the journalists indicates who York's assailant was. Clark's field notes hasten to insist that the sand was thrown "in fun." Since no further reference is made to York's eyesight, Clark's early alarm was apparently exaggerated. York emerges in the journals as a man of considerable human sympathy. Clark's field notes indicate that York ministered to Sergeant Charles Floyd in his final illness. On August 19, 1804, one day before Floyd's death, Clark wrote, "every man is attentive to him ~~york prlly~~." These words, though crossed out, appear to all journal editors to mean "York principally." When one of the Shoshone women (presumably Sacagawea) in residence at Fort Mandan was ill on January 20, 1805, Clark wrote, "I ordered my Servent to, give her Some froot Stewed and tee at dift Tims." The journals indicate that York was permitted to carry a gun while hunting. Presumably he was sometimes alone away from the expedition with his gun. What would have been unusual, and in some places illegal within the jurisdiction of the existing states of the United States, had come to seem unexceptional in the West. On May 29, 1805, in eastern Montana, a buffalo thundered into camp and nearly trampled some of the men as they slept. The buffalo had first swum across the Missouri River and lumbered over one of the pirogues. Meriwether Lewis matter-of-factly mentions that York had neglected to remove his rifle from the pirogue at the end of the day and that the buffalo had damaged it considerably. If the journals tell the whole story, neither of the captains rebuked York for this act of negligence. And that York has a gun that he calls his own is simply taken for granted. When Clark and the Charbonneau family were caught in a sudden plains storm at the Great Falls of the Missouri on June 29, 1805, York was deeply concerned. According to Meriwether Lewis, "when this gust came on he [York] returned in such of them & not being able to find them for some time was much alarmed." Clark, Sacagawea, Charbonneau, and their son, Jean Baptiste, were caught in a ravine and nearly drowned by the flash flood. When at last they climbed out to safety, Clark wrote, "I found my servent in serch of us greatly agitated, for our wellfar." Fortunately York was carrying whiskey in a canteen. Clark administered "a little spirits" to the Charbonneaus to calm them after the ordeal. Together with the other members of the expedition (including Sacagawea), York was consulted about the critical issue of just where to spend the winter of 1805–06. Whether Clark's listing of the views of the individual members of the expedition constitutes a "democratic vote on the shores of the Pacific Ocean" is a contested issue. It is clear, however, that York's opinion was by now considered worth recording. The West that Lewis and Clark explored was beyond the boundaries of American civilization. Just as the eating, clothing, and privacy protocols relaxed in the wilderness, so too there appears to have been a relaxation of codes of social stratification. Several places were named for York. Somewhere near the Three Forks of the Missouri in southwestern Montana, Clark listed "Yorks 8 Islands" in a record of distances. On the return journey William Clark named a small tributary of the Yellowstone "York's dry river." The name for York's Islands was recently restored. The other site no longer bears his name. At some point York was married. Probably this occurred before the expedition, but we have no way of knowing for sure. We do not know his wife's name. And though there has been endless speculation about York's supposed progeny among the Indians of the West, we have no certain knowledge of the progeny of his marriage, if any. After the expedition York apparently asserted himself. According to contemporary accounts he became something of a raconteur in St. Louis taverns. He told vivid tales of the expedition's adventures and apparently emphasized his own contributions to the success of the Voyage of Discovery. He made it clear to William Clark that he no longer wished to be separated from his wife. He may even have demanded manumission for his services in the expedition. It is certain that he was not willing to jettison whatever measure of status and independence he had earned in the wilderness. After experiencing a world of lightened enslavement, York made it clear that he did not intend to return to a more emphatic servitude without protest. York was probably never more equal to his peers than on the shores of the Pacific Ocean, literally a continent away from slavery and segregation. The first indication of trouble between York and his master came in November 1808. Clark wrote his brother Jonathan that he would soon be sending "York . . . and promit him to Stay a fiew weeks with his wife. He wishes to Stay there altogether and hire himself which I have refused. he prefers being Sold to return here, he is Serviceable to me at this place, and I am determined not to Sell him to gratify him, and have derected him to return in John H. Clarks Boat if he Sends goods to this place, this fall . . . if any attempt is made by York to run off, or refuse to pervorm his duty as a Slave, I wish him Sent to New Orleans and Sold, or hired out to Some Sevare Master until he thinks better of Such Conduct I do not wish him to know my determination if he conduct well (This choice I must request you to make to you if his Conduct deservs Severity)." This whole episode reveals the dark side of William Clark's character. Clark was a superb leader, a good friend, a loving husband, but he was also a Kentuckian and a slave-holder. By 1809 York had been hired out in Louisville. By 1810 things had broken down entirely. To his brother Jonathan, Clark wrote, "He is here but of verry little Service to me . . . insolent and Sulky, I gave him a Severe trouncing the other Day and he has much mended Sence." Clark may even have had York jailed or locked up during this period. On July 22, 1809, he writes that he has "taken York out of the Caleboos and he has for two or three weeks been the finest Negrow I ever had." Clark granted York his freedom sometime after 1811. According to Clark, York failed in business and decided to rejoin his former master in St. Louis. Washington Irving interviewed William Clark in St. Louis on September 13, 1832. Irving's notes indicate: "His slaves—set them free—one he placed at a ferry—another on a farm, giving him land, horses, &c.—a third he gave a large wagon & team of 6 horses to ply between Nashville and Richmond. They all repented & wanted to come back. The waggoner was York, the hero of the Missouri expedition & adviser of the Indians. He could not get up early enough in the morning—his horses were ill kept—two died—the others grew poor. He sold them, was cheated—entered into service—fared ill. Damn this freedom, said York. I have never had a happy day since I got it. He determined to go back to his old master—set off for St. Louis, but was taken with the cholera in Tennessee & died. Some of the traders think they have met traces of York's crowd, on the Missouri." The tradition that York returned to the upper Missouri and spent a part of his life among the Crow Indians is almost certainly without foundation. York is usually considered the only African American on the Lewis and Clark Expedition, but there is some reason to doubt whether that is strictly true. A North West Company employee named Charles McKenzie had ample occasion to observe the men of the expedition during the winter at Fort Mandan. He wrote, "A mulatto, who spoke bad French and worse English, served as interpreter to the Captains, so that a single word to be understood by the party required to pass from the Natives to the woman, from the woman to the husband, from the husband to the mulatto, from the mulatto to the captains." Assuming, as seems certain, that McKenzie could not be referring here to York, there must have been a second dark-skinned man on the expedition. The Corps of Discovery member Meriwether Lewis most often employed as a translator from English to French was a man named François Labiche. It is possible that Labiche was a mulatto dark enough to get McKenzie's attention. On October 26, 1804, Clark wrote: "they [Mandan] appeared delighted with the Steel—ill which we were obliged to use, also with my black Servent, Capt Lewis returned late—" And on October 24, 1804, he wrote, ". . . and entertained Several of the Curious Chiefs whome, wished to See the Boat which was verry Curious to them viewing it as great medison, as they also viewed my black Servent." See McKenzie, Charles.

References: Betts; Moulton, vols. 1, 3; Wood and Thiessen

Appendix I
List of Indian Presents Carried by the Corps

(FROM DONALD JACKSON,
LETTERS OF THE LEWIS AND CLARK EXPEDITION)

5 lbs. White Wampum

5 lbs. White Glass Beads mostly small

20 lbs. Red Do. Do. Assorted

5 lbs. Yellow or Orange Do. Do. Assorted

30 Calico Shirts

*12 Pieces of East India muslin Hanckerchiefs striped or check'd
with brilliant Colours*

12 Red Silk Hanckerchiefs

144 Small cheap looking Glasses

100 Burning Glasses

4 Vials of Phosforus

288 Steels for striking fire

144 Small cheap Scizors

20 Pair large Do.

12 Groces Needles Assorted No.1 to 8 Common points

12 Groces Do. Assorted with points for sewing leather

288 Common brass thimbles

10 lbs. Sewing Thread assorted

24 Hanks Sewing Silk

8 lbs. Red lead

2 lbs. Vermillion

*288 Knives Small such as are generally used for the Indian
trade with fix'd blades & handles inlaid with brass*

36 Large knives

36 Pipe Tomahawks

12 lbs. Brass wire Assorted

12 lbs. Iron do. do. generally large

6 Belts of narrow Ribbons colours assorted

50 lbs. Spun Tobacco

20 Small falling axes

40 fish Giggs such as the Indians use with a single barbed point

3 Groce fishing Hooks assorted

4 Groce Mockerson awls assorted

50 lbs. Powder secured in a Keg covered with oil Cloth

24 Belts of Worsted feiret or Gartering Colours brilliant and Assorted

15 Sheets of Copper Cut into strips of an inch in width & a foot long

20 Sheets of Tin

12 lbs. Strips of Sheet iron 1 In. wide 1 foot long

1 Pc. red Cloth second quality

1 Nest of 8 or 9 small copper kettles

100 Block-tin rings cheap kind ornamented with Colour'd Glass or Mock-Stone

2 Groces of brass Curtain Rings & sufficiently large for the Finger

1 Groce Cast Iron Combs

18 Cheap brass Combs

24 Blankets

12 Arm Bands Silver

12 Wrist do. do. Do.

36 Ear Trinkets Do. part do.

36 Nose Do. Do.

6 Groces Drops of Do. part Do.

4 doz Rings for Fingers of do.

4 Groces Broaches of do.

12 Small Medals Do.

Appendix II
Some of the Tribes Visited by Lewis and Clark

(FROM THE NATIONAL GEOGRAPHIC WEBSITE,
WWW.NATIONALGEOGRAPHIC.COM/LEWISANDCLARK/RESOURCES
DISCOVERIES TRIBE.HTML)

People

Alsea Indians

Amahami Indians
(Anahami, Ahahar-
way, Wattasoon)

Arikara Indians (Sahnish)

Assiniboin Indians

Atsina Indians (Gros
Ventre)

Bannock Indians

Blackfeet Indians

Cathlamet Indians
(Kathlamet)

Cayuse Indians

Chehalis Indians
(Chilwitz, Chiltz)

Cheyenne Indians

Chinook Indians

Clackamas Indians

Clatskanie Indians

Clatsop Indians

Cowlitz Indians

Crow Indians (Absaroka)

Flathead Indians (Salish)

Hidatsa Indians

Kickapoo Indians

Klickitat Indians
(Klikitat)

Kootenai Indians
(Kootenay, Kutenai)

Mandan Indians

Minitari Indians (Min-
netaree)

Missouri Indians

Multnomah Indians

Nez Perce Indians
(Sahaptin, Shahaptin)

Omaha Indians

Oto Indians

Palouse Indians (Palus)

Pawnee Indians

Quinault Indians

Shoshone Indians (Snake)

Siletz Indians

Siuslaw Indians

Skilloot Indians

Tenino Indians

Teton Sioux Indians

Tillamook Indians

Umatilla Indians

Umpqua Indians

Wahkiakum Indians
(Wahkiaku)

Walla Walla Indians
(Walula)

Wanapum Indians
(Wanapam, Sokulks)

Wasco Indians (Kiksht)

Wishram Indians
(Wishham, Tlakluit)

Yakima Indians

Yankton Sioux Indians
(Nakota)

Language Groups

Algonquian

Athabascan

Caddoan

Chinookian

Sahaptian

Salishan

Shoshonian

Siouan

Bibliography

Books

Abel, Annie H., ed. *Chardon's Journal at Fort Clark 1834–1839.* Pierre: State of South Dakota, 1932.

———. *Tabeau's Narrative of Loisel's Expedition to the Upper Missouri.* Norman: University of Oklahoma Press, 1939.

Albers, Everett C. *The Saga of Seaman: The Story of the Dog Who Went with Lewis and Clark.* Bismarck, N.D.: Northern Lights Press, 2002.

Allen, John Logan. *Passage through the Garden: Lewis and Clark and the Image of the American Northwest.* Urbana: University of Illinois Press, 1975.

Alt, David, and Donald W. Hyndman. *Roadside Geology of Montana.* Missoula, Mont.: Mountain Press Publishing, 1986.

Ambrose, Stephen E. *Undaunted Courage: Meriwether Lewis, Thomas Jefferson, and the Opening of the American West.* New York: Simon and Schuster, 1996.

Anderson, Irving. *Fort Clatsop: A Charbonneau Family Portrait.* Fort Clatsop, Ore.: Fort Clatsop Historical Association, 1988.

Appleman, Roy E. *Lewis and Clark; Historic Places Associated with Their Transcontinental Exploration (1804–1806).* Washington, D.C.: United States Department of the Interior National Park Service, 1975.

Bakeless, John. *Lewis and Clark: Partners in Discovery.* New York: William Morrow, 1947.

Bedini, Silvio. *Thomas Jefferson: Statesman of Science.* New York: Macmillan, 1990.

Benson, Guy Meriwether, with William Irwin and Heather Moore. *Exploring the West from Monticello: A Perspective in Maps from Columbus to Lewis and Clark.* Charlottesville: University of Virginia, 1995.

Berman, Karen. *American Indian Traditions and Ceremonies.* Greenwich, Conn.: Brompton Books, 1997.

Berman, Morris. *The Reenchantment of Nature.* Ithaca, N.Y.: Cornell University Press, 1981.

Betts, Robert B. *In Search of York: The Slave Who Went to the Pacific with Lewis and Clark.* With a new epilogue by James J. Holmberg. Boulder: University Press of Colorado, revised edition, 2000.

Biddle, Nicholas. *History of the Expedition under the Command of Captains Lewis and Clark. . . .* 2 vols. Ed. Paul Allen. Philadelphia: Bradford and Inskeep; New York: Abm. H. Inskeep, 1814.

Black Elk. *The Sacred Pipe.* Ed. Joseph Epes Brown. Norman: University of Oklahoma Press, 1953.

Blevins, Win. *Dictionary of the American West.* Seattle: Sasquatch Books, 2001.

Boone, Lalia Phipps. *Idaho Place Names: A Geographical Dictionary*. Moscow, Idaho: University of Idaho Press, 1988.

Botkin, Daniel B. *Our Natural History: The Lessons of Lewis and Clark*. New York: Berkley Publishing Group, 1995.

―――. *Passage of Discovery*. New York: Berkley Publishing Group, 1999.

Brackenridge, H. M. *Views of Louisiana: Together with a Journal of a Voyage Up the Missouri River in 1811*. Pittsburgh: Cramer, Spear and Eichbaum, 1814.

Bruchac, Joseph. *The Native American Sweat Lodge: History and Legends*. Freedom, Calif.: The Crossing Press, 1993.

―――. *Sacajawea*. San Diego: Silver Whistle, Harcourt Inc., 2000.

Burns, David. *Gateway: Dr. Thomas Walker and the Opening of Kentucky*. Middlesboro, Ky.: Bell County Historical Society, 2000.

Burroughs, Raymond Darwin. *The Natural History of the Lewis and Clark Expedition*. East Lansing: Michigan State University Press, 1961.

Carver, Jonathan. *Travels through the Interior Parts of North America in the Years 1766, 1767, and 1768*. London, 1781.

Catlin, George. *Letters and Notes on the Manners, Customs, and Conditions of the North American Indians*. 2 vols. London: privately published, 1841.

―――. *North American Indians*. Edinburgh, Scotland: John Grant, 1926.

Cheney, Roberta Carkeek. *Names on the Face of Montana*. Missoula, Mont.: Mountain Press Publishing, 1983.

Chern, Margaret Booth. *The New Complete Newfoundland*. New York: Howell Books, 1975.

Chittenden, Hiram Martin. *The American Fur Trade of the Far West*. Vols. 1–2. New York: Harper, 1902.

Chuinard, E. G. *Only One Man Died: The Medical Aspects of the Lewis and Clark Expedition*. Glendale, Calif.: The Arthur Clark Company, 1979.

Clark, Ella E., and Margot Edmonds. *Sacagawea of the Lewis and Clark Expedition*. Berkeley: University of California Press, 1979.

Clark, W. P. *The Indian Sign Language*. Lincoln: University of Nebraska Press, 1982.

Clarke, Charles G. *The Men of the Lewis and Clark Expedition*. Glendale, Calif.: The Arthur Clark Company, 1970.

Cokinos, Christopher. *Hope Is the Thing with Feathers: A Personal Chronicle of Vanished Birds*. New York: Warner Books, 2000.

Colter-Frick, L. R. *Courageous Colter and Companions*. Washington, Mo.: Self-published, 1997.

Coues, Elliott, ed. *The History of the Expedition under the Command of Captains Lewis and Clark*. 3 vols. New York: Dover Publications, 1965. First published by Harper in 1893.

―――. *New Light on the Early History of the Greater Northwest. The Manuscript Journals of Alexander Henry, Fur Trader of the Northwest Company, and of David Thompson, Official Geographer and Explorer of the Same Company, 1799–1814*. 3 vols. New York: Harper, 1897.

Cox, Ross. *The Columbia River*. Norman: University of Oklahoma Press, 1957.

Craighead, John J., Frank C. Craighead, and Ray J. Davis. *A Field Guide to Rocky Mountain Wildflowers*. Boston: Houghton Mifflin, 1963.

Cramer, Zadoc. *The Navigator*. 8th ed. New York: Readex Microprint Corporation, 1966.

Criswell, Elijah Harry. *Lewis and Clark—Pioneering Linguists*. The University of Missouri Studies, vol. 15. Columbia: University of Missouri Press, 1940.

Culin, Stewart. *Games of the North American Indians*. Toronto: General Publishing, 1975.

Cutright, Paul Russell. *A History of the Lewis and Clark Journals*. Norman: University of Oklahoma Press, 1976.

———. *Lewis and Clark: Pioneering Naturalists*. Urbana: University of Illinois Press, 1969.

Dahlinger, Charles W. *Pittsburgh: A Sketch of Its Early Social Life*. New York: G. P. Putnam's Sons, 1916.

Daniels, Jonathan. *The Devil's Backbone: The Story of the Natchez Trace*. New York: McGraw Hill, 1962.

De Voto, Bernard, ed. *The Journals of Lewis and Clark*. Boston: Houghton Mifflin, 1953.

Dear, Elizabeth. *The Grand Expedition of Lewis and Clark as Seen by C. M. Russell*. Great Falls, Mont.: C. M. Russell Museum, 1998.

Denig, Edwin T. *Indian Tribes of the Upper Missouri*. Ed. J. N. B. Hewitt. Bureau of American Ethnology, 46th Annual Report. Washington, D.C., 1940.

DeSanto, Jerry. *Bitterroot: The Montana State Flower*. Babb, Mont.: Lere Press, 1993.

Dietrich, William. *Northwest Passage: The Great Columbia River*. New York: Simon and Schuster, 1995.

Dillon, Richard. *Meriwether Lewis*. New York: Coward-McCann, 1965.

Dubin, Lois Sherr. *North American Indian Jewelry and Adornment from Prehistory to the Present*. New York: Henry N. Abrams, 1999.

Duncan, Dayton. *Lewis and Clark: An Illustrated History Based on a Documentary Film by Ken Burns. . . .* New York: Alfred A. Knopf, 1997.

Eide, Ingvard H. *American Odyssey: The Journey of Lewis and Clark*. Chicago: Rand McNally, 1969.

Ewers, John C. *Artists of the Old West*. New York: Doubleday, 1965.

———. *The Blackfeet: The Northwestern Plains*. Norman: University of Oklahoma Press, 1958.

———. *The Horse in Blackfoot Indian Culture*. Washington, D.C.: Smithsonian Institution Press, 1980.

Fanselow, Julie. *Traveling the Lewis and Clark Trail*. Helena, Mont.: Falcon Press, 1998.

Fazio, James R. *Across the Snowy Ranges: The Lewis and Clark Expedition in Idaho and Western Montana*. Moscow, Idaho: Woodland Press, 2001.

———, ed. *The Mystery of Lost Trail Pass: A Quest for Lewis and Clark's Campsite of September 3, 1805*. Great Falls, Mont.: Lewis and Clark Trail Heritage Foundation, 2000.

Fifer, Barbara. *Going Along with Lewis and Clark*. Helena, Mont.: MT Magazine, 2000.

Fischer, Hank, and Carol Fischer. *The Floater's Guide to Montana*. Helena, Mont.: Falcon Press, 1986.

Fletcher, Alice C. *Indian Games and Dances with Native Songs*. Lincoln: University of Nebraska Press, 1994.

Flexner, John Thomas. *Doctors on Horseback: Pioneers of American Medicine*. New York: Dover Publications, 1969.

Forrest, Earle R. *Patrick Gass: Lewis and Clark's Last Man*. Independence, Mo.: Mrs. A. M. Painter, 1950.

Frazier, Neta Lohnes. *Sacajawea: The Girl Nobody Knows*. New York: D. McKay, 1967.

Freedman, Russell. *An Indian Winter*. New York: Scholastic, 1992.

Furtwangler, Albert. *Acts of Discovery: Visions of America in the Lewis and Clark Journals*. Urbana: University of Illinois Press, 1999.

Gilmore, Melvin R. *Uses of Plants by the Indians of the Missouri River Region*. Lincoln: University of Nebraska Press, 1977.

Hafen, Leroy R., ed. *French Fur Traders and Voyageurs in the American West*. Lincoln: University of Nebraska Press, 1987.

———. *Fur Traders, Trappers and Mountain Men of the Upper Missouri*. Norman: University of Oklahoma Press, 1995.

———. *The Mountain Men and the Fur Trade of the Far West*. 10 vols. Glendale, Calif.: Arthur H. Clark, 1965.

Hart, Jeff. *Montana Native Plants and Early Peoples*. Helena: Montana Historical Society, 1976.

Hasselstrom, Linda. *Bison: Monarch of the Plains*. Portland, Ore.: Graphic Arts Center Publishing, 1997.

Haverstock, Mary Sayre. *Indian Gallery: The Story of George Catlin*. New York: Four Winds Press, 1973.

Hawke, David Freeman. *Those Tremendous Mountains: The Story of the Lewis and Clark Expedition*. New York: W. W. Norton, 1980.

Holmberg, James J., ed. *Dear Brother: Letters of William Clark to Jonathan Clark*. New Haven: Yale University Press, 2002.

Hosmer, James K. *The History of the Louisiana Purchase*. New York: Appleton, 1902.

Howard, Ella Mae. *Lewis and Clark: Exploration of Central Montana*. Great Falls, Mont.: Lewis and Clark Interpretive Association, 1993.

Howard, Harold P. *Sacajawea*. Norman: University of Oklahoma Press, 1971.

Hoxie, Frederick E., ed. *Encyclopedia of North American Indians*. Boston: Houghton Mifflin, 1996.

Hunsaker, Joyce Badgley. *Sacagawea Speaks: Beyond the Shining Mountains with Lewis and Clark*. Guilford, Conn.: Globe Pequot Press, 2001.

Hutchens, Alma R. *A Handbook of Native American Herbs*. Boston: Shambhala, 1992.

———. *Indian Herbology of North America*. Boston: Shambhala, 1991.

Irving, Washington. *The Adventures of Captain Bonneville*. Philadelphia, 1837.

————. *The Rocky Mountains*. Philadelphia, 1836.

Jackson, Donald Dean. *Among the Sleeping Giants, Occasional Pieces on Lewis and Clark*. Urbana: University of Illinois Press, 1987.

————. *Thomas Jefferson and the Stony Mountains: Exploring the West from Monticello*. Urbana: University of Illinois Press, 1981, 1993.

————, ed. *Letters of the Lewis and Clark Expedition, with Related Documents, 1783–1854*, 2 vols. Urbana: University of Illinois Press, 1962, 1978.

Jewitt, John R. *A Journal Kept at Nootka Sound*. Farfield, Wash.: Ye Galleon Press, 1996.

Johansen, Bruce E., and Donald A. Grinde Jr. *The Encyclopedia of Native American Biography*. New York: Da Capo Press, 1998.

Johnson, Allen, and Dumas Malone, eds. *Dictionary of American Biography*. New York: Charles Scribner's Sons, 1930.

Josephy, Alvin. *The Nez Perce Indians and the Opening of the Northwest*. Lincoln: University of Nebraska Press, 1979.

Karwoski, Gail. *Seaman: The Dog Who Explored the West with Lewis and Clark*. Atlanta: Peachtree Publishing, 1999.

Kershaw, Linda. *Edible and Medicinal Plants of the Rockies*. Edmonton, Canada: Lone Pine Publishing, 2000.

Kessler, Donna J. *The Making of Sacagawea: A Euro-American Legend*. Tuscaloosa: The University of Alabama Press, 1996.

Kessler, Dorothy S. *Lewis and Clark: The Fincastle Connection*. Fincastle, Va.: Historic Fincastle, Inc., 1995.

Kramer, Carl E. *Visionaries, Adventurers, and Builders: Historical Highlights of the Falls of the Ohio*. Jeffersonville, Ind.: Sunnyside Press, 2000.

Lamar, Howard R. *The New Encyclopedia of the American West*. New Haven: Yale University Press, 1998.

Landeen, Dan, and Allen Pinkham. *Salmon and His People: Fish and Fishing in Nez Perce Culture*. Lewiston, Idaho: Confluence Press, 1999.

Lavender, David. *Land of Giants: The Drive to the Pacific Northwest, 1750–1950*. Lincoln: University of Nebraska Press, 1956.

————. *The Way to the Western Sea*. New York: Harper & Row, 1988.

Little, Elbert L. *The Audubon Society Field Guide to North American Trees*. New York: Alfred A. Knopf, 1980.

Luttig, John. *Journal of a Fur Trading Expedition on the Upper Missouri 1812–1813*. Ed. Stella Drum. St. Louis: Missouri Historical Society, 1920.

Lyon, William S. *Encyclopedia of Native American Healing*. New York: W. W. Norton, 1996.

MacGregor, Carol Lynn, ed. *The Journals of Patrick Gass: Member of the Lewis and Clark Expedition*. Missoula, Mont.: Mountain Press Publishing, 1997.

Mackenzie, Alexander. *Voyages from Montreal, on the River St. Lawrence, Through the Continent of North America, to the Frozen and Pacific Ocean*. 1801.

Malouf, Carling. *The Shoshone. The Gosiute Indians*. New York: Garland Publishing, 1974.

Manning, Richard. *Grassland: The History, Biology, Politics, and Promise of the American Prairie*. New York: Penguin Books, 1995.

Masson, L. R., ed. *Les Bourgeois de la Compagnie du Nord-Ouest: Recits de voyages, lettres et rapports inedits relatifs au Nord-Ouest Canadien.* 2 vols. Quebec: de L'Imprimière Générale A. Côte et Cie., 1889–1890; reprinted in 2 vols., New York: Antiquarian Press, 1960.

McCracken, Harold. *George Catlin and the Old Frontier.* New York: Dial Press, 1959.

Merrill, Andrea, and Judy Jacobson. *Montana Almanac.* Helena, Mont.: Falcon Press, 1997.

Moulton, Gary, ed. *The Journals of the Lewis and Clark Expedition.* 13 vols. Lincoln: University of Nebraska Press, 1990.

Munford, Kenneth. *John Ledyard: An American Marco Polo.* Portland, Ore.: Binfords & Mort, 1939.

Nasatir, A. P. *Before Lewis and Clark: Documents Illustrating the History of the Missouri, 1785–1804.* 2 vols. Lincoln: University of Nebraska Press, 1990.

Nell, Donald, and John Taylor. *Lewis and Clark in the Three Rivers Valleys.* Tucson, Ariz.: Lewis and Clark Trail Heritage Foundation, 1996.

Nisbet, Jack. *Sources of the River: Tracking David Thompson across Western North America.* Seattle: Sasquatch Books, 1994.

Nye, Virgil. *Fort on the Prairie: Fort Atkinson on the Council Bluff, 1819–1827.* Washington, D.C.: Command Publications, 1978.

Oglesby, Richard Edward. *Manuel Lisa and the Opening of the Missouri Fur Trade.* Norman: University of Oklahoma Press, 1963.

Orr, William J. *Karl Bodmer's America.* Japan: Joslyn Art Museum and University of Nebraska Press, 1984.

Osgood, Ernest S. *The Field Notes of Captain William Clark 1803–1805.* New Haven: Yale University Press, 1964.

Parks, Douglas R. *Myths and Traditions of the Arikara Indians.* Lincoln: University of Nebraska Press, 1996.

Paton, Bruce C. *Lewis and Clark: Doctors in the Wilderness.* Golden, Colo.: Fulcrum Publishing, 2001.

Peck, David. *Or Perish in the Attempt: Wilderness Medicine in the Lewis and Clark Expedition.* Helena, Mont.: Far Country Press, 2002.

Peters, Virginia Bergman. *Women of the Earth Lodges: Tribal Life on the Plains.* Norman: University of Oklahoma Press, 1995.

Peterson, Larry Len. *Charles M. Russell: Legacy.* Helena, Mont.: Two Dot Press, Falcon, 1999.

Peterson, Merrill. *Writings / Thomas Jefferson.* New York: Literary Classics of the United States, 1984.

Plamondon, Martin. *Lewis and Clark Trail Maps.* Vols. 1–2. Pullman: Washington State University Press, 2001.

Prucha, Francis Paul. *Indian Peace Medals in American History.* Lincoln: University of Nebraska Press, 1971.

Pursh, Frederick. *Flora Americae Septentrionalis; Or a Systematic Arrangement and Description of the Plants of North America.* 2 vols. London: White, Cochrane, and Co., 1814.

Quaife, Milo, ed. *Journals of Lewis and Ordway*. Madison: State Historical Society of Wisconsin, 1916.

Reid, Russell. *Lewis and Clark in North Dakota*. Bismarck: State Historical Society of North Dakota, 1988.

———. *Sakakawea, the Bird Woman*. Bismarck: State Historical Society of North Dakota, 1986.

Rogers, Ann. *Lewis and Clark in Missouri*. St. Louis: Meredco, 1981.

Ronda, James. *Jefferson's West: A Journey with Lewis and Clark*. Monticello, Va.: Thomas Jefferson Foundation, 2000.

———. *Lewis and Clark among the Indians*. Lincoln: University of Nebraska Press, 1984.

———, ed. *Voyages of Discovery: Essays on the Lewis and Clark Expedition*. Helena: Montana Historical Society Press, 1998.

Ruby, Robert H., and John A. Brown. *The Chinook Indians, Traders of the Lower Columbia River*. Norman: University of Oklahoma Press, 1976.

———. *Indians of the Pacific Northwest: A History*. Norman: University of Oklahoma Press, 1981.

Russell, Carl P. *Firearms, Traps and Tools of the Mountain Men*. New York: Alfred A. Knopf, 1967.

Salisbury, Albert, and Jane Salisbury. *Lewis and Clark: The Journey West*. New York: Promontory Press, 1950.

Schneider, Mary Jane. *The Hidatsa*. New York: Chelsea House Publishers, 1989.

Schullery, Paul. *Lewis and Clark among the Grizzlies*. Helena, Mont.: Falcon Press, 2002

Sierra Club. *What's Lost, What's Left: A Status Report on the Plants and Animals of the Lewis and Clark Expedition*. Seattle: Sierra Club, 2002.

Sivertson, Howard. *The Illustrated Voyageur*. Duluth, Minn.: Lake Superior Port Cities, 1999.

Skarsten, M. O. *George Drouillard, Hunter and Interpreter for Lewis and Clark and Fur Trader, 1807–1810*. Glendale, Calif.: A. H. Clark, 1964.

Snyder, Gerald S. *In the Footsteps of Lewis and Clark*. Washington, D.C.: National Geographic Society, 1970.

Society of Gentlemen. *A New and Complete Dictionary of Arts and Sciences. . . .* Vols. 1–4. London: W. Owen, 1753.

Space, Ralph S. *The Lolo Trail*. 2nd ed. Missoula, Mont.: Historic Montana Publishing, 2001.

Speck, Gordon. *Breeds and Half Breeds*. New York: Clarkson N. Potter, 1969.

Sprague, Marshall. *So Vast So Beautiful a Land: Louisiana and the Purchase*. Boston: Little, Brown, 1974.

Steffen, Jerome O. *William Clark, Jeffersonian Man on the Frontier*. Norman: University of Oklahoma Press, 1977.

Stevens, Walter B. *St. Louis, the Fourth City, 1764–1909*. St. Louis: S. J. Clarke Publishing, 1909.

Stoddard, Amos. *Sketches, Historical and Descriptive of Louisiana*. Philadelphia: Mathew Carey, 1812.

Strong, Ruth, and Emory Strong. *Seeking Western Waters: The Lewis and Clark Trail from the Rockies to the Pacific.* N.p.: Oregon Historical Society Press, 1995.

Sufrin, Mark. *Geoge Catlin: Painter of the Indian West.* New York: Atheneum, 1991.

Swayne, Zoa L. *Do Them No Harm.* Orofino, Idaho: Legacy House, 1990.

Thrapp, Dan L. *Encyclopedia of Frontier Biography.* Lincoln: University of Nebraska Press, 1991.

Thwaites, Rueben Gold, ed. *Early Western Travels.* 32 vols. Cleveland: Arthur Clark, 1904–07.

———. *Original Journals of the Lewis and Clark Expedition, 1804–1806.* 8 vols. New York: Dodd, Mead, 1904–05.

Turney-High, Harry H. *The Flathead Indians of Montana.* Menasha, Wisc.: American Anthropological Association, 1937.

Tyrrell, J. B., ed. *David Thompson's Narrative of His Explorations in Western America, 1784–1812.* Toronto: The Champlain Society, 1916.

Udvarty, Miklos D. F. *National Audubon Society Field Guide to North American Birds.* Revised by John Farrand Jr. New York: Alfred A. Knopf, 1994.

Walcheck, Kenneth C. *The Lewis and Clark Expedition: Montana's First Bird Inventory through the Eyes of Lewis and Clark.* Great Falls, Mont.: Lewis and Clark Interpretive Association, 1999.

Waldman, Carl. *Atlas of the North American Indian.* New York: Facts on File, 1985.

———, ed. *Encyclopedia of Native American Tribes.* New York: Chessmark Books, 1999.

Wheeler, Olin D. *The Trail of Lewis and Clark, 1804–1904.* New York: Putnam and Sons, 1904.

Whitaker, John O., Jr., ed. *National Audubon Society Field Guide to North American Mammals.* New York: Alfred A. Knopf, 1996.

Williams, Glyndwr, ed. *Hudson's Bay Miscellany 1670–1870.* Vol. 30. Winnipeg, Canada: Hudson's Bay Record Society, 1975.

Wilson, Alexander. *American Ornithology.* Philadelphia: Bradford, Inskeep, 1808–1814.

Wishart, David J. *The Fur Trade of the American West 1807–1840.* Lincoln: University of Nebraska Press, 1979.

Wood, Raymond W., and Thomas D. Thiessen, eds. *Early Fur Trade on the Northern Plains: Canadian Traders among the Mandan and Hidatsa Indians 1738–1818.* Norman: University of Oklahoma Press, 1985.

Articles

Allen, John Logan. "Of this Enterprize: The American Images of the Lewis and Clark Expedition." Address delivered at the Lewis and Clark College Symposium, "Enlightenment Science in the Pacific Northwest," Portland, Ore., February 1984.

Anderson, Irving W. "Probing the Riddle of the Bird Woman." *Montana Magazine of Western History,* Autumn 1973.

Bedini, Silvio A. "The Scientific Instruments of the Lewis and Clark Expedition." *Great Plains Quarterly,* Winter 1984.

Beeman, Robert. "Proceeding On to the Lewis and Clark Airgun." *Airgun Review* 6, April 2000.

Benton, Fay E. "Popular Poplars Are Wide-Ranging." *Great Falls Tribune*, June 7, 2001.

Brown, JoAnn. "New Light on Some of the Expedition Engagés." *We Proceeded On*, August 1996.

Byram, Scott, and David G. Lewis. "Ourigan, Wealth of the Northwest Coast." *Oregon Historical Quarterly*, vol. 102, no. 2, Summer 2001.

Carrick, Michael. "Lewis and Clark Question and Answer." *Oregon Chapter Newsletter*, vol. 1, no. 11, March 1999.

Charbonneau, L. "Seaman's Trail: Fact vs. Fiction." *We Proceeded On*, November 1989.

Chatters, R. M. "The Not-So-Enigmatic LC Airgun." *We Proceeded On*, May 1977.

Cheney, Roberta Carkeek. "Lewis and Clark Place Names." *Montana Magazine of Western History*, Winter 1970.

Chuinard, E. G. "Thomas Jefferson and the Corps of Discovery: Could He Have Done More?" *American West*, November 1975.

Cleary, Rita. "Charbonneau Reconsidered." *We Proceeded On,* February 2000.

Craft, R. D. "Lewis and Clark's Wapato: Endangered Plant Fights for Survival." *We Proceeded On*, February 1982.

Cutright, Paul R. "Lewis and Clark and Du Pratz." *Missouri Historical Society Bulletin*, October 1964.

———. "Lewis and Clark: Portraits and Portraitists." *Montana Magazine of Western History*, Spring 1969.

———. "Lewis and Clark's Indian Peace Medals." *Missouri Historical Society Bulletin*, January 1968.

———. "Meriwether Lewis, Naturalist." *Oregon Historical Society Quarterly*, 1968.

David, Norman. "Lewis and Clark Expedition Medicine Chest Drugs." Unpublished manuscript, courtesy of Lewis and Clark College, Portland, Oregon.

Davis, Nancy. "Caspar Wistar." *We Proceeded On,* February 2000.

Denny, James M. "Lewis and Clark in the Boonslick." *Boons Lick Heritage*, vol. 8, no. 2–3, June–September 2000.

Dickson, Frank H. "Hard on the Heels of Lewis and Clark." *Montana Magazine of Western History*, Winter 1976.

Diller, Aubrey. "Maps of the Missouri River before Lewis and Clark." In *Studies and Essays . . . in Homage to George Sarton*. New York, 1946.

Furtwangler, Albert. "Sacagawea's Son as a Symbol." *Oregon Historical Quarterly*, Fall 2001.

———. "Sacagawea's Son: New Evidence from Germany." *Oregon Historical Quarterly*, Winter 2001.

Gasque, Thomas J. "Lewis and Clark's Onomastic Assumptions." *Midwestern Folklore*, Spring–Fall 1995.

Gravelines, Paul. "Joseph Gravelines and the Lewis and Clark Expedition." *We Proceeded On*, October 1977.

Great Falls Tribune staff. "Sifting the Sonic Sands of Time." *Great Falls Tribune*, March 4, 2001.

Guinness, Ralph. "The Purpose of the Lewis and Clark Expedition." *Mississippi Historical Review*, June 1933.

Hafen, Ann. "The Fur Trade and the Mountain Men." In Leroy Hafen, *Mountain Men and the Fur Trade of the Far West*. Glendale, Calif.: Arthur H. Clark, 1965.

Hafen, Leroy R. "Raton Pass, an Historic Highway." *Colorado Magazine*, November 1930.

Hoffman, Wilbur. "The Gravesite of the Expedition's Alexander Hamilton Willard." *We Proceeded On*, May 1980.

Holbrook, Stewart. "Lost Notes of the Lewis and Clark Exploration." *American Weekly*, November 8, 1953.

Holmberg, James. "Seaman's Fate." *We Proceeded On*, November 1989.

Hunt, Robert R. "The Espontoon: Captain Lewis's Magic Stick." *We Proceeded On*, February 1990.

———. "Gills and Drams of Consolation." *We Proceeded On*, August–November 1991.

———. "Hoofbeats & Nightmares: A Horse Chronicle of the Lewis and Clark Expedition." *We Proceeded On*, November 1994 and February 1995.

———. "Merry to the Fiddle: The Musical Amusement of the Lewis and Clark Party." *We Proceeded On*, November 1988.

———. "Mockersons: An Unspoken Tongue." *We Proceeded On*, August 1990.

Jackson, Donald. "Call Him a Good Old Dog but Don't Call Him Scannon." *We Proceeded On*, special publication no. 10, September 1990.

———. "Some Books Carried by Lewis and Clark." *Missouri Historical Bulletin*, October 1959.

Johnson, Willie. "Keelboats and Pirogues." Unpublished material for the Keelboat Exhibit in Clarksville, Indiana, 2001.

"Joslyn Art Museum Is Given Maximilian / Bodmer Collection." *We Proceeded On*, February 1987.

Keith, A. B. "The Legend of Giant Spring." *Great Falls Daily Tribune*, December 15, 1901.

Kirkpatrick, Glen. "Stupendious Columbia Gorge." *We Proceeded On*, May 2001.

Knowles, Charles. "Lewis and Clark's Guide Old Toby." *Idaho Yesterdays*, Summer 1999.

Lange, Robert E. "The Expedition's Brothers: Joseph and Rueben Field." *We Proceeded On*, July 1978.

———. "The Three Forks of the Missouri River: Jefferson, Madison, and Gallatin." *We Proceeded On*, May 1981.

Large, Arlen J. "Captain Lewis and the Hopeful Cadet." *We Proceeded On*, November 1989.

———. "History's Two Nicholas Biddles." *We Proceeded On*, May 1990.

———. "The Humboldt Connection." *We Proceeded On*, November 1990.

———. "Vancouver's Legacy to Lewis and Clark." *We Proceeded On*, January 1992.

Laycock, Ron. "Lewis and Clark's First Big Mistake." Paper presented at the Lewis and Clark Trail Heritage Foundation annual meeting, Pierre, South Dakota, 2001.

Lecompte, Janet. "August Pierre Chouteau." In Leroy Hafen, *French Fur Traders and Voyagers in the American West*. Lincoln: University of Nebraska, 1987.

Lewis, M. N. "Meriwether Lewis, Devoted Son." *We Proceeded On*, May 1990.

Long, Michael E. "The Vanishing Prairie Dog." *National Geographic*, April 1998.

Loos, John Louis. "William Clark's Part in the Preparation of the Lewis and Clark Expedition." *Missouri Historical Society Bulletin*, July 1954.

MacGregor, Carol Lynn. "The American Philosophical Society and Thomas Jefferson." *We Proceeded On*, August 1992.

McDermott, John F. "William Clark's Struggle with Place Names in Upper Louisiana." *Missouri Historical Society Bulletin*, April 1978.

Minnick, Harriet D. "Francois Rivet." In Leroy Hafen, *Mountain Men and the Fur Trade of the Far West*. 10 vols. Glendale, Calif.: Arthur H. Clark, 1965.

Missouri Historical Review. "William Clark's Museum." July 1933.

Montana Magazine of Western History. "What Are the Facts? Photo of William Clark's Nez Perce 'son.' " Summer 1955.

Montana Outdoors. "Pronghorn Facts." November–December 2001.

Moulton, Gary. "On Reading Lewis and Clark: The Last Twenty Years." *Montana Magazine of Western History*, Summer 1988.

Nasatir, A. P. "Jacques D'Eglise." In Leroy Hafen, *Mountain Men and the Fur Trade of the Far West*. 10 vols. Glendale, Calif.: Arthur H. Clark, 1965.

———. "Jean Baptiste Truteau." Op cit.

Osgood, Ernest S. "Our Dog Scannon: Partner in Discovery." *Montana Magazine of Western History*, Summer 1976.

Pollard, Lancaster. "Jack Ramsey." *The Oregonian*, April 22, 1956.

Rasmussen, Jay. "Corps of Discovery." *Oregon Chapter Newsletter*, vol. 3, no. 1, January 2001.

Rees, John. "The Shoshoni Contribution to Lewis and Clark." *Idaho Yesterdays*, Summer 1958.

Robinson, Doane. "Sac-a-jawe vs. Sa-kaka-wea." South Dakota Historical Collection, 1924.

Ronda, James. "Calculating Ouragon." *Oregon Historical Quarterly*, Summer–Fall 1993.

———. "In Memoriam." *We Proceeded On,* February 1988.

Rose, Donald W. "Captain Lewis's Iron Boat: The Experiment." *We Proceeded On*, May 1981.

Saindon, Bob. "Old Menard." *We Proceeded On*, May 1987.

———. "The River Which Scolds All Others." *Montana Magazine of Western History*, Summer 1976.

Schontzler, Gail. "Historian: Idaho Drove Lewis Crazy." *Bozeman Daily Chronicle*, March 27, 1997.

Shoemaker, Arthur. "The Many Faces of Nathaniel Pryor." *True West*, September 1988.

Slosberg, Daniel. "Pierre Cruzatte: Fiddling Around with Lewis and Clark." *FolkWorks*, January–February 2001.

Smith, James S., and Kathryn Smith. "Sedulous Sergeant Patrick Gass." *Montana Magazine of Western History*, July 1955.

Thwaites, Rueben Gold. "William Clark: Soldier, Explorer, Statesman." *Missouri Historical Society Bulletin*, July 1954.

Walcheck, Ken. "Wapati." *We Proceeded On*, August 2000.

We Proceeded On. Great Falls: Lewis and Clark Trail Heritage Foundation, 1976–2002. (See entries for specific article references.)

Wesselius, Allen. "A Lasting Legacy: The Lewis and Clark Place Names of the Pacific Northwest." *Columbia*, Spring 2000–Winter 2001.

Wetmore, Mark. "Spirit Mound Hill of Little Devils." *We Proceeded On*, February 1996.

Will, Drake W. "Lewis and Clark: Westering Physicians." *Montana Magazine of Western History*, Summer 1971.

———. "The Medical and Surgical Practice of the Lewis and Clark Expedition." *Journal of the History of Medicine and Allied Sciences*, 1959.

Williams, David. "John Evans' Strange Journey." *American Historical Review*, January–April 1949.

Wilson, Alexander. "Particulars of the Death of Capt. Lewis." *The Port Folio*, January 1812, vol. 7. Published by Oliver Oldschool and Asbury Dickens in Philadelphia, Pa.

Wood, Raymond W. "The John Evans 1796–97 Map of the Missouri River." *Great Plains Quarterly*, Winter 1981.

———. "John Thomas Evans: An Overlooked Precursor to Lewis and Clark." *North Dakota History*, vol. 68, no. 2, November 2001.

———. "John Thomas Evans and William Clark: Two Early Western Explorers' Maps Re-examined." *We Proceeded On*, March 1983.

Yater, George H., and Carolyn S. Denton. "Nine Young Men from Kentucky." *We Proceeded On*, May 1992.

Websites

For information related to Lewis and Clark on the World Wide Web see Jay Rasmussen's comprehensive website, www.lcarchive.org, "Lewis and Clark on the Information Superhighway," especially the ones he has marked as "well presented, interesting and informative," including "Firearms of the Lewis and Clark Expedition."

Peabody Museum, "Ethnography of Lewis and Clark," www.peabody.harvard .edu/Lewis_and_Clark

National Geographic, www.nationalgeographic.com

Personal Communications

Burroughs, Raymond Darwin. Lewis and Clark Interpretive Center Information.

Carrick, Michael. List of firearms carried on the Lewis and Clark Expedition in letter, January 4, 2002.

Doerk, Robert. Lecture, 2001.

Henley, Page. Letter, August 23, 2001.

Holmberg, James. Letter, May 2002

Karsminski, Ken. Conversation, Fall 2000.

Matchet, Randy. Conversation, Summer 2002.

Moore, Bob. Letter, February 21, 2003.

Peck, Daniel. E-mail, February 4, 2003.

Slosberg, Daniel. Letter, January 14, 2002.

Venso, Mikall. Letter, April 24, 2002.

Wendlick, Roger. Rare printed material from private collection, October 2001.

Other

Reiten, Jon, and Robert Bergentino. Montana Bureau of Mines and Technology, informational poster text.

Acknowledgments

In addition to our patient and supportive families, we would like to thank the following individuals for their timely encouragement, guidance, and expertise: James Holmberg, Bob Doerk, Marty Erickson, Michael Carrick, Doug Erickson, Stephen Dow Beckham, Roger Wendlick, Ron Laycock, Charles Fritz, Elizabeth Stein, Mike Venso, Tim and Doris Crawford, Page and Jane Henley, Phyllis Yeager, Dave Peck, Bob Moore, Dan Slosberg, and Lanny Jones.

About the Authors

STEPHENIE AMBROSE TUBBS is a veteran traveler on the Lewis and Clark trail and was the assistant researcher on her father's three-volume biography, *Nixon*. She serves on the board of the Lewis and Clark Interpretive Center Foundation and lives in Helena, Montana, with her husband, John, and sons, Alex and Riley.

CLAY STRAUS JENKINSON is a nationally respected Jefferson scholar whose previous books include *The Paradox of Thomas Jefferson, Message on the Wind*, and *The Character of Meriwether Lewis*. He has portrayed Meriwether Lewis in first-person historical characterizations throughout the country. He lives in Reno, Nevada.